Family Law: Practice and Procedure

JoAnn Kurtz, LLB

2004
EMOND MONTGOMERY PUBLICATIONS LIMITED
TORONTO, CANADA

Printed in Canada.

Edited, designed, and typeset by WordsWorth Communications, Toronto.
Cover design by Susan Darrach, Darrach Design.

We acknowledge the financial support of the Government of Canada through the Book Publishing Industry Development Program (BPIDP) for our publishing activities.

National Library of Canada Cataloguing in Publication

Kurtz, JoAnn, 1951-
Family law : practice and procedure / JoAnn Kurtz.

Includes index.
ISBN 1-55239-081-0

1. Domestic relations — Ontario. I. Title.

KEO213.K87 2004 346.71301'5 C2003-907101-4
KF505.ZB3K87 2004

*To my (thankfully intact) family — my husband Daniel Henry,
and my three sons, Jacob, Max, and Ely.*

Contents

Preface

For many years, my colleagues at Seneca College and I have taught family law to students in our law clerk program using a patchwork of texts, statutes, rules, and precedents. No one text discussed both the substantive law and the practice and procedure in the area. I wrote this book so that my family law students could have the text I always wanted them to have.

This text covers all of the material that we teach in our two family law courses at Seneca College. It starts with an overview of a marriage breakdown, to place the study of family law in a practical context, and a brief history of family law, to place the study of family law in a historical context. Chapters 3 through 9 discuss the substantive law of marriage, separation, and divorce. Chapters 10 and 11 deal with the substantive law and procedure of settlement in family law matters — negotiation, separation, and financial disclosure. Chapters 12 through 16 cover the practice and procedure in a variety of family law proceedings before both the Family Court of the Ontario Superior Court of Justice and the Ontario Superior Court of Justice, by examining the relevant court rules and forms in the context of client fact situations. Chapters 17 and 18 deal with the substantive law and practice regarding enforcement, variation, and indexing of family law orders. Appendix A highlights the recent changes in the law with respect to same-sex relationships.

This book is designed to be as comprehensive as possible. The three major statutes in the family law area are reproduced in full in appendix C. For a complete understanding of the area, however, students will also need access to the *Family Law Rules*, the *Rules of Civil Procedure*, and a precedent separation agreement.

The text is not meant to serve as a blueprint for the teaching of a family law course. It is not necessary, nor is it even recommended, that the chapters be taught or studied in sequence. Rather, the professor and students should move between the substantive law and procedure in the different areas.

JoAnn Kurtz
Toronto, 2003

CHAPTER 1

Overview of a Marriage Breakdown

Harold and Wendy have been married for five years. They have two children — Sam, age three, and Deb, age six — and a cat and a dog. Harold is a partner in a small and successful accounting firm. Wendy gave up the practice of law to be a full-time mother. The couple owns a house, a cottage, a sailboat, and a variety of investments. Harold has just told Wendy that he is leaving her for a Canada Customs and Revenue Agency investigator whom he met when one of his clients was audited. Wendy is emotionally devastated, but she is also a lawyer and realizes the issues that have to be resolved with Harold:

- Who will get custody of the children?
- How much child support will the other spouse be required to pay?
- Will Harold have to pay her spousal support; if so, how much and for how long?
- How will their property be divided?
- Will they divorce and, if so, when?

If Harold and Wendy are like the majority of separating couples, they will negotiate a settlement of all these issues and incorporate the terms of their settlement into a separation agreement without going to court, except to get a divorce. At some point after the separation agreement is signed, Harold, Wendy, or the two of them together will start divorce proceedings, and a divorce will be granted by the court without a trial.

If Harold and Wendy cannot agree on a settlement, either of them can start a court proceeding. They can ask the court to deal with the issues of support, custody, and property in a divorce proceeding, or they can ask the court to deal with support, custody, and property issues without seeking a divorce.

In this book we will be studying the substantive law and procedure involved in resolving the issues that arise when domestic relationships break down. In this chapter, we will look at

- the law that governs these issues, and
- the courts' jurisdiction over these issues.

SOURCES OF FAMILY LAW

Whether Harold and Wendy settle their outstanding issues themselves or leave them for the courts to decide, both must know their legal rights and responsibilities. In Ontario, family law is governed by both statute law and case law.

Because of Canadian constitutional law, some family law issues are governed by federal legislation, some are governed by provincial legislation, and some are governed by both.

Sections 91 and 92 of the *Constitution Act, 1867* divide statute-making power between the federal and the provincial governments. The Act gives jurisdiction over marriage and divorce to the federal government and jurisdiction over marriage and property rights to the provincial governments. As a result, the legislation governing divorce is federal, while the legislation governing the division of property is provincial. Custody and support (both spousal and child) are addressed in both federal and provincial statutes.

The jurisdiction over family law is divided between the federal and provincial governments as set out in figure 1.1.

If a claim for custody and/or support is made in a divorce proceeding, the federal divorce legislation governs. If a claim for custody and/or support is made while the marriage continues, it is dealt with under the provincial legislation.

Figure 1.2 sets out the relevant federal and provincial family law statutes.

There have been many court decisions that have interpreted and applied the provisions of these statutes. These decisions form a part of Ontario family law as well.

JURISDICTION OF THE COURTS

If Harold and Wendy cannot settle the issues that arise from the breakdown of their marriage on their own, a court proceeding must be started. Although Ontario is moving toward the creation of a unified family court across the province, for now there are three Ontario courts with jurisdiction over family law:

1. Family Court of the Superior Court of Justice,
2. Superior Court of Justice, and
3. Ontario Court of Justice.

The party who starts the proceeding must know which court to use.

History

Historically, jurisdiction over family law matters was split between the province's superior court (then called the Ontario Court (General Division)) and the province's provincial court. The superior court had jurisdiction over all family breakdown matters — divorce, property, custody, and support — while the provincial court's jurisdiction was limited to custody and support issues. (The provincial court also had jurisdiction over adoption, child protection, and young offenders.)

This split in jurisdiction was confusing, and for many years there was talk of consolidating jurisdiction over all family matters into one court. In 1977, a Unified Family Court was established in Hamilton-Wentworth as a three-year pilot project. The Hamilton court was made a permanent entity in 1982, and the province promised

FIGURE 1.1 JURISDICTION OVER FAMILY LAW IN CANADA

	Federal jurisdiction	Provincial jurisdiction
Divorce	X	
Division of property		X
Custody	X	X
Child support	X	X
Spousal support	X	X

FIGURE 1.2 RELEVANT FAMILY LAW LEGISLATION

Federal

- *Divorce Act*, which deals with dissolution of marriage, custody, and support.

Provincial

- *Family Law Act*, which deals with division of property and support.
- *Children's Law Reform Act*, which deals with custody.

to create more unified family courts across the province. However, it was not until 1995 that the Unified Family Court was expanded to include four more sites.

As part of the most recent set of Ontario court reforms, the province committed itself to the creation of the Family Court of the Superior Court of Justice, a single family court at the superior court level across the province. In addition, as part of its child-centred family justice strategy announced in December 2002, the federal government pledged additional funding to the provinces to assist in the expansion of unified family courts.

Present Situation

At the time of this book's publication, the Family Court of the Superior Court of Justice is up and running in 18 of the province's 49 counties and judicial districts. Toronto and Peel are among the counties and judicial districts in which the Family Court does not yet operate.

In those places where it has been established, the Family Court of the Superior Court of Justice has jurisdiction over all family law matters. The goal of the court is to deal with family problems in an integrated manner with mediation, resource, informational, and legal services attached to each court site.

In those areas of Ontario where the Family Court of the Superior Court of Justice does not exist, jurisdiction over family law matters continues to be divided between the Superior Court of Justice and the Ontario Court of Justice. Cases that include divorce or property claims must be brought before the Superior Court of Justice. Cases that involve only custody and/or support claims may be brought before either the Superior Court of Justice or the Ontario Court of Justice.

Appendix B lists those provincial jurisdictions with the Family Court and those without.

REFERENCES

Children's Law Reform Act, RSO 1990, c. C.12.
Constitution Act, 1867, 30 & 31 Vict., c. 3 (UK).
Divorce Act, RSC 1985, c. 3 (2d Supp.).
Family Law Act, RSO 1990, c. F.3.

REVIEW QUESTIONS

1. What legal issues must a separating couple resolve?
2. How do the majority of separating couples resolve the issues between them?
3. What are the sources of family law in Ontario?
4. Why are some family law issues dealt with under federal legislation, some under provincial legislation, and some under both?
5. What family law issues are dealt with under federal legislation only?
6. What family law issues are dealt with under provincial legislation only?
7. What family law issues are dealt with under both federal and provincial legislation?
8. Name the federal family law statute. What issues does this statute deal with?
9. Name two provincial family law statutes. What issues do each of these statutes deal with?
10. What are the three Ontario courts with jurisdiction over family law matters?

CHAPTER 2

A Brief History of Family Law in Ontario

Before beginning a study of contemporary family law in Ontario, it is important to realize that this law has been in effect for a relatively short time. Ontario's family law, like most of our law, has its origins in England during the late Middle Ages. The law has changed a great deal since that time as our society and its values have changed. Until recently, the history of family law has been the history of the relationship between husbands and wives. It was not until the latter part of the 20th century that the law began to recognize first the relationships between cohabiting couples of the opposite sex and then those of the same sex. It is only in the last few months that the law has recognized the validity of same-sex marriages.[1]

In this chapter, we will look at how family law has evolved in the following areas:

- the legal status of the husband and wife,
- the physical relationship between the husband and wife,
- the property of the husband and wife,
- the custody of the children,
- the support of one spouse by the other, and
- divorce.

ENGLISH LAW BEFORE THE 19TH CENTURY

The family in pre-19th-century England was an important social and economic unit. It was the family, not society or government, that educated its children and cared for the sick, disabled, and old. The economy was largely rural, and all members of the family worked to provide for the family unit. The division of labour was based on sex and age. The husband and father, as the head of the family, made all decisions affecting family members and could enforce those decisions through the use of corporal punishment.

Marriages — at least among the middle and upper classes[2] — were usually arranged by the families of the bride and groom. The choice of a spouse was based largely

1 In the case of *Halpern v. Canada (Attorney General)* (2003), 65 OR 161 (CA).

2 What we know about marriages of the time comes from written records such as journals, correspondence, marriage contracts, and land deeds. As a result, we don't know very much about marriage among the lower classes, who did not leave records of this kind.

on economic factors: Could the prospective husband provide financially for the wife? Would the prospective bride bring any money or property with her in the form of a dowry?

Romantic love, though it existed, was not thought of as a basis for marriage and was not expected in the marriage relationship. While it was hoped that a husband and wife would come to love each other, that love was not expected to be of a romantic nature. In fact, romantic love between husband and wife was not much heard of until the beginning of the 19th century, when it started to appear in literature.

Women had few prospects outside marriage. There were not many jobs available to them. Single women past marriageable age (referred to as spinsters) were pitied. If their families were unable to support them, they were forced to take one of the few low-paying jobs open to women, such as teacher, governess, or domestic help.

Marriage was based on Christian principles and was viewed as an oath taken before God. Marriage was for life: "Whom God hath joined together, let no man put asunder." According to Christian doctrine, the husband was considered the "head" of the marriage.

The legal aspects of the marriage relationship reflected the values of the time.

Legal Status of the Husband and Wife

unity of legal personality
a doctrine by which a husband and wife were considered to be one person in law

A husband and a wife were considered to be one person in law — and that person was the husband. This doctrine was referred to as the **unity of legal personality**. A married woman had no right to enter into contracts on her own behalf, although she could enter into contracts on her husband's behalf for necessities for herself. She could neither sue nor be sued. Her husband was responsible for her debts and for any torts she might commit. Because a husband and wife were one person, spouses could not sue each other.

Physical Relationship Between the Husband and Wife

ecclesiastical courts
a system of church courts in England

Both husband and wife had a duty to have sexual relations with each other. This was both a legal and a religious duty that either the husband or wife could enforce in the church courts (called **ecclesiastical courts**). A wife had no legal right to refuse to have sex with her husband, and it was not considered rape if a man had sexual intercourse with his wife without her consent.

criminal conversation
a tort action by which a husband could claim damages against a man who had sexual intercourse with the husband's wife

If a wife had sexual intercourse with a man other than her husband, her husband had the right to sue the man for damages in an action for **criminal conversation**. A man who enticed a wife away from her husband or who offered her shelter and support could also be sued for damages.

right of physical chastisement
the right of a husband to use physical force to discipline his wife

The husband, as head of the family, had the right of **physical chastisement**: in other words, the right to use physical force to discipline his wife.

Property of the Husband and Wife

In keeping with the view that the husband and the wife were one person — namely, the husband — on marriage, the wife's personal property became the husband's. The wife's real property became his to use; he had the right to use her land and buildings, including the right to mortgage them to raise money. Married women were not legally able to own property. On separation or divorce, the husband kept all property that was originally his or that had become his by virtue of the marriage.

To protect against this loss of property, a wealthy family would either give no property to a daughter or would make arrangements before marriage to keep the property in trust for her. That way, her husband would have access to the income from the property but would not be able to deal with the property itself.

Custody of the Children

Children were traditionally seen as property and, as with all other property of a married couple, they were the property of the husband. The husband had the absolute right to determine the children's religious training, general education, choice of career, and choice of marriage partner.

A woman had no right to custody of her children. If she left the marriage, the husband had the absolute right to custody.

Support of One Spouse by the Other

Support flowed only from the husband as supporter to the wife as dependant. It was based on principles of reward and punishment, not on financial need.

A husband was required to support his wife while the couple were living together, but a wife who left her husband was not entitled to receive any support from him. If the breakdown of the marriage relationship was caused by the husband, a wife could, in limited circumstances, bring a common law action for **alimony**.

A wife would be awarded alimony only if she could prove that

- the parties were living separate and apart; and
- the husband
  - had committed adultery, or
  - was guilty of cruelty (physical or mental injury to the wife), or
  - had deserted the wife for two or more years; and
- the wife had not herself committed a matrimonial offence (adultery, cruelty, or desertion).

alimony
a common law action by a wife for support from her husband

A wife was not entitled to alimony unless she was willing to take her husband back to live with her. However, if she actually took him back and resumed the marriage relationship with knowledge of his misconduct, she was considered to have **condoned** (forgiven) the misconduct and would also be disentitled to alimony.

Alimony, if awarded, was not designed to meet all of a wife's financial needs. Rather, the amount was meant to be sufficient only to allow her to live "modestly and in retirement." A wife was not awarded alimony if she had enough income to maintain herself. Alimony payments continued only so long as the wife remained chaste: she lost all right to support if she had sexual intercourse with another man.

condonation
forgiveness of a matrimonial offence by continuing or resuming cohabitation with the guilty spouse, with knowledge of the offence

Divorce

Originally, there was no divorce. A marriage ended only with the death of one party or with an **annulment** (a declaration that the marriage was never valid). In the latter case, the ecclesiastical courts issued a **divorce *a vinculo matrimonii*** (from the bonds of marriage).

annulment
a declaration that the marriage was never valid

divorce *a vinculo matrimonii*
an order of the ecclesiastical courts, following a declaration that a marriage was not valid, by which the parties were released from the bonds of marriage

divorce *a mensa et thoro*
an order of the ecclesiastical courts by which the parties to a valid marriage were relieved of their obligation to cohabit, but were still legally married

If the marriage was valid, either party could apply to the ecclesiastical courts for a **divorce *a mensa et thoro*** (from bed and board), which was granted for adultery, extreme cruelty, or desertion, but this decree did *not* terminate the marriage. The parties no longer had the duty to live together, but they remained married. The husband continued to have a duty to support the wife if the decree was issued at the wife's request and based on the husband's misconduct. If the decree was granted at the husband's request and based on the wife's misconduct, the husband was not obliged to support the wife.

Thanks to Henry VIII,[3] eventually it became possible to terminate a marriage by divorce. It was not possible, however, to obtain a divorce through civil court proceedings. Instead, a divorce was obtained through a combination of an ecclesiastical court proceeding and a private member's bill in Parliament.

A husband could obtain a divorce based on his wife's adultery. First he had to sue the other man for damages for criminal conversation. Then he was required to apply to the ecclesiastical courts for a divorce *a mensa et thoro*, a judicial order permitting him to live separately from his wife. Finally, he had to get his member of Parliament to put through a private member's bill for divorce. In other words, the husband needed a law passed that divorced him from his wife. The process was long and expensive, and it was not available to those without money and connections. It was also not available to women. There was no remedy available to a wife to divorce her husband on any ground.

19TH-CENTURY REFORMS

The first major reforms in family law took place in the mid- to late 19th century as the economic and intellectual changes brought about by the Industrial Revolution led to a move for greater rights for women.

Legal Status of the Husband and Wife

Reforms of the 19th century started to give a married woman a legal identity separate from that of her husband. A married woman became entitled to buy and own property and to sue and be sued in her own name, although spouses still could not sue each other.

Physical Relationship Between the Husband and Wife

During the 19th century, a husband's right to physically discipline his wife ended.

presumption of advancement
the presumption, created by the *Married Women's Property Act*, that a husband who placed property in the name of his wife intended to make a gift of the property to her

Property of the Husband and Wife

In the 1880s, both England and Ontario passed statutes called the *Married Women's Property Act*, which provided that married women could own property separately from their husbands.

The *Married Women's Property Act* also created the **presumption of advancement** between a husband and wife: if a husband placed property in the

3 He founded his own church, separate from the Roman Catholic Church, so that he could divorce Catherine of Aragon and marry Anne Boleyn (whom he dispatched not long after by beheading).

name of his wife, it was presumed that he intended to make a gift of the property to her. Before the *Married Women's Property Act*, transfers of property from a husband to a wife were treated like transfers of property between unrelated parties. It was presumed that a person who paid for property and placed it in the name of another person intended the other person to hold the property in trust for the donor. (This presumption is called the **presumption of resulting trust**.)

presumption of resulting trust
an equitable principle under which it is presumed that a person who places property in the name of another person intends that person to hold the property in trust for the donor

In the event of a marriage breakdown, property was divided between the spouses strictly on the basis of ownership. Under common law, that meant that a wife could keep only property that was registered in her name. Under the law of equity, she might also be given an interest in property if she had contributed money or money's worth directly to the creation, improvement, or acquisition of the property. There was no recognition of an interest based on indirect contributions that the wife may have made to the marriage. The result was that ordinarily the husband would get most of the property.

Custody of the Children

During the 19th century, there was a change in the way children were viewed by society. Whereas children had previously been thought of as miniature adults, now childhood began to be seen as a distinct stage in human development during which children needed special care and nurturing. There was also a growing recognition of the need to consider the best interests of the children in the event of a separation of their parents. Children were no longer viewed as the property of the father, and courts began to make decisions about custody on the basis of psychological and emotional factors.

In 1886, the *Infants Custody Act* made "the best interests of the child" the basis on which custody was to be awarded. As a result, fathers no longer had an absolute right to custody, and mothers, as the parents responsible for raising children, were usually granted custody of young children ("children of tender years").

Support of One Spouse by the Other

Alimony continued through the 19th century and beyond, and continued to be tied to the conduct of the wife. There was no legislation passed in this area. However, judges effected changes in the common law through their decisions over time.

One judicial innovation was the **doctrine of constructive desertion**. Under the original alimony rules, if a wife left her husband for any reason, it was considered to be desertion. Desertion was a matrimonial offence that disentitled a wife to alimony. Under the doctrine of constructive desertion, if a wife left the marriage because of her husband's misconduct, the husband was deemed to have deserted the wife, and the wife did not lose her entitlement to alimony.

doctrine of constructive desertion
a doctrine related to alimony under which it was deemed that the husband had deserted the wife if a wife left her husband because of his misconduct

Another judicial innovation relaxed the requirement that a wife be willing to take her husband back in order to be entitled to alimony. Eventually, the courts decided that a wife was required to accept her husband's return only for a reasonable time.

Divorce

In England, judicial divorce (divorce through the civil courts) was established in 1857 by the *Divorce and Matrimonial Causes Act*. The ecclesiastical courts were abolished, and private members' bills were no longer required. The action of criminal conversation was also abolished.

A husband could divorce his wife on the ground of her adultery. Until 1925, a wife could not divorce her husband unless she could prove that he had committed incestuous adultery, bigamy, sodomy, bestiality, rape, adultery with cruelty, or adultery coupled with desertion for at least two years. A husband's adultery alone was not a ground; neither was his desertion alone, nor his cruelty alone. The 1925 *Divorce Act* made the grounds for divorce the same for both spouses, thus allowing a wife to divorce her husband on the ground of adultery alone.

Canada did not follow suit, in large part because of the opposition of Roman Catholic Quebec. Judicial divorce and the abolition of the action of criminal conversation did not come to Canada until the 20th century.

20TH-CENTURY CHANGES

The 20th century brought major changes in the role of women in society, and in the way the law dealt with women and marriage. Ontario family law was drastically reformed in 1978 with the passage of the *Family Law Reform Act* and was further reformed in 1986 by the *Family Law Act*. The first Canada-wide *Divorce Act* was passed in 1968 and reformed in 1985.

Legal Status of the Husband and Wife

The *Family Law Reform Act* abolished the unity of legal personality between husband and wife by stating that for all purposes a married person has a legal personality that is independent, separate, and distinct from that of his or her spouse. Husbands and wives were also given the right to sue each other in tort.

Physical Relationship Between the Husband and Wife

Before 1983, the *Criminal Code* defined the offence of rape as involving sexual intercourse by a male person with "a female person who is not his wife." In 1983, this provision was replaced by a general sexual assault provision. A husband no longer has a special right to sexual intercourse with his wife, and either a husband or a wife can be charged with sexual assault against the other party.

Property of the Husband and Wife

In 1975, the Supreme Court of Canada decided the case of *Murdoch v. Murdoch*. Mr. and Mrs. Murdoch were married from 1943 until 1968. During the course of the marriage, Mr. Murdoch bought and sold a series of ranches. Mrs. Murdoch worked on all of them. At the time of the separation, Mr. Murdoch owned a valuable ranch that was registered in his name only. Mrs. Murdoch claimed an interest in the ranch based on her contribution to the various ranches in the form of her labour over the years. The court decided that she had not made a substantial contribution to the acquisition of the ranch since the work she had done "was the work done by any ranch wife." Many people considered the decision unfair. Within several years, the Supreme Court of Canada took a different approach to the division of property on a marriage breakdown,[4] and the legislatures of most provinces, including Ontario, passed statutes reforming the law as it related to the property of a married couple.

The 1978 *Family Law Reform Act* recognized for the first time in Ontario that the division of property on a marriage breakdown should not be decided simply on the basis of ownership of or direct contribution to property. Instead, the Act acknowledged that marriage is a partnership to which both spouses make a contribution—whether by working outside the home or by assuming responsibility for child care and household management—and that by contributing to the partnership, the spouses were entitled to a share of the "partnership property." Under this Act, assets owned by the spouses were categorized as either "family assets" or "non-family assets," depending on how the assets were used by the family. On a marriage breakdown, family assets were divided equally between the parties. Non-family assets were not divided unless a court found that a division of only the family assets was inequitable.

The *Family Law Act*, which is the current legislation in Ontario, came into force on March 1, 1986. It continues to recognize the partnership aspect of marriage. However, it takes a different approach to property division. Property is no longer categorized on the basis of its use, and instead of dividing property, the Act divides the profits of the marriage. An accounting, called an **equalization of net family property**, takes place in which both spouses calculate the value of the assets they have on leaving the marriage as compared with the value of the assets they had on entering the marriage. If the value has gone up, the profit must be shared with the other party.

equalization of net family property
a process under the *Family Law Act* under which spouses share equally in the value of most property acquired during the marriage

Custody of the Children

Custody continues to be decided on the basis of the best interests of the child. The current statute, the *Children's Law Reform Act*, sets out a number of factors for the court to consider when deciding what those best interests might be. The biggest change in this area is more judicial than legislative, in that the courts have recently begun to grant custody, even of young children, to fathers.

Support of One Spouse by the Other

Starting with the *Family Law Reform Act* in 1978 and continuing with the *Family Law Act*, support is now based solely on the need of the dependent party and the ability of the other party to pay. Conduct is not an issue, except in the most unusual cases. Support can be paid by either a husband or a wife.

The term "alimony" is no longer used. Now the term "support" applies to payments ordered under the *Family Law Act* and the *Divorce Act*.

Divorce

In Ontario, there was no judicial divorce until 1930. Before then, a party seeking a divorce had to obtain a private member's bill in Parliament. The grounds for divorce were the same as those in England.

4 In the case of *Rathwell v. Rathwell*, [1978] 2 SCR 436, the court relied upon principles of unjust enrichment and constructive trust to give a wife a share in property acquired by her husband during the marriage.

The *Divorce Act (Ontario)* of 1930 brought judicial divorce to Ontario. The only ground available to a husband was his wife's adultery. A wife could obtain a divorce on the grounds of adultery, rape, sodomy, bestiality, or bigamy.

The first Canada-wide divorce legislation, the *Divorce Act*, was passed in 1968. That Act allowed divorce on both fault and no-fault grounds. The fault grounds included adultery, physical or mental cruelty, sodomy, bestiality, rape, and homosexual acts. The no-fault grounds included three years of separation, although a deserting spouse had to wait five years before being able to start a divorce action based on separation. The same grounds were available to both husbands and wives. The Act also dealt with child custody and support on the basis of the needs of the spouses and children.

A new *Divorce Act* came into effect in June 1986. It also provides for fault and no-fault grounds. The only fault grounds are adultery and cruelty. The no-fault ground requires a separation of one year.

REFERENCES

Children's Law Reform Act, RSO 1990, c. C.12.
Divorce Act, RSC 1985, c. 3 (2d Supp.).
Divorce and Matrimonial Causes Act (repealed).
Family Law Act, RSO 1990, c. F.3.
Family Law Reform Act (repealed).
Halpern v. Canada (Attorney General) (2003), 65 OR 161 (CA).
Infants Custody Act (repealed).
Married Women's Property Act (repealed).
Murdoch v. Murdoch, [1975] 1 SCR 423.
Rathwell v. Rathwell, [1978] 2 SCR 436.

REVIEW QUESTIONS

1. What is the "unity of legal personality"?
2. Before the 19th century, what right did a married woman have to own property?
3. Before the 19th century, what right did a woman have to custody of her children?
4. Before the 19th century, under what circumstances would a wife be awarded alimony?
5. Before the 19th century, what right did a woman have to divorce her husband? What right did a husband have to divorce his wife?
6. What is the *Married Women's Property Act*?
7. What is the "presumption of advancement"?
8. What is the "presumption of resulting trust"?
9. What is the *Infants Custody Act*?
10. What is the doctrine of constructive desertion?
11. When was the first Canada-wide divorce legislation passed?
12. What is the *Family Law Reform Act*?
13. What is the *Family Law Act*?
14. What is the *Children's Law Reform Act*?

DISCUSSION QUESTIONS

1. Ontario's family law has its origins in England during the late Middle Ages. The law has changed a great deal since that time as our society and its values have changed. Discuss.
2. The 1978 *Family Law Reform Act* recognized for the first time in Ontario that the division of property on a marriage breakdown should not be decided simply on the basis of ownership of or direct contribution to property. Discuss.

CHAPTER 3

Marriage

Family law deals with the legal rights and responsibilities of family members, and focuses primarily on the legal consequences of family breakdown. Before we can examine what happens when there is a family breakdown, we have to look at how a family is created.

What is meant by the word "family"? Is marriage a necessary element? Certainly a man and a woman who marry form a family unit, but in Canada today, families take other forms as well. In Ontario, same-sex couples may also marry. Many unmarried couples of the same or opposite sex live together in "common law" relationships. The partners in all of these family relationships have certain legal rights and responsibilities, whose nature depends on a number of factors, the most significant of which is whether the parties are, in fact, married.

In this chapter, we will look at one of the ways that families are created—through marriage—and in particular:

- the meaning of marriage,
- the requirements for a valid marriage, and
- the difference between marriage and other forms of family arrangements.

DEFINITION OF MARRIAGE

The definition of marriage comes from English common law. Historically, marriage was defined in Canada as "the voluntary union for life of one man and one woman to the exclusion of all others." In other words, marriage required a man and a woman, and there was no valid same-sex marriage.

On June 10, 2003, in the case of *Halpern v. Canada (Attorney General)*, the Ontario Court of Appeal ruled that this common law definition of marriage is contrary to the *Canadian Charter of Rights and Freedoms*. Courts in British Columbia and Quebec had already made similar rulings. One week later, the federal government announced that it would not be appealing these rulings, and would instead be proposing legislation to change the common law definition of marriage to allow for same-sex marriage.[1] As of December 2003, the federal government has referred draft legislation to the Supreme Court of Canada to ensure that it is within federal jurisdiction and is consistent with the Charter.

1 Under the *Constitution Act, 1867*, the federal government has legislative authority over marriage. Therefore, federal legislation is required to change the common law definition of marriage.

Marriage is a contract and, like any contract, confers legal rights and responsibilities on the parties. However, unlike other contracts, the rights and obligations of the parties are largely defined by statute, rather than by the parties themselves.

Marriage is subject to the same rules that govern all contracts, and so the parties to a marriage must have the **legal capacity** to enter into the contract and must comply with certain **legal formalities** for the contract to be valid.

legal capacity to marry
legal ability to enter into the contract of marriage

legal formalities of marriage
the form a marriage ceremony must take

LEGAL JURISDICTION OVER MARRIAGE

Under the *Constitution Act, 1867,* the federal government has jurisdiction over marriage and divorce, including matters relating to the capacity to marry, while the provinces have jurisdiction over the solemnization of marriage — in other words, the formal requirements of licensing and ceremony.

LEGAL CAPACITY TO MARRY

When we talk about the legal capacity to marry, we are talking about matters such as

- age,
- mental capacity,
- consent,
- consanguinity (blood relationship), and
- marital status.

Whether or not the parties have the legal capacity to marry is determined according to the law of the **domicile** (permanent residence) of the parties at the time of the marriage.

domicile
permanent residence

Age

Pursuant to the Ontario *Marriage Act*, a person must be at least 18 years old to be married without the consent of his or her parents. A person who is 16 or 17 years old may marry with the written consent of both parents. If the parents are not available or if they unreasonably withhold their consent to the marriage, the person may apply to a judge to dispense with parental consent.

Mental Capacity

A person entering a marriage must have the capacity to understand the nature of a marriage and its duties and responsibilities. A person who lacks this understanding at the time of the marriage, either as a result of an inherent lack of mental capacity or as a result of drugs or alcohol, cannot enter into a valid marriage.

duress
force or threats that cause a person to do something he or she would not ordinarily do

Consent

To be valid, a marriage must be entered into freely, without **duress** (force or threats). A person marries under duress if:

- the person is so afraid as to remove the element of consent,
- the fear is reasonable, and
- the fear is caused by a circumstance for which the person is not responsible.

In addition, the marriage must be entered into without any mistake as to the identity of the other party at the time of the ceremony or the nature of the ceremony. For example, if a party goes through a ceremony in a foreign country without realizing that it is a marriage ceremony, the party is not married. However, a mistake about certain characteristics of the other party, such as wealth or background, does not make a marriage invalid.

If a person goes through a marriage ceremony knowing the identity of the other person and the nature of the ceremony, the person's motives for doing so are irrelevant. For example, a marriage entered into for the sole objective of immigration is a valid marriage.

Consanguinity

The parties to a marriage may not be too closely related to each other, either by blood (consanguinity) or by adoption. Under the federal *Marriage (Prohibited Degrees) Act*, a man may not marry his

- grandmother,
- mother,
- daughter,
- sister, or
- granddaughter.

A woman may not marry her

- grandfather,
- father,
- son,
- brother, or
- grandson.

These prohibitions apply to relationships by whole or half blood or by adoption. Historically, marriage between parties closely related by marriage (affinity) was also prohibited. That is no longer the case.

Marital Status

A party to a marriage may not already be married to someone else. Any previous marriage must have been ended by death, divorce, or annulment.

FORMALITIES

The formalities of marriage involve such matters as:

- the persons authorized to perform a marriage ceremony,
- the nature of the ceremony,
- licence requirements, and
- residency requirements (in some jurisdictions).

The formalities of a valid marriage are determined by the law of the jurisdiction in which the marriage takes place. In Ontario, the formalities required of marriages are set out in the *Marriage Act.*

Persons Authorized To Perform a Marriage Ceremony

A couple marrying in Ontario may have a civil marriage or a religious marriage. A civil marriage can be performed by a judge or a justice of the peace. A religious marriage can be performed by a person who is recognized by a religious body to perform marriages and who is registered to perform marriages in Ontario under the *Marriage Act.*

The person who performs a marriage, whether it is civil or religious, is required to send documentation to the Office of the Registrar General for registration.

Nature of the Ceremony

Under Ontario law, each of the parties must at some point in the ceremony, in the presence of the person solemnizing the marriage and witnesses, declare: "I do solemnly declare that I do not know of any lawful impediment why I, AB, may not be joined in matrimony to CD," and must say to the other: "I call upon these persons here present to witness that I, AB, do take you CD, to be my lawful wedded wife (*or* husband)," after which the person solemnizing the marriage must say: "I, EF, by virtue of the powers vested in me by the *Marriage Act*, do hereby pronounce you AB and CD to be husband and wife."[2] Otherwise, no particular form is required for a civil marriage.

Any religious marriage performed by a properly registered person according to the rites, usages, and customs of the particular religion is valid.

Licence Requirements

A civil marriage can be performed only under the authority of a marriage licence. A religious marriage can be performed under the authority of a marriage licence or, depending on the religious denomination, the publication of banns,[3] provided that neither of the parties was previously in a marriage that ended in divorce or annulment.

A marriage licence can be obtained from the clerk of most cities, townships, towns, or villages.

2 In the absence of legislative amendment, terminology such as "married spouses" is currently being substituted for "husband and wife" at the marriages of same-sex couples.

3 The publication of banns involves proclaiming the intention to marry during church services.

Residency Requirements

In some jurisdictions, the parties must reside in the jurisdiction for a minimum period of time before they may be married in that jurisdiction. There are no residency requirements for marriage in Ontario.

RIGHTS AND OBLIGATIONS OF MARRIAGE

Like all contracts, marriage confers rights and obligations on the parties. The main rights and obligations of the parties to a marriage involve support and property. In Ontario, each spouse has an obligation to provide financial support for him- or herself and for the other spouse, in accordance with the other spouse's need, to the extent that he or she is capable of doing so. Husbands and wives in Ontario are also given the right to a share of the value of property acquired during the marriage and to possession of their matrimonial home (the home in which they live).[4] Married couples also have rights to share in each other's estates, as well as rights under various statutes regarding taxes, pensions, insurance, and benefits.

"COMMON LAW MARRIAGE"

The term "common law marriage" is sometimes used to describe the relationship between people who live in a marital relationship but who have not gone through a marriage ceremony. Parties in these relationships may consider themselves married, and others may think of them as married, but they are not. No matter how long they live together, and whether or not they have children, people who have not gone through a formal marriage ceremony are not married and do not have all of the rights and obligations that married people have.

Under federal and provincial statutes, unmarried same-sex and opposite-sex couples who cohabit have been given many of the same rights as married couples when it comes to taxes, pensions, insurance, and other benefits. After a certain period of time, they may also have the same obligation as married people to support each other and the same right to claim support from the estate of the deceased partner.

Parties who cohabit without being married do *not* have the same property rights as parties to a marriage.[5] In fact, they do not have *any* statutory right to a share of their partner's property or to possession of the home in which the parties live. Parties in these non-marriage relationships can, however, choose to give each other these rights by entering into a cohabitation agreement (discussed in chapter 10).

4 At present, this right has not been extended to married couples of the same sex.

5 Nor, at present, do married parties of the same sex.

REFERENCES

Canadian Charter of Rights and Freedoms, part I of the *Constitution Act, 1982*, RSC 1985, app. II, s. 44.

Constitution Act, 1867, 30 & 31 Vict., c. 3 (UK).

Halpern v. Canada (Attorney General) (2003), 65 OR 161 (CA).

Marriage Act, RSO 1990, c. M.3.

Marriage (Prohibited Degrees) Act, SC 1990, c. 46.

REVIEW QUESTIONS

1. Which level of government has jurisdiction over the legal capacity to marry?
2. Which level of government has jurisdiction over marriage licences and marriage ceremonies?
3. Describe how *Halpern v. Canada (Attorney General)* affected the laws of marriage in Ontario.
4. How old must a person be to be married in Ontario without the consent of his or her parents?
5. What must a person have the capacity to understand in order to form a valid marriage?
6. By the law of which place are the formalities of a valid marriage determined?
7. What statute governs the formalities of marriage in Ontario?
8. Who may perform a civil marriage in Ontario? Who may perform a religious marriage?
9. Describe the form required for a civil and a religious marriage ceremony in Ontario.
10. Is a marriage licence always required?
11. Are there any residency requirements for marriage in Ontario?
12. What are the main rights and obligations of the parties to a marriage?
13. Do parties who cohabit without being married have the right to be supported by each other?
14. Do parties who cohabit without being married have a statutory right to a share of the other party's property?

DISCUSSION QUESTIONS

1. In the Bible, Jacob fell in love with Rachel and asked to marry her. At the ceremony, Rachel's father substituted her older sister Leah for Rachel. Leah was covered in a heavy veil, and Jacob, thinking he was marrying Rachel, was married to Leah instead. Would this be a valid marriage in Ontario?
2. Susan Sarandon and Tim Robinson have lived together for many years and have had several children together, but they have never married. In Ontario, would either of them have a statutory right to share in each other's property?

CHAPTER 4

Dissolution of Marriage by Annulment

A marriage can be terminated in only three ways: annulment, divorce, or the death of one of the parties. While a divorce puts an end to a valid marriage, an annulment declares that a marriage is invalid and, therefore, void. Both divorce and annulment require a court judgment.

The law of annulment[1] developed when it was virtually impossible to get a divorce on any ground. It continued to be an important remedy when divorce was available only on fault grounds. Annulment is now a rarely used remedy, since divorce is available on the basis of a one-year separation.

In this chapter, we will look at

- the grounds for annulment, and
- the remedies available in an annulment proceeding.

WHAT IS AN ANNULMENT?

An annulment is a judgment that declares that a marriage is void. A marriage may be **void *ab initio*** or it may be **voidable**. In the latter case, the parties can choose whether to treat the marriage as void or as valid. If a marriage is void *ab initio*, it is as if the marriage had never taken place. A voidable marriage, however, is treated as a valid marriage unless and until it is annulled by a court.

void *ab initio*
void, or having no legal force, from the beginning

voidable
may be declared void but is otherwise not void

Marriages That Are Void ab Initio

A marriage is void *ab initio* if one of the parties did not have the legal capacity to marry. The factors affecting capacity, which are discussed more fully in chapter 3, are the following:

- *Age*. A marriage is void *ab initio* if either of the parties was too young. Even though the *Marriage Act* of Ontario states that a marriage licence cannot be issued to a minor without parental consent, a marriage that has been performed without parental consent is void *ab initio* only if one of the parties was younger than 7 years old. (If a female party is between the ages of 7 and

1 Annulment is a common law remedy — that is, all of the law in this area comes from case decisions. There is no legislation that deals with annulment.

12 or a male party is between the ages of 7 and 14, the marriage, while not void, is voidable at the option of the underage party.)

- *Mental capacity*. A marriage is void *ab initio* if, at the time of the marriage ceremony, one of the parties was incapable of understanding the nature of a marriage and its obligations, either as a result of an inherent lack of mental capacity or as a result of drugs or alcohol.
- *Consent*. A marriage is void *ab initio* if either of the parties did not freely consent to the marriage because of mistake or fraud, and is voidable if either of the parties did not consent because of duress.
- *Consanguinity*. A marriage is void *ab initio* if the parties are too closely related to each other by blood or adoption.
- *Marital status*. A marriage is void *ab initio* if either of the parties was married to another person at the time of the marriage ceremony. This is the reason that most marriages are declared void *ab initio*. In some cases, one of the parties lies about his or her marital status at the time of the wedding, but more commonly, a party enters into a marriage in the honest belief that his or her prior marriage has been terminated. For example, a party may have participated in a divorce proceeding that is not recognized as valid in Canada.

Marriages That Are Voidable

A marriage is voidable if one of the parties is unable to consummate the marriage at the time of the ceremony.[2] Either party may apply to have the marriage annulled on this ground. (In other words, an applicant may rely on his or her own inability to consummate.)

The applicant must prove that the other party to the marriage has an incurable inability or incapacity to consummate the marriage. The inability may be physical or mental, but a simple refusal to have sexual intercourse is not enough.

EFFECT OF AN ANNULMENT

A marriage that is void *ab initio* was never valid, and the parties to a void marriage were never validly married. The judicial decree of nullity merely confirms the status of the parties as unmarried.

A marriage that is voidable continues to be valid, and the parties continue to be married unless and until the marriage is declared to be invalid by a court. Once a decree of nullity is granted, it is as if the marriage never took place.

RIGHTS OF THE PARTIES

Under s. 1(1) of the *Family Law Act*, the definition of "spouse" includes "either of a man and woman who . . . have together entered into a marriage that is voidable or

2 A marriage is consummated when ordinary and complete sexual intercourse takes place between the spouses after the marriage ceremony.

void, in good faith on the part of the person relying on this clause to assert any right." In other words, a person who entered into a void or voidable marriage in good faith can assert the same property and support claims as a person who is validly married.

PROCEDURE

A party wishing to annul a marriage may do so by way of an application in the Family Court of the Superior Court of Justice or by way of a statement of claim in the Superior Court of Justice. The proceeding may include claims for custody, support, and property rights.

REFERENCES

Family Law Act, RSO 1990, c. F.3.
Marriage Act, RSO 1990, c. M.3.

REVIEW QUESTIONS

1. What is an annulment?
2. What does void *ab initio* mean?
3. What marriages are void *ab initio*?
4. What marriages are voidable?
5. What is the effect of an annulment?
6. What type of proceeding is required to obtain an annulment?

DISCUSSION QUESTIONS

Jude loved Sue and so he married her. Unfortunately, he neglected to tell her that he was already married to Arabella. Is this a valid marriage? Does Sue have any property or support rights against Jude? Does Jude have any property or support rights against Sue?

CHAPTER 5

Dissolution of Marriage by Divorce

A valid marriage may be terminated in only two ways: by the death of one of the parties or by divorce.[1]

In this chapter, we will look at

- the legislative jurisdiction over divorce,
- the jurisdiction of the courts in divorce matters,
- the grounds for divorce,
- the bars to divorce,
- the statutory duties regarding reconciliation,
- the effective date of a divorce,
- the legal effect of a divorce, and
- the recognition of foreign divorce decrees.

The law relating to custody and support under the *Divorce Act* and procedure in divorce proceedings are discussed later in this book.

LEGISLATIVE JURISDICTION OVER DIVORCE

Divorce is a matter of federal jurisdiction. The first Canada-wide statute dealing with divorce was passed in 1968. The current *Divorce Act* has been in effect since 1986.

Once a divorce proceeding is commenced, questions of spousal support, child support, and custody are dealt with under the *Divorce Act*. Issues relating to the property of the parties are dealt with under provincial legislation (and not under the *Divorce Act*).

1 The *Divorce Act* has not yet been amended to apply to same-sex marriages. At present, proceedings under the Act may be brought only by a "spouse," which is defined as "either of a man or woman who are married to each other."

JURISDICTION OF THE COURTS IN DIVORCE MATTERS

A party seeking a divorce must know which court has jurisdiction to deal with the matter. This involves two questions:

1. Which province has jurisdiction?
2. If Ontario has jurisdiction, which Ontario court has jurisdiction?

Which Province Has Jurisdiction?

The *Divorce Act* is a federal statute that governs divorce throughout Canada. The spouses may live anywhere in Canada, and may even be living in different provinces. The statute sets out which province has jurisdiction to deal with their divorce.

Section 3(1) of the Act states:

> A court in a province has jurisdiction to hear and determine a divorce proceeding if either spouse has been ordinarily resident in the province for at least one year immediately preceding the commencement of the proceeding.

In other words, if one spouse has lived in a province for at least *one* year immediately before the commencement of the divorce, then *either* spouse can start a divorce proceeding in that province.

Dharma and Greg were married in Ontario and lived there until their separation a little more than a year ago. Immediately after their separation, Dharma moved to British Columbia, while Greg stayed in Ontario.

Dharma can start a divorce action in British Columbia since she has resided in that province for at least one year, and Greg can start a divorce action in Ontario for the same reason. But Dharma can also start her divorce action in Ontario, and Greg can also start his divorce action in British Columbia.

Section 3(1) is very useful if the person who wants to start the divorce action has not lived in one province long enough to be able to rely on his or her own residency.

Fred and Ethel were married in Alberta and lived there until their separation a little more than one year ago. After the separation, Fred moved to British Columbia and stayed there. Ethel, however, decided to work her way across Canada, moving first to Manitoba, where she lived for three months, then to Ontario, where she lived for the next three months, then on to Quebec, where she lived for four months, and finally to Newfoundland, where she has lived ever since. Ethel now wants a divorce. What can she do?

Clearly Fred can start a divorce action in British Columbia since he has resided in that province for at least one year. But what if Ethel wants to start the divorce action? She cannot start an action in any of the provinces she has lived in during the marriage or since the separation because she has not lived in any of them for the year leading up to the divorce action. But Ethel, like Fred, can start a divorce action in British Columbia, relying on the fact that Fred has resided there for at least one year before she commences the divorce action.

As you can see in the Greg and Dharma example, it is possible for more than one province to have jurisdiction to start a divorce proceeding. What happens if two spouses both start divorce proceedings in different provinces? Under s. 3(2) of the Act, the divorce proceeding that was started first continues, while the one that was started second is deemed to be discontinued. If the proceedings are both started on the same day and neither spouse discontinues his or her action, the divorce is dealt with by the Federal Court Trial Division under s. 3(3) of the Act.

Which Ontario Court Has Jurisdiction?

In Ontario, the Superior Court of Justice (including the Family Court of the Superior Court of Justice) has jurisdiction over divorce actions.

GROUNDS FOR DIVORCE

The grounds for divorce are dealt with in s. 8 of the *Divorce Act*. The Act speaks of one ground only: breakdown of the marriage (in s. 8(1)), but there are three ways to establish marriage breakdown. One is a no-fault ground, and two are fault grounds.

No-Fault Ground

Spouses may divorce on the ground of separation. This ground involves no allegation of fault against either party.

Under s. 8(2)(a), breakdown of a marriage is established if

> the spouses have lived separate and apart for at least one year immediately preceding the determination of the divorce proceeding and were living separate and apart at the commencement of the proceeding.

Either spouse can start a divorce action any time after the parties have separated, but the parties must have been living separate and apart for at least one year by the time the matter is dealt with by the judge. In other words, a spouse can *start* a divorce proceeding on the day of separation, but a judge cannot *grant* a divorce until the parties have been separated for at least one year.

Spouses are considered to be living separate and apart only if they are both physically separated, and at least one of them has an intention to be separate and apart. Spouses who live in different places are not living separate and apart if they have an intention to remain married.

Lucy and Ricky were married and lived together in Toronto. Ricky got a job as a band leader in Cuba and set up an apartment there. Lucy and Ricky continued to consider themselves married. Lucy flew to Cuba twice a year, and Ricky returned to Toronto twice a year.

Lucy and Ricky are not living separate and apart under the *Divorce Act*.

Sometimes it is difficult for the courts to decide when spouses have separated.

Lynn and Keith were married in 1985. After many difficulties in the marriage, Lynn moved out in 1995, telling Keith she needed "some space." Over the next three and a half years, Lynn and Keith maintained separate households, cars, and bank accounts, but they also continued to have a sexual relationship and regularly went out, travelled, and spent weekends together. They never told Keith's parents that they had separated, and they spent Christmas with his family, pretending they were still living together. One night in January 1998, Lynn and Keith had an argument. She told him that she did not want to have sex with him, and she realized that she wanted her marriage to end.

The judge who presided at the couple's divorce decided that Lynn's desire to end the marriage and the cessation of sexual relations marked the point at which the couple began to live separate and apart.

It is even possible for spouses to be living separate and apart under the same roof as long as there are two households or the spouses are living separate lives. It is not enough for the spouses simply to have ceased having a sexual relationship. There must be a mutual repudiation of the marriage relationship. Spouses living under the same roof who rarely communicate, eat separately, do not share social activities, and occupy separate bedrooms have been found to be living separate and apart.

Under s. 8(3)(b)(ii) of the *Divorce Act*, if the spouses resume cohabitation, in an attempt at reconciliation, for a period or periods of not more than 90 days, the period during which the spouses have lived separate and apart is not considered to have been interrupted or ended.

Fault Grounds

There are two grounds for divorce that involve an allegation of fault against one of the spouses: adultery and cruelty.

ADULTERY

Pursuant to s. 8(2)(b)(i) of the Act, breakdown of a marriage can also be established if the spouse against whom the divorce action is brought has committed adultery. Adultery has been defined by the courts to mean voluntary sexual intercourse between a married person and another person of the opposite sex other than his or her spouse. The adultery must be committed by the respondent spouse. The spouse who starts the divorce proceeding cannot rely on his or her own adultery as a ground for divorce.

CRUELTY

Pursuant to s. 8(2)(b)(ii) of the Act, breakdown of a marriage can also be established if the spouse against whom the divorce action is brought has treated the other spouse with physical or mental cruelty of such a kind as to render intolerable the continued cohabitation of the spouses.

A spouse who by his or her conduct "causes wanton, malicious or unnecessary infliction of pain or suffering upon the body, the feelings or emotions of the other" may be guilty of cruelty.[1] To constitute cruelty, the conduct must be of a grave and weighty nature; it cannot be trivial. At the same time, the test for cruelty is subjective. The question is whether particular conduct by a particular party against his or her spouse is cruelty. Isolated acts that are not in themselves cruelty can amount to cruelty if they are part of an ongoing course of conduct whose cumulative effect is to make continued cohabitation intolerable.[2]

Examples of conduct found to constitute cruelty include:

- a series of assaults,
- one savage attack,
- persistent harassment and abuse,
- a husband's transvestism,
- a husband's pedophilia,
- a spouse's persistent refusal to have sexual relations with the other,
- a husband's forcing his wife to engage in fellatio against her will, and
- a wife's ongoing ridicule of her husband's sexual performance.

BARS TO DIVORCE

There are certain circumstances in which a court will not grant a divorce, even if the spouse who started the proceeding proves that one or more of the grounds for divorce exist. The three major bars to divorce, which are dealt with in s. 11 of the Act, are:

- collusion,
- condonation, and
- connivance.

Collusion

Collusion is defined in s. 11(4) of the Act as

> an agreement or conspiracy to which an applicant for a divorce is ... a party for the purpose of subverting the administration of justice, and includes any agreement, understanding or arrangement to fabricate or suppress evidence or to deceive the court.

Harry and Sally have just separated. They do not want to wait for a divorce until they've been separated for one year, so Sally suggests to Harry that he sue her for divorce based on adultery. They agree that Sally will give

1 *Knoll v. Knoll* (1970), 1 RFL 141 (Ont. CA).

2 *Powell v. Powell* (1971), 5 RFL 195 (Sask. CA) and *Wittstock v. Wittstock*, [1971] 2 OR 472 (CA).

evidence that she committed adultery with a co-worker even though that is not the case. This agreement constitutes collusion.

It would also be collusion if Harry and Sally agreed to lie about the date on which they separated so that they could get a divorce early.

It is the duty of the court to satisfy itself that there has been no collusion in relation to the application for a divorce. If the court finds collusion on the part of the applicant, the court must dismiss the divorce claim. Collusion is an absolute bar to a divorce whether the divorce is brought on a fault or a no-fault ground.

Connivance

Connivance is not defined in the Act, but it takes place when the spouse bringing the proceeding encourages the other spouse to commit a matrimonial offence so that there are grounds for a divorce.

Harry and Sally have just separated. They don't want to wait until they've been separated for one year, so Sally suggests to Harry that he have sexual intercourse with a co-worker so that she can sue him for divorce based on adultery. Harry agrees. The couple's actions here constitute connivance.

Unlike collusion, connivance is not an absolute bar to divorce. Pursuant to s. 11(1)(c), the court may grant a divorce notwithstanding connivance on the part of the spouse bringing the proceeding if, in its opinion, "the public interest would be better served by granting the divorce." Connivance applies only to a divorce brought on the fault grounds of adultery or cruelty.

Condonation

Condonation, which may also be a bar to a divorce, applies only to a divorce brought on the fault grounds of adultery or cruelty. Condonation is not defined in the Act, but at common law, condonation takes place when a spouse, with knowledge of the offence, forgives the offence and continues or resumes cohabitation with the guilty spouse.

In order to encourage spouses to attempt to reconcile before commencing divorce proceedings, s. 11(3) provides that a continuation or resumption of cohabitation during a period or periods totalling no more than 90 days with reconciliation as its primary purpose is not considered to constitute condonation.

Angelina and Billy Bob have been married a short time when Angelina discovers that Billy Bob has been having an affair with a co-worker. Angelina is furious and moves out, threatening to start divorce proceedings immediately. Billy Bob begs for forgiveness and promises to change. Angelina relents and moves back in with Billy Bob in an attempt at reconciliation. After two months, she notices him flirting with other women whenever they go out together, and she decides that he has not changed at all. She moves out again.

Angelina can still rely on Billy Bob's affair as a ground for divorce. Even though she resumed cohabitation with him with full knowledge that he had committed adultery, her behaviour does not constitute condonation because of the exception in s. 11(3). However, if the couple had resumed cohabitation for four months instead of two, Angelina could not rely on Billy Bob's original affair and would need new grounds for divorce.

Condonation, like connivance, is not an absolute bar to a divorce. Pursuant to s. 11(1)(c), the court may grant a divorce notwithstanding condonation on the part of the spouse who brings the proceeding if, in its opinion, "the public interest would be better served by granting the divorce."

Failure To Make Reasonable Arrangements for Child Support

If the parties to the divorce have children, pursuant to s. 11(1)(b), the court has a duty to satisfy itself that reasonable arrangements have been made for the support of the children. If arrangements have not been made, the court must stay the granting of the divorce until arrangements are made.

ENCOURAGEMENT OF RECONCILIATION UNDER THE DIVORCE ACT

There are a number of provisions of the *Divorce Act* designed to encourage reconciliation by the spouses. We have examined two already:

- Under s. 8(3)(b)(ii), the one-year period of separation is not interrupted by a resumption of cohabitation, with reconciliation as its primary purpose, for a period or periods totalling no more than 90 days.
- Under s. 11(3), a resumption of cohabitation, with reconciliation as its primary purpose, for a period or periods totalling no more than 90 days does not constitute condonation of a matrimonial offence.

How do these provisions encourage reconciliation? It is presumed that spouses will be more willing to attempt to reconcile if they know that they have nothing to lose (in terms of their grounds for divorce) if the reconciliation fails.

In addition to these provisions, the Act imposes a duty on legal advisers and the court to encourage the parties to reconcile:

- Under s. 9, except in cases where it would clearly not be appropriate to do so, it is the duty of every legal adviser who acts on behalf of a spouse in a divorce proceeding to draw the provisions in s. 8(3) and s. 11(3) to the attention of the spouse, to discuss with the spouse the possibility of reconciliation, and to advise the spouse about marriage counselling or guidance facilities. The legal adviser must certify that he or she has done this.
- Under s. 10, except in cases where it would clearly not be appropriate to do so, it is the duty of the court, before hearing the evidence in the divorce

proceeding, to satisfy itself that there is no possibility of the reconciliation of the spouses. If the court is of the opinion that there is a possibility of reconciliation, it must adjourn the proceedings to allow the spouses an opportunity to achieve a reconciliation.

EFFECTIVE DATE OF DIVORCE

Under the provisions of s. 12 of the Act, a divorce generally takes effect on the 31st day after the divorce judgment is granted. If the court is of the opinion that special circumstances exist, it can order that the judgment take effect earlier. In order for the court to grant this kind of order, the spouses must file a document with the court by which they agree and undertake not to appeal the judgment.

Because a divorce takes effect on the 31st day, a party who wishes to appeal a judgment granting a divorce must file his or her appeal (or an application to extend the appeal period) within the 31-day period. If no appeal is filed within the time limit, the divorce judgment becomes effective.

When a court grants a divorce, it signs a formal divorce judgment. The judgment document itself does not prove that the divorce has become effective because it does not indicate whether or not the judgment was appealed. As a result, the Act provides that once a divorce becomes effective, the court must issue on request a certificate that the divorce was effective as of a specified date. A party requires this certificate to prove that he or she is divorced.

EFFECT OF DIVORCE

Pursuant to s. 14 of the Act, on taking effect, a divorce dissolves the marriage of the spouses. According to s. 13 of the Act, a divorce has legal effect throughout Canada.

RECOGNITION OF FOREIGN DIVORCES

Not all divorces granted by other jurisdictions are considered valid in Canada. "Quickie" foreign divorces are frowned upon. Canada requires some legitimate connection between the parties and the jurisdiction that granted the divorce before a foreign divorce judgment will be recognized.

Under the provisions of s. 22(1) of the Act, a divorce granted by a foreign jurisdiction is recognized in Canada if either party was resident in the jurisdiction for at least one year immediately before the proceeding was commenced. (Note that this is the same basis on which jurisdiction of the Canadian courts is based.)

Another basis for recognizing foreign divorce judgments is found in s. 22(3) of the Act, which provides that common law rules for recognition of foreign divorces are preserved. The common law test, which was stated in the 1969 House of Lords decision of *Indyka v. Indyka*, was adopted by the Canadian courts. In that case, it was decided that a foreign divorce is recognized if there is a real and substantial connection between the spouse bringing the proceeding and the jurisdiction granting the divorce unless the divorce was obtained by fraud, or unless recognition of the divorce would offend the rules of natural justice.

REFERENCES

Divorce Act, RSC 1985, c. 3 (2d Supp.).
Indyka v. Indyka, [1969] AC 33 (HL).
Knoll v. Knoll (1970), 1 RFL 141 (Ont. CA).
Powell v. Powell (1971), 5 RFL 195 (Sask. CA).
Wittstock v. Wittstock, [1971] 2 OR 472 (CA).

REVIEW QUESTIONS

1. What statute governs divorce? Is it a federal statute or a provincial statute?
2. Under what legislation are issues of spousal support, child support, and custody dealt with once a divorce proceeding is commenced?
3. Under what legislation are issues relating to property dealt with once a divorce proceeding is commenced?
4. How does a party determine which province has jurisdiction to deal with his or her divorce?
5. In the province of Ontario, which court has jurisdiction over divorce actions?
6. When may a spouse start a divorce on the grounds of separation? When may the divorce be granted?
7. Is it possible for spouses to live separate and apart under the same roof?
8. Can the spouse who starts a divorce proceeding rely on his or her own adultery as a ground for the divorce?
9. What is collusion?
10. What is connivance?
11. What is condonation?
12. What provisions of the *Divorce Act* encourage reconciliation of the spouses?
13. When does a divorce generally take effect?
14. What is a certificate of divorce, and why is one necessary?
15. Under what circumstances is a divorce granted by a foreign jurisdiction recognized in Canada?

DISCUSSION QUESTION

Helen caught her husband Hank in bed with her former best friend Jamie. In an ensuing argument, Hank punched Helen in the eye, something that he has done several times before. Helen has just left Hank and wants a divorce. Name all possible grounds for divorce that are available to Helen. For each ground, state when Helen may commence divorce proceedings and when a divorce may be granted.

CHAPTER 6

Custody and Access

When a two-parent family is intact, the children live with and are cared for by both parents. When the parents separate, a decision must be made as to which parent will live with and care for the children. If the parents cannot make this decision, a court will make it for them.

In this chapter, we will be looking at the law of custody and access, including:

- the applicable legislation,
- the jurisdiction of the Ontario courts,
- the meaning of custody and access,
- the relevant factors in determining custody,
- interim and permanent custody orders,
- custody under the *Divorce Act*,
- custody under the *Children's Law Reform Act*,
- custody assessments,
- mediation,
- enforcement of custody orders, and
- variation of custody orders.

WHICH LEGISLATION APPLIES?

Custody and access are dealt with in both the provincial *Children's Law Reform Act* and the federal *Divorce Act*. Custody and access are determined under the *Divorce Act* if divorce proceedings have been commenced by either spouse. If a spouse has not started a divorce proceeding, custody and access are determined under part III of the *Children's Law Reform Act*.

JURISDICTION OF THE ONTARIO COURTS

Before an Ontario court considers the issue of custody, whether under the *Divorce Act* or under the *Children's Law Reform Act*, it must be satisfied that it is appropriate to assume jurisdiction.

Under the Divorce Act

As discussed in chapter 5, a court has jurisdiction to hear a divorce proceeding if either spouse has been ordinarily resident in the province for at least one year immediately preceding the commencement of the divorce proceeding. A court that has jurisdiction to hear a divorce proceeding has jurisdiction over a custody application included in the proceeding. However, under s. 6 of the *Divorce Act*, if the custody application is opposed, the court has the power to transfer the divorce proceeding to another province if it is of the opinion that the child is most substantially connected with the other province.

Under the Children's Law Reform Act

jurisdiction shopping
the practice of choosing a jurisdiction in which to start a proceeding based on a party's view of his or her chances of success in that jurisdiction rather than on the jurisdiction's connection with the subject matter of the proceeding

The provisions of the *Children's Law Reform Act* concerning the jurisdiction of the Ontario courts are designed to discourage child abduction and "**jurisdiction shopping**" in custody matters. To that end, the provisions of the Act require the return of any child to the appropriate jurisdiction if the court is of the opinion that the child has inappropriately come before the Ontario courts.

Under s. 22 of the Act, Ontario courts may take jurisdiction only if

- the child is "habitually resident" in Ontario, or
- although the child is not habitually resident in Ontario,
    - ❑ the child is physically present in Ontario at the commencement of the proceedings,
    - ❑ substantial evidence concerning the best interests of the child is available in Ontario,
    - ❑ no application for custody or access is pending in a jurisdiction where the child is habitually resident,
    - ❑ no foreign custody or access order has been recognized by an Ontario court,
    - ❑ the child has a real and substantial connection with Ontario, and
    - ❑ on the balance of convenience it is appropriate for jurisdiction to be exercised in Ontario.

"Habitual residence" is defined in s. 22(2) as the place where the child resided with both parents. If the parents are separated, the child's habitual residence is the place where the child has resided with one parent under a separation agreement or court order or, if there is no agreement or order, with the consent or acquiescence of the other parent. A parent may not alter a child's habitual residence by abducting the child (taking the child without the consent of the other parent) unless the other parent has acquiesced to the abduction or has unduly delayed in taking steps to have the child returned.

Section 23 of the Act also allows an Ontario court to assume jurisdiction, even though the criteria of s. 22 have not been met, if the child is physically present in Ontario and the court is satisfied that the child would otherwise suffer serious harm.

On the flip side, s. 25 of the Act allows an Ontario court to decline jurisdiction, even though the criteria of s. 22 have been met, if the court is of the opinion that it would be more appropriate for jurisdiction to be exercised outside Ontario.

MEANING OF CUSTODY AND ACCESS

When the parents of a child reside together, both parents have **custody**: the right and responsibility to make decisions affecting the well-being of the child. It is only when the parents separate that custodial issues arise. Then the parties must answer questions such as the following:

custody
the rights and responsibilities of a parent, including the right and responsibility to make decisions affecting the well-being of the child

- Where will the child reside (with one parent or both parents)?
- When will each parent see the child?
- Who has the right to make decisions affecting the child: one parent or both parents? If both parents, what happens if the parents disagree?
- If one parent leaves the child to be cared for by the other parent, how are the first parent's custody rights affected?

These issues have been addressed in the *Divorce Act*, the *Children's Law Reform Act*, and court decisions over the years. They will be discussed in detail later in this chapter.

Custody involves more than where a child lives. It involves the right to make decisions affecting the child's welfare on matters such as place of residence, health, education, and religion. **Access** is the right to visit with the child and to obtain information regarding the child's health, education, and welfare.

access
the right to visit with the child and to obtain information regarding the child's health, education, and welfare

Custody arrangements can take various forms. At one extreme, one parent may have total care of and decision-making power over the child, while the other parent is not allowed even to see the child. At the other extreme, both parents may share care and decision making equally. More commonly, however, the arrangements involve the child's residing primarily with one parent while spending some time, such as every weekend or alternate weekends, with the other parent.

If we are told that one parent has total care and decision-making power, it is easy to determine that that parent has **sole custody**. If we are told that both parents share care and decision-making power, it is easy to determine that the parents have **joint custody**. But if we are told that a child lives primarily with one parent and spends weekends with the other parent, we do not have enough information to determine who has custody. Custody is not a matter of how much time is spent with the child. Rather, it is a matter of decision-making authority. If both parents share decision-making authority, the parents have joint custody, even though the child spends considerably more time with one parent than the other.

sole custody
when one parent has total care of and decision-making power over the child

joint custody
when both parents share care of and decision-making power over the child

PRINCIPLES IN DETERMINING CUSTODY

When a court decides a custody case, the same principles apply whether the case is decided under the *Children's Law Reform Act* or the *Divorce Act*.

Under both statutes, the issue of custody is determined on the basis of the "best interests of the child." The *Children's Law Reform Act* lists a number of factors in s. 24(2) that the court should consider when deciding what those best interests are. The *Divorce Act* does not.

Although each case is decided on its individual merits, a number of principles have emerged over the years:

- As a general rule, siblings are not separated.
- The wishes of the child, especially an older child, are considered.
- Past conduct of the parents is not relevant unless it has an impact on the parent's ability to be a parent to the child.

The most important factor in any custody dispute is the status quo. Generally, a judge will change existing custody arrangements only if it is clear that the status quo is not working.

INTERIM OR TEMPORARY CUSTODY ORDERS

A decision must be made about the custody of children at the time the parents separate. If the parties cannot agree on the issue of custody, either of them can ask the court to decide the issue, either by starting a custody proceeding under the *Children's Law Reform Act* or by claiming custody in a divorce proceeding. However, the question of custody will not be finally decided until the matter comes to trial, which can take a year or more.

The decision regarding interim custody is extremely important in light of the courts' reluctance to interfere with the status quo when deciding custody at trial. Generally speaking, the parent who is awarded interim custody will win permanent custody at the trial (unless that parent has made a mess of things).

de facto custody
actual custody, or custody in fact

In fact, even at the interim custody stage, the courts will not, generally speaking, disturb the status quo. As a result, the person who has ***de facto* custody** (custody in fact) of a child at the time of the interim custody motion is generally allowed to keep the child until the trial.

CUSTODY UNDER THE DIVORCE ACT

Application of the Act

The issues of custody and access are dealt with under the *Divorce Act*[1] if divorce proceedings have been commenced by a spouse. The court may make an order respecting any "child of the marriage."

"Child of the marriage" is defined in s. 2(1) of the Act to mean a child of two spouses or former spouses who, at the material time,

- is under the age of majority and who has not withdrawn from their charge, or
- is the age of majority or over and under their charge but unable, by reason of illness, disability, or other cause, to withdraw from their charge or to obtain the necessaries of life.

Accordingly, the court has jurisdiction to make a custody order with respect to a disabled child over the age of 18 who is in the care of one or both parents.

Under s. 2(2) of the Act, a child of two spouses or former spouses includes

1 The federal government is proposing changes to the custody provisions of the *Divorce Act*. See the end of the chapter for a discussion of these changes.

- any child for whom the spouses both stand in the place of parents, and
- any child of whom one is the parent and for whom the other stands in the place of a parent.

Accordingly, a child of only one spouse is considered to be a child of the marriage if the other spouse acted as a parent to the child, even if that spouse never formally adopted the child.

Definition of Custody and Access

The *Divorce Act* does not give a definition of either custody or access. However, s. 16(5) of the Act states that unless ordered otherwise, a spouse who is granted access to a child has the right to make inquiries and to be given information about the health, education, and welfare of the child.

Who May Apply for Custody?

Pursuant to ss. 16(2) and (3) of the Act, an application for custody may be made by either or both spouses or by any other person. However, a person other than a spouse may not make a custody application without leave of the court.

Orders That May Be Made

Under s. 16(4) of the Act, the court may make an order granting custody of, or access to, any or all children of the marriage to any one or more persons. (This section authorizes the court to make an order granting joint custody.) Section 16(6) gives the court the power to impose terms, conditions or restrictions as it thinks fit and just.

Pursuant to s. 16(7), the court may require a person who has custody of a child to give at least 30 days' notice to any person who has access of an intention to change the child's place of residence. This notice period gives non-custodial parents and others with access time to take steps to prevent the move if they wish. (For a more complete discussion of the right of a custodial parent to change the child's place of residence, see the section entitled "Variation of Custody Orders" below.)

Section 16(2) provides for the making of interim orders with respect to custody and access.

Factors in Deciding Custody

Section 16(8) of the Act states that, in making an order for custody or access,

> the court shall take into consideration only the best interests of the child of the marriage as determined by reference to the condition, means, needs and other circumstances of the child.

The Act does not give a definition of "best interests of the child," nor does it direct the court to any specific factors to consider. However, in s. 16(9), the court is directed not to take into consideration the past conduct of any person unless the conduct is relevant to the ability of that person to act as a parent of a child.

In addition, in s. 16(10), the court is directed to give effect to the principle that a child of the marriage should have as much contact with each spouse as is consistent with the best interests of the child and for that purpose to take into consideration

the willingness of the person seeking custody to facilitate that contact. Accordingly, it is important for a parent seeking custody to demonstrate a willingness to provide access to the other parent.

CUSTODY UNDER THE CHILDREN'S LAW REFORM ACT

Application of the Act

If no divorce proceeding has been started, custody of a child is determined under part III of the *Children's Law Reform Act*.

If a proceeding for custody is started under the *Children's Law Reform Act* and a divorce proceeding is subsequently commenced, any custody or access application that has not been determined is stayed except by leave of the court pursuant to s. 27 of the *Children's Law Reform Act*.

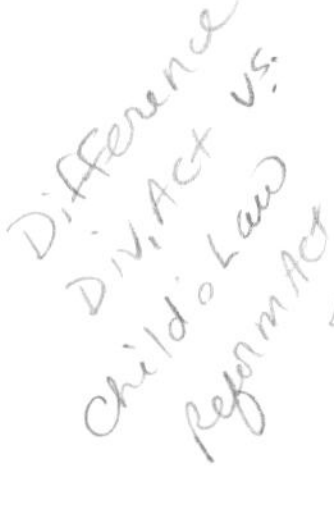

A child is defined by s. 18(2) of the Act to mean a child under the age of 18. Unlike the *Divorce Act*, the *Children's Law Reform Act* confers no jurisdiction on a court to make a custody order with respect to an adult child who is disabled.

Definition of Custody and Access

According to s. 20(2) of the Act, a person entitled to custody of a child has the rights and responsibilities of a parent with respect to that child, and must exercise those rights and responsibilities in the best interests of the child.

The Act sets out the custody rights of the respective parents during cohabitation and following a separation. It starts, in s. 20(1) with the statement that the father and the mother of a child are equally entitled to custody. In s. 20(3), it states that where more than one person is entitled to custody, any one of them may exercise the rights of custody on behalf of both. Accordingly, if both parents are residing together, they both have custody, and either one of them can make decisions with respect to the child.

Section 20(4) of the Act clarifies the rights of the parties after a separation and before any court order is made. If the child lives with one parent with the consent or acquiescence of the other parent, the right of that other parent to custody is suspended until a separation agreement or court order provides otherwise. A parent who leaves a child in the care of the other parent cannot unilaterally return and take the child away. That parent's custody rights are suspended unless he or she gets a court order or enters into a separation agreement giving him or her custody.

The term "access" is defined in s. 20(5) to include the right to visit with and be visited by the child and the same right as a parent to make inquiries and to be given information as to the health, education, and welfare of the child.

Who May Apply for Custody?

Under s. 21 of the Act, a parent of a child or any other person may apply to the court for custody or access. A non-parent does not require leave of the court to make an application as is necessary under the *Divorce Act*.

Orders That May Be Made

The powers of the court on an application are set out in s. 28. The court may

- grant custody or access to one or more persons,
- determine any aspect of the incidents of the right to custody or access, and
- make any other order it considers necessary and proper in the circumstances.

Factors in Deciding Custody

Pursuant to s. 24, an application for custody or access is to be determined on the basis of the best interests of the child. Unlike the *Divorce Act*, the *Children's Law Reform Act* lists a number of factors that the court should take into account. The court is directed to consider "all the needs and circumstances of the child," including

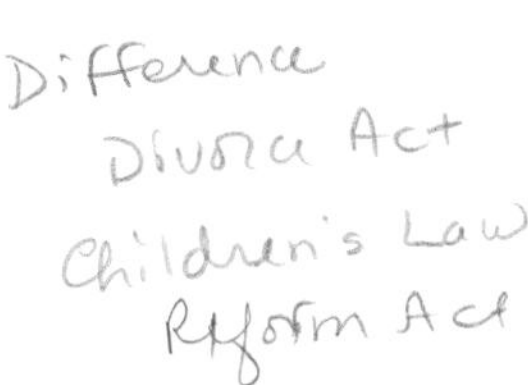

- the love, affection, and emotional ties between the child and each person claiming custody or access and others;
- the views and preferences of the child;
- the length of time the child has lived in a stable home environment;
- the ability and willingness of each person applying for custody to provide the child with guidance and education, the necessaries of life, and any special needs of the child;
- proposed plans for the care and upbringing of the child;
- the permanence and stability of the proposed custodial family unit; and
- the relationship by blood or adoption between the child and the person applying for custody.

The past conduct of the person applying for custody is not to be considered unless it is relevant to the ability of the person to act as a parent of a child.

CUSTODY ASSESSMENTS

What is a court to do when presented with two parents who seek custody of a child? How is a court to decide who is the better parent and what arrangements will be in the best interests of the child?

Under the Children's Law Reform Act

Under s. 30 of the *Children's Law Reform Act*, the court can appoint a person who has "technical or professional skill" (such as a psychiatrist, psychologist, or social worker) to assess and report to the court on the needs of the child and the "ability and willingness" of the parties to satisfy the needs of the child.

If an assessment is ordered, a professional meets with the parents and the child separately and in various combinations, and then writes a report for the court containing his or her observations, conclusions, and recommendations.

An assessment report can help a court in deciding the issue of custody. It can also encourage settlement by allowing a parent to withdraw a custody claim if that parent becomes satisfied that it would be in the best interests of the child for the other parent to have custody. An assessment report does not necessarily determine the issue. Parties have been known to fight on in the face of a negative report. It is the responsibility of the judge, not the assessor, to make the decision regarding custody. The judge is not bound to follow the recommendations in an assessment report, but it is an uphill battle to overcome an assessment report that has been made by a qualified and responsible professional.

Notwithstanding the usefulness of assessment reports, the court will not automatically order an assessment if one of the parties opposes it. For some time, the courts have held that the costs of an assessment and the length of time required to complete it are generally not warranted unless there are "clinical issues" to be determined.

The mechanics of getting an assessment are set out in s. 30. The court can order an assessment on the request of either party or on its own motion. The court chooses the assessor, a person agreed upon by the parties if possible. The assessor must consent to the appointment. The court makes an order regarding payment for the assessment. The order may require the attendance of the parties, the child, or any other person. Adverse inferences may be drawn if a party fails to attend.

Once the report is prepared, the assessor is required to file it with the court, which then gives a copy to the parties. The report is admissible in the hearing of the custody application, and either party may require the assessor to testify. Either party is entitled to lead other expert evidence on the issue of custody.

Under the Divorce Act

There is no provision in the *Divorce Act* for the ordering of an assessment. However, the court has inherent jurisdiction to do so if it is of the opinion that an assessment is necessary.

MEDIATION

Mediation is a process in which a neutral third party meets with the parties to a dispute to help them reach an agreement. The mediator assists the parties in identifying the matters underlying their dispute and the possible solutions. It is up to the parties to arrive at a voluntary agreement. The mediator does not impose a solution.

Parties to a mediation decide in advance whether the mediation is to be open or closed. In an open mediation, the mediator is allowed to disclose to the court anything the parties say during the mediation. In a closed mediation, anything said by the parties is confidential, and the mediator can disclose to the court only whether or not an agreement was reached.

Under s. 9 of the *Divorce Act*, every legal adviser who acts for a spouse in a divorce action has a duty to tell the spouse of the advisability of negotiating a settlement of custody (and support) matters, and to inform him or her of mediation facilities that might be able to assist the spouses to achieve a reconciliation.

Under s. 31 of the *Children's Law Reform Act*, the court may appoint a mediator at the request of the parties. A court will make the order only if both parties agree to mediation and to the mediator, and if the mediator consents to act. Before entering into mediation, the parties decide whether the mediation is to be open or closed.

ENFORCEMENT OF CUSTODY ORDERS

Under the Children's Law Reform Act

Sections 34 to 39 deal with enforcement of custody and access orders.

Under s. 34, the court may order that custody or access be supervised by a person, a children's aid society, or another body if there is a concern that a child will be harmed or abducted while in a party's custody or while access is being exercised. The supervising party must consent to act before an order is made.

Under s. 35, the court may make an order restraining a person from molesting, annoying, or harassing the applicant or the children in the applicant's lawful custody.

Under s. 36, the court may direct the sheriff or the police force to locate, apprehend, and deliver a child to the person lawfully entitled to custody or access, if a court is satisfied that there are reasonable and probable grounds for believing that someone is unlawfully withholding the child from that person, or is proposing to remove the child from Ontario contrary to a separation agreement or court order.

Section 37 gives the court the power to make orders with respect to property, support payments, and passports in order to prevent a party from unlawfully removing a child from Ontario.

Section 38 gives the Ontario Court of Justice powers to punish willful contempt of custody or access orders by fine or imprisonment or both.

Under s. 39, the court may make orders requiring any person or public body to provide the court with particulars of the address of the respondent, where the court is of the opinion that the information is necessary for the purpose of bringing a custody or access application or enforcing a custody or access order.

Under the Divorce Act

Pursuant to s. 20 of the *Divorce Act*, a custody or access order has legal effect throughout Canada. It may be registered in any court in a province and enforced as an order of that court.

VARIATION OF CUSTODY ORDERS

A custody or access order, whether made under the *Divorce Act* or under the *Children's Law Reform Act*, is never final and is always subject to variation if the circumstances of the parties and/or the children change.

Variation Under the Divorce Act

A custody order made under the *Divorce Act* must be varied under that Act by way of a variation proceeding. Variation of custody (and support) orders is dealt with under s. 17 of the Act.

A variation proceeding may be commenced by either or both former spouses or any other person, although a person other than a former spouse requires leave of the court. The court has the power to vary, rescind, or suspend a custody order or any provision thereof. A court may include in a variation order any provisions that could be included in a custody order.

Section 17(5) sets out the factors that a court is to consider in a variation proceeding. It states that before a court makes a variation order, the court must satisfy itself that there has been a change in the condition, means, needs, or other circumstances of the child since the making of the custody order. The section also states that in making the variation order, the court shall take into consideration only the best interests of the child as determined by reference to that change.

As in the making of a custody order, the court may not take into consideration the past conduct of any person unless the conduct is relevant to the ability of that person to act as a parent of the child. The court is also directed to give effect to the principle that a child should have as much contact with each former spouse as is consistent with the best interests of the child. Where the variation order would grant custody of the child to a person who does not currently have custody, the court is directed to take into consideration the willingness of the person seeking custody to facilitate that contact.

Variation Under the Children's Law Reform Act

A custody order made under the *Children's Law Reform Act* must be varied under that Act. Variation of custody orders is dealt with in s. 29. According to that section, a court must not make an order that varies a custody or access order unless there has been a material change in circumstances that affects or is likely to affect the best interests of the child.

Principles Applied in Varying Custody Orders

While the language of the statutes differs, courts apply the same principles whether a case is decided under the *Children's Law Reform Act* or the *Divorce Act*.

Under either statute, the party who applies to vary the original order must show that a material change in circumstances that affects the best interests of the child has occurred since the original order was made. If the applicant meets this threshold test, the court will consider whether a variation in the existing order is necessary to meet the best interests of the child under these changed circumstances.

A variation application is not an appeal. It is not designed to correct an error made by the trial judge. A court hearing a variation application assumes that the original order was correctly made.

The Right of a Custodial Parent To Move the Child's Residence

Many variation applications arise because a parent who has been granted custody wishes to move with the child, but the other parent objects because the move will make it difficult or impossible for that parent to exercise access rights. An application to vary the custody order may be brought by the custodial parent to seek permission of the court to relocate, or it may be brought by the access parent to prevent the move.

Should the court give greater weight to the right of the custodial parent to get on with his or her life, even if that involves moving the child far away from the access parent? Should it give greater weight to the right of the access parent to continue an established pattern of access visits? In the case of *Goertz v. Gordon*, the Supreme Court of Canada made it clear that there is no legal presumption in favour of the custodial parent. In fact, the issue does not involve the parents' rights. The primary concern is the best interests of the child in the particular circumstances of the case. The court should consider, among other things:

- the relationship between the child and the custodial parent;
- the existing access arrangement and the relationship between the child and the access parent;
- the desirability of maximizing contact between the child and both parents;
- the views of the child;
- the custodial parent's reason for moving only if it is relevant to that parent's ability to meet the needs of the child;
- the disruption that would be caused to the child if custody were changed; and
- the disruption that would be caused to the child if the child were moved away from family, schools, and community.

Ultimately, the court must weigh the benefits of the child's remaining in the care of the custodial parent in a new location against the benefits of a change in custody that maintains contact with the access parent, extended family, and community.

A court has at least three options:

- The parent wishing to move keeps custody and is given permission to move.
- The parent wishing to move keeps custody and is denied permission to move.
- The parent wishing to move is given an option: either stay and keep custody or move and lose custody.

PROPOSED CHANGE TO THE DIVORCE ACT

In December 2002, the federal government announced a child-centred family justice strategy whose objective is to help parents focus on the needs of their children following separation and divorce, and thereby minimize the potentially negative impact of separation and divorce.

As part of this strategy, the government is proposing amendments to the *Divorce Act*.[2] The Act will contain a list of specific criteria to be considered in determining the best interests of children. The terms "custody" and "access" will be eliminated from the Act. Instead, the Act will use the term "parenting arrangements," under which the parties allocate "parenting time" and "decision-making responsibilities." Courts will make "parenting orders" rather than custody orders.

changes shelved for now.

2 Bill C-22 was given first reading in December 2002.

REFERENCES

Children's Law Reform Act, RSO 1990, c. C.12.

Divorce Act, RSC 1985, c. 3 (2d Supp.).

Goertz v. Gordon, [1996] 2 SCR 27.

REVIEW QUESTIONS

1. When do the Ontario courts have jurisdiction over custody under the *Divorce Act*?
2. When do the Ontario courts have jurisdiction over custody under the *Children's Law Reform Act*?
3. What is meant by "custody"?
4. What is meant by "access"?
5. What is the primary factor in determining custody?
6. Why do courts make interim or temporary custody awards?
7. What is the definition of "child of the marriage" under the *Divorce Act*?
8. Does a court have jurisdiction to make a custody order with respect to a disabled child over the age of 18 under the *Divorce Act*?
9. Who may apply for custody under the *Divorce Act*?
10. What is the definition of a "child" under the *Children's Law Reform Act*?
11. Does a court have jurisdiction to make a custody order with respect to a disabled child over the age of 18 under the *Children's Law Reform Act*?
12. Who may apply for custody under the *Children's Law Reform Act*?
13. When and how can a party obtain an order for a custody assessment under the *Children's Law Reform Act*?
14. What is mediation?
15. What provisions of the *Divorce Act* address mediation? What provisions of the *Children's Law Reform Act* address mediation?
16. Summarize the provisions of the *Children's Law Reform Act* that deal with enforcement of custody and access orders.
17. What factors must a court consider in varying a custody order under the *Divorce Act*?
18. What factors must a court consider in varying a custody order under the *Children's Law Reform Act*?
19. Summarize the proposed changes to the custody provisions of the *Divorce Act*.

DISCUSSION QUESTIONS

1. Hugh and Elizabeth were married in England and lived there after the marriage. They had one child and subsequently separated. In England, Elizabeth won custody of the child and Hugh was granted access. Hugh then moved to Ontario. While exercising access on a visit to England, Hugh decided he should have custody of the child. He did not return the child to Elizabeth at the end of his access period, but instead took the child with him back to Ontario. On the day after he returned, Hugh commenced a custody proceeding under the *Children's Law Reform Act*. Should the Ontario courts assume jurisdiction in this matter? Discuss.
2. What is the concern of the courts in determining custody? What are some of the factors that a court might consider under the *Children's Law Reform Act*? What factors is the court directed to ignore under that Act? How can a court obtain objective information to help it determine the issue of custody?
3. Calista and Harrison divorced several years ago. The divorce judgment gave Calista custody of the children with access to Harrison. It contained no other provisions about custody. Calista is getting married again, and she and her new husband want to move to Hollywood, California. What right does Calista have to move with the children? Can Harrison do anything to stop her? Discuss.

CHAPTER 7

Spousal Support

In Ontario, every spouse[1] has an obligation to be self-supporting to the extent that he or she is able. Once a spouse satisfies that obligation, he or she has an obligation, to the extent that he or she is able, to support the other spouse in accordance with that person's need. The obligation to support one's spouse continues after the parties separate, and a court may order one spouse to pay support to the other.

Spousal support is dealt with under both the *Family Law Act* and the *Divorce Act*. Support is decided on the basis of the need of the spouse applying for support, and the ability of the other spouse to pay.

In this chapter we will be looking at the law of spousal support, including:

- the parties entitled to claim support,
- the applicable legislation,
- the factors that determine support entitlement,
- the types of support orders,
- the amount and duration of support payments,
- the tax treatment of support orders, and
- the variation of support orders.

PARTIES ENTITLED TO CLAIM SUPPORT

The parties entitled to assert a claim for support differ under the *Divorce Act* and the *Family Law Act*.

Under the Divorce Act

Under the *Divorce Act*, "spouse" is defined as "either of a man or woman who are married to each other" and includes a former spouse. Accordingly, only spouses who are or were validly married to each other have the right to make a claim for spousal support.[2] To make a claim for support, one of the parties must have started

1 In this chapter, the term "spouse" and related terms are used with respect to support payments under both the *Divorce Act* and the *Family Law Act*. When referring to support payments under the *Divorce Act*, the term includes only a husband or wife in a valid marriage. When referring to support payments under the *Family Law Act*, the term may also include parties of the same or opposite sex who are cohabiting.

2 Until the definition of spouse is amended or interpreted to extend to a same-sex spouse, support issues between married same-sex couples cannot be dealt with under the *Divorce Act*.

limitation period
a certain time allowed by a statute for the commencement of a court proceeding

a divorce action. The right to assert a claim for support continues indefinitely, even after the parties divorce. There is no **limitation period** set out in the Act.

Under the Family Law Act

The definition of a "spouse" is much broader under the support provisions of the *Family Law Act*. "Spouse" is defined to mean either of a man and woman:

- who are married to each other, or
- who have entered into a void or voidable marriage in good faith on the part of the person asserting the claim for support, or
- who are not married to each other and have cohabited
    - continuously for a period of not less than three years, or
    - in a relationship of some permanence, if they are the parents of a child.

Same-sex partners[3] are also given the right to claim support if they have cohabited

- continuously for a period of not less than three years, or
- in a relationship of some permanence if they are the parents of a child.

The right to support arises as soon as one satisfies the definition of a "spouse" or a "same-sex partner." The right can be asserted before or after separation, although, under s. 50, the right to bring a support action ends after two years from the day the spouses or partners separate. (If the parties enter into a separation agreement, the right to claim support ends two years after a default occurs under the agreement.)

APPLICABLE LEGISLATION

Courts apply the same principles in deciding the amount and duration of spousal support under both the *Divorce Act* and the *Family Law Act*. The circumstances of the parties determine which statute applies.

The *Divorce Act* applies only to validly married spouses of the opposite sex. Married couples of the same sex and spouses who are not validly married must apply for spousal support under the *Family Law Act*.

For the *Divorce Act* to apply, one of the spouses must start a divorce proceeding. To be able to do so, he or she must have been resident in the province in which the proceeding is started for at least one year immediately before the commencement of the proceeding. If neither spouse can satisfy the residence requirements of the *Divorce Act*, any application for spousal support must be made under the *Family Law Act*.

If the parties have already divorced, and no support claim was made at the time, subsequent claims for support must be made in corollary relief proceedings under the *Divorce Act*.

3 The *Family Law Act* has not yet been amended to address the situation of married same-sex couples. Until that occurs, married same-sex couples will have to seek support as "same-sex partners."

Section 36(1) of the *Family Law Act* sets out what happens when a support application is started under the *Family Law Act* before a divorce proceeding in which one of the spouses seeks support is commenced.

- Any support application under the *Family Law Act* that has not been adjudicated is stayed unless the court gives permission for it to continue.
- Any interim order made under the *Family Law Act* continues in force unless and until it is superseded by an order under the *Divorce Act*. Neither party can apply to vary the *Family Law Act* order, nor can either party apply for a final order under the *Family Law Act*.
- Any final support order obtained under the *Family Law Act* before the divorce proceeding was commenced continues in force unless and until it is superseded by an order under the *Divorce Act*. If neither party seeks a support order under the *Divorce Act*, the *Family Law Act* order continues in effect. If one of the parties seeks a support order under the *Divorce Act*, the *Family Law Act* order can be incorporated into the divorce judgment or replaced with a new and different order.

FACTORS THAT DETERMINE SUPPORT ENTITLEMENT

Both the *Divorce Act* and the *Family Law Act* set out factors to be taken into account in determining whether a party is entitled to a support order.

Language of the Divorce Act

A claim for spousal support under the *Divorce Act* is made under s. 15.2. Section 15.2(1) gives the court the power to make an order requiring a spouse to pay an amount that the court thinks reasonable for the support of the other spouse.

In making an order for spousal support, the court is directed by s. 15.2(4) to take into consideration "the condition, means, needs and other circumstances of each spouse," including

- the length of time the spouses cohabited,
- the role played by each spouse during the marriage, and
- any orders or agreements with respect to support that may exist between the parties.

Section 15.2(6) sets out the objectives of a spousal support order as follows:

- to recognize any economic advantages or disadvantages to the spouses arising from the marriage or its breakdown,
- to apportion between the spouses any financial consequences arising from child care,
- to relieve economic hardship arising from the marriage breakdown, and
- to promote the economic self-sufficiency of the spouses as far as is practicable within a reasonable period of time.

Section 15.2(5) makes it clear that misconduct of a spouse is not a factor in determining spousal support.

Language of the Family Law Act

Under s. 30 of the *Family Law Act*, every spouse has an obligation to provide support for himself or herself and for the other spouse, in accordance with need, to the extent that he or she is capable of doing so. In other words, an award of support is based on the dependent spouse's need and the other spouse's ability to pay, while still meeting his or her own needs.

A claim for support under the *Family Law Act* is made under s. 33, which gives the court the power to order a person to provide support for his or her dependants.

Section 33(8) sets out the purposes of a support order, which is

- to recognize the spouse's contribution to the relationship and the economic consequences to the spouse of the relationship,
- to share the economic burden of child support equitably,
- to assist the spouse to become able to contribute to his or her own support, and
- to relieve financial hardship (if this has not been done by orders dividing the property of the spouses).

Under s. 33(10), the obligation to provide support for a spouse exists without regard to the conduct of either spouse.

How the Courts Decide

The factors in the *Divorce Act* and the *Family Law Act* are similar, and a court considering a support claim would make the same decision under both statutes.

Although both statutes base entitlement to support on need, for some time, starting with the Supreme Court of Canada's decision in *Moge v. Moge*, the need of a spouse alone was not enough to warrant a support order. The courts looked for a causal connection between a spouse's need for support and the spousal relationship. Support orders were seen as a way to compensate a spouse for economic disadvantages, such as abandoned careers and missed opportunities, that arose as a result of the marriage or its breakdown. However, in *Bracklow v. Bracklow*, the Supreme Court of Canada made it clear that a spouse who needs support, but who has not been handicapped by the marriage, may still be entitled to support if the other spouse has the ability to pay.

Rob and Laura were married when they were in their mid-20s. Laura was working as a keypunch operator (entering data on computer cards), and Rob was working as a television comedy writer. Rob and Laura had their first child three years later. The couple agreed that Laura should stop working to care for the child. Over the next nine years, Rob and Laura had three more children. Laura continued to stay home as a full-time mother. Rob continued to work in television and was very successful. Over time, Rob became the producer of a number of successful television shows and movies. Now Rob and Laura have recently separated after more than 25 years of marriage.

The only child still at home is the youngest, aged 16. The oldest child is living on his own, and the other two children are in university. Laura would like spousal support from Rob.

The court should have no difficulty in finding Laura entitled to spousal support. While Laura no longer needs to stay at home to care for the children, she will find it very difficult to be self-supporting. She has not worked for 25 years because of the role she and Rob agreed she should play in the family, and her only previous work experience is in a job that is now obsolete.

AMOUNT AND DURATION OF SUPPORT

Once it is established that a spouse is entitled to support, a court must decide the **quantum** of support (how much support should be paid) and the duration of the support payments (how long support should be paid).

quantum
amount

When a support order is made under the *Family Law Act*, the court is directed to consider the factors set out in s. 33(9) of the Act, which include:

- the parties' current assets and means,
- the respondent's ability to pay,
- the dependant's needs with reference to the parties' accustomed standard of living,
- the dependant's ability to contribute to his or her own support,
- the measures available for the dependant to become self-supporting,
- the dependant's age and health, and
- contribution by the dependant to the realization of the respondent's career potential.

While the conduct of the couple is not a factor in determining entitlement to support, the court may, under s. 33(10), "have regard to a course of conduct that is so unconscionable as to constitute an obvious and gross repudiation of the relationship." Under this section, such conduct of the dependent spouse could serve to reduce the support that might otherwise be paid. Poor conduct on the part of the respondent spouse does not increase the amount of support. The kind of conduct required to reduce support is such that could reasonably be expected to destroy the relationship.

When a support order is made under the *Divorce Act*, the quantum and duration of the support is determined in accordance with the factors set out in s. 15.2(4) and the objectives set out in s. 15.2(6). Under s. 15.2(5), conduct is not a factor in determining the quantum and duration of support.

Although both the *Divorce Act* and the *Family Law Act* speak of an obligation to be self-supporting, in deciding on the quantum and duration of support payments, the courts have recognized that a person who has been out of the work force for a number of years may never be able to be completely self-supporting.

The court requires information about the assets and debts and the income and expenses of both the parties in order to determine the amount of support. The rules of procedure of the Ontario courts require the parties to make full and complete financial disclosure to each other and to the court so that this information is available. See chapter 13 for a discussion of financial disclosure in connection with support applications.

TYPES OF SUPPORT ORDERS

The courts are empowered to make a variety of support orders under both the *Divorce Act* and the *Family Law Act*.

Periodic Support Payments

Most support orders are for periodic support payments. In these orders, the paying spouse is ordered to make payments of a fixed amount of support at regular intervals, usually monthly.

The court's authority to order periodic support under the *Divorce Act* is found in s. 15.2(1), and under the *Family Law Act* is found in s. 34(1)(a).

Time-Limited Support

Under s. 15.2(3) of the *Divorce Act* and s. 34(1)(a) of the *Family Law Act*, the court may order that periodic support be paid either for an indefinite period of time or for a definite or time-limited period.

Time-limited support orders are generally made in the context of short relationships without children to force dependent spouses to gain economic self-sufficiency. Time-limited support is generally not ordered for women who have been out of the workforce for a long time.

Lump-Sum Support

Section 15.2(1) of the *Divorce Act* and s. 34(1)(b) of the *Family Law Act* give the court the power to order payment of support by way of a lump sum. Generally, lump-sum payments are ordered only where the parties' relationship has been short (to encourage a clean break between the parties) or where there are serious concerns that the paying spouse will not make periodic payments.

Indexing Orders

Section 34(5) of the *Family Law Act* gives the court the power to order that periodic support payments be indexed to the cost of living. While the *Divorce Act* does not contain a provision specifically authorizing indexing, the Supreme Court of Canada in *Richardson v. Richardson* held that the court has the power to order indexing under the *Divorce Act*.

When a periodic support payment is indexed to the cost of living, the amount of support is increased automatically on its anniversary date in an amount proportionate to the annual increase in the cost of living. See chapter 16 for an explanation of how the increase in support payments is calculated.

Securing Support

Under s. 15.2(1) of the *Divorce Act*, the court has the power to make an order "to secure or pay, or to secure and pay," support. Accordingly, the court may order a spouse to make periodic payments of support and to post security that can be looked to if he or she defaults in making the periodic payments. Similar power is given to the court under s. 34(1)(k) of the *Family Law Act*.

Interim Support

A final determination of support is not made until trial, yet the need for support may arise as soon as the parties separate. In that case, the dependent party may apply for interim support until the trial. The court has power to make interim support orders under both s. 15.2(2) of the *Divorce Act* and s. 34(1) of the *Family Law Act*.

TAX TREATMENT OF SUPPORT ORDERS

Under the *Income Tax Act*, periodic support payments paid pursuant to a court order or separation agreement for a spouse or common law partner are taxable as income in the hands of the receiving person and are deductible from the paying person's income. The tax implications of support payments are considered by the court when it determines the amount of these payments. The dependent party will need enough support to cover the additional income tax he or she must pay as a result of receiving that additional income. The payer's ability to pay support is increased by the fact that his or her income tax payments will be reduced because of the deductibility of the support payments.

VARIATION OF SUPPORT ORDERS

Support orders under both the *Divorce Act* and the *Family Law Act* may be varied by the court if there has been a change in circumstances of either or both of the parties.

Under s. 17 of the *Divorce Act*, a court must be satisfied that there has been "a change in the condition, means, needs or other circumstances" of either person since the making of the support order. Under s. 37 of the *Family Law Act*, a court must be satisfied that there has been "a material change in the dependant's or respondent's circumstances or that evidence not available on the previous hearing has become available."

See chapter 16 for a more complete discussion of variation applications.

REFERENCES

Bracklow v. Bracklow, [1999] 1 SCR 420.
Divorce Act, RSC 1985, c. 3 (2d Supp.).
Family Law Act, RSO 1990, c. F.3.
Income Tax Act, RSC 1985, c. 1 (5th Supp.).
Moge v. Moge, [1992] 3 SCR 813.
Richardson v. Richardson, [1987] 1 SCR 857.

REVIEW QUESTIONS

1. What is the definition of "spouse" under the *Divorce Act*?
2. What is the definition of "spouse" under the support provisions of the *Family Law Act*?
3. What is the definition of "same-sex partner" under the support provisions of the *Family Law Act*?
4. When must a spousal support application be dealt with under the *Divorce Act*?
5. When must a spousal support application be dealt with under the *Family Law Act*?
6. What factors is the court directed to take into consideration when making an order for spousal support under the *Divorce Act*?
7. What are the purposes of an order for spousal support under the *Family Law Act*?
8. What factors must a court consider when making an order for spousal support under the *Family Law Act*?
9. What is periodic support?
10. What is time-limited support, and when is it likely to be ordered?
11. What is lump-sum support, and when is it likely to be ordered?
12. What authority does the court have to order spousal support payments under the *Family Law Act*?
13. What authority does the court have to order spousal support payments under the *Divorce Act*?
14. What is the tax treatment of spousal support payments?

CHAPTER 8

Child Support

Parents have an obligation to provide support for their children. A parent's obligation to support his or her children continues after a separation, even if the parent does not get custody of the children. After separation, the obligation to provide support is satisfied by the payment of child support to the party who has custody.

Child support is dealt with under both the *Family Law Act* and the *Divorce Act*. Unlike spousal support, which is calculated by taking into account the assets and debts and the income and expenses of both the dependent spouse and the paying spouse, child support is determined in accordance with child support guidelines. These guidelines calculate support in accordance with tables that set out amounts of support based on the income of the paying party and the number of children for whom support is being paid. The income of the recipient party is, generally speaking, irrelevant.

In this chapter, we will be looking at the law of child support, including:

- the obligation to provide child support,
- the applicable legislation,
- the types of support orders,
- the federal and provincial *Child Support Guidelines*,
- the tax treatment of child support orders, and
- the variation of child support orders.

OBLIGATION TO PROVIDE CHILD SUPPORT

The *Family Law Act* and the *Divorce Act* each require parents to provide support for their children, but the obligation is defined somewhat differently under each Act.

Under the Divorce Act

Under the *Divorce Act*, a spouse has the obligation to provide support for any "child of the marriage."

A "child of the marriage" is defined in s. 2(1) to be a child of two spouses or former spouses who is

- under the age of majority (18 years in Ontario) and who has not withdrawn from their charge, or is
- the age of majority or over and under their charge but unable, by reason of illness, disability, or other cause, to withdraw from their charge or to obtain the necessaries of life.

Accordingly, the obligation to provide support continues past the age of 18 if the child is unable to support him- or herself for any reason — for example, if the child is ill, disabled, or a full-time student.

Under s. 2(2), a child of the marriage includes

- any child for whom both spouses or former spouses stand in the place of parents, and
- any child of whom one spouse or former spouse is the parent and for whom the other stands in the place of a parent.

In other words, a spouse or former spouse who has acted as a parent to his or her spouse's or former spouse's child may have an ongoing obligation to provide support for that child, even if he or she did not formally adopt the child.

Under the Family Law Act

Under s. 31 of the *Family Law Act*, every parent has an obligation to provide support for his or her unmarried child who is a minor or is enrolled in a full-time program of education, to the extent that the parent is capable of doing so. Accordingly, the obligation to provide support for a child over the age of 18 does not extend to a disabled child unless the child is in full-time attendance at school. The obligation does not extend to a child 16 years of age or older who has withdrawn from parental control.

Like the *Divorce Act*, the *Family Law Act* uses an extended definition of "child." Under s. 1(1), a child is defined to include a person whom a parent has demonstrated a settled intention to treat as a child of his or her family.

APPLICABLE LEGISLATION

As stated above, child support is dealt with by both the *Divorce Act* and the *Family Law Act*, and the courts apply the same principles in deciding the quantum of child support under both statutes. As with spousal support, the circumstances of the parties determine which statute applies.

Because the *Divorce Act* applies only to validly married opposite-sex spouses, all other parties must apply for child support under the *Family Law Act*.

There is no obligation for a parent to support a disabled adult child under the *Family Law Act*. Accordingly, a parent seeking support for such a child would have to do so under the *Divorce Act*.

For the *Divorce Act* to apply, one of the spouses must start a divorce proceeding and meet the residence requirements of the Act — that is, one of them must have been resident in the province in which the proceeding is started for at least one year immediately before the commencement of the proceeding. If neither spouse can satisfy the residence requirements of the *Divorce Act*, an application for child support must be made under the *Family Law Act*.

If the parties have already divorced, and no support claim was made at the time, any subsequent claim for support must be made as a corollary relief proceeding under the *Divorce Act*.

Section 36(1) of the *Family Law Act* sets out what happens when a support application is started under the *Family Law Act* before the commencement of a divorce proceeding in which one of the spouses seeks child support.

- Any support application under the *Family Law Act* that has not been adjudicated is **stayed** unless the court gives permission for it to continue.
- An interim order made under the *Family Law Act* continues in force unless and until it is superseded by an order under the *Divorce Act*. Neither party can apply to vary the *Family Law Act* order, nor can either party apply for a final order under the *Family Law Act*.
- Any final support order obtained under the *Family Law Act* before the divorce proceeding was commenced continues in force unless and until it is superseded by an order under the *Divorce Act*. If neither party seeks a support order under the *Divorce Act*, the *Family Law Act* order continues in effect. If one of the parties seeks a support order under the *Divorce Act*, the *Family Law Act* order can be incorporated into the divorce judgment or replaced with a new and different order.

stayed
temporarily stopped or suspended

SUPPORT ORDERS

The court's power to make a child support order is found in s. 15.1(1) of the *Divorce Act* and in s. 33(1) of the *Family Law Act*. Under both acts, the courts are empowered to make a variety of support orders.

Periodic Support Payments

Most support orders are for periodic support payments. In these orders the paying party is ordered to make payments of a fixed amount of support at regular intervals, usually monthly.

The court's authority to order periodic support under the *Divorce Act* is found in s. 15.1(1), and under the *Family Law Act* in s. 34(1)(a).

Time-Limited Support

Under s. 15.1(4) of the *Divorce Act* and s. 34(1)(a) of the *Family Law Act*, the court may order that periodic support be paid either for an indefinite period of time or for a definite or time-limited period.

Lump-Sum Support

Section 11 of the *Federal Child Support Guidelines*, which are made under the *Divorce Act*, and s. 34(1)(b) of the *Family Law Act* give the court the power to order payment of support by way of a lump sum. Generally, a lump-sum child support payment is ordered only if there are serious concerns that the paying party will fail to make periodic payments.

Securing Support

Under s. 12 of the *Federal Child Support Guidelines*, the court has the power to order that the amount payable "be paid or secured, or paid and secured, in the manner specified in the order." Accordingly, the court may order a party to make periodic payments of support and to post security that can be looked to if he or she defaults in making the periodic payments. Similar power is given to the court under s. 34(1)(k) of the *Family Law Act* to require that payment be secured "by a charge on property or otherwise."

Indexing Orders

There is no provision for the indexing of child support orders under either statute. Under both the federal and provincial *Child Support Guidelines*, the amount of child support payments is tied solely to the income of the paying party. If the income of the paying party goes up, the receiving party may apply to have the amount of child support increased.

Interim Support

A final determination of child support is not made until trial, yet the need for support may arise as soon as the parties separate. In that case, the party in need may apply for interim support until the trial. The court has power to make interim support orders under s. 15.1(2) of the *Divorce Act* and s. 34(1) of the *Family Law Act*.

THE CHILD SUPPORT GUIDELINES

Under both s. 15.1(3) of the *Divorce Act* and s. 33(11) of the *Family Law Act*, child support orders are determined in accordance with child support guidelines. The *Federal Child Support Guidelines* are a regulation made pursuant to the *Divorce Act*, and the Ontario *Child Support Guidelines* are a regulation made pursuant to the *Family Law Act*. The guidelines under both statutes are essentially the same.

The guidelines contain provisions addressing

- the calculation of child support in a variety of situations,
- the elements of a child support order,
- the variation of child support orders,
- the determination of income for the purposes of calculating child support orders, and
- child support tables.

Child Support Tables

The child support tables, which are schedules to the guidelines, set out the amount of monthly child support payments calculated on the basis of the annual income of the paying party and the number of children for whom support is being paid. There is a separate table for each province and territory, and the amounts vary from one province to another because of differences in provincial income tax rates.

In calculating child support, the courts use the table for the province in which the paying party ordinarily resides at the time the application is made. If the paying party resides outside Canada, the courts use the table for the province in which the applicant ordinarily resides at the time of the application.

The amounts in the tables are based on economic studies of the average spending on children in families at different income levels in Canada. They are calculated using a formula that reflects the average expenses of a parent with a particular number of children and a particular level of income.

Figures 8.1 and 8.2 (at the end of the chapter) set out the Ontario child support tables for one child and two children, respectively.

Consider two examples of how child support is calculated using the tables. Notice that the amount of support payable for two children is not double the amount of support payable for one child.

David and Lisa both live in Ontario, and Lisa has custody of their one child. David earns $72,500.

The basic amount of support paid by a parent earning $72,000 is $585 per month.

The percentage for amounts in excess of $72,000 is 0.67.

David's monthly child support obligation is calculated as follows:

$585 + [0.67% × (72,500 − 72,000)]
$585 + [0.67% × 500]
$585 + 3.35
$588.35

Assume now that David and Lisa have two children.

The basic amount of support paid by a parent earning $72,000 is $948 per month.

The percentage for amounts in excess of $72,000 is 1.04.

David's monthly child support obligation is calculated as follows:

$948 + [1.04% × (72,500 − 72,000)]
$948 + [1.04% × 500]
$948 + 5.20
$953.20

Application of Child Support Tables

Generally, child support is calculated by using the amount set out in the appropriate child support table. In some circumstances, the court may also order an additional amount to cover special or extraordinary expenses for the child, and in other circumstances the table amounts may not be applicable.

The court is given discretion not to apply the table amounts in the following situations:

- the child is over the age of majority,
- the income of the paying party is over $150,000,
- the paying party is not the natural parent of the child,
- the parties split or share custody of the children,
- the application of the guideline amounts would result in undue hardship,
- a court order or agreement exists with respect to support, or
- the parties consent to an order in a different amount.

SPECIAL OR EXTRAORDINARY EXPENSES

Section 7 of the guidelines provide that the court may order the payment of an amount in addition to the table amount to cover all or a portion of the following special or extraordinary expenses:

- child care expenses if incurred as a result of the custodial parent's employment, illness, disability, or education or training for employment;
- the portion of medical and dental insurance premiums if attributable to the child;
- health-related expenses that exceed insurance reimbursement by at least $100 annually — for example, orthodontic treatment, professional counselling, physiotherapy, occupational therapy, speech therapy, prescription drugs, hearing aids, prescription glasses, or contact lenses;
- extraordinary expenses for primary or secondary school education or for any other education programs that meet the child's particular needs — for example, private school or religious school tuition fees and tutoring costs;
- expenses for post-secondary education (unlike primary or secondary school expenses, these do not need to be "extraordinary"); and
- expenses for extracurricular activities over and above those activities anticipated for a child in the economic bracket reflected in the table amount.

In making an order to cover these expenses, s. 7 of the guidelines requires the court to take into account the necessity of the expense in relation to the child's best interests and the reasonableness of the expense in relation to the means of the parents or spouses and those of the child and to the spending pattern of the parents or spouses in respect of the child during cohabitation. In other words, the court looks at the family's historical spending patterns.

If the court decides that an expense falls within this section, the guiding principle is that the expense is shared by each parent or spouse in proportion to his or her income after deducting any contribution from the child.

CHILD OVER THE AGE OF MAJORITY

Under s. 3(2) of the guidelines, if the child is over 18, the amount of support is to be determined in accordance with the tables (plus any amount for special or extraordinary expenses) unless the court considers that approach to be inappropriate. In such a case, the court may order the amount that it considers appropriate, having regard to the condition, means, needs, and other circumstances of the child and the financial ability of each parent or spouse to contribute to the support of the child.

INCOMES OVER $150,000

It is possible to calculate child support using the tables even if the income of the paying party is over $150,000. The child support tables set out incremental support payment amounts for paying parents whose incomes range from $6,730 up to $150,000. For incomes over $150,000, the tables set out a basic monthly amount for the first $150,000 and a percentage applicable to the portion of income that is greater than $150,000.

Under s. 4 of the guidelines, a court may order support in that amount (plus any amount for special or extraordinary expenses). However, if a court considers that amount to be inappropriate, it may order:

- the table amount in respect of the first $150,000 of the paying parent's income;
- the amount the court considers appropriate, having regard to the condition, means, needs, and other circumstances of the child and the financial ability of each parent or spouse to contribute to the support of the child in respect of the balance of the parent's income; and
- any amount for special or extraordinary expenses.

PAYING PARTY IS NOT THE NATURAL PARENT OF THE CHILD

If a paying party is not the natural parent of a child, but stands in the place of a parent of the child, the amount of support is not automatically determined in accordance with the tables. Under s. 5 of the guidelines, the court is to order the amount the court considers appropriate, having regard to the guidelines and any other parent's legal duty to support the child. In these cases, the courts consider the financial circumstances and roles of the step-parent and the natural parent in the child's life.

SPLIT OR SHARED CUSTODY

The term "split custody" refers to the situation where the parties have more than one child, and each party has custody of one or more children. In this case, s. 8 of the guidelines provides that the amount of child support is the difference between the amount that each parent would otherwise pay if a child support order were sought against each of the parents. For example, a court would calculate the support that Parent 1 would be entitled to from Parent 2 based on the number of children in her custody and the income of Parent 2. The court would then calculate the support that Parent 2 would be entitled to from Parent 1 based on the number of children in his custody and the income of Parent 1. The parent with the obligation to pay the higher amount would pay the difference between the two amounts to the parent with the obligation to pay the lower amount.

"Shared custody" refers to a situation where a parent exercises access to or has physical custody of a child for not less than 40 percent of the time over the course of a year. In that case, s. 9 of the guidelines directs the court to set the amount of support by taking into account:

- the amounts set out in the applicable tables for each parent;
- the increased costs of shared custody arrangements; and
- the "condition, means, need and other circumstances" of each parent and of the child.

UNDUE HARDSHIP

Under s. 10 of the guidelines, on the application of either parent, the court may award an amount of child support that is different from the amount under the guidelines if the court finds that the party making the request or the child would otherwise suffer undue hardship.

The section states that the following circumstances may cause undue hardship:

- an unusually high level of debt reasonably incurred to earn a living or support the parents or spouses and their children before the separation;
- unusually high expenses in relation to exercising access to a child;
- a legal duty under a judgment, order, or separation agreement to support someone;
- a legal duty to support a child, other than a child of the marriage; or
- a legal duty to support someone who is ill or disabled.

If a court is satisfied that there is undue hardship, it must then compare the standards of living of the households of the two parents. If the household of the party who claims undue hardship would, after setting support in accordance with the guidelines, have a higher standard of living than the household of the other party, the application to award a different amount of support must be denied. In other words, to succeed in an application under this section, the applicant must not only establish undue hardship; he or she must also establish that the standard of living of his or her household is lower than that of the respondent's household.

In comparing standards of living for the purpose of this section, the court may use the comparison of household standards of living test in schedule II of the guidelines. Using this test, a court examines the income of every person in the household, including domestic partners and children.

The test sets out the following series of steps:

Step 1: Establish the annual income of each person in each household. This involves determining the income in accordance with ss. 15 to 20 of the guidelines, and then deducting federal and provincial income taxes.

Step 2: Adjust the annual income of each party by

a. deducting

- any amount relied on by the court as a factor that resulted in the determination of undue hardship,
- the amount that would be payable by the person for child support if no finding of undue hardship were made, and
- any amount of support that is paid by the person under a judgment, order, or written separation agreement that is not already included as a hardship amount above, and by

b. adding

- the amount of child support that would be received by the person if no finding of undue hardship were made, and
- any amount of child support that the person receives under a judgment, order, or written separation agreement.

Step 3: Add all adjusted incomes in the household.

Step 4: Determine the applicable "low-income measures amount" for each household as set out in the schedule.

Step 5: Divide the household income amount (from step 3) by the low-income measures amount (from step 4).

Step 6: Compare the household income ratios. The household that has the higher ratio has the higher standard of living.

Fred and Wilma are divorced. Wilma has custody of their two children. Fred earns $40,000, on which he pays income tax of $15,000. He is remarried to Betty, who does not earn a salary. They have one child. Wilma earns $30,000, on which she pays income tax of $10,000. She lives with Barney, who earns $40,000, on which he pays income tax of $10,000. In the absence of a finding of undue hardship, Fred would be required to pay child support in the taxable amount of $570 per month, $6,840 per year.

Fred's Household

Step 1

Fred's income	$40,000
Subtract taxes	(15,000)
	$25,000

Step 2: Fred's after-tax income

Subtract hardship amounts	0
Subtract child support	(6,840)
	$18,160

Step 3

Add income of other household members	0
	$18,160

Step 4

Low-income measures amount (for two adults and one child) = $17,649

Step 5

$$\frac{\$18,160}{\$17,649} = 1.03$$

Wilma's Household

Step 1

Wilma's income	$30,000
Subtract income tax	(10,000)
Wilma's after-tax income	$20,000
Barney's income	$40,000
Subtract income tax	(15,000)
Barney's after-tax income	$25,000

Step 2

Add child support to Wilma's after-tax income	$6,840
	$26,840

Step 3

Add income of other household members (Barney)	$25,000
	$51,840

Step 4

Low-income measures amount (for two adults and two children) = $20,764

Step 5

$$\frac{\$51,840}{\$20,764} = 2.50$$

Wilma's household has a higher standard of living than Fred's household.

EXISTING COURT ORDER OR AGREEMENT WITH RESPECT TO SUPPORT

Under both s. 15.1(5) of the *Divorce Act* and s. 33(12) of the *Family Law Act*, a court may order an amount of child support that is different from the amount that would be determined under the guidelines if the court is satisfied that special provisions in an order or a written agreement with respect to the financial obligations of the parents, or the division or transfer of their property, directly or indirectly benefit a child, or that special provisions have otherwise been made for the benefit of a child, and that the application of the child support guidelines would result in an amount of child support that is inequitable given those special provisions.

CONSENT OF THE PARTIES

Under s. 15.1(7) of the *Divorce Act* and s. 33(14) of the *Family Law Act*, the court may award an amount different from the amount that would be determined under the guidelines on the consent of both parents if the court is satisfied that reasonable arrangements have been made for the support of the child. Under s. 15.1(8) of the *Divorce Act* and s. 33(15) of the *Family Law Act*, the court is to have regard to the applicable guidelines in determining whether reasonable arrangements have been made. However, the court may not consider the arrangements to be unreasonable only because the amount of support agreed to is not the same as the guideline amount.

Income Information

Under s. 21 of the guidelines, a person against whom an application for child support is made has an obligation to provide information about his or her income so that a determination of the appropriate level of support may be made.

The applicant, on the other hand, is required to provide income information only in those circumstances in which the guidelines require the court to consider the income of the applicant:

- if the applicant is seeking an additional amount for special or extraordinary expenses;
- if the child is over the age of majority and it is determined that the table amount of support is inappropriate;
- if the income of the paying party is over $150,000 and the court considers the table amount of support to be inappropriate;
- if there is split or shared custody; or
- if there is a claim of undue hardship (in which case income information from any domestic partners would also be required).

TAX TREATMENT OF CHILD SUPPORT ORDERS

Unlike spousal support payments, child support payments are neither taxable in the hands of the receiving party nor deductible by the paying party for income tax purposes.

VARIATION OF CHILD SUPPORT ORDERS

Both s. 17.1 of the *Divorce Act* and s. 37 of the *Family Law Act* provide for variation of child support orders in the event of a change of circumstances as provided for in the child support guidelines.

Section 14 of the guidelines sets out the changes in circumstances that justify a variation:

- if child support was previously determined in accordance with the tables, any change in circumstances that would result in a different child support order; or
- if child support was previously determined without reference to the tables, any change in the condition, means, needs, or other circumstances of either parent or of any child who is entitled to support.

See chapter 18 for a more complete discussion of variation applications.

REFERENCES

Divorce Act, RSC 1985, c. 3 (2d Supp.).
Family Law Act, RSO 1990, c. F.3.
Federal Child Support Guidelines, SOR/97-175.
Ontario *Child Support Guidelines*, O. Reg. 391/97.

REVIEW QUESTIONS

1. In what circumstances can a parent be required to support a child over the age of 18 under the *Divorce Act*?
2. In what circumstances can a parent be required to support a child over the age of 18 under the *Family Law Act*?
3. When must a child support application be dealt with under the *Divorce Act*?
4. When must a child support application be dealt with under the *Family Law Act*?
5. Why is there no provision for the indexing of child support orders under either the *Divorce Act* or the *Family Law Act*?
6. What are the *Federal Child Support Guidelines* and the Ontario *Child Support Guidelines*?
7. What do the child support guidelines contain?
8. What are the child support tables?
9. Under what circumstances is the court given discretion not to apply the table amounts in determining child support?
10. Under what circumstances may the court order the payment of an additional amount over and above the table amount?
11. Give examples of "extraordinary expenses."
12. How is child support calculated if the child is over the age of majority?
13. How is child support calculated if the income of a paying parent is over $150,000?
14. How is child support calculated if a paying party is not the natural parent of the child?
15. What is "split custody"? How is child support calculated in the case of split custody?
16. What is "shared custody"? How is child support calculated in the case of shared custody?
17. What may the court do in the case of undue hardship?
18. What is the effect of an existing court order or agreement on the making of a child support order?

19. When must a person against whom an application for child support is made provide income information?

20. When must the applicant provide income information?

21. What is the tax treatment of child support?

DISCUSSION QUESTIONS

1. Tristan and Isolde were married and have one child, who is 19 years old and mentally disabled. Tristan and Isolde have separated, and the child lives with Tristan. Tristan wants child support from Isolde. Can Tristan obtain child support? Under what statute? Explain.

2. Will and Grace both live in Ontario and Will has custody of their one child. Grace earns $97,500. Based on the child support tables, how much support will Grace be required to pay?

FIGURE 8.1 CHILD SUPPORT TABLE FOR ONE CHILD IN ONTARIO

Income ($)		Monthly award ($)			Income ($)		Monthly award ($)			Income ($)		Monthly award ($)		
From	To	Basic amount	Plus (%)	of Income over	From	To	Basic amount	Plus (%)	of Income over	From	To	Basic amount	Plus (%)	of Income over
0	6729	**0**			54000	54999	**461**	0.72	54000	103000	103999	**793**	0.67	103000
6730	6999	**0**	5.00	6730	55000	55999	**468**	0.73	55000	104000	104999	**799**	0.67	104000
7000	7999	**14**	4.81	7000	56000	56999	**475**	0.80	56000	105000	105999	**806**	0.67	105000
8000	8999	**62**	0.86	8000	57000	57999	**483**	0.80	57000	106000	106999	**813**	0.67	106000
9000	9999	**70**	0.86	9000	58000	58999	**492**	0.80	58000	107000	107999	**820**	0.67	107000
10000	10999	**79**	0.86	10000	59000	59999	**500**	0.75	59000	108000	108999	**826**	0.67	108000
11000	11999	**87**	0.86	11000	60000	60999	**507**	0.74	60000	109000	109999	**833**	0.67	109000
12000	12999	**96**	0.86	12000	61000	61999	**514**	0.74	61000	110000	110999	**840**	0.67	110000
13000	13999	**105**	0.86	13000	62000	62999	**522**	0.74	62000	111000	111999	**846**	0.67	111000
14000	14999	**113**	0.68	14000	63000	63999	**529**	0.70	63000	112000	112999	**853**	0.67	112000
15000	15999	**120**	0.68	15000	64000	64999	**536**	0.67	64000	113000	113999	**860**	0.67	113000
16000	16999	**127**	0.68	16000	65000	65999	**543**	0.51	65000	114000	114999	**866**	0.67	114000
17000	17999	**134**	0.68	17000	66000	66999	**548**	0.52	66000	115000	115999	**873**	0.67	115000
18000	18999	**140**	0.72	18000	67000	67999	**553**	0.55	67000	116000	116999	**880**	0.67	116000
19000	19999	**148**	1.50	19000	68000	68999	**559**	0.64	68000	117000	117999	**887**	0.67	117000
20000	20999	**163**	1.50	20000	69000	69999	**565**	0.67	69000	118000	118999	**893**	0.67	118000
21000	21999	**178**	1.50	21000	70000	70999	**572**	0.67	70000	119000	119999	**900**	0.67	119000
22000	22999	**192**	1.06	22000	71000	71999	**578**	0.67	71000	120000	120999	**907**	0.67	120000
23000	23999	**203**	0.95	23000	72000	72999	**585**	0.67	72000	121000	121999	**913**	0.67	121000
24000	24999	**213**	0.95	24000	73000	73999	**592**	0.67	73000	122000	122999	**920**	0.67	122000
25000	25999	**222**	0.95	25000	74000	74999	**599**	0.67	74000	123000	123999	**927**	0.67	123000
26000	26999	**232**	0.88	26000	75000	75999	**605**	0.67	75000	124000	124999	**933**	0.67	124000
27000	27999	**240**	0.88	27000	76000	76999	**612**	0.67	76000	125000	125999	**940**	0.67	125000
28000	28999	**249**	0.88	28000	77000	77999	**619**	0.67	77000	126000	126999	**947**	0.67	126000
29000	29999	**258**	0.80	29000	78000	78999	**625**	0.67	78000	127000	127999	**954**	0.67	127000
30000	30999	**266**	0.71	30000	79000	79999	**632**	0.67	79000	128000	128999	**960**	0.67	128000

FIGURE 8.1 CONCLUDED

Income ($)		Monthly award ($)			Income ($)		Monthly award ($)			Income ($)		Monthly award ($)		
From	To	Basic amount	Plus (%)	of Income over	From	To	Basic amount	Plus (%)	of Income over	From	To	Basic amount	Plus (%)	of Income over
31000	31999	**273**	0.76	31000	80000	80999	**639**	0.67	80000	129000	129999	**967**	0.67	129000
32000	32999	**281**	0.83	32000	81000	81999	**645**	0.67	81000	130000	130999	**974**	0.67	130000
33000	33999	**289**	0.83	33000	82000	82999	**652**	0.67	82000	131000	131999	**980**	0.67	131000
34000	34999	**297**	0.79	34000	83000	83999	**659**	0.67	83000	132000	132999	**987**	0.67	132000
35000	35999	**305**	0.78	35000	84000	84999	**666**	0.67	84000	133000	133999	**994**	0.67	133000
36000	36999	**313**	0.81	36000	85000	85999	**672**	0.67	85000	134000	134999	**1000**	0.67	134000
37000	37999	**321**	0.81	37000	86000	86999	**679**	0.67	86000	135000	135999	**1007**	0.67	135000
38000	38999	**329**	0.81	38000	87000	87999	**686**	0.67	87000	136000	136999	**1014**	0.67	136000
39000	39999	**337**	0.81	39000	88000	88999	**692**	0.67	88000	137000	137999	**1020**	0.67	137000
40000	40999	**345**	0.84	40000	89000	89999	**699**	0.67	89000	138000	138999	**1027**	0.67	138000
41000	41999	**354**	0.84	41000	90000	90999	**706**	0.67	90000	139000	139999	**1034**	0.67	139000
42000	42999	**362**	0.84	42000	91000	91999	**712**	0.67	91000	140000	140999	**1041**	0.67	140000
43000	43999	**371**	0.84	43000	92000	92999	**719**	0.67	92000	141000	141999	**1047**	0.67	141000
44000	44999	**379**	0.84	44000	93000	93999	**726**	0.67	93000	142000	142999	**1054**	0.67	142000
45000	45999	**387**	0.84	45000	94000	94999	**733**	0.67	94000	143000	143999	**1061**	0.67	143000
46000	46999	**396**	0.84	46000	95000	95999	**739**	0.67	95000	144000	144999	**1067**	0.67	144000
47000	47999	**404**	0.84	47000	96000	96999	**746**	0.67	96000	145000	145999	**1074**	0.67	145000
48000	48999	**413**	0.84	48000	97000	97999	**753**	0.67	97000	146000	146999	**1081**	0.67	146000
49000	49999	**421**	0.84	49000	98000	98999	**759**	0.67	98000	147000	147999	**1087**	0.67	147000
50000	50999	**429**	0.84	50000	99000	99999	**766**	0.67	99000	148000	148999	**1094**	0.67	148000
51000	51999	**438**	0.84	51000	100000	100999	**773**	0.67	100000	149000	149999	**1101**	0.67	149000
52000	52999	**446**	0.76	52000	101000	101999	**779**	0.67	101000	150000 or greater		**1108**	0.67	150000
53000	53999	**454**	0.72	53000	102000	102999	**786**	0.67	102000					

FIGURE 8.2 CHILD SUPPORT TABLE FOR TWO CHILDREN IN ONTARIO

Income ($)		Monthly award ($)			Income ($)		Monthly award ($)			Income ($)		Monthly award ($)		
From	To	Basic amount	Plus (%)	of Income over	From	To	Basic amount	Plus (%)	of Income over	From	To	Basic amount	Plus (%)	of Income over
0	6729	**0**			54000	54999	**750**	1.17	54000	103000	103999	**1271**	1.04	103000
6730	6999	**0**	5.42	6730	55000	55999	**762**	1.18	55000	104000	104999	**1281**	1.04	104000
7000	7999	**15**	5.23	7000	56000	56999	**774**	1.25	56000	105000	105999	**1292**	1.04	105000
8000	8999	**67**	3.54	8000	57000	57999	**786**	1.25	57000	106000	106999	**1302**	1.04	106000
9000	9999	**102**	1.65	9000	58000	58999	**799**	1.25	58000	107000	107999	**1313**	1.04	107000
10000	10999	**119**	2.86	10000	59000	59999	**811**	1.16	59000	108000	108999	**1323**	1.04	108000
11000	11999	**147**	2.90	11000	60000	60999	**823**	1.15	60000	109000	109999	**1334**	1.04	109000
12000	12999	**176**	2.21	12000	61000	61999	**834**	1.15	61000	110000	110999	**1344**	1.04	110000
13000	13999	**198**	1.24	13000	62000	62999	**846**	1.15	62000	111000	111999	**1354**	1.04	111000
14000	14999	**211**	1.24	14000	63000	63999	**857**	1.10	63000	112000	112999	**1365**	1.04	112000
15000	15999	**223**	1.24	15000	64000	64999	**868**	1.07	64000	113000	113999	**1375**	1.04	113000
16000	16999	**236**	1.24	16000	65000	65999	**879**	0.91	65000	114000	114999	**1386**	1.04	114000
17000	17999	**248**	1.24	17000	66000	66999	**888**	0.91	66000	115000	115999	**1396**	1.04	115000
18000	18999	**260**	1.24	18000	67000	67999	**897**	0.94	67000	116000	116999	**1406**	1.04	116000
19000	19999	**273**	1.24	19000	68000	68999	**907**	1.02	68000	117000	117999	**1417**	1.04	117000
20000	20999	**285**	1.24	20000	69000	69999	**917**	1.04	69000	118000	118999	**1427**	1.04	118000
21000	21999	**297**	1.24	21000	70000	70999	**927**	1.04	70000	119000	119999	**1438**	1.04	119000
22000	22999	**310**	1.24	22000	71000	71999	**938**	1.04	71000	120000	120999	**1448**	1.04	120000
23000	23999	**322**	1.80	23000	72000	72999	**948**	1.04	72000	121000	121999	**1459**	1.04	121000
24000	24999	**340**	1.96	24000	73000	73999	**959**	1.04	73000	122000	122999	**1469**	1.04	122000
25000	25999	**360**	1.95	25000	74000	74999	**969**	1.04	74000	123000	123999	**1479**	1.04	123000
26000	26999	**379**	1.85	26000	75000	75999	**979**	1.04	75000	124000	124999	**1490**	1.04	124000
27000	27999	**398**	1.85	27000	76000	76999	**990**	1.04	76000	125000	125999	**1500**	1.04	125000
28000	28999	**416**	1.66	28000	77000	77999	**1000**	1.04	77000	126000	126999	**1511**	1.04	126000
29000	29999	**433**	1.25	29000	78000	78999	**1011**	1.04	78000	127000	127999	**1521**	1.04	127000
30000	30999	**446**	1.10	30000	79000	79999	**1021**	1.04	79000	128000	128999	**1531**	1.04	128000

FIGURE 8.2 CONCLUDED

Income ($)		Monthly award ($)			Income ($)		Monthly award ($)			Income ($)		Monthly award ($)		
From	To	Basic amount	Plus (%)	of Income over	From	To	Basic amount	Plus (%)	of Income over	From	To	Basic amount	Plus (%)	of Income over
31000	31999	**456**	1.15	31000	80000	80999	**1031**	1.04	80000	129000	129999	**1542**	1.04	129000
32000	32999	**468**	1.26	32000	81000	81999	**1042**	1.04	81000	130000	130999	**1552**	1.04	130000
33000	33999	**481**	1.26	33000	82000	82999	**1052**	1.04	82000	131000	131999	**1563**	1.04	131000
34000	34999	**493**	1.26	34000	83000	83999	**1063**	1.04	83000	132000	132999	**1573**	1.04	132000
35000	35999	**506**	1.26	35000	84000	84999	**1073**	1.04	84000	133000	133999	**1584**	1.04	133000
36000	36999	**518**	1.30	36000	85000	85999	**1084**	1.04	85000	134000	134999	**1594**	1.04	134000
37000	37999	**531**	1.30	37000	86000	86999	**1094**	1.04	86000	135000	135999	**1604**	1.04	135000
38000	38999	**544**	1.26	38000	87000	87999	**1104**	1.04	87000	136000	136999	**1615**	1.04	136000
39000	39999	**557**	1.26	39000	88000	88999	**1115**	1.04	88000	137000	137999	**1625**	1.04	137000
40000	40999	**570**	1.31	40000	89000	89999	**1125**	1.04	89000	138000	138999	**1636**	1.04	138000
41000	41999	**583**	1.31	41000	90000	90999	**1136**	1.04	90000	139000	139999	**1646**	1.04	139000
42000	42999	**596**	1.31	42000	91000	91999	**1146**	1.04	91000	140000	140999	**1656**	1.04	140000
43000	43999	**609**	1.31	43000	92000	92999	**1156**	1.04	92000	141000	141999	**1667**	1.04	141000
44000	44999	**622**	1.31	44000	93000	93999	**1167**	1.04	93000	142000	142999	**1677**	1.04	142000
45000	45999	**635**	1.31	45000	94000	94999	**1177**	1.04	94000	143000	143999	**1688**	1.04	143000
46000	46999	**648**	1.31	46000	95000	95999	**1188**	1.04	95000	144000	144999	**1698**	1.04	144000
47000	47999	**661**	1.31	47000	96000	96999	**1198**	1.04	96000	145000	145999	**1709**	1.04	145000
48000	48999	**674**	1.31	48000	97000	97999	**1209**	1.04	97000	146000	146999	**1719**	1.04	146000
49000	49999	**687**	1.31	49000	98000	98999	**1219**	1.04	98000	147000	147999	**1729**	1.04	147000
50000	50999	**700**	1.31	50000	99000	99999	**1229**	1.04	99000	148000	148999	**1740**	1.04	148000
51000	51999	**713**	1.31	51000	100000	100999	**1240**	1.04	100000	149000	149999	**1750**	1.04	149000
52000	52999	**726**	1.22	52000	101000	101999	**1250**	1.04	101000	150000 or greater		**1761**	1.04	150000
53000	53999	**739**	1.17	53000	102000	102999	**1261**	1.04	102000					

CHAPTER 9

Property Rights

When spouses separate, they have the right to seek a division of their property. If the parties are married,[1] the property division takes place in accordance with a formula set out in the Act. If the parties are not married, their property is divided on the basis of common law principles of property ownership and equitable principles of trust.

In this chapter we will be looking at the law of property rights including:

- an overview of property rights under the *Family Law Act*,
- the equalization of net family property on marriage breakdown,
- equitable property rights,
- the matrimonial home,
- the rights of unmarried couples, and
- the tax consequences of property transfers.

OVERVIEW OF PROPERTY RIGHTS UNDER THE FAMILY LAW ACT

Family property is dealt with in part I of the *Family Law Act*. Section 5(7) states that the purpose of the property provisions of the Act is

> to recognize that child care, household management and financial provision are the joint responsibilities of the spouses and that inherent in the marital relationship there is equal contribution, whether financial or otherwise, by the spouses to the assumption of these responsibilities.

The property provisions of the *Family Law Act* allow spouses to share equally in the value of most property acquired during the marriage, and in the increase in value during the marriage of previously owned property. With the exception of the matrimonial home (discussed below), the spouses do not share the value of property that they bring into the marriage; they share only in the increase in value during the marriage of that property. Here's an example:

> George and Elaine were married. During the marriage, George bought a painting for $10,000. George and Elaine later separate, at which time the painting is worth $100,000. The entire $100,000 value of the painting is

1 The property provisions of the *Family Law Act* apply only to spouses as defined in the Act. The definition of spouse does not yet include a spouse in a same-sex marriage.

divided between George and Elaine because the painting was acquired during the marriage. If George had bought the painting before the marriage, the result would be different. George would have to share with Elaine only the amount by which the painting had increased in value during the marriage. So, if he paid $10,000 for the painting, and it was worth $50,000 at the time of the marriage and $100,000 at the time of separation, Elaine would be entitled to share only in the increase in value of the painting during the marriage, or $50,000, which would then be divided between George and Elaine.

Certain property, such as gifts or inheritances from third parties, even though acquired during marriage, is not shared. One category of property, the matrimonial home, is shared fully even if it was acquired before the marriage.

The division of property under the Act is achieved through a series of calculations. The purpose of these calculations is (subject to certain excluded property) to arrive at the dollar amount of

- the value of the property acquired by each spouse during the marriage and
- the increase in value during the marriage of property owned by each spouse at the time of the marriage

and then to divide that dollar amount equally between the spouses.

This dollar value is arrived at by calculating the net worth (subject to exclusions under the Act) of each spouse both at the time of separation and at the time of marriage. The difference between a spouse's net worth at separation and his or her net worth at marriage is the amount by which the spouse's net worth has gone up in value over the course of the marriage, either because of property acquired by the spouse during the marriage or because of the increase in value of property owned by the spouse during the marriage.

This process of calculation and division is called "equalization of net family property."

EQUALIZATION OF NET FAMILY PROPERTY

Who May Apply for an Equalization and When

The property provisions of the *Family Law Act* apply only to spouses as defined under s. 1(1). Under that section, a spouse means either of a man or woman who are married to each other, or who have gone through a marriage that is voidable or void, in good faith on the part of the person asserting a right to property. In other words, the provisions of the Act *do not* apply to parties who are simply cohabiting, regardless of the length of their relationship.

Section 5 of the Act sets out the five triggering events that give rise to a spouse's right to seek an equalization of net family property (NFP):

- a divorce is granted,
- a marriage is declared a nullity,
- the spouses are separated and there is no reasonable prospect that they will resume cohabitation,

- one of the spouses dies, or
- a "serious danger" arises, during cohabitation, that one spouse may "improvidently deplete" his or her net family property.

This chapter discusses only the triggering events that arise from the breakdown of a marriage.

Section 7 sets out the right of a spouse, a former spouse, or a deceased spouse's personal representative to apply to court for an equalization of NFP. Pursuant to s. 7(3), an application cannot be brought after the earliest of:

- two years after the date the marriage is terminated,
- six years after the day the spouses separate and there is no reasonable prospect of their resuming cohabitation, and
- six months after the death of the first spouse.

There is no limitation period for an application based on an improvident depletion of assets.

There have, however, been many successful applications to extend the time limit for bringing an application for equalization.

Powers of the Court on an Equalization Application

The powers of the court on an equalization application are set out in s. 9 of the Act. The court's primary power is to order the spouse with the higher NFP to pay the equalization amount to the spouse with the lower NFP. The court does not have the power to order the transfer of specific assets except as a means of satisfying the obligation to make the equalization payment. Accordingly, a spouse in an equalization application seeks an order that the other spouse make an equalization payment; a spouse does not claim a share in any particular asset or assets.

Net Family Property Definitions

Section 4 of the Act contains a number of definitions that give us the formula for calculating the net family property of the spouses. Each spouse has his or her own net family property. The calculation of net family property is done with respect to each spouse. The equalization takes place when comparing the net family properties of the two spouses.

It is necessary to be familiar with the definitions of terms under the Act before using the formula for NFP calculation.

"Net family property" is defined in s. 4(1) to mean the value of all property, except property excluded by s. 4(2), that a spouse owns on the valuation date (see below), after deducting

- the spouse's debts and other liabilities, and
- the value of property, other than a matrimonial home, that the spouse owned on the date of the marriage, after deducting the spouse's debts and other liabilities, calculated as of the date of the marriage.

"Property" is defined in s. 4(1) to mean "any interest, present or future, vested or contingent, in real or personal property." The definition is broad and is meant to include real estate, vehicles, cash, bank accounts, RRSPs, stocks, bonds, pensions, annuities, businesses, and equipment. Cases have held that the definition also includes:

- a right to receive income from a trust,
- accounts receivable, and
- an interest in a professional practice.

It does not include a professional degree or a licence to practise.

"Valuation date" is defined in s. 4(1) to mean the earliest of the following dates:

- the date the spouses separate and there is no reasonable prospect of their resuming cohabitation,
- the date their divorce is granted,
- the date the marriage is declared a nullity,
- the date one of the spouses commences an application based on improvident depletion of assets, and
- the date before the date on which the first spouse dies.

In other words, the valuation date (V-day) is the date of the triggering event that gives rise to the application. In the case of a marriage breakdown, that date is usually the date of separation.

Undefined Terms

Although the definition of net family property refers to the value of property, s. 4 does not define the term "value," which can have the following different meanings:

- replacement value — what it would cost to replace the piece of property;
- book value — the value of a piece of property as shown in the financial statements of the business that owns the property (usually, the purchase price less depreciation);
- fair market value — the price for which the property could be sold on the open market; and
- fair value — the value that is just and equitable in the circumstances, which might mean intrinsic value, value to the owner, fair market value, or some other amount.

The value of particular pieces of property is often arrived at with the help of professional valuations and appraisals. A law clerk will not generally be required to assign a value to a piece of property, but will be asked to calculate net family property based on values provided by the supervising lawyer.

The definition of net family property talks about property that was owned as of the relevant dates, but does not define what is meant by "owned." Ownership can mean *legal ownership*, in which case the owner of property is the person who is the registered owner, or it can mean *equitable ownership*, in which case ownership is decided on the basis of equitable principles of trust law. (These principles are discussed later in this chapter under the heading "Equitable Property Rights.")

It is necessary to decide who owns or owned the various pieces of property before an NFP calculation can be done. However, a law clerk will not be required to make a determination of ownership. Rather, the clerk will be asked to calculate the NFP on the basis of decisions about ownership made by the supervising lawyer.

Excluded Property

Under s. 4(2), the value of the following property that a spouse owns on V-day does not form part of the spouse's NFP:

- Property, other than a matrimonial home, that was acquired by gift or inheritance from a third party after the date of the marriage — for example, a gift of a car to the wife from her parents, or a rental property left to the husband by his mother during the marriage.
- Income from property acquired by gift or inheritance (as described above) if the **donor** or **testator** has expressly stated that it is to be excluded from the spouse's net family property — for example, the rental income from the inherited rental property, if the husband's mother's will specifically stated that the income was to be excluded from the husband's net family property.
- Damages received for personal injuries, nervous shock, mental distress, or loss of guidance, care, and companionship, or the part of a settlement that represents those damages — for example, damages awarded to the husband for injuries suffered as a result of medical malpractice.
- Proceeds of a life insurance policy that are payable on the death of the life insured — for example, life insurance proceeds payable to the wife on the death of her father.
- Property, other than a matrimonial home, into which any of the property referred to above can be traced — for example, corporate shares bought by the wife using the life insurance proceeds she received on the death of her father.
- Property that the spouses have agreed by way of domestic contract to exclude from a spouse's NFP.

donor
one who makes a gift

testator
one who makes a will; one who leaves property to another by will

Financial Disclosure

Section 8 of the Act requires each party to a s. 7 application to make full and complete financial disclosure to the other side of the matters necessary to calculate that party's NFP.

Each party is required to serve on the other and file with the court a statement verified by oath or statutory declaration disclosing particulars of the following:

- the party's property, debts, and other liabilities
  - as of the date of the marriage,
  - as of V-day, and
  - as of the date of the statement;
- the deductions claimed by the party under the definition of net family property;

- the exclusions claimed by the party under s. 4(2); and
- all property that the party disposed of during the two years immediately preceding the making of the statement, or during the marriage, whichever period is shorter.

See chapter 14 for a more complete discussion of the financial statements required in an NFP application.

Calculating NFP

The actual calculation of NFP involves listing the various categories of property and their values. There are two main ways of doing the actual mathematical calculations involved, both of which arrive at identical NFP amounts.

FORMULA SET OUT IN THE ACT

Working with the wording of s. 4, these are the steps to calculate the NFP of a spouse.

Step 1: List and value in V-day amounts all property owned by the spouse at V-day.

Step 2: List and value in V-day amounts all excluded property, and deduct the value of property excluded under s. 4(2) from the step 1 total. Because of the disclosure requirements of s. 8, it is necessary to list all property owned on V-day in step 1 (even though it is excluded property) and then to list and deduct the value of the excluded property in step 2.

Step 3: List and value in V-day amounts all debts owed by the spouse at V-day, and deduct the total of those debts.

Step 4: Arrive at a value of assets owned less debts owed by the spouse at the date of marriage:

a. List and value in marriage-date amounts all property other than a matrimonial home owned by the spouse at the date of marriage.
b. List and value in marriage-date amounts all debts owed by the spouse at the date of marriage.
c. Deduct the total value of the debts from the total value of the assets.

If the value of the debts owed at marriage is greater than the value of the property owned at marriage, this total will be a negative number.

Step 5: Deduct the step 4 total from the step 3 total. The total you arrive at is the spouse's NFP. Pursuant to s. 4(5), this figure cannot be less than zero. If the calculation produces a result that is less than zero, the spouse's NFP is deemed to be zero.

Repeat steps 1 through 5 for the other spouse.

FORMULA SET OUT IN THE NET FAMILY PROPERTY STATEMENT

The parties to an equalization application are required to serve on each other and file with the court a net family property statement. (See chapter 14 for a more detailed discussion of this statement.) The statement takes the parties through an NFP calculation in a somewhat different sequence of steps as follows:

Step 1: List and value in V-day amounts all property owned by the spouse at V-day.

Step 2: List and value in V-day amounts all debts and liabilities owed by the spouse at V-day.

Step 3: Calculate the net value in marriage-day amounts of all property owned (other than a matrimonial home) and debts owed on the date of marriage.

a. List and value in marriage-date amounts all property other than a matrimonial home owned by the spouse at the date of marriage.

b. List and value in marriage-date amounts all debts owed by the spouse at the date of marriage.

c. Deduct the total value of the debts from the total value of the assets.

If the value of the debts owed at marriage is greater than the value of the property owned at marriage, this total will be a negative number.

Step 4: List and value in V-day amounts all property excluded under s. 4(2).

Step 5: Add step 2 total, step 3 total, and step 4 total.

Step 6: Subtract step 5 total from step 1 total to arrive at the spouse's NFP. Pursuant to s. 4(5), this figure cannot be less than zero. If the calculation produces a result that is less than zero, the spouse's NFP is deemed to be zero.

Repeat steps 1 through 6 for the other spouse.

EQUALIZATION OF NFP

Section 5 of the Act states that, on the happening of one of the triggering events, the spouse whose NFP is the lesser of the two NFPs is entitled to one-half of the difference between them. In other words, that spouse is entitled to an equalization of the NFPs. Accordingly, once the NFP of each spouse is calculated, the next step is to equalize the NFPs.

This equalization is accomplished by subtracting the lesser NFP from the greater NFP and dividing the difference by two. The spouse with the greater NFP is required to pay that amount to the spouse with the lesser NFP. Each spouse gets to keep the assets he or she owns as of the date of separation, although the spouse with the greater NFP may have to sell some property in order to come up with the cash necessary to make the equalization payment. In most cases, jointly owned assets are disposed of and the cash divided in accordance with ownership.

Determination of Excluded Property

Property is excluded under s. 4(2) only if it was acquired by a spouse during the marriage. Property of the same type is treated differently if it was acquired before the marriage. Here's an example to illustrate the difference between property inherited before the marriage and property inherited during the marriage.

During Harry and Sally's marriage, Sally's father died, leaving Sally Microsoft shares worth $20,000. When Harry and Sally separated, the shares were worth $50,000. Because these shares were inherited during the marriage, they are excluded from Sally's NFP, and Harry does not get to share in their value. If Sally's father had died before her marriage to Harry, the result would be different. Sally would have to share with Harry the increase in value of the shares because the shares would not be excluded from Sally's NFP. Sally would be allowed to deduct only the value of the shares as of the time of the marriage. If the shares were worth $20,000 when she inherited them, $30,000 when she married Harry, and $50,000 when she and Harry separated, the shares would be included in Sally's NFP at the V-day value of $50,000, and she would be able to deduct their marriage-day value of $30,000. Harry would be entitled to a share of the $20,000 increase in value during the marriage.

Impact of Ownership on NFP Calculations

When spouses acquire property during the marriage, title may be put into the name of one or both spouses for a variety of reasons, such as tax considerations, business considerations, or convenience. For example, income-producing property may be put into the name of the spouse with the lower taxable income so that the income from the property will be taxed at a lower tax bracket. Real estate may be put in the name of one spouse because the other spouse is starting a new business, and the spouses don't want to risk losing the property if the business should fail.

Spouses generally do not intend their property to be treated differently on a marriage breakdown because of these decisions. However, the following example shows that the way in which title is held can have a major impact on the NFP of each spouse.

Peter and Wendy were married. At the time of the marriage Peter had $100,000 in cash and Wendy had nothing. At the time of their separation their only asset was their matrimonial home worth $150,000.

(1) If the home is in Peter's name only:

Peter's NFP

Value of property at separation	$150,000
Less value of property at marriage	(100,000)
	$50,000

Peter's NFP is $50,000
Wendy's NFP is 0
Peter has to pay Wendy an equalization payment of $25,000.
Peter winds up with the following assets:

The house	$150,000
Less a loan to cover the NFP payment to Wendy	(25,000)
	$125,000

Wendy winds up with $25,000

(2) If the home is in Wendy's name only:

Peter's NFP	
Value of property at separation	$ 0
Less value of property at marriage	100,000
	($100,000)
Peter's NFP is 0 (NFP can't be less than 0)	
Wendy's NFP	
Value of property at separation	$150,000
Less value of property at marriage	0
	$150,000
Wendy's NFP is $150,000	
Wendy has to pay Peter an equalization payment of $75,000	
Peter winds up with the following assets:	
Cash	$75,000
Wendy winds up with the following assets:	
The house	150,000
Less a loan to cover the NFP payment to Peter	(75,000)
	$75,000

(3) If the home is in the name of Peter and Wendy jointly:

Peter's NFP	
Value of property at separation	75,000
Less value of property at marriage	(150,000)
	($75,000)
Peter's NFP is 0	
Wendy's NFP	
Value of property at separation	$75,000
Less value of property at marriage	0
	75,000
Wendy's NFP is $75,000	
Wendy has to pay Peter an equalization payment of $37,500. Assuming they sell the matrimonial home, Peter ends up with:	
Cash from half-interest in matrimonial home	$75,000
Cash from equalization payment	37,500
	$112,500
Wendy ends up with:	
Cash from half-interest in matrimonial home	$75,000
Less payment to Peter	(37,500)
	$37,500

Special Treatment of the Matrimonial Home

The matrimonial home is defined in s. 18 of the Act to be a property in which one or both of the spouses has an interest and that is or, if the parties have separated, was at the time of the separation ordinarily occupied by the spouses as their family residence.

The matrimonial home of the spouses is given special treatment in the calculation of NFP:

- If property that is the matrimonial home of the parties was owned by a spouse before the marriage, the spouse cannot deduct its marriage-date value from his or her NFP.
- Property that is the matrimonial home of the parties is not excluded from equalization even though it may have been acquired during marriage by gift or inheritance from a third party, or though it may have been purchased with the proceeds of property excluded under s. 4(2).

Here's an example of the treatment of a matrimonial home owned by a spouse before the marriage.

At the time of her marriage to Louis, Thelma had $100,000 in cash. Louis had nothing. The day after the wedding, Thelma bought a home which she put in her name alone. The house became the couple's matrimonial home. The home is worth $150,000 at the time of their separation. Louis still has nothing.

Thelma's NFP	
Value of the house at separation	$150,000
Less assets other than matrimonial home owned at time of marriage	(100,000)
Thelma's NFP is	$50,000
Louis's NFP is 0	
Thelma must pay Louis an equalization payment of $25,000	
Thelma winds up with the following assets:	
The house	$150,000
Less loan to pay NFP	(25,000)
	$125,000
Louis winds up with the following assets:	
NFP payment of $25,000	
If Thelma had bought the house before the marriage:	
Thelma's NFP	
Value of the house at separation	$150,000
Less assets other than matrimonial home owned at time of marriage	0
	$150,000
Louis's NFP is still 0	

Thelma must pay Louis an equalization payment of $75,000. Louis ends up with $75,000 and Thelma also ends up with $75,000 (the house less the $75,000 payment).

Here's an example of the treatment of a matrimonial home purchased with the proceeds of property excluded under s. 4(2).

Neither Homer nor Marge had any assets at the time of their marriage. During their marriage, Homer inherited $100,000. He used the money to purchase a house in his name alone, which became the couple's matrimonial home. The matrimonial home is worth $150,000 at the time of the separation.

Homer cannot exclude the $100,000 inheritance from his NFP because it no longer exists, nor can he exclude the asset into which the inheritance is traceable, because that asset is the matrimonial home. Accordingly, Homer's NFP is $150,000 (the value of the matrimonial home) and Marge's NFP is 0. Homer will be able to keep the house, but will have to pay Marge an equalization payment of $75,000.

If Homer had used the same $100,000 to purchase shares, the result would be different. If the shares are worth $150,000 at the time of the separation, Homer would be able to exclude the full value of the shares from his NFP because the shares are property other than a matrimonial home into which Homer's inheritance can be traced. In this case, Homer's NFP would be 0. He would not have to make an equalization payment to Marge and would get to keep the shares.

If the parties have separated, this special treatment extends only to property that was the matrimonial home of the parties at the time of separation. If property was occupied as a matrimonial home during the marriage, but was no longer being used as a family residence at the time of separation, the property will not be considered a matrimonial home.

Putting It All Together

The best way to gain an understanding of NFP calculations is to do one, so here's a fact situation:

Husband's Financial Situation

At the date of the marriage

- Owned a home worth $400,000 subject to a $75,000 mortgage
- Had a savings account with a balance of $5,000
- Had a student loan with a balance of $10,000

During the marriage

- Sold the home owned at the date of marriage for $475,000
- Purchased a new home jointly with wife for $500,000

At the date of the separation

- Owned home jointly with wife, now worth $750,000
- Had a savings account with a balance of $10,000
- Had a joint savings account with wife with a balance of $10,000
- Had a credit card balance owing of $10,000

Wife's Financial Situation

At the date of the marriage

- Had a stock portfolio left to her by her mother worth $20,000
- Had a student loan with a balance of $3,000

During the marriage

- Inherited shares from her father worth $75,000 (father's will was silent on the issue of income from the shares)
- Purchased home jointly with husband for $500,000

At the date of the separation

- Owned home jointly with husband, now worth $750,000
- Had a joint savings account with husband with a balance of $10,000
- Owned shares inherited from mother now worth $50,000
- Owned shares inherited from father now worth $100,000
- Had $15,000 in dividends earned on her father's shares
- Had a credit card balance owing of $3,000

(1) Here's how to do the NFP calculation using the formula as set out in the Act:

Calculation of Husband's NFP

Step 1: List and value in V-day amounts all property owned by the husband at V-day:

Matrimonial home (1/2 interest)	$375,000
Joint savings account (1/2)	5,000
Savings account	10,000
	$390,000

Step 2: List and value in V-day amounts all excluded property, and deduct the value of property excluded under s. 4(2) from the step 1 total:

Value of excluded property	0
	$390,000

Step 3: List and value in V-day amounts all debts owed by the husband at V-day and deduct the total of those debts:

Credit card balance	$10,000
	$380,000

Step 4: Arrive at a value of assets owned less debts owed by the spouse at the date of marriage:

a. List and value in marriage-day amounts all property other than a matrimonial home owned by the spouse at the date of marriage:

Home	$400,000
Savings	5,000
	$405,000

b. List and value in marriage-date amounts all debts owed by the husband at the date of marriage:

Student loan	$10,000
Mortgage	75,000
	$85,000

c. Deduct the total value of the debts from the total value of the assets:

	$405,000
	(85,000)
	$320,000

Step 5: Deduct the step 4 total from the step 3 total.

	$380,000
	(320,000)
Husband's NFP	$60,000

Calculation of Wife's NFP

Step 1: List and value in V-day amounts all property owned by the wife at V-day:

Matrimonial home (1/2 interest)	375,000
Joint account (1/2)	5,000
Shares from mother	50,000
Shares from father	100,000
Dividends	15,000
	$545,000

Step 2: List and value in V-day amounts all excluded property, and deduct the value of property excluded under s. 4(2) from the step 1 total:

Shares from father	(100,000)
	$445,000

Step 3: List and value in V-day amounts all debts owed by the wife at V-day and deduct the total of those debts:

Credit card balance	(3,000)
	$442,000

Step 4: Arrive at a value of assets owned less debts owed by the wife at the date of marriage:

a. List and value in marriage-day amounts all property other than a matrimonial home owned by the spouse at the date of marriage:

Shares from mother	$20,000
	$20,000

b. List and value in marriage-date amounts all debts owed by the wife at the date of marriage:

Student loan	$3,000
	$3,000

c. Deduct the total value of the debts from the total value of the assets:

	$20,000
	(3,000)
	$17,000

Step 5: Deduct the step 4 total from the step 3 total.

	$442,000
	(17,000)
Wife's NFP	$425,000

(2) Here's how to do the net family property calculation using the formula as set out in the net family property statement:

Calculation of Husband's NFP

Step 1: List and value in V-day amounts all property owned by the husband at V-day:

Matrimonial home (1/2 interest)	$375,000
Joint savings account (1/2)	5,000
Savings account	10,000
	$390,000

Step 2: List and value in V-day amounts all debts and liabilities owed by the husband at V-day:

Credit card balance	$10,000
	$10,000

Step 3: Calculate the net value in marriage-date amounts of property owned (other than a matrimonial home) and debts owed on the date of marriage:

a. List and value in marriage-date amounts all property (other than a matrimonial home) owned at the date of marriage:

Home	$400,000
Savings	5,000
	$405,000

b. List and value in marriage-date amounts all debts owed at the date of marriage:

Student loan	$10,000
Mortgage	75,000
	$85,000

c. Deduct the total value of the debts from the total value of the assets:

$405,000
(85,000)
$320,000

Step 4: List and value in V-day amounts all property excluded under s. 4(2):

Value of excluded property	0

Step 5: Add step 2 total + step 3 total + step 4 total:

Step 2 total	$10,000
Step 3 total	320,000
Step 4 total	0
	$330,000

Step 6: Subtract step 5 total from step 1 total to arrive at the husband's net family property:

Step 1 total	$390,000
Step 5 total	(330,000)
Husband's NFP	$60,000

Calculation of Wife's NFP

Step 1: List and value in V-day amounts all property owned by the wife at V-day:

Matrimonial home (1/2 interest)	$375,000
Joint account (1/2)	5,000
Shares from mother	50,000
Shares from father	100,000
Dividends	15,000
	$545,000

Step 2: List and value in V-day amounts all debts and liabilities owed by the wife at V-day:

Credit card balance	$3,000
	$3,000

Step 3: Calculate the net value in marriage-date amounts of property owned (other than a matrimonial home) and debts owed on the date of marriage:

a. List and value in marriage-date amounts all property (other than a matrimonial home) owned at the date of marriage:

Shares from mother	$20,000
	$20,000

b. List and value in marriage-date amounts all debts owed at the date of marriage:

Student loan	$3,000
	$3,000

c. Deduct the total value of the debts from the total value of the assets:

	$20,000
	(3,000)
	$17,000

Step 4: List and value in V-day amounts all property excluded under s. 4(2):

Shares from father	$100,000
	$100,000

Step 5: Add step 2 total + step 3 total + step 4 total:

Step 2 total	$3,000
Step 3 total	17,000
Step 4 total	100,000
	$120,000

Step 6: Subtract step 5 total from step 1 total to arrive at the wife's net family property:

Step 1 total	$545,000
Step 5 total	(120,000)
Wife's NFP	$425,000

Equalization of NFP

However you calculate the net family property, the calculation of the equalization payment is as follows:

Wife's NFP	$425,000
Husband's NFP	(60,000)

$$\frac{\$365{,}000}{2} = \$182{,}500$$

The wife must pay the husband an equalization payment of $182,500.

Orders the Court May Make

Section 9 of the Act sets out the orders the court may make on an application for an equalization of NFP. A court's primary power is to order one spouse to pay money to the other spouse. In addition, the court may order that

- security be given for the performance of any obligation imposed by the order;
- if it is necessary to avoid hardship, an amount payable be paid in instalments during a period not exceeding 10 years, or that payment of all or part of the amount be delayed for a period not exceeding 10 years; and
- if it is needed to satisfy an obligation imposed by the order,
  - property be transferred to or in trust for or vested in a spouse, or
  - property be **partitioned** or sold.

partition
divide

EQUITABLE PROPERTY RIGHTS

Historically, if one person pays for property but places title to the property in the name of another person, there is a presumption that the second person holds title in trust for the person who paid for the property. This is called the **presumption of a resulting trust**, and it is an attempt to give effect to the intention of both parties. Under s. 14 of the *Family Law Act*, the presumption of a resulting trust applies in questions of property ownership between husband and wife, as if they were not married.

More recently, equitable principles have been applied to impose on the legal owner of property a **constructive trust** in favour of another person who has contributed work, money, or money's worth to the acquisition, preservation, or maintenance of a piece of property. The remedy of constructive trust is available to married spouses in determining questions of ownership of property under the *Family Law Act*.

Here's an example:

presumption of resulting trust
the presumption that, when one person pays for property but places title to the property in the name of another person, the second person holds title to the property in trust for the person who paid for the property

constructive trust
a trust imposed on the legal owner of property in favour of another person who has contributed work, money, or money's worth to the acquisition, preservation, or maintenance of the property

> Lucy and Ricky were married. Ricky bought and paid for a small apartment building that he registered in his name alone. Lucy did not contribute any money to the purchase of the building; however, she managed the building throughout the marriage — finding tenants, collecting rents, evicting troublesome tenants, maintaining the building, and making repairs. On separation, Lucy may make a claim that she has an ownership interest in the building because of her contribution of work and money's worth to the preservation and maintenance of the property. A court would determine a value for her contribution and decide that Ricky holds that portion of the value of the property in trust for Lucy. That portion of the property would form part of Lucy's NFP.

THE MATRIMONIAL HOME

In addition to the right to seek an equalization of NFP, married spouses[2] are given special rights under part II of the *Family Law Act* with respect to the matrimonial home.

2 Not yet, however, married same-sex spouses.

Definition of Matrimonial Home

The matrimonial home is defined in s. 18 of the Act to be "[e]very property in which a person has an interest and that is or, if the spouses have separated, was at the time of separation ordinarily occupied by the person and his or her spouse as their family residence." Subject to the effects of a designation of a matrimonial home (discussed below), it is possible for spouses to have any number of matrimonial homes.

Designation of Matrimonial Home

Under s. 20, one or both spouses may designate a property owned by one or both of them as a matrimonial home by registering the prescribed designation form on the title to the property.

On registration of a designation made by both spouses, the property becomes the matrimonial home of the spouses, and any other property that otherwise satisfies the definition of matrimonial home, but is not also designated by both spouses, ceases to be a matrimonial home. If the parties subsequently cancel the designation, all properties that satisfy the definition of matrimonial home again become the matrimonial homes of the spouses.

If only one spouse registers a designation, it does not affect the status of other potential matrimonial homes. Why would one spouse designate a property as a matrimonial home? To alert prospective purchasers or mortgagees that the property is a matrimonial home and subject to the rights of the spouse.

Right to Possession of the Matrimonial Home

Under s. 19, both spouses have an equal right to possession of a matrimonial home. This right exists even if title to the matrimonial home is registered in the name of only one of the spouses, although in that case the right of the other spouse to possession is personal as against the titled spouse — that is, the right can be asserted only against the spouse who holds title to the property — and ends when the couple ceases to be spouses, unless a separation agreement or court order provides otherwise.

exclusive possession the sole right to reside in the home to the exclusion of the other spouse

Under s. 24, regardless of ownership of the matrimonial home, and despite s. 19, a court may make an order granting one spouse **exclusive possession** of the matrimonial home or part of it for a period stipulated by the court. Without this order, one spouse, even if he or she is the sole registered owner of the property, does not have the right to force the other spouse to leave the matrimonial home on a marriage breakdown.

In determining whether to make an order for exclusive possession, the court is required to consider the following:

- the best interests of the children who are affected,
- the existence of any property and support orders,
- the financial positions of both spouses,
- any written agreement between the spouses,
- the availability of other affordable and suitable accommodation, and
- any violence committed by one spouse against the other spouse or against the children.

In determining the best interests of a child, the court is required to consider the following:

- the possible disruptive effects on the child of a move to other accommodation, and
- the views and preferences of the child, if they can be reasonably ascertained.

Orders for exclusive possession are generally made only if it can be shown that there is domestic violence or that the order is required in the best interests of a child.

Disposition and Encumbrance of the Matrimonial Home

Whichever spouse is the registered owner of the matrimonial home, s. 21 forbids the spouses from disposing of or encumbering an interest in the home unless:

- the other spouse consents to the transaction,
- the other spouse has released all rights under part II of the Act by way of a separation agreement,
- a court order authorizes the transaction or releases the property from the application of part II of the Act, or
- another property has been designated by both spouses to be their matrimonial home.

If a spouse tries to transfer title or mortgage a matrimonial home without complying with s. 21, the court may hold that the mortgage or transfer is not valid if the transferee or mortgagee was aware of the fact that the property was a matrimonial home or was acting in concert with the spouse. If, however, the transferee or mortgagee actually paid for the property or advanced money under a mortgage, was not acting in concert with the spouse, and had no knowledge that the property was a matrimonial home, the transaction will not be considered invalid.

Joint Tenancy in Matrimonial Home

Ordinarily, if title to property is held in **joint tenancy** and one of the joint tenants dies, the other joint tenant receives full title to the property by right of survivorship. Under s. 26 of the Act, however, the right of survivorship does not apply if a spouse dies while owning an interest in a matrimonial home as a joint tenant with a third person and not with the surviving spouse. In this case, the joint tenancy is considered to have been severed immediately before the spouse's death.

joint tenancy
property is owned by two or more people and, on the death of one owner, the property passes to the other(s) automatically and not to the estate of the owner who died

RIGHTS OF UNMARRIED COUPLES

As stated earlier, only married spouses are entitled to seek an equalization of their net family properties under the *Family Law Act*. The property provisions of the Act do not apply to parties who are simply cohabiting, regardless of the length of their relationship.[3]

3 The property provisions of the Act also do not yet apply to married same-sex couples.

The division of property between unmarried spouses is determined purely on the basis of ownership, using legal and equitable principles. Generally speaking, each unmarried spouse is entitled to the property registered in his or her name, unless the non-titled spouse can prove that the property is being held in trust for him or her under either a resulting trust (because the non-titled spouse in fact paid for the property) or a constructive trust (because the non-titled spouse contributed work, money, or money's worth to the acquisition, preservation, or maintenance of the property).

In addition, the definition of matrimonial home does not apply to non-married spouses,[4] so they have no special rights with respect to their family residence.

TAX CONSEQUENCES OF PROPERTY TRANSFERS

Although the *Family Law Act* provides for the making of an equalization payment rather than the transfer of property between spouses, most separating spouses settle the equalization issue by transferring various properties between them. There are income tax implications to these transfers.[5]

Spousal Rollovers

capital gain
the profit made on the sale or other disposition of capital property

adjusted cost base
the cost at which capital property was acquired

adjusted sale price
the value at which capital property is transferred

In ordinary circumstances, when a person transfers a piece of property (whether by way of a sale or a gift) that has increased in value since it was acquired, a **capital gain** results. The capital gain is the difference between the cost at which the property was acquired (the **adjusted cost base**) and the value at which it is transferred (the **adjusted sale price**). One-half of any capital gain is added to the person's income and taxed.

There is no capital gain, however, when a person transfers property to his or her spouse. Instead, the government treats the property as if it had been originally acquired by the transferee spouse at the same time and at the same cost as it was actually acquired by the transferor spouse. When the transferee spouse ultimately disposes of the property, he or she bears the full tax liability for any capital gain calculated from the original acquisition cost. This is called a "spousal rollover." There is an automatic spousal rollover for all transfers of property between spouses during marriage or as part of a family law settlement.

The spouses may choose to opt out of the automatic rollover provisions of the *Income Tax Act*. In that case, the transfer is treated as a transfer between non-spouses. The transferring spouse will be liable for tax on any capital gain based on the increase in value between the date the property was acquired and the date it is transferred to his or her spouse. When the transferring spouse disposes of the property, he or she is liable for tax on any capital gain based on the increase in value between the date the property was transferred to him or her and the date he or she disposes of the property. If the spouses do not want the automatic rollover provisions to apply, one of them must file an election to that effect with his or her tax return for the year.

4 Nor, as yet, to married same-sex couples.

5 These provisions also apply to a "common-law partner" — a person of the same or opposite sex with whom the taxpayer has a relationship and has been living with the taxpayer for 12 continuous months.

Attribution of Capital Gains

If there is a spousal rollover, and the transferee spouse disposes of the property before the end of the year in which the original transfer took place, the tax department can choose not to tax the capital gain in the hands of the transferee spouse, but rather to **attribute** the capital gain to the transferor spouse — in other words, to treat the capital gain as if it were that of the transferor spouse. The tax department will do this if the transferor's income is higher than the transferee's because the capital gain will then be taxed at the transferor's higher tax rate. When the transfer of property comes about as a result of a separation, the parties can avoid this risk of attribution of capital gains by filing a joint election with their income tax returns for the year.

attribution of capital gains
the decision by the Canada Customs and Revenue Agency to treat the capital gain of one spouse as the capital gain of the other spouse

Principal Residence Exemption

There is no capital gain when a taxpayer disposes of his or her **principal residence**. A property qualifies as a principal residence if a taxpayer or other family member has resided in the property during the taxation year. A taxpayer may have only one principal residence for any given period. Spouses are allowed only one principal residence between them until the year after they separate.

principal residence
under the *Income Tax Act*, a residential property in which the taxpayer or other family member has resided during the taxation year

If the spouses own more than one property that could qualify as a principal residence, they should agree which property should be designated as the principal residence for each of the relevant years.

Registered Retirement Savings Plans

Ordinarily, a person who wishes to transfer his or her RRSP to another person must "collapse" the plan by withdrawing all of the money in the plan. When a person withdraws money from his or her RRSP, the amount is taxed as income. However, when an RRSP is transferred as a result of a marriage breakdown under a separation agreement or court order, there is no tax payable.

REFERENCES

Family Law Act, RSO 1990, c. F.3.
Income Tax Act, RSC 1985, c. 1 (5th Supp.).

REVIEW QUESTIONS

1. Who may apply for an equalization of NFP? Who may not apply? Why not?
2. What triggering events give rise to the right to seek an equalization of NFP?
3. What is the definition of "net family property" in the *Family Law Act*?
4. What is the definition of "property" in the *Family Law Act*?
5. What is the definition of "valuation date" in the *Family Law Act*?
6. How may the term "value" be defined? Is a definition provided in the *Family Law Act*?
7. How may the term "ownership" be defined? Is a definition of "ownership" provided in the *Family Law Act*?
8. What property is excluded from a spouse's NFP?
9. What financial disclosure are the spouses required to make on an NFP application?
10. How is "matrimonial home" defined in the *Family Law Act*?
11. What special treatment is the matrimonial home given in the equalization of NFP?
12. What orders may a court make on an equalization application?
13. What is a "resulting trust"?
14. What is a "constructive trust"?
15. How many matrimonial homes may spouses have?
16. How do spouses designate property as a matrimonial home? What is the effect of such a designation?
17. What rights of possession does a spouse have to a matrimonial home?
18. What rights does a spouse have with respect to the disposal or encumbrance of a matrimonial home?
19. What is a "capital gain"?
20. What is the "adjusted cost base" of a property?
21. What is the "adjusted sale price" of a property?
22. What is a "spousal rollover"?
23. What is meant by "attribution of capital gains"?
24. What is the "principal residence exemption"?

DISCUSSION QUESTIONS

Using the following facts, calculate the NFPs of the spouses and the equalization of their NFPs.

Husband's Financial Situation

At the date of the marriage

- Owned a home worth $400,000 subject to a $75,000 mortgage.
- Had a stock account at Merrill Lynch worth $400,000.
- Had shares (private corporation) in a sales business worth $500,000.
- Had a savings account with a balance of $80,000.

During the marriage

- Took $300,000 from his Merrill Lynch account and purchased a condominium in Florida, taking title jointly with the wife.
- Took the remaining $100,000 in the Merrill Lynch account and placed it in the joint names of the husband and wife.
- Received a settlement for a personal injury claim in the amount of $60,000.
- Lost his business, which went bankrupt.

At the date of separation

- Continues to own the same home he owned at marriage. (The parties reside there most of the year.) Home is now worth $600,000 and is subject to a mortgage of $50,000.
- Has the condominium in Florida (jointly owned with the wife) worth $400,000. The parties reside there during the winter months.
- Has the joint stock account (with the wife) at Merrill Lynch, now worth $200,000.
- Has the personal injury settlement of $60,000.
- Has a savings account with a balance of $10,000.

Wife's Financial Situation

At the date of the marriage

- Had no assets and no debts.

During the marriage

- The husband purchased a condominium in Florida for $300,000 and took title jointly with her.
- The husband placed $100,000 into a Merrill Lynch account in joint names with her.

At the date of the separation

- Has the condominium in Florida (jointly owned with the husband) worth $400,000. The parties reside there during the winter months.
- Has the joint stock account (with the husband) at Merrill Lynch, now worth $200,000.
- Has a savings account with a balance of $10,000.

CHAPTER 10

Negotiation and Separation Agreements

Most separating couples negotiate a settlement of all their outstanding issues and incorporate the terms of their settlement into a separation agreement. Lawyers usually try to negotiate a settlement before starting court proceedings, and many separating couples settle without court proceedings. Even in cases where court proceedings are started, negotiations generally continue, and the vast majority of these cases settle before or at trial.

In this chapter we will be looking at

- the law of domestic contracts,
- the negotiation process,
- the organization and content of a separation agreement, and
- how to work with a precedent separation agreement.

THE LAW OF DOMESTIC CONTRACTS

Separation agreements are dealt with in part IV of the *Family Law Act*, along with other domestic contracts. "**Domestic contract**" is the generic term used in the Act, and is defined in s. 51 to mean a marriage contract, separation agreement, or cohabitation agreement. Paternity agreements are also dealt with in part IV of the Act, although they are not considered domestic contracts.

domestic contract
a marriage contract, separation agreement, or cohabitation agreement

Part IV of the Act sets out the formal requirements for domestic contracts and the matters with which each of the various domestic contracts may deal.

Marriage Contracts

Marriage contracts are dealt with in s. 52. A **marriage contract** is an agreement between a man and a woman who are married to each other or intend to marry in which they agree on their respective rights and obligations under the marriage or on separation, annulment, divorce, or death, including

- property ownership or division,
- support obligations,
- the right to determine the education and moral training of their children, and
- any other matter with regard to the settlement of their affairs.

marriage contract
an agreement between parties who are married or who intend to marry, in which they agree on their respective rights and obligations under the marriage or on separation, annulment, divorce, or death

A marriage contract may *not*

- deal with child custody or access rights (on separation), or
- purport to limit a spouse's right to possession of the matrimonial home under part II of the Act.

Cohabitation Agreements

cohabitation agreement
an agreement between two persons (of the same or opposite sex) who are cohabiting or intend to cohabit and who are not married to each other in which they agree on their respective rights and obligations during cohabitation, on ceasing to cohabit, or on death

Cohabitation agreements are dealt with in s. 53. A **cohabitation agreement** is an agreement between two persons (of the opposite sex or the same sex) who are cohabiting or intend to cohabit and who are not married to each other in which they agree on their respective rights and obligations during cohabitation, or on ceasing to cohabit or on death, including:

- property ownership or division,
- support obligations,
- the right to determine the education and moral training of their children, and
- any other matter with regard to the settlement of their affairs.

A cohabitation agreement may *not* deal with child custody or access rights (on separation).

If opposite-sex parties to a cohabitation agreement marry each other, the agreement is deemed to be a marriage contract.

Separation Agreements

separation agreement
an agreement between parties who have cohabited, in or out of marriage, and who have separated, in which they agree on their respective rights and obligations

Separation agreements are dealt with in s. 54. A **separation agreement** is an agreement between parties who cohabited (in or out of marriage) and who have separated,[1] in which they agree on their respective rights and obligations, including:

- property ownership or division,
- support obligations,
- the right to determine the education and moral training of their children,
- child custody and access rights, and
- any other matter with regard to the settlement of their affairs.

Formal Requirements

Pursuant to the provisions of s. 55, any domestic contract or agreement to amend or rescind a domestic contract must be in writing, signed by the parties, and witnessed.

Limitations on Freedom of Contract

Section 56 of the Act contains a number of provisions that effectively limit the freedom of the parties to set the terms of their domestic contract:

1 The parties to a separation agreement must be separated at the time the agreement is entered into. An agreement in which parties who are still cohabiting agree to separate in the future is either a cohabitation agreement or a marriage contract; it is not a separation agreement.

- Any provisions of a domestic contract dealing with the education, moral training, or custody of or access to a child may be disregarded by a court if they are not in the best interests of the child.
- Any child support provision may be disregarded by a court if it is unreasonable having regard to the child support guidelines (see chapter 8) and any other child support provisions in the agreement.
- Any provision taking effect on separation that stipulates that any right of a party is dependent upon his or her remaining chaste is unenforceable, although provisions tied to remarriage or cohabitation are enforceable.[2]

In addition, s. 56(4) states that a court may set aside a domestic contract or a provision in it

- if one party failed to disclose to the other significant assets, or significant debts or other liabilities, existing when the domestic contract was made,[3]
- if one party did not understand the nature or consequences of the domestic contract, or
- for other reasons that are in accordance with the law of contracts.[4]

THE NEGOTIATION PROCESS

The first step in the negotiation process is the exchange of financial information. The practice is for the parties to exchange the same sworn financial statements that would be filed in a court proceeding, together with supporting documents such as income tax returns, bank statements, investment statements, and credit card statements. It may be necessary to obtain professional evaluations of some of the assets.

Lawyers for the parties negotiate on behalf of their clients by letter, by telephone, and/or in person over a period of time. At some point, the parties may hold a four-way meeting with both lawyers and clients, or the parties may decide to try to resolve certain issues such as custody and access by **mediation**.

mediation
a method of dispute resolution in which the parties meet with a neutral third party who will help them try to come to an agreement

In mediation, the parties meet with a neutral third party who will meet with the parties to help them try to come to an agreement. The mediator's role is to help the parties explore the situation and see if there is a solution that can satisfy the needs of both parties (and, in custody matters, the needs of the children). It is up to the parties to arrive at a settlement voluntarily. A mediator does not take sides and does not judge who is right or wrong. If the parties cannot come to an agreement, the mediator does

2 As discussed in chapter 2, historically a wife receiving alimony lost her right to payments if she had sexual intercourse with a man who was not her husband. Accordingly, it was not uncommon for separation agreements to contain a clause stating that a wife's support payments would continue only as long as she was chaste. These clauses, called *dum casta* clauses, continued to be used until they were declared unenforceable by the *Family Law Reform Act* in 1978. The abolition of *dum casta* clauses does not affect clauses that state that support will end if the recipient remarries or cohabits with another person. These continue to be enforceable.

3 This is the reason that full and complete financial disclosure is so important in the negotiation of a separation agreement.

4 Grounds for setting aside a contract include duress, undue influence, and fraud.

not make a decision for the parties. Mediation must be entered into voluntarily and is not appropriate in cases involving domestic violence.

While they are collecting the necessary financial information to negotiate a final settlement, the parties may enter into an interim agreement — without prejudice to the rights of either party — on matters such as custody, access, and support.

When a final settlement is arrived at, the lawyers for the parties will work on drafting a separation agreement that incorporates the terms of their settlement.

THE ORGANIZATION AND CONTENT OF A SEPARATION AGREEMENT

There is no such thing as a standard separation agreement. There are many issues that arise on the breakdown of a domestic relationship and the facts of each situation are unique. As a result, a separation agreement must be carefully tailored to meet the needs of the particular couple.

Notwithstanding the uniqueness of each separation agreement, most separation agreements contain similar types of clauses, and are organized in a similar fashion.

Preliminary Matters

Separation agreements usually start with clauses that set out background matters such as:

- the date of the marriage or commencement of cohabitation,
- the date of the separation,
- the names and dates of birth of any children,
- definitions of terms used in the agreement, and
- the agreement of the parties to continue to live separate and apart.

Custody and Access

These clauses set out the agreement of the parties with respect to custody of and access to their children, and deal with the following issues:

- the parent with whom the child will reside,
- how much time the child will spend with the other parent, and
- which parent has the right to make decisions about the child's health, education, and moral upbringing.

The parties may agree that one parent will have sole custody while the other parent will have access rights. In that case, the child will reside with the custodial parent and visit with the access parent. In addition, the custodial parent will have the sole right to make decisions concerning the child. The agreement may set out a strict schedule of access visits, or may simply state that access is to be reasonable or to be as agreed by the parties, depending on the relationship between the parties and how well they expect to be able to cooperate on this matter.

Instead, the parties may agree to shared or joint custody (see chapter 8). In some shared custody situations, the child will spend equal amounts of time with each parent, while in others the child will reside primarily with one parent and visit with the other parent. In any case, both parents will share the right to make decisions concerning the upbringing of the child.

As a result of the child-centred family justice strategy announced by the federal government in December 2002, some lawyers are moving away from the use of the terms "custody" and "access" in their separation agreements. Instead, they are using the terms "parenting arrangements," "parenting time," and "decision-making responsibilities."

The custody and access clauses of the agreement may also address such related matters as:

- the right of the parties to obtain information with regard to the child,
- the right of the parties to communicate with the child while he or she is spending time with the other parent,
- the right of either party to remove the child from the province, either permanently or on vacations,
- the right to obtain a passport for the child,
- the right to change the name of the child,
- the nature of the child's religious upbringing,
- custody of the child in the event of the death of the parents, and
- a method for resolving disputes relating to custody and/or access.

Here's an example of a custody and access clause giving the wife custody and the husband access according to a set schedule:

3.0 CUSTODY AND ACCESS

3.1 The wife will have custody of the children. The husband will have access to the children (which will include the right to have them stay overnight) as follows:

(a) Every second weekend from Friday after school to Sunday at 8:00 p.m.
(b) During the entire spring holiday and entire Christmas holiday in every odd-numbered year. He will not exercise weekend access during these holidays in even-numbered years.
(c) For one month of his choice during the summer school holiday, and he will advise the wife in writing of his choice by no later than the preceding March 1st.

3.2 The wife will have the right to have the children with her for a continuous and uninterrupted period of one month during the summer school holiday.

3.3 The husband will have the right to communicate with the children at any reasonable time by telephone and letter.

3.4 The husband will have the right to be fully advised of the school progress (including the right to have copies of report cards and notices of school events) and the health and general welfare of the children.

Child Support

These clauses set out the agreement of the parties with respect to payment of child support, and they should be drafted to reflect the provisions of the child support guidelines (see chapter 8). The clauses must take into account the provisions of the guidelines that relate to the particular situation of the parties.

The parties may agree to support in the table amount, in which case:

- if one party has sole custody, the agreement should provide for payment of the table amount and should also address the paying party's share of special or extraordinary expenses;
- if the parties have split custody, the agreement should state how the table amounts for the children are being set off against each other, and how the parties are apportioning special or extraordinary expenses for the children; and
- if the parties have shared custody, the agreement should set out the percentage of the time the children spend with the paying party and state that the parties have set the child support amount taking into account the increased costs of the shared custody arrangement.

If the parties agree to an amount of support that is different from the table amount, the agreement should contain enough information for a court to conclude that the arrangements are reasonable. If the amount of child support is lower than the table amount because of undue hardship, the agreement should set out details of the undue hardship and provide for a review of the hardship issue at a set date in the future.

Whatever the circumstances of the parties, the child support clauses should

- specify the income of the parties,
- provide for ongoing disclosure of income information, and
- identify the events that will terminate child support payments, and, if there is more than one child, state how support for the remaining children will be calculated at that time.

The parties may also wish to include provisions that

- set out their agreement on how insurance claims are to be processed if either or both of the parties have health or dental insurance coverage for the children,
- provide for variation of child support in the event of a material change in circumstances, and
- state that the child support payments will be made by post-dated cheques.

Here's an example of a child support clause in which the husband, who earns $70,000 per year, agrees to pay $927 per month as support for two children in accordance with the child support guideline tables. (There are no special or extraordinary expenses.) The parties have agreed that support for each child will be paid until the completion of the child's first post-secondary degree up to a maximum age of 22, but that support will end at the age of 18 if the child does not continue in school. The parties agree that the support payments will end if the husband dies because he will be providing life insurance to take the place of the support payments.

4.0 CHILD SUPPORT

4.1 Commencing on September 1, 2003, and on the first day of each subsequent month, the husband will pay to the wife for the support of the two children the sum of $927 in accordance with the child support guideline tables.

4.2 The husband will no longer be obliged to pay support for a child referred to in paragraph 4.1 above when one of the following events occurs:

(a) the child ceases to reside full time with the wife. "Reside full time" includes the child living away from home to attend an educational institution, pursue summer employment, or take a vacation while otherwise maintaining a residence with the wife;

(b) the child becomes 18 years of age and ceases to be in full-time attendance at an educational institution;

(c) the child obtains his or her first post-secondary degree or diploma;

(d) the child becomes 22 years of age;

(e) the child marries;

(f) the child dies; or

(g) the husband dies, so long as he has complied with his obligations pursuant to paragraph 12.0 of this agreement to provide life insurance.

3. The husband represents that his income (as defined by the child support guidelines) at the date of this agreement is $70,000 per year.

Spousal Support

These clauses set out the agreement of the parties concerning their responsibility to provide support for each other. The parties may agree that

- neither spouse will pay support to the other,
- one spouse will make a lump-sum payment of support to the other,
- one spouse will make periodic (usually monthly) support payments to the other, but for a limited time only, or
- one spouse will make periodic support payments to the other for an indefinite period of time.

Generally, parties agree that no support will be paid because both parties are financially self-sufficient. If the parties have agreed that neither of them will pay support to the other, the agreement must specifically say so.

The parties may agree that one of them should make a lump-sum payment in satisfaction of his or her obligation to pay spousal support, after which both parties will be financially self-sufficient. If the parties agree that one of them will make a lump-sum payment, the agreement will set out the amount and the date on which the payment is to be made, and will state that the payment is in full satisfaction of the paying party's spousal support obligation.

In both the case of no support and of a lump-sum payment, the agreement will contain a clause in which the parties release each other from any responsibility for future support payments.

In some cases, the parties will agree that one of them requires support for a fixed period of time to enable him or her to become self-sufficient. In that case, the agreement will provide for payment of a specified amount per month, starting on a specific date and ending on a specific date. The support clause will go on to state that the spouse receiving support releases the paying spouse from any claims for support beyond that termination date. The purpose of the release is to prevent the receiving spouse from making a claim for additional spousal support at the end of the fixed term. It is, however, impossible to prevent a court from considering an application for additional support.

If the parties have agreed to support for an indefinite period, the agreement will set out the amount to be paid per month and the date on which the payments are to start. Instead of setting a fixed date for termination, the agreement will set out the circumstances in which support will end, such as the death, cohabitation, or remarriage of the spouse who is receiving support. The support payments may end when the paying spouse dies — if the parties have made arrangements for insurance for the surviving spouse. (See below for a discussion of insurance clauses.) If support payments are not stated to end on the death of the paying spouse, his or her estate will be obligated to continue making the support payments.

The agreement may also provide for variation of the amount of support in the event of a material change in circumstances and/or for the increase of the amount of support in accordance with changes in the cost of living.

Here's an example of a support clause in which the husband agrees to pay the wife support for an unlimited time in the amount of $500 per month.

5.0 SPOUSAL SUPPORT

5.1 Commencing on September 1, 2003, and on the first day of each subsequent month, the husband will pay to the wife for her support $500.

5.2 The support in paragraph 5.1 of this agreement ends when:

(a) the wife remarries,
(b) the wife cohabits with another person and has become a spouse or same-sex partner pursuant to the provisions of s. 29 of the *Family Law Act*,
(c) the wife dies, or
(d) the husband dies, so long as he has complied with his obligations pursuant to paragraph 12.0 of this agreement to provide life insurance.

Finality of Support Release Clauses

Whatever the agreement of the parties on the subject of spousal support, the party who is liable to pay support wants as much finality as possible.

Separation agreements often contain a clause in which the parties release each other from any responsibility for future support payments. The purpose of the release clause is to prevent either party from making a claim for spousal support in the future.

Until the Ontario Court of Appeal decision in *Miglin v. Miglin*, the courts followed the *Pelech* trilogy of cases,[5] and would not override a release of support in a separation agreement unless there had been a radical change of circumstances that was

5 Named for three cases including *Pelech v. Pelech*.

somehow causally connected to the marriage. In the *Miglin* case, however, the Ontario Court of Appeal held that a simple material change in circumstances was all that was necessary to allow a court to override a release of support in a separation agreement.

This case was appealed to the Supreme Court of Canada, which heard the appeal on October 29, 2002, and released its decision on April 17, 2003. The court ruled that it was no longer necessary to prove a radical and unforeseen change in circumstances that was causally connected to the marriage, as required under the *Pelech* trilogy of cases. However, a simple material change in circumstances alone was not enough to justify a variation.

Instead, the court's view was that courts should examine both the circumstances surrounding the negotiation of the agreement and the circumstances at the time of the court application, stating that

> unimpeachably negotiated agreements that represent the intentions and expectations of the parties and that substantially comply with the objectives of the *Divorce Act* as a whole should receive considerable weight.

When examining the negotiation,

> the court should look at the circumstances in which the agreement was negotiated and executed to determine whether there is any reason to discount it, including any circumstances of oppression, pressure or other vulnerabilities. Circumstances less than "unconscionability" in the commercial law context may be relevant, but a court should not presume an imbalance of power. Further, the degree of professional assistance received by the parties may be sufficient to overcome any systemic imbalances between the parties.

When looking at the circumstances at the time of the court application,

> the court must assess whether the agreement still reflects the original intentions of the parties and the extent to which it is still in substantial compliance with the objectives of the Act. Accordingly, the party seeking to set aside the agreement will need to show that these new circumstances were not reasonably anticipated by the parties, and have led to a situation that cannot be condoned.

As a result of the decision of the Supreme Court of Canada in *Miglin*, it has again become more difficult to persuade a court to make an order that varies the spousal support provisions of a separation agreement, but not as difficult as it was previously under the *Pelech* trilogy.

Lawyers are constantly refining the wording of their release clauses in an effort to persuade any court that might consider a future support application that the parties did not want the courts to interfere.

Life Insurance

When a separation agreement provides for the payment of ongoing child and/or spousal support, it is important to consider what will happen to the support payments if the paying party dies.

An agreement to pay child support or spousal support does not end with the death of the paying party, unless the support clause states that it does. Instead, the estate of the paying party is obligated to continue to make the support payments. However, having the estate make support payments may cause problems for both parties.

The estate may not have enough money to continue making the support payments, which will cause problems for the dependants. The paying party's estate could be tied up as long as the support payments are owing, which will cause problems for the estate.

There is an alternative to this arrangement, and that is to end support payments on the death of the paying party, while requiring the party to provide life insurance to take the place of support payments if he or she dies while still obligated to make payments. The amount of the insurance should be enough to satisfy the support obligation as long as it would otherwise last.

Insurance clauses in separation agreements generally require the paying spouse to take out a policy in the appropriate amount with the recipient spouse or the child (through a trustee) as beneficiary, to maintain the policy or a replacement policy until the obligation to provide support ends, and to provide proof, if requested by the other spouse, of payment of policy premiums. If the paying spouse fails to pay a premium, the other spouse is generally given the right to make the payment and be repaid. The clauses also usually provide that, if the paying party dies without having the insurance in place, the estate is bound to continue to make support payments.

Health Insurance

Often, at least one party has medical and/or dental insurance through his or her place of employment. It is customary to require that party to maintain coverage for the other party and children as long as the coverage is available. The obligation to provide coverage will end when the insured party no longer has the insurance or when the other party and/or children no longer qualify as beneficiaries under the policy.[6]

Matrimonial Home

If the parties own a matrimonial home, the agreement will identify the property and confirm how title is currently held — either by one spouse alone or by both spouses, either as joint tenants or as **tenants in common** — and then state what is to happen to the property. The parties may agree that

tenants in common
two or more people who own property and on the death of one owner the owner's share passes to his or her estate

- the home, which is owned by one spouse only, will stay in the name of the registered owner;
- the home, which is owned by one or both spouses, will be transferred to the name of one spouse only; or
- the home, which is owned by both spouses, will be sold, either immediately or after a period of exclusive possession by one spouse.

If the parties agree that the sole current owner of the house will retain sole ownership, the separation agreement will state that the other spouse releases any claim to ownership or possession of the property.

If the parties agree that the matrimonial home will be transferred into the name of one spouse only, the agreement will set out the obligation of the transferring

6 When the parties have been married, coverage is usually available for the separated spouse until the parties divorce. Sometimes, a former spouse can continue to be covered until the insured party adds a new spouse to the policy. For unmarried or same-sex couples, coverage will depend on the terms of the individual policy.

spouse to sign the transfer document, and state which of the spouses is to pay the cost of preparation and registration of the transfer. If there are any outstanding mortgages, the agreement must state whether the mortgages are to be discharged or assumed by the new owner.

If the parties agree that the matrimonial home is to be sold, the agreement must set out all of the mechanics of the sale including the choice of a real estate agent and the determination of a listing price. The agreement must also set out how the proceeds of sale are to be applied — for example, to pay any taxes, encumbrances, lawyers' fees, and real estate commission — and then how the balance of the proceeds is to be divided between the spouses. The agreement should state which spouse has the right to occupy the home until its sale, and who is to pay the costs of the home until sale.

If the parties agree that the house should not be sold immediately, but that one spouse is to have exclusive possession of the matrimonial home for an extended period of time, the agreement should specify when the right to exclusive possession ends, and that the house is to be sold at that time.

Here's an example of a matrimonial home clause in which a husband and wife own a mortgage-free matrimonial home as joint tenants, and the wife agrees to transfer her interest to the husband.

6.0 MATRIMONIAL HOME

6.1 The husband and wife own the matrimonial home located at 145 Ellsworth Avenue, Toronto, jointly.

6.2 The wife hereby transfers all of her right, title, and interest in the matrimonial home to the husband.

6.3 Concurrently, with the signing of this agreement, the wife will sign a transfer of the matrimonial home.

6.4 The husband will pay the cost of the preparation and registration of the transfer.

Other Property

The agreement should specify how all of the property of the parties is to be divided. Depending on the property they own, there may be clauses dealing with:

- other real estate,
- the contents of the matrimonial home,
- bank accounts,
- corporate securities,
- RRSPs,
- pensions,
- cars,
- boats,
- air miles, etc.

On the breakdown of a marriage, either spouse is entitled to apply for a division of the Canada Pension Plan credits of the two spouses. The parties cannot contract out of this right.

Equalization of Net Family Property

The agreement may state that one spouse will make an equalization payment to the other spouse, or it may state that the transfers of property in the agreement are made in satisfaction of the right of either party to an equalization payment.

Income Tax Implications

In chapter 9, we discussed the income tax implications of property transfers between spouses. The separation agreement should contain clauses that address these implications.

The parties should consider whether or not they wish the automatic spousal rollover provisions of the *Income Tax Act* to apply to the transfer of various properties. If they do not want the provisions to apply, they must specifically opt out of the provisions and the transferring spouse must agree to file the appropriate election with his income tax return for that year. If the automatic rollover provisions do apply, the parties should take steps to protect each other from possible capital gains attribution by agreeing to sign and file the appropriate joint election with their income tax returns.

If the parties own more than one property that could qualify for the principal residence exemption, they should agree which property will be designated as their principal residence for each of the relevant taxation years.

Debts

The separation agreement should list the debts of the parties and state who will be responsible for the payment of each debt. The parties should agree to cancel any joint credit cards. They should also agree to indemnify each other if called on to pay a debt that the other party has agreed to pay.

Releases

Separation agreements ordinarily contain several clauses by which the parties release each other from any future claims arising out of their relationship, including property claims and claims to a share in each other's estates.

Dispute Resolution

Parties often agree to a method of dispute resolution if they cannot agree on any matters — such as custody and access provisions and child support — that are subject to change under the agreement. They may wish to have these matters arbitrated or mediated rather than decided by a court.

General Terms

The agreement usually concludes with a number of general clauses in which the parties acknowledge that

- they have made and received adequate financial disclosure,
- they have received or have had the opportunity to receive independent legal advice,
- they understand the nature and consequences of the agreement,
- the agreement is fair and reasonable, and
- the agreement is being entered into voluntarily and without duress or undue influence.

WORKING WITH A PRECEDENT SEPARATION AGREEMENT

Because of the length and complexity of separation agreements, lawyers usually work with a precedent agreement when they prepare a separation agreement for a client. Lawyers often also use checklists to make sure that they have addressed all relevant matters or they may use their precedent agreement as a checklist.

In 2002, the Law Society of Upper Canada published a new precedent separation agreement. The agreement was prepared with the assistance of an editorial board made up of senior family law lawyers, and contains clauses to cover most situations and issues together with commentary and explanations.

When working with a precedent separation agreement, use a checklist or the precedent itself to determine which issues need to be addressed. Then choose the most appropriate paragraph or combination of paragraphs from the precedent for each issue. Keep in mind that the paragraphs in the precedent may require modification to reflect the agreement arrived at by the parties to your agreement.

It is important to carefully proofread the document you create — even clauses that have been computer-generated — to make sure that the precedent clause has been reprinted correctly.

REFERENCES

Family Law Act, RSO 1990, c. F.3.
Federal Child Support Guidelines, SOR/97-175.
Income Tax Act, RSC 1985, c. 1 (5th Supp.).
Miglin v. Miglin (2001), 53 OR 641 (CA), appealed (2003), 224 DLR (4th) 193 (SCC).
Ontario *Child Support Guidelines*, O. Reg. 391/97.
Pelech v. Pelech, [1987] 1 SCR 801.

REVIEW QUESTIONS

1. What part of the *Family Law Act* deals with separation agreements?
2. What is the definition of a "domestic contract"?
3. What is the definition of a "marriage contract"?
4. What may a marriage contract not do?
5. What is the definition of a "cohabitation agreement"?
6. What may a cohabitation agreement not do?
7. What are the formal requirements for domestic contracts?
8. In what ways do the provisions of the *Family Law Act* limit the freedom of the parties to set the terms of their domestic contract?
9. What is the first step in the process when lawyers try to negotiate a separation agreement for their clients?
10. What preliminary matters are usually dealt with in a separation agreement?
11. What issues do the custody and access clauses of a separation agreement deal with?
12. What should be included in the child support clauses of a separation agreement?
13. Under what circumstances, generally, will the parties agree that they will provide no spousal support for each other?
14. Under what circumstances, generally, will the parties agree that spousal support should be paid in a lump sum?
15. What is the purpose of a spousal support release clause?
16. Why do separation agreements contain life insurance clauses?
17. If the parties wish to transfer title of the matrimonial home from both spouses to one spouse, what matters should the matrimonial home clause of a separation agreement address?
18. If the parties wish the matrimonial home to be sold, what matters should the matrimonial home clause of a separation agreement address?
19. What should a separation agreement specify with respect to the other property of the parties?
20. What should a separation agreement specify with respect to an equalization of net family property?
21. What should a separation agreement specify with respect to the debts of the parties?

DISCUSSION QUESTIONS

1. The husband has agreed to pay $1,000 per month for the support of the wife for a period of five years, whether or not the wife remarries or cohabits with another person. The parties agree that the support payments will end if the husband dies because he will be providing life insurance to take the place of the support payments. Working with a precedent separation agreement, draft the support clauses. What other clauses should the agreement contain?
2. A husband and wife jointly own a matrimonial home at 25 Lyndhurst Avenue in Toronto. The parties have agreed that the matrimonial home is to be sold as soon as possible. They have agreed to accept the first reasonable offer they receive, and to split the proceeds of sale equally after paying off the mortgage on the property and any costs of the sale. They have also agreed that the wife will have exclusive possession of the home until it is sold. During that time, the wife will be responsible for the utilities, mortgage, and insurance payments, and both parties will be equally responsible for the realty taxes and any repairs. Working with a precedent separation agreement, draft the matrimonial home clauses. What tax clauses should this agreement contain?

CHAPTER 11

Financial Disclosure

Whenever the parties have claims against each other for support and/or equalization of net family property, they must make full and complete financial disclosure of all of their assets and liabilities and their incomes and expenses.

In this chapter we will look at

- the history of financial disclosure in family cases,
- the legislative requirements for financial disclosure,
- the specific financial statements required by the *Family Law Rules*, and
- the completion of the financial statement forms.

HISTORY OF FINANCIAL DISCLOSURE

Financial disclosure in family law cases is now routine — the usual first step in the negotiation of a separation agreement, and an integral part of any litigation. However, this was not always the case.

Historically, it was up to the plaintiff to prove all elements of his or her claim. So, if a plaintiff asserted a claim to a share in the property of his or her spouse, it was up to the plaintiff to prove that the property existed, that the defendant owned the property, that the property had a certain value, and that part of this value was owing to the plaintiff. If the plaintiff claimed support for him- or herself or for a child, in addition to proving his or her need for support, the plaintiff had to prove that the defendant had the ability to pay support by establishing what the defendant earned.

This approach to family law litigation changed when the *Family Law Reform Act* was passed in 1978, requiring parties to a family law matter to serve and file financial statements on each other. Early on, the courts made it clear that what was required under the Act was full, complete, and up-to-date disclosure, and that failure to make such disclosure could have unfavourable consequences.

In *Silverstein v. Silverstein*, Mr. Justice Galligan stated:

> [T]he legislature of Ontario ... intended to require that full, complete and up-to-date information be provided to the opposite party and to the court at the earliest possible opportunity. ... Such statements must not be perfunctory *pro forma* documents, but they must be real, complete, up-to-date and meaningful. ... [A]ny party who does not comply with the letter and the spirit of [the legislation] must realize that a court might very well draw unfavourable inferences against that party if a statement under those sections is less than frank and complete. Any unnecessary prolonging of proceedings because of the failure of such statements to be full, frank and complete ought to be at the cost of the person whose statement or statements are deficient.

Since 1978 the financial disclosure process has been an important part of all family law cases.

LEGISLATIVE REQUIREMENTS FOR FINANCIAL DISCLOSURE

The current requirements for financial disclosure are found in the *Family Law Act*, the *Child Support Guidelines*, the *Rules of Civil Procedure*, and the *Family Law Rules*.

Family Law Act

Section 8 of the *Family Law Act* governs disclosure in net family property equalization applications. The parties are required to serve and file a statement under oath disclosing particulars of:

- each party's property and debts and other liabilities,
    - as of the date of the marriage,
    - as of the valuation date (see chapter 9), and
    - as of the statement date;
- the deductions that each party claims under the definition of "net family property";
- the exclusions claimed by each party under s. 4(2); and
- all property disposed of during the previous two years or the period of the marriage (whichever is shorter).

Section 41 of the Act also requires disclosure in support applications, by requiring the parties to serve and file a financial statement under oath in the form required by the rules of the court.

There is no legislative requirement that the parties exchange financial statements if they decide to negotiate a separation agreement without starting court proceedings. However, under s. 56(4) of the Act, a court may set aside a domestic contract if one party failed to disclose to the other party significant assets, or significant debts or other liabilities that existed when the domestic contract was made. As a result, most lawyers insist on full and complete financial disclosure before entering into negotiations — usually by the exchange of the sworn financial statements that would be filed in a court proceeding.

The Child Support Guidelines

Section 21 of the Ontario *Child Support Guidelines* requires the parent or spouse against whom a support claim is made to provide a copy of his or her personal income tax return and notice of assessment and reassessment for each of the three most recent taxation years. A self-employed parent or spouse is required to provide supporting financial statements for his or her business. The applicant parent or spouse must also provide this information if it is necessary to determine his or her income for the purpose of calculating the amount of support.

The Family Law Rules

Rule 13 of the *Family Law Rules* sets out the requirement for financial statements in proceedings before the Family Court of the Superior Court of Justice and before the Ontario Court of Justice Family Court.

Form 13 — Financial Statement (Support Claims) — must be served and filed if there is a claim for support, but no claim for property or exclusive possession of the matrimonial home. If the only claim is for child support in the table amount under the *Child Support Guidelines*, no financial statement is required by the applicant. However, the respondent must file a statement.

The longer form 13.1 — Financial Statement (Property and Support Claims) — must be filed where there is a claim for property and/or exclusive possession of the matrimonial home, whether or not support is also claimed. In addition, the parties to a net family property equalization must file form 13B — Net Family Property Statement.

Under rule 13(1), both parties are required to serve and file the appropriate financial statement (form 13 or form 13.1) if an application, answer, reply, or notice of motion contains a claim for support, property, or exclusive possession whether or not the matter is defended. The applicant must serve and file the financial statement with his or her application,[1] and the respondent must serve and file the financial statement within the time for serving and filing his or her reply.

Pursuant to rule 13(6), each party must make full and frank disclosure of his or her financial situation, and attach any documents to prove his or her income that the financial statement requires. Under rule 13(7), the court will not accept a financial statement for filing unless it includes copies of the party's income tax returns and notices of assessment for the three previous taxation years, or a direction authorizing the tax department to release copies of those documents to the court. Under rule 13(10), if the rules require the delivery of a financial statement, the court will not accept an application, answer, reply, notice of motion, or affidavit for filing without the financial statement.

A party who believes that the other party's financial statement does not contain enough information for a full understanding of the other party's financial circumstances, may ask for additional information. If the other party does not comply within seven days, under rule 13(11) the dissatisfied party may apply to the court for an order that the other party give the information. One party may question the other party on his or her financial statement under rule 20, but only after a request for additional information has been made.

The parties are required to update their financial statements as the proceeding progresses. Under rules 13(12), (12.1), and (12.2), before any case conference, motion, settlement conference, or trial, the parties must serve and file new financial statements, or affidavits that the information in their financial statements has not changed. Rule 13(15) also requires the parties to correct immediately any information that has materially changed or that is discovered to be incorrect or incomplete.

Under rule 13(14), the parties to a property claim under part I of the *Family Law Act* must also serve and file a net family property statement before a settlement conference or trial.

1 Unless the only claim is for child support in the table amount under the *Child Support Guidelines*.

The Rules of Civil Procedure

The *Rules of Civil Procedure* set out the requirement for financial statements in proceedings before the Superior Court of Justice. Rule 69.14 deals with financial disclosure in divorce proceedings and rule 70.04 deals with financial disclosure in family law proceedings. The provisions of these rules are similar to those in the *Family Law Rules*.

There are three financial statement forms under the *Rules of Civil Procedure*:

- form 69K — this long form is used in most proceedings,
- form 69M — this short form is used in custody actions, if the court requires a financial statement, and
- form 69N — this net family property statement must be filed seven days before any pre-trial, motion for judgment, or trial in a net family property equalization proceeding.

COLLECTING INFORMATION

The preparation of financial statements is time-consuming and must be done meticulously. Often the client has little knowledge of his or her financial affairs or how to go about finding the information necessary to complete the statements. The task of completing the statement usually falls to the lawyer — who often delegates the task to an articling student, law clerk, or secretary.

The law firm prepares the financial statement using documents and information provided by the client. The client must be advised of the requirement to provide full, complete, and up-to-date financial information, and that failure to make proper disclosure can result in a judge making adverse findings of fact against the client and/or cost penalties. The client must also understand that he or she is likely to be cross-examined on the contents of his or her statement. For all of these reasons, it is important for the client to provide as much information as possible and for that information to be accurate and current.

The client must collect all of his or her financial documents, such as:

- income tax returns and notices of assessment and reassessment for the previous three years,
- current pay stubs,
- financial statements for any businesses owned by the party,
- copies of all bills and credit card statements,
- bank statements, chequebook registers, and cancelled cheques,
- statements for any investments,
- title documents, and
- mortgage and loan documents.

These documents should be organized and kept in the client's file so that copies are available for delivery to the lawyer for the opposing party.

If the client is cross-examined on the financial statement, he or she is likely to be asked how various amounts in the financial statement were arrived at. As a result, it is important to make and keep notes on these calculations. See figure 11.1 for an example of notes to a financial statement.

FIGURE 11.1 NOTES TO FINANCIAL STATEMENT OF LAURA PETRIE

Food (Weekly)	
• One weekly trip to supermarket	$150.00
• Fresh fruits and vegetables	25.00
• Butcher	50.00
	$225.00
Gifts (Yearly)	
• Children's birthdays (2 @ $75.00)	$150.00
• Children's Christmas (2 @ $100.00)	200.00
• Family birthdays (5 @ $40.00)	200.00
• Family Christmas (5 @ $75.00)	375.00
• Children's friends' birthdays (10 @ $25.00)	250.00
	$1,175.00

FORM 13: FINANCIAL STATEMENT (SUPPORT CLAIMS)

This financial statement must be filed by

- a party who is making or responding to a claim for spousal support,
- a party who is responding to a claim for child support, or
- a party who is making a claim for child support in an amount different from the table amount specified under the *Child Support Guidelines*.

A copy of form 13 can be found at the end of this chapter. Because the form is used for support claims only, it focuses primarily on the income and expenses of the parties.

The party must complete all parts of the form unless he or she is only responding to a claim for child support in the table amount specified under the *Child Support Guidelines* and agrees with the claim. In that case, the party must complete only parts 1, 2, and 3 of the financial statement.

General Information: Form 13

The first page of the form sets out information about the proceeding and the parties. Complete page one as follows:

- Set out the name of the court—the Superior Court of Justice Family Court—and the court office address.
- Insert the court file number if the application has already been started and a court file number has been assigned.
- Set out the full legal name and complete address of each of the parties, along with telephone and fax numbers, and e-mail address, if any.
- Set out the name, address, telephone and fax numbers, and e-mail address of each party's lawyer.
- In paragraph 1, set out:
    - ❑ the full legal name of the party completing the financial statement,
    - ❑ the municipality and province where the party resides,

- the length of the financial statement in number of pages, and
- the date for which the information in the financial statement is accurate.

Part 1: Income

Part 1 details the party's income on a monthly basis over a stated 12-month period. The party must choose the 12-month period that provides the most current information available — if possible, the 12 months starting with the date of the statement. A party who is self-employed or receives an annual bonus may not know what his or her earnings will be in the next 12 months, in which case the most accurate figures may be those for the previous year. The start date and end date of the 12-month period must be set out.

The party must set out his or her *monthly* income. It is important to accurately convert payments received at other intervals to monthly amounts. For example:

- If income is received annually, obtain the monthly income by dividing the yearly income by 12.
- If income is received weekly, multiply the weekly income by 4.33, *not* by 4 — there are more than four weeks in each month.
- If income is received every two weeks, divide the biweekly amount by 2 and then multiply by 4.33.

Part 1 of the form requires the party to state all income and other money that he or she gets from all sources whether taxable or not, including:

1. Pay, wages, and salary, including overtime — This information can be found by looking at the party's pay stubs. Usually, salary is paid weekly or biweekly. Set out the *gross* wages — the amount shown on the pay stub *before* deductions are taken for income tax, Canada Pension Plan, employment insurance, etc.
2. Bonuses, fees, and commissions — If the party receives bonuses, fees, or commissions, calculate the total amount of these items received during the stated 12-month period, and divide by 12 to get a monthly figure. The party may estimate his or her income if the party's income fluctuates or cannot be ascertained. State on the form when a figure is an estimate.
3. Social assistance, employment insurance, and workers' compensation — If the party receives any of these benefits, set out the monthly amount of the payments.
4. Pensions — If the party receives pension benefits, set out the monthly amount of the payments.
5. Dividends and interest — If the party receives dividends and/or interest, calculate the total payments during the stated 12-month period and divide by 12 to get a monthly figure.

Here's an example.

Facts

Laura Petrie is employed as a computer programmer. According to her latest pay stub, her gross salary is $2,692.30 every second week. Her salary is reviewed annually, and she received her last raise on July 1 of this year. Laura usually receives a bonus every December. Her last bonus was $1,500, and she thinks it will be 5 percent higher this year. In addition to her salary, Laura owns shares in a corporation named CruiseCo on which she received dividends of $240 last year. She expects to be paid the same amount this year.

Preparation

- Choose a 12-month period for the financial statement. Given the date of Laura's annual salary review, the most current information available is for the 12-month period starting July 1 of this year.
- Convert Laura's salary to a monthly figure

  Biweekly salary of $2,692.30 ÷ 2 = weekly salary $1,346.15 × 4.33 = monthly salary of $5,828.83
- Estimate the amount of Laura's bonus for this year, and then convert it to a monthly figure:

  Last year's bonus $1,500.00 x 1.05 = expected bonus for this year of $1,575.00

  Expected bonus of $1,575.00 ÷ 12 = monthly bonus of $131.25
- Convert Laura's dividends to a monthly figure:

  Annual dividends of $240.00 ÷ 12 = monthly dividends of $20.00

Laura's financial statement

Assuming that the financial statement is prepared on November 15 of this year, part 1 of Laura's financial statement would look like this:

PART 1: INCOME

for the 12 months from *(date)* July 1, Year 0 to *(date)* July 1, Year +1

Include all income and other money that you get from all sources, whether taxable or not. Show the gross amount here and show your deductions in Part 3.

	CATEGORY	Monthly
1.	Pay, wages, salary, including overtime (before deductions)	5,828.83
2.	Bonuses, fees, commissions	131.25
3.	Social assistance	
4.	Employment insurance	
5.	Workers' compensation	
6.	Pensions	
7.	Dividends	20.00
8.	Interest	

	CATEGORY	Monthly
9.	Rent, board received	
10.	Canada Child Tax Benefit	
11.	Support payments actually received	
12.	Income received by children	
13.	G.S.T. refund	
14.	Payments from trust funds	
15.	Gifts received	
16.	Other *(Specify. If necessary, attach an extra sheet.)*	
17.	**INCOME FROM ALL SOURCES**	5,980.08

Part 2: Other Benefits

Part 2 sets out the party's non-cash benefits, such as the use of a company car, health benefits, a club membership, or room and board that the party's employer or someone else provides for the party or that are charged through or written off by the party's business.

This information can frequently be found on the party's T4 slip. If it is not there, contact the party's employee benefits or payroll officer for the information.

Here's an example that continues Laura Petrie's financial statement.

Facts

Assume that Laura's employer pays premiums for health and dental care insurance totalling $1,200 per year.

Preparation

- Convert the insurance premiums to a monthly figure:

  Annual premiums of $1,200.00 ÷ 12 = $100.00

Laura's financial statement

Part 2 of Laura's financial statement will look like this:

PART 2: OTHER BENEFITS

Show your non-cash benefits — such as the use of a company car, a club membership or room and board that your employer or someone else provides for you or benefits that are charged through or written off by your business.

ITEM	DETAILS	Monthly Market Value
Health and dental insurance	Premiums paid by employer	100.00
	18. TOTAL	100.00

19. GROSS MONTHLY INCOME AND BENEFITS *(Add* **[17]** *plus* **[18]***.)* $ 6,080.08

Part 3: Automatic Deductions from Income

Part 3 of form 13 details the amounts automatically deducted from the party's pay. The party must choose a 12-month period — the same 12-month period that was used for detailing his or her income. Get information about these deductions from the party's pay stubs. Note that deductions for Canada Pension Plan and employment insurance are taken out of every paycheque for part of the year only — until the maximum amount is reached for the year. Accordingly, don't use the pay stub figures, but instead find out the maximum for these items for the current year (this information is available from the Canada Customs and Revenue Agency). Convert all amounts to monthly figures.

Here's an example that continues Laura Petrie's financial statement.

CPP- need find max + ÷ 12

Fact Situation

According to Laura's pay stub, the following amounts are deducted from the paycheque that she receives every second week:

- Income tax $668.90
- Canada Pension Plan 99.48
- Employment insurance 64.45
- Union dues 45.00

Preparation

Convert all amounts to monthly figures, keeping in mind that Laura is paid every second week:

- Biweekly income tax of $668.90 ÷ 2 = $334.45 × 4.33 = monthly tax of $1,448.17
- Canada Pension Plan current annual maximum of $1,673.20 ÷ 12 = monthly CPP of $139.43
- Employment insurance current annual maximum of $858.00 ÷ 12 = $71.50
- Biweekly union dues of $45.00 ÷ 2 = $22.50 × 4.33 = $97.43

Laura's financial statement

Part 3 of Laura's financial statement will look like this:

PART 3: AUTOMATIC DEDUCTIONS FROM INCOME

for the 12 months from *(date)* July 1, Year 0 to *(date)* July 1, Year +1

	TYPE OF EXPENSE	Monthly		TYPE OF EXPENSE	Monthly
20.	Income tax deducted from pay	1,448.17	25.	Group insurance	
21.	*Canada Pension Plan*	139.43	26.	Other *(Specify. If necessary, attach an extra sheet.)*	
22.	Other pension plans				
23.	Employment insurance	71.50			
24.	Union or association dues	97.43	27.	**TOTAL AUTOMATIC DEDUCTIONS**	1,756.53

28. NET MONTHLY INCOME ***(Do the subtraction:*** **[19]** ***minus*** **[27].*)*** $ 4,323.55

Part 4: Total Expenses

Part 4 details the party's living expenses on a monthly basis over a stated 12-month period. The party must choose the 12-month period that provides the most current information available. This period may be different from the period for which income was reported.

The party should include all living expenses, including expenses of any children living with the party. If the party is living with someone else, give the total household expense, not just the party's share. (Part 6 sets out the amount of the other party's contribution to the expenses.)

The party should use current expenses or, if the actual expenses cannot be ascertained, his or her best estimate. He or she should not simply guess at amounts, but should review past bills and chequing account records to get as much information as possible about the expenses. If the party has absolutely no idea of the amount of a particular expense, direct him or her to the proper place to find out the amount of a particular expense — for example, the cable company or telephone company for standard monthly rates — or make the inquiries yourself. In addition, Statistics Canada publishes material documenting standard expenses in various cities. Estimated amounts should be clearly indicated on the form.

It is very important that the expenses be as accurate as possible because, as stated earlier, the party will likely be cross-examined on his or her financial statement. For the same reason, it is a good idea to make and keep notes about expenses that are not based simply on regular monthly bills, such as food, clothing, gifts, and entertainment. That way, when the party is cross-examined, he or she will be able to remember and explain how a particular figure was arrived at. See figure 11.1 for an example of these notes.

If the other party is paying some of the expenses directly — for example, mortgage, utilities, or taxes — the expenses should be included in the financial statement so that the court gets an idea of the actual lifestyle of the party. But mark these expenses with an asterisk and put a note at the bottom of the statement stating that the expenses are paid by the other party.

The party's current expenses may not accurately reflect his or her accustomed standard of living. For example, he or she may have been forced to reduce expenses in the short term, or his or her expenses may be changing in the near future because the matrimonial home has been sold. In such a case, a proposed budget should also be completed. To prepare a proposed budget, photocopy part 4 of the form, change the title to "Proposed Budget," and attach it to the financial statement form.

The party must set out his or her *monthly* expenses. It is important to accurately convert expenses paid at other intervals to monthly amounts:

- If an expense is paid annually, obtain the monthly expense by dividing the yearly expense by 12.
- If an expense is paid weekly, multiply the weekly expense by 4.33, *not* by 4.

There are five major categories of expenses listed in the financial statement:

- Housing — this category includes rent or mortgage, property taxes, condominium fees, utilities, home insurance, and home repairs.
- Food, clothing, and transportation — this category includes groceries, general household supplies, meals outside the home, grooming expenses, car expenses, and other transportation expenses. Sometimes an expense could be listed under more than one category — household cleaning supplies, for example, could be placed under groceries or under general household supplies. It doesn't really matter which category is used, as long as the expense is claimed only once, and notes are kept so that the client knows how each category was calculated.
- Health and medical — this category includes expenses of the party only, not of the children.
- Child(ren) — this category includes school, camp, activities, babysitting, and medical expenses.

- Miscellaneous and other — this category includes books, newspapers, gifts, charities, alcohol and tobacco, pet expenses, tuition, entertainment and recreation, savings, credit card payments (other than for expenses already mentioned in the statement), support payments being made to others, additional income tax not deducted from pay, and any other expense not covered in the form.

Here's an example that continues Laura Petrie's financial statement.

Fact Situation

Since the separation, Laura has remained in the matrimonial home and her housing expenses are as follows:

- Her husband Rob has been making the monthly mortgage payments of $1,072.
- Rob has also been paying the property taxes, which will be $4,500 this year.
- Her municipal water bill comes twice a year. On the basis of last year's bills, she estimates this year's water bill will be $600.
- Her electric bill comes every two months and averages about $375.
- Her gas heating bill is $200 each month.
- Her basic telephone service is $50 per month and she averages about $35 per month in long-distance charges.
- Her home insurance costs $800 for the year.
- She and Rob have usually spent about $2,500 each year on home repairs and maintenance. In addition, she has a gardener who is paid $100 per month for the months of May through September.

Preparation

- Convert the property tax expense to a monthly figure:
  Yearly taxes of $4,500.00 ÷ 12 = $375.00
- Convert the water expense to a monthly figure:
  Yearly water bill of $600.00 ÷ 12 = $50.00
- Convert the electric expense to a monthly figure:
  Average bimonthly electric bill of $375.00 ÷ 2 = $187.50
- Convert the home insurance expense to a monthly figure:
  Yearly insurance expense of $800.00 ÷ 12 = $66.67
- Convert the repair, maintenance, and gardening expense to a monthly figure:
  Yearly maintenance and repairs of $2,500.00 ÷ 12 = $208.33
  Monthly gardening expense of $100.00 × 5 months = $500.00 per year ÷ 12 = $41.67

Laura's financial statement

Here's what the housing portion of part 4 of Laura's financial statement will look like:

	TYPE OF EXPENSE	Monthly
Housing		
29.	Rent/mortgage	1,072.00*
30.	Property taxes & municipal levies	375.00*
31.	Condominium fees & common expenses	
32.	Water (est.)	50.00
33.	Electricity & heating fuel	387.50
34.	Telephone	85.00
35.	Cable television & pay television	
36.	Home insurance	66.67
37.	Home repairs, maintenance, gardening	250.00
	Sub-total of items [29] to [37]	2,286.17

* Expenses being paid by husband.

Summary of Income and Expenses

This part of the financial statement compares the party's net monthly income with his or her actual monthly expenses to determine whether the party has a monthly surplus or deficit.

If Laura's total monthly expenses were $5,987.22, the summary would look like this:

SUMMARY OF INCOME AND EXPENSES

Net monthly income (item [28]) =	$4,323.55
Subtract actual monthly expenses (item [82]) =	$5,987.22
ACTUAL MONTHLY ~~SURPLUS~~/DEFICIT =	$(1,663.67)

Part 5: Other Income Information

This part sets out further information about the party's source of income and proof of that income. Fill out this part by stating:

- Whether the party is employed, self-employed, or unemployed.
- What supporting tax documentation is being provided: tax returns and assessments for three years, a statement from the Canada Customs and Revenue Agency that the party has not filed income tax returns for the past three years or a direction to the Taxation Branch of the Canada Customs and Revenue Agency to provide copies of tax returns and assessments for the past three years.
- What proof of current income is being provided — for example, the most current paycheque stub.

Part 6: Other Income Earners in the Home

This part is completed only if the party is making a claim for spousal support or is claiming undue hardship under the *Child Support Guidelines*. In that case, the party must state whether he or she lives alone or with another person. If the party lives with another person, he or she must state:

- whether the person works outside the home,
- whether the person earns any money, and if so the amount, and
- whether the person contributes any money toward the household expenses, and if so the amount.

Part 7: Property

In this part, the party must give details and the estimated market value of all property that he or she owns as of the date of the statement under the following categories:

- Land — set out the percentage of the party's interest and the estimated market value of that interest.
- General items and vehicles — including household goods and furniture, jewellery, cars, boats, tools, and sports and hobby equipment.
- Bank accounts, savings, securities, and pensions — including RRSPs, other savings plans, accounts in financial institutions, stocks, bonds, term deposits, and any controlling interest in an incorporated business.
- Life and disability insurance policies.
- Business interests — include any interest in an unincorporated business.
- Money owed to the party — including any court judgments in the party's favour, any estate money, and any income tax refunds owed to the party.
- Other property — include any other property owned that does not fit into any of the previous categories.

Part 8: Debts and Other Liabilities

In this part, the party must give details and the current balance of any debts and other liabilities owed by the party at the date of the statement, such as loans, credit card debts, and other debts. The party may include any money owed to the Canada Customs and Revenue Agency, any unpaid legal or professional bills as a result of the family law case, mortgages, charges, liens, notes, and accounts payable. The party may set out **contingent liabilities** such as guarantees or warranties, but must indicate that they are contingent.

contingent liability
a liability that is not fixed and absolute but will become fixed and absolute when a specified event occurs

Part 9: Summary of Assets and Liabilities

This part calculates the party's net worth by deducting the total debts and other liabilities in part 8 from the total assets in part 7.

Concluding Information

This part states whether or not the party expects changes in his or her financial situation, and if so details of the expected changes. The party must also state whether a proposed budget is included as part of the financial statement.

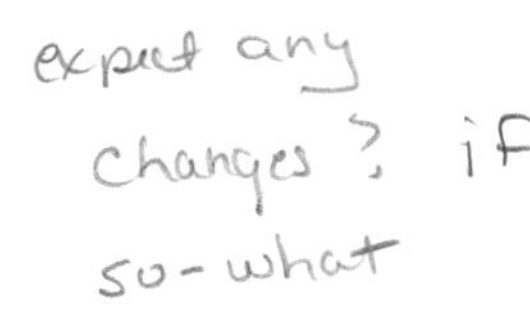

Jurat

The financial statement must be sworn or affirmed under oath and must, therefore, be signed in the presence of a lawyer, justice of the peace, notary public, or commissioner for taking affidavits.

FORM 13.1: FINANCIAL STATEMENT (PROPERTY AND SUPPORT CLAIMS)

This financial statement must be filed by a party who is making or responding to a claim for property or exclusive possession of the matrimonial home and its contents, with or without a claim for other relief. A copy of form 13.1 can be found at the end of this chapter.

Parts 1 through 6 of the form deal with the income and expenses of the party and are identical to parts 1 through 6 of form 13. The balance of the form deals with the assets and debts of the party. The information set out in this form is more extensive than the asset and debt information in form 13.

Part 7: Assets In and Outside Ontario

Part 7 details all property owned by the party, and starts with a statement of:

- the date of marriage,

- the valuation date, and
- the date of commencement of cohabitation (if different from the date of marriage).

List all property the party owned either at the valuation date or the date of the statement or both. (If the party owned property earlier in the marriage but disposed of it before the valuation date, do not include it.) If the party owns only a percentage of the property, state that fact clearly and show the value of the party's percentage only. Whenever the form asks for a value of property, give the *market* value of the property — the amount for which the property could be sold to an interested third party. Do not use the purchase price or the replacement value of the property.

Part 7(a): Land

Include any interest in land owned, including leasehold interests and mortgages[2] by setting out:

encumbrances
mortgages or other liens registered against the property

costs of disposition
costs of disposing of the property, including real estate commission and legal fees

- the nature and type of ownership and percentage interest where relevant — sole owner, joint tenant, tenant in common, etc.;
- the address of the property; and
- the estimated market value of the party's interest on the date of marriage, on the valuation date, and as of the date of the statement, as relevant — do not deduct **encumbrances** or **costs of disposition**.

2 List only mortgages under which money is owing to the party as mortgagee.

Here's an example.

During their marriage, Laura and her husband Rob bought a home at 123 Maple Avenue, Toronto, as joint tenants for $100,000. At the time of the separation, the home was worth $250,000 and as of the date of the financial statement it is worth $275,000.

Part 7(a) of Laura's financial statement will look like this:

Nature & Type of Ownership *(Give your percentage interest where relevant.)*	Address of Property	Estimated Market Value of YOUR Interest		
		on date of marriage	on valuation date	today
Joint tenancy (50%)	Matrimonial home at 123 Maple Avenue, Toronto		125,000.00	137,500.00
		83. TOTAL VALUE OF LAND	$ 125,000.00	

Part 7(b): General Household Items and Vehicles

List and give values for the following types of property:

- Household goods and furniture — it is sufficient to group all household contents together under the description "contents of matrimonial home" unless there are items of particular value. Items of particular value should be listed separately. Give the estimated market value at the relevant dates, keeping in mind that household contents are generally worth very little — half or less of the original purchase price. In most cases, household contents are owned equally by the spouses (in which case show half the total value only), although some items may be owned by one spouse alone.
- Cars, boats, and vehicles — include only cars, boats, or vehicles registered in the party's name. You can determine the value at the relevant dates by looking at newspaper ads or by calling a dealer.
- Jewellery, art, electronics, tools, and sports and hobby equipment — obtain market values from appropriate dealers.

Here's an example.

Laura and her husband Rob bought most of their furniture and household contents together during their marriage. Laura estimates that their furniture, linens, kitchen supplies, and other household items have a market value of about $6,000. Laura also has a baby grand piano that she inherited from her grandmother during the marriage, with a market value of about $2,500. Laura and Rob each own a car. Laura's car is a five-year-old Dodge Caravan worth about $11,000. Laura has some jewellery, but nothing special or very valuable. She estimates the resale value of all of her jewellery to be no more than $500.

Part 7(b) of Laura's financial statement will look like this:

Item	Description	Indicate if NOT in your possession	Estimated Market Value of YOUR Interest		
			on date of marriage	on valuation date	today
Household goods & furniture	One-half of contents of matrimonial home			3,000.00	3,000.00
Cars, boats, vehicles	Year -5 Dodge Caravan			11,000.00	11,000.00
Jewellery, art, electronics, tools, sports & hobby equipment	Jewellery			500.00	500.00
Other special items	Baby grand piano			2,500.00	2,500.00
84. TOTAL VALUE OF GENERAL HOUSEHOLD ITEMS AND VEHICLES			$	17,000.00	

Part 7(c): Bank Accounts, Savings, Securities, and Pensions

Show these items by category — for example, cash, accounts in financial institutions, pensions, registered retirement or other savings plans, deposit receipts, any other savings bonds, warrants, options, notes, and other securities.

The party must disclose all bank accounts, even if they contain only a small amount of money. Look at the client's passbooks or get statements from the bank to determine the balances as of the appropriate dates. If an account is a joint account, show one-half of the balance as the value of the account.

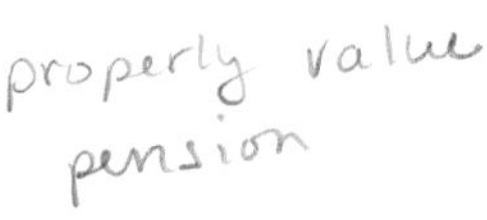

If the party has a pension, it must be properly valued — the value is not simply the total of the employee and employer contributions. It may be possible to get a valuation of the pension from the party's employer, or it may be necessary to hire an expert to value the pension. If no valuation is available at the time the statement is prepared, give details of the pension and under value state "to be valued."

Show the current market value of any securities.

Here's an example.

Laura has a joint chequing account with Rob at ScotiaBank, account number 12345. The account balance at separation was $1,200.00 and the current balance is $600.00. Laura also has had a small savings account at the Bank of Montreal, account number 2468 since before her marriage. At the date of marriage the balance was $5,000, the balance at separation was $1,000, and the balance today is $1,200. In addition, she owns 500 shares in CruiseCo Inc. These shares were worth $5,000 at the time of separation and are worth $4,500 today.

Part 7(c) of Laura's financial statement will look like this:

Category	INSTITUTION (including location)/ DESCRIPTION (including issuer and date)	Account number	Amount/Estimated Market Value		
			on date of marriage	on valuation date	today
Joint chequing account	ScotiaBank, 4000 Yonge Street, Toronto	12345		600.00	300.00
Savings Account	Bank of Montreal, 4200 Yonge Street, Toronto	2468	5,000.00	1,000.00	1,200.00
Shares	CruiseCo Inc. — 500 shares			5,000.00	4,500.00
85. TOTAL VALUE OF ACCOUNTS, SAVINGS, SECURITIES AND PENSIONS			$	6,600.00	

Part 7(d): Life and Disability Insurance

List all life and disability insurance policies and give the cash surrender value as of the relevant dates.

Here's an example.

Laura owns a $50,000 whole-life insurance policy with Metropolitan Life, policy number 369. Rob is the beneficiary, and the policy has a cash surrender value of $20,000. She also owns a $100,000 term-life policy with Canada Life, policy number 567. Rob is the beneficiary, and the policy has no cash surrender value.

Part 7(d) of Laura's financial statement will look like this:

Company, Type & Policy No.	Owner	Beneficiary	Face Amount	Cash Surrender Value		
				on date of marriage	on valuation date	today
Metropolitan Life — whole life — policy no. 369	Wife	Husband	50,000		20,000.00	20,000.00
Canada Life — term life — policy no. 567	Wife	Husband	100,000		0	0
86. TOTAL CASH SURRENDER VALUE OF INSURANCE POLICIES				$	20,000.00	

Part 7(e): Business Interests

Show any interest in an unincorporated business. An interest in an incorporated business may be shown in this part or in part 7(c). Give the market value of the party's interest in the business.

Here's an example.

In addition to her full-time job, Laura carries on a small business from her home as a computer programmer, called Petrie's 'Puters. The business owns some computer equipment, and has one or two clients. Laura estimates that the business is worth only $1,000.

Part 7(e) of her financial statement will look like this:

Name of Firm or Company	Interest	Estimated Market Value of YOUR Interest		
		on date of marriage	on valuation date	today
Petrie's 'Puters	Sole proprietor		1,000.00	1,000.00
87. TOTAL VALUE OF BUSINESS INTERESTS		$	1,000.00	

Part 7(f): Money Owed to the Party

Give details of all money that other persons owe to the party, whether because of business or from personal dealings. The party must include any court judgments in his or her favour, any estate money, and any income tax refunds owed to him or her.

Here's an example.

Laura's business is owed $750 by a client named Jerry Mathers. In addition, Laura is expecting a tax refund of $375.

Part 7(f) of her financial statement will look like this:

Details	Amount Owed to You		
	on date of marriage	on valuation date	today
Owing to Petrie's 'Puters by Jerry Mathers		750.00	750.00
Expected income tax refund		375.00	375.00
88. TOTAL OF MONEY OWED TO YOU		$ 1,125.00	

Part 7(g): Other Property

Show any other property here that has not already been listed.

Here's an example.

Laura has had a stamp collection since she was a child. At the date of the marriage, the collection was worth $150. At the time of separation and today, the collection is worth $1,000.

Part 7(g) of her financial statement will look like this:

Category	Details	Estimated Market Value of YOUR interest		
		on date of marriage	on valuation date	today
Stamp collection		150.00	1,000.00	1,000.00
	89. TOTAL VALUE OF OTHER PROPERTY		$ 1,000.00	

Value of All Property Owned on the Valuation Date

After completing parts 7(a) through 7(g), add items [83] to [89] to get the total value of all property owned on the valuation date.

Laura's total would be as follows:

90. VALUE OF ALL PROPERTY OWNED ON THE VALUATION DATE *(Add items* **[83]** *to* **[89]**.*)*	$ 171,725.00	

Part 8: Debts and Other Liabilities

Set out the party's debts and other liabilities at the relevant dates, listing them by such categories as mortgages, charges, liens, notes, credit cards, and accounts payable. The party should include any money owed to the Canada Customs and Revenue Agency, any contingent liabilities such as guarantees or warranties (indicating that they are contingent), and any unpaid legal or professional bills as a result of the family law case. If a debt is jointly owed, show only one-half of the outstanding balance.

For example:

Laura and Rob have a mortgage on the matrimonial home on which $97,000 was owing at the date of separation. The balance owing today is $96,500. Laura also has an outstanding Visa balance of $1,000. At the time of separation her balance was $750.00.

Part 8 of her financial statement will look like this:

Category	Details	Amount Owing		
		on date of marriage	on valuation date	today
Mortgage Visa	Matrimonial home Outstanding balance		48,500.00 750.00	48,250.00 1,000.00
		91. TOTAL OF DEBTS AND OTHER LIABILITIES	$ $49,250.00	

Part 9: Property, Debts, and Other Liabilities on Date of Marriage

This part details the party's assets and debts as of the date of marriage; this is information that is needed to calculate the party's net family property. The party must not include the value of a matrimonial home (or associated mortgage) that was owned on the date of marriage if this property is still a matrimonial home on valuation date.

If the parties married young, they probably had very little in the way of assets or debts at the date of marriage.

For example:

When Laura married Rob, her only assets were a savings account with a balance of $5,000 and a stamp collection worth $150. In addition, she had an outstanding student loan of $2,000, which she has since repaid.

Part 9 of her financial statement will look like this:

Category and details	Value on date of marriage	
	Assets	Liabilities
Land		
General household items & vehicles		
Bank accounts, savings, securities & pensions **Bank of Montreal no. 2468**	5,000.00	
Life & disability insurance		
Business interests		
Money owed to you		
Other property *(Specify.)* **Stamp collection**	150.00	
Debts and other liabilities *(Specify.)* **Student loan**		2,000.00
TOTALS	$ $5,150.00	$ $2,000.00
92. NET VALUE OF PROPERTY OWNED ON DATE OF MARRIAGE *(From the total of the "Assets" column, subtract the total of the "Liabilities" column.)*	$ $3,150.00	

Total Value of All Deductions

In this part, the party adds together the total of the deductions he or she is entitled to claim in calculating his or her net family property — the debts and liabilities at the valuation date and the net value of property owned on the date of marriage.

For example:

> Laura's total debts on valuation day were $49,250. The net value of her property on the date of marriage was $3,150. This part of her financial statement will look like this:

93. VALUE OF ALL DEDUCTIONS *(Add items* **[91]** *and* **[92]**.)	$ $52,400.00	

Part 10: Excluded Property

Show by category the value of property owned on the valuation date that is excluded from the definition of net family property. Excluded property is defined in s. 4(2) of the *Family Law Act* to include:

- property, other than a matrimonial home, that was acquired by gift or inheritance from a third person after the date of the marriage;
- damages or a right to damages for personal injuries, nervous shock, mental distress, or loss of guidance, care, and companionship;
- proceeds or a right to proceeds of a life insurance policy;

- property, other than a matrimonial home into which property referred to above can be traced; and
- property that the spouses have agreed by a domestic contract is not to be included in the spouse's net family property.

For example:

During the marriage, Laura inherited a baby grand piano from her grandmother. At the time of separation, the piano was worth $2,500.

Part 10 of her financial statement would look like this:

Category	Details		Value on valuation date
Inheritance	Baby grand piano inherited from grandmother during marriage		2,500.00
	94. TOTAL VALUE OF EXCLUDED PROPERTY	$	$2,500.00

Part 11: Disposed Of Property

Show by category the value of all property the party disposed of during the two years immediately preceding the making of the statement, or during the marriage, whichever period is shorter.[3]

Part 12: Calculation of Net Family Property

This part calculates the party's net family property by starting with the total value of all property owned on the valuation date and deducting the value of all deductions and the value of excluded property calculated earlier in the financial statement.

Using the figures from Laura's financial statement, part 12 would look like this:

		Deductions		BALANCE
Value of all property owned on valuation date *(from item* **[90]** *above)*	$		$	171,725.00
Subtract value of all deductions *(from item* **[93]** *above)*	$	52,400.00	$	119,325.00
Subtract total value of excluded property *(from item* **[94]** *above)*	$	2,500.00	$	116,825.00
		96. NET FAMILY PROPERTY	$	$116,825.00

Concluding Information

This part states whether or not the party expects changes in his or her financial situation, and if so details of the expected changes. The party must also state whether a proposed budget is included as part of the financial statement.

3 The requirement to disclose this information is found in s. 8(d) of the *Family Law Act*.

Jurat

The financial statement must be sworn or affirmed under oath, and must, therefore, be signed in the presence of a lawyer, justice of the peace, notary public, or commissioner for taking affidavits.

FORM 13B: NET FAMILY PROPERTY STATEMENT

This statement must be served and filed by each party to a property claim under part I of the *Family Law Act*

- not less than 7 days before a settlement conference, and
- not more than 30 days and not less than 7 days before a trial.

If the party has already served a net family property statement, the party may instead serve and file an affidavit saying that the information on the statement has not changed and is still true.

A copy of form 13B can be found at the end of this chapter.

This unsworn statement summarizes the contents of form 13.1 for both spouses in four tables:

- table 1 — value of assets owned on valuation date,
- table 2 — value of debts and liabilities on valuation date,
- table 3 — net value of property (other than a matrimonial home) and debts on date of marriage, and
- table 4 — value of property excluded under s. 4(2) of the *Family Law Act*.

Each table lists the categories and category totals from each spouse's financial statement. The table figures are then used to calculate the net family property of both spouses.

Using the information from Laura's form 13.1, the Wife's column of her net family property statement would like this:

Table 1: Value of assets owned on valuation date *(List in the order of the categories in the financial statement.)*		
ITEM	**HUSBAND**	**WIFE**
1. Land	$	$ 125,000
2. General household items and vehicles		3,000
3. Bank accounts, savings, securities, and pensions		6,600
4. Life and disability insurance		20,000
5. Business interests		1,000
6. Money owed to you		1,125
7. Other property		1,000
TOTAL 1		171,725

Table 2: Value of debts and liabilities on valuation date *(List in the order of the categories in the financial statement.)*		
ITEM	**HUSBAND**	**WIFE**
1. Mortgage	$	$ 48,500
2. Visa		750
TOTAL 2		49,250

Table 3: Net value of property (other than a matrimonial home) and debts on date of marriage *(List in the order of the categories in the financial statement.)*		
3(a) PROPERTY ITEM	**HUSBAND**	**WIFE**
Bank accounts, savings, securities, and pensions	$	$ 5,000
Other property		150
TOTAL OF PROPERTY ITEMS		5,150
3(b) DEBIT ITEM		
1. Student loan		2,000
TOTAL OF DEBIT ITEMS		2,000
NET TOTAL 3 [3(a) minus 3(b)] **NET TOTAL 3** *[3(a) minus 3(b)]*		3,150

Table 4: Value or property excluded under subsection 4(2) of the *Family Law Act* *(List in the order of the categories in the financial statement.)*		
ITEM	**HUSBAND**	**WIFE**
1. Inheritance	$	$ 2,500
TOTAL 4		2,500

TOTAL 2 *(from page 2)*		49,250
TOTAL 3 *(from page 2)*		3,150
TOTAL 4 *(from above)*		2,500
TOTAL 5 *([Total 2] + [Total 3] + [Total 4])*		54,900

TOTAL 1 *(from page 1)*		171,725
TOTAL 5 *(from above)*		54,900
TOTAL 6: NET FAMILY PROPERTY *([Total 1] minus [Total 5])*		116,825

REFERENCES

Family Law Act, RSO 1990, c. F.3.

Family Law Rules, O. Reg. 114/99.

Federal Child Support Guidelines, SOR/97-175.

Ontario *Child Support Guidelines*, O. Reg. 391/97.

Rules of Civil Procedure, RRO 1990, reg. 194.

Silverstein v. Silverstein (1978), 1 RFL (2d) 239 (Ont. HC).

REVIEW QUESTIONS

1. What are the requirements for financial disclosure under the *Family Law Act*?
2. What are the requirements for financial disclosure under the *Child Support Guidelines*?
3. Under the *Family Law Rules*, when must form 13 be served and filed?
4. Under the *Family Law Rules*, when must form 13.1 be served and filed?
5. Under the *Family Law Rules*, under what circumstances is the court directed not to accept a financial statement for filing?
6. Under the *Family Law Rules*, what is the responsibility of the parties to update their financial statements as the proceeding progresses?
7. Under the *Family Law Rules*, when must the parties serve and file a net family property statement?
8. What are the three types of financial statements under the *Family Law Rules*?
9. What are the three types of financial statements under the *Rules of Civil Procedure*?
10. Why is it important to make and keep notes on the calculations used in completing a financial statement?

DISCUSSION QUESTIONS

1. You are completing a financial statement (form 13.1) under the *Family Law Rules* for a client. Working with a blank financial statement form, set out the following information in the appropriate places:

    a. The client is paid a gross salary of $1,346.15 every two weeks.

    b. The client spends $150 every week on groceries.

    c. The client pays home insurance premiums of $1,200 per year.

    d. The client and her husband jointly own the matrimonial home, located at 10579 Canarsie Avenue, Toronto. They bought the home during the marriage for $200,000. When they separated the property was worth $350,000. At the time the financial statement is prepared, the property is worth $380,000.

    e. The matrimonial home is subject to a first mortgage held by the Bank of Montreal. The original amount of the mortgage was $150,000. When they separated, the outstanding balance was $100,000. At the time the statement is prepared, the balance is $98,000.

ONTARIO

Court File Number

(Name of Court)

at

Court office address

Family Law Rules, O. Reg. 114/99

Form 13: Financial Statement (Support Claims) sworn/affirmed

Applicant(s)

Full legal name & address for service — street & number, municipality, postal code, telephone & fax numbers and e-mail address (if any).	*Lawyer's name & address — street & number, municipality, postal code, telephone & fax numbers and e-mail address (if any).*

Respondent(s)

Full legal name & address for service — street & number, municipality, postal code, telephone & fax numbers and e-mail address (if any).	*Lawyer's name & address — street & number, municipality, postal code, telephone & fax numbers and e-mail address (if any).*

INSTRUCTIONS

1. YOU DO NOT NEED TO COMPLETE THIS FORM IF:
   - your only claim for support is for child support in the table amount specified under the Child Support Guidelines and you are not making or responding to a claim described in paragraph 3 below.
2. USE THIS FORM IF:
   - you are making or responding to a claim for spousal support; or
   - you are responding to a claim for child support; or
   - you are making a claim for child support in an amount different from the table amount specified under the Child Support Guidelines.

   You must complete all parts of the form **UNLESS** you are **ONLY** responding to a claim for child support in the table amount specified under the Child Support Guidelines **AND** you agree with the claim. In that case only complete Parts 1, 2 and 3.
3. DO NOT USE THIS FORM AND INSTEAD USE FORM 13.1 IF:
   - you are making or responding to a claim for property or exclusive possession of the matrimonial home and its contents; or
   - you are making or responding to a claim for property or exclusive possession of the matrimonial home and its contents together with other claims for relief.

1. **My name is** *(full legal name)* ______________________

   I live in *(municipality & province)* ______________________

   and I swear/affirm that the following is true:

   My financial statement set out on the following *(specify number)* __________ pages is accurate to the best of my knowledge and belief and sets out the financial situation as of *(give date for which information is accurate)*

   ______________________ for

   Check one or more boxes, as circumstances require.

   ☐ me

   ☐ the following person(s): *(Give name(s) and relationship to you.)*

   ____

   ____

   ____

Continued on next sheet →

(Français au verso)

Form 13: Financial Statement (Support Claims) (page 2)

Court file number

NOTE: *When you show monthly income and expenses, give the current actual amount if you know it or can find out. To get a monthly figure you must multiply any weekly income by 4.33 or divide any yearly income by 12.*

PART 1: INCOME

for the 12 months from *(date)* .... to *(date)* ....

Include all income and other money that you get from all sources, whether taxable or not. Show the gross amount here and show your deductions in Part 3.

	CATEGORY	Monthly
1.	Pay, wages, salary, including overtime (before deductions)	
2.	Bonuses, fees, commissions	
3.	Social assistance	
4.	Employment insurance	
5.	Workers' compensation	
6.	Pensions	
7.	Dividends	
8.	Interest	

	CATEGORY	Monthly
9.	Rent, board received	
10.	Canada Child Tax Benefit	
11.	Support payments actually received	
12.	Income received by children	
13.	G.S.T. refund	
14.	Payments from trust funds	
15.	Gifts received	
16.	Other *(Specify. If necessary, attach an extra sheet.)*	
17.	**INCOME FROM ALL SOURCES**	

PART 2: OTHER BENEFITS

Show your non-cash benefits — such as the use of a company car, a club membership or room and board that your employer or someone else provides for you or benefits that are charged through or written off by your business.

ITEM	DETAILS	Monthly Market Value
	18. TOTAL	

19. GROSS MONTHLY INCOME AND BENEFITS ***(Add*** **[17]** ***plus*** **[18].)** **$** ....

PART 3: AUTOMATIC DEDUCTIONS FROM INCOME

for the 12 months from *(date)* .... to *(date)* ....

	TYPE OF EXPENSE	Monthly
20.	Income tax deducted from pay	
21.	*Canada Pension Plan*	
22.	Other pension plans	
23.	Employment insurance	
24.	Union or association dues	

	TYPE OF EXPENSE	Monthly
25.	Group insurance	
26.	Other *(Specify. If necessary, attach an extra sheet.)*	
27.	**TOTAL AUTOMATIC DEDUCTIONS**	

28. NET MONTHLY INCOME ***(Do the subtraction:*** **[19]** ***minus*** **[27].)** **$** ....

Continued on next sheet →

(Français au verso)

FLR 13 (Rev. 04/03)

Form 13: Financial Statement (Support Claims) (page 3)

Court file number

PART 4: TOTAL EXPENSES

for the 12 months from *(date)* ________________ to *(date)* ________________

***NOTE**: If you need to complete this Part (see instructions on page 1), you must set out your TOTAL living expenses, including those expenses involving any children now living in your home. This part may also be used for a proposed budget. To prepare a proposed budget, photocopy Part 4, complete as necessary, change the title to "Proposed Budget" and attach it to this form.*

	TYPE OF EXPENSE	Monthly
Housing		
29.	Rent/mortgage	
30.	Property taxes & municipal levies	
31.	Condominium fees & common expenses	
32.	Water	
33.	Electricity & heating fuel	
34.	Telephone	
35.	Cable television & pay television	
36.	Home insurance	
37.	Home repairs, maintenance, gardening	
	Sub-total of items [29] to [37]	
Food, Clothing and Transportation etc.		
38.	Groceries	
39.	Meals outside home	
40.	General household supplies	
41.	Hairdresser, barber & toiletries	
42.	Laundry & dry cleaning	
43.	Clothing	
44.	Public transit	
45.	Taxis	
46.	Car insurance	
47.	Licence	
48.	Car loan payments	
49.	Car maintenance and repairs	
50.	Gasoline & oil	
51.	Parking	
	Sub-total of items [38] to [51]	
Health and Medical ***(do not include child(ren)'s expenses)***		
52.	Regular dental care	
53.	Orthodontics or special dental care	
54.	Medicine & drugs	
55.	Eye glasses or contact lenses	
56.	Life or term insurance premiums	
	Sub-total of items [52] to [56]	

	TYPE OF EXPENSE	Monthly
Child(ren)		
57.	School activities (field trips, etc.)	
58.	School lunches	
59.	School fees, books, tuition, *etc.* (for children)	
60.	Summer camp	
61.	Activities (music lessons, clubs, sports)	
62.	Allowances	
63.	Baby sitting	
64.	Day care	
65.	Regular dental care	
66.	Orthodontics or special dental care	
67.	Medicine & drugs	
68.	Eye glasses or contact lenses	
	Sub-total of items [57] to [68]	
Miscellaneous and Other		
69.	Books for home use, newspapers, magazines, videos, compact discs	
70.	Gifts	
71.	Charities	
72.	Alcohol & tobacco	
73.	Pet expenses	
74.	School fees, books, tuition, *etc.*	
75.	Entertainment & recreation	
76.	Vacation	
77.	Credit cards *(but not for expenses mentioned elsewhere in the statement)*	
78.	R.R.S.P. or other savings plans	
79.	Support actually being paid in any other case	
80.	Income tax and *Canada Pension Plan (not deducted from pay)*	
81.	Other *(Specify. If necessary attach an extra sheet.)*	
	Sub-total of items [69] to [81]	
82.	**Total of items [29] to [81]**	

SUMMARY OF INCOME AND EXPENSES

Net monthly income *(item* **[28]** *above)* =$ ________________

Subtract actual monthly expenses *(item* **[82]** *above* =$ ________________

ACTUAL MONTHLY SURPLUS/DEFICIT =$ ________________

Continued on next sheet →
(Français au verso)

Form 13: Financial Statement (Support Claims) (page 4)

Court file number

PART 5: OTHER INCOME INFORMATION

1. I am ☐ employed by *(name and address of employer)*

☐ self-employed, carrying on business under the name of *(name and address of business)*

☐ unemployed since *(date when last employed)*

2. I attach the following required information *(if you are filing this statement to update or correct an earlier statement, then you do not need to attach income tax returns that have already been filed with the court.):*
   - ☐ a copy of my income tax returns that were filed with the Canada Customs and Revenue Agency for the past 3 taxation years, together with a copy of all material filed with the returns and a copy of any notices of assessment or re-assessment that I have received from the Canada Customs and Revenue Agency for those years; or
   - ☐ a statement from the Canada Customs and Revenue Agency that I have not filed any income tax returns from the past 3 years; or
   - ☐ a direction in Form 13A signed by me to the Taxation Branch of the Canada Customs and Revenue Agency for the disclosure of my tax returns and notices of assessment to the other party for the past 3 years.

   I attach proof of my current income, including my most recent
   - ☐ pay cheque stub. ☐ employment insurance stub. ☐ worker's compensation stub.
   - ☐ pension stub. ☐ Other. *(Specify.)*

3. ☐ *(check if applicable)* I am an Indian within the meaning of the *Indian Act* (Canada) and all my income is tax exempt and I am not required to file an income tax return. I have therefore not attached an income tax return for the past three years.

PART 6: OTHER INCOME EARNERS IN THE HOME

Complete this part only if you are making a claim for undue hardship or spousal support. Indicate at paragraph 1 or 2, whether you are living with another person (for example, spouse, same sex partner, roommate or tenant). If you complete paragraph 2, also complete paragraphs 3 to 6.

1. ☐ I live alone.
2. I am living with *(full legal name of person)* ____________
3. This person has *(give number)* ____________ child(ren) living in the home.
4. This person ☐ works at *(place of work or business)* ____________
   ☐ does not work outside the home.
5. This person ☐ earns *(give amount)* $ ____________ per ____________
   ☐ does not earn anything.
6. This person ☐ contributes about $ ____________ per ____________ towards the household expenses.
   ☐ contributes no money to the household expenses.

Continued on next sheet →
(Français au verso)

Form 13: Financial Statement (Support Claims) (page 5)

Court file number

PART 7: PROPERTY

LAND

Kind of Property	Address of Property	Type of Ownership *(Give your percentage of interest)*	Estimated Market Value of Your Interest
		83. TOTAL VALUE	

GENERAL ITEMS AND VEHICLES (including household goods and furniture, jewellery, cars, boats, tools, sports and hobby equipment)

Description (including where located, year and make)	Estimated Market Value *(not replacement cost)*
84. TOTAL VALUE	

BANK ACCOUNTS, SAVINGS, SECURITIES AND PENSIONS (including R.R.S.P.'s other savings plans, cash, accounts in financial institutions, stocks, bonds, term deposits and controlling interest in an incorporated business)

Item/Type	Institution (include location)/ Description (including issuer and date)	Account Number	Date of Maturity	Amount/Estimated Market Value
			85. TOTAL VALUE	

LIFE AND DISABILITY INSURANCE (List all policies now in existence.)

Company, Type & Policy No.	Beneficiary	Face Amount	Today's Cash Surrender Value
		86. TOTAL VALUE	

BUSINESS INTERESTS (Show any interest in an unincorporated business owned today.)

Name of Firm or Company	Nature and Location of Business	Interest	Estimated Market Value of Your Interest
		87. TOTAL VALUE	

MONEY OWED TO YOU (including any court judgments in your favour, any estate money and any income tax refunds owed to you.)

Details (including name of debtors)	Amount Owed to You
88. TOTAL OF MONEY OWED TO YOU	

OTHER PROPERTY

Type of Property	Description and Location	Estimated Market Value
	89. TOTAL VALUE OF OTHER PROPERTY	

90. TOTAL VALUE OF ALL PROPRETY *Add items* **[83]** *to* **[89]**	

Continued on next sheet →

FLR 13 (Rev. 04/03)

(Français au verso)

Form 13: Financial Statement (Support Claims) (page 6)

Court file number

PART 8: DEBTS AND OTHER LIABILITIES

Debts and other liabilities may include any money owed to the Canada Customs and Revenue Agency, contingent liabilities such as guarantees or warranties given by you (but indicated that they are contingent), any unpaid legal or professional bills as a result of this case, mortgages, charges, liens, notes, credit cards and accounts payable.

Type of Debt	Creditor	Details	Monthly Payments	Full Amount Now Owing
Bank, trust or finance company, or credit union loans				
Amounts owed to credit card companies				
Other debts				
			91. TOTAL OF DEBTS AND OTHER LIABILITIES:	

PART 9: SUMMARY OF ASSETS AND LIABILITIES

	Amounts
TOTAL ASSETS *(from item* **[90]** *above)*	$
Subtract TOTAL DEBTS *(from item* **[91]** *above)*	$
92. NET WORTH	$

☐ I do not expect changes in my financial situation.

☐ I do expect changes in my financial situation as follows:

☐ I attach a proposed budget in the format of Part 4 of this form.

NOTE: As soon as you find out that the information in this financial statement is incorrect or incomplete, or there is a material change in your circumstances that affects or will affect the information in this financial statement, you MUST serve on every other party to this case and file with the court:

- ***a new financial statement with updated information, or***
- ***if changes are minor, an affidavit in Form 14A setting out the details of these changes.***

Sworn/Affirmed before me at ____________________
municipality

in ____________________
province, state or country

on ____________ ____________________
date *Commissioner for taking affidavits*
(Type or print name below if signature is illegible.)

____
Signature
(This form is to be signed in front of a lawye justice of the peace, notary public or commissioner for taking affidavits.)

FLR 13 (Rev. 04/03) (Français au verso)

ONTARIO

Court File Number

(Name of court)

at

Court office address

Family Law Rules, O. Reg. 114/99

Form 13.1: Financial Statement (Property and Support Claims) sworn/affirmed

Applicant(s)

Full legal name & address for service — street & number, municipality, postal code, telephone & fax numbers and e-mail address (if any).	*Lawyer's name & address — street & number, municipality, postal code, telephone & fax numbers and e-mail address (if any).*

Respondent(s)

Full legal name & address for service — street & number, municipality, postal code, telephone & fax numbers and e-mail address (if any).	*Lawyer's name & address — street & number, municipality, postal code, telephone & fax numbers and e-mail address (if any).*

INSTRUCTIONS

1. USE THIS FORM IF:
   - you are making or responding to a claim for property or exclusive possession of the matrimonial home and its contents; or
   - you are making or responding to a claim for property or exclusive possession of the matrimonial home and its contents together with other claims for relief.
2. DO NOT USE THIS FORM AND INSTEAD USE FORM 13 IF:
   - you are making or responding to a claim for support but NOT making or responding to a claim for property or exclusive possession of the matrimonial home and its contents.

1. **My name** is *(full legal name)* ____________

   I live in *(municipality & province)* ____________

   and I swear/affirm that the following is true:

   My financial statement set out on the following *(specify number)* ________ pages is accurate to the best of my knowledge and belief and sets out the financial situation as of *(give date for which information is accurate)* ____________ for

   Check one or more boxes, as circumstances require.

   ☐ me
   ☐ the following person(s): *(Give name(s) and relationship to you.)*

Continued on next sheet →
(Français au verso)

Form 13.1: Financial Statement (Property and Support Claims) (page 2)

Court file number

NOTE: *When you show monthly income and expenses, give the current actual amount if you know it or can find out. To get a monthly figure you must multiply any weekly income by 4.33 or divide any yearly income by 12.*

PART 1: INCOME

for the 12 months from *(date)* .... to *(date)* ....

Include all income and other money that you get from all sources, whether taxable or not. Show the gross amount here and show your deductions in Part 3.

	CATEGORY	Monthly
1.	Pay, wages, salary, including overtime (before deductions)	
2.	Bonuses, fees, commissions	
3.	Social assistance	
4.	Employment insurance	
5.	Workers' compensation	
6.	Pensions	
7.	Dividends	
8.	Interest	

	CATEGORY	Monthly
9.	Rent, board received	
10.	Canada Child Tax Benefit	
11.	Support payments actually received	
12.	Income received by children	
13.	G.S.T. refund	
14.	Payments from trust funds	
15.	Gifts received	
16.	Other *(Specify. If necessary, attach an extra sheet.)*	
17.	**INCOME FROM ALL SOURCES**	

PART 2: OTHER BENEFITS

Show your non-cash benefits — such as the use of a company car, a club membership or room and board that your employer or someone else provides for you or benefits that are charged through or written off by your business.

ITEM	DETAILS	Monthly Market Value
	18. TOTAL	

19. GROSS MONTHLY INCOME AND BENEFITS ***(Add*** **[17]** ***plus*** **[18].)** **$** ....

PART 3: AUTOMATIC DEDUCTIONS FROM INCOME

for the 12 months from *(date)* .... to *(date)* ....

	TYPE OF EXPENSE	Monthly
20.	Income tax deducted from pay	
21.	*Canada Pension Plan*	
22.	Other pension plans	
23.	Employment insurance	
24.	Union or association dues	

	TYPE OF EXPENSE	Monthly
25.	Group insurance	
26.	Other *(Specify. If necessary, attach an extra sheet.)*	
27.	**TOTAL AUTOMATIC DEDUCTIONS**	

28. NET MONTHLY INCOME ***(Do the subtraction:*** **[19]** ***minus*** **[27].)** **$** ....

Continued on next sheet →

FLR 13.1 (Rev. 04/03) (Français au verso)

Form 13.1: Financial Statement (Property and Support Claims) **(page 3)**

Court file number

PART 4: TOTAL EXPENSES

for the 12 months from *(date)* ______________ to *(date)* ______________

NOTE: *This part must be completed in all cases. You must set out your TOTAL living expenses, including those expenses involving any children now living in your home. This part may also be used for a proposed budget. To prepare a proposed budget, photocopy Part 4, complete as necessary, change the title to "Proposed Budget" and attach it to this form.*

	TYPE OF EXPENSE	Monthly
Housing		
29.	Rent/mortgage	
30.	Property taxes & municipal levies	
31.	Condominium fees & common expenses	
32.	Water	
33.	Electricity & heating fuel	
34.	Telephone	
35.	Cable television & pay television	
36.	Home insurance	
37.	Home repairs, maintenance, gardening	
	Sub-total of items [29] to [37]	
Food, Clothing and Transportation etc.		
38.	Groceries	
39.	Meals outside home	
40.	General household supplies	
41.	Hairdresser, barber & toiletries	
42.	Laundry & dry cleaning	
43.	Clothing	
44.	Public transit	
45.	Taxis	
46.	Car insurance	
47.	Licence	
48.	Car loan payments	
49.	Car maintenance and repairs	
50.	Gasoline & oil	
51.	Parking	
	Sub-total of items [38] to [51]	
Health and Medical *(do not include child(ren)'s expenses)*		
52.	Regular dental care	
53.	Orthodontics or special dental care	
54.	Medicine & drugs	
55.	Eye glasses or contact lenses	
56.	Life or term insurance premiums	
	Sub-total of items [52] to [56]	

	TYPE OF EXPENSE	Monthly
Child(ren)		
57.	School activities (field trips, etc.)	
58.	School lunches	
59.	School fees, books, tuition, *etc.* (for children)	
60.	Summer camp	
61.	Activities (music lessons, clubs, sports)	
62.	Allowances	
63.	Baby sitting	
64.	Day care	
65.	Regular dental care	
66.	Orthodontics or special dental care	
67.	Medicine & drugs	
68.	Eye glasses or contact lenses	
	Sub-total of items [57] to [68]	
Miscellaneous and Other		
69.	Books for home use, newspapers, magazines, videos, compact discs	
70.	Gifts	
71.	Charities	
72.	Alcohol & tobacco	
73.	Pet expenses	
74.	School fees, books, tuition, *etc.*	
75.	Entertainment & recreation	
76.	Vacation	
77.	Credit cards *(but not for expenses mentioned elsewhere in the statement)*	
78.	R.R.S.P. or other savings plans	
79.	Support actually being paid in any other case	
80.	Income tax and *Canada Pension Plan (not deducted from pay)*	
81.	Other *(Specify. If necessary attach an extra sheet.)*	
	Sub-total of items [69] to [81]	
82.	**Total of items [29] to [81]**	

SUMMARY OF INCOME AND EXPENSES

Net monthly income *(item* **[28]** *above)* =$ ______________

Subtract actual monthly expenses *(item* **[82]** *above)* =$ ______________

ACTUAL MONTHLY SURPLUS/DEFICIT =$ ______________

Continued on next sheet →

FLR 13.1 (Rev. 04/03)

(Français au verso)

Form 13.1: Financial Statement (Property and Support Claims) (page 4)

Court file number

PART 5: OTHER INCOME INFORMATION

1. I am ☐ employed by *(name and address of employer)*

☐ self-employed, carrying on business under the name of *(name and address of business)*

☐ unemployed since *(date when last employed)*

2. I attach the following required information *(if you are filing this statement to update or correct an earlier statement, then you do not need to attach income tax returns that have already been filed with the court):*

☐ a copy of my income tax returns that were filed with the Canada Customs and Revenue Agency for the past 3 taxation years, together with a copy of all material filed with the returns and a copy of any notices of assessment or re-assessment that I have received from the Canada Customs and Revenue Agency for those years; or

☐ a statement from the Canada Customs and Revenue Agency that I have not filed any income tax returns from the past 3 years; or

☐ a direction in Form 13A signed by me to the Taxation Branch of the Canada Customs and Revenue Agency for the disclosure of my tax returns and notices of assessment to the other part for the past 3 years.

I attach proof of my current income, including my most recent

☐ pay cheque stub. ☐ employment insurance stub. ☐ worker's compensation stub.
☐ pension stub. ☐ Other. *(Specify.)*

3. ☐ *(check if applicable)* I am an Indian within the meaning of the *Indian Act* (Canada) and all my income is tax exempt and I am not required to file an income tax return. I have therefore not attached an income tax return for the past three years.

PART 6: OTHER INCOME EARNERS IN THE HOME

Complete this part only if you are making a claim for undue hardship or spousal support. Indicate at paragraph 1 or 2, whether you are living with another person (for example, spouse, same sex partner, roommate or tenant). If you complete paragraph 2, also complete paragraphs 3 to 6.

1. ☐ I live alone.
2. I am living with *(full legal name of person)* ....
3. This person has *(give number)* .... child(ren) living in the home.
4. This person ☐ works at *(place of work or business)* ....
☐ does not work outside the home.
5. This person ☐ earns (give amount) $ .... per ....
☐ does not earn anything.
6. This person ☐ contributes about $ .... per .... towards the household expenses.
☐ contributes no money to the household expenses.

Continued on next sheet →

Form 13.1: **Financial Statement (Property and Support Claims)** **(page 5)**

Court file number

PART 7: ASSETS IN AND OUT OF ONTARIO

If any sections of Parts 7 to 12 do not apply, do not leave blank, print "NONE" in the section.

The date of marriage is: *(give date)* ____________

The valuation date is: *(give date)* ____________

The date of commencement of cohabitation is (if different from date of marriage): *(give date)* ____________

PART 7(a): LAND

*Include any interest in land **owned** on the dates in each of the columns below, including leasehold interests and mortgages. Show estimated market value of your interest, but do not deduct encumbrances or costs of disposition; these encumbrances and costs should be shown under Part 8, "Debts and Other Liabilities".*

Nature & Type of Ownership *(Give your percentage interest where relevant.)*	Address of Property	Estimated Market Value of YOUR Interest		
		on date of marriage	on valuation date	today
	83. TOTAL VALUE OF LAND	$		

PART 7(b): GENERAL HOUSEHOLD ITEMS AND VEHICLES

Show estimated market value, not the cost of replacement for these items owned on the dates in each of the columns below. Do not deduct encumbrances or costs of disposition; these encumbrances and costs should be shown under Part 8, "Debts and Other Liabilities".

Item	Description	Indicate if NOT in your possession	Estimated Market Value of YOUR Interest		
			on date of marriage	on valuation date	today
Household goods & furniture					
Cars, boats, vehicles					
Jewellery, art, electronics, tools, sports & hobby equipment					
Other special items					
		84. TOTAL VALUE OF GENERAL HOUSEHOLD ITEMS AND VEHICLES	$		

Continued on next sheet →

(Français au verso)

Form 13.1: Financial Statement (Property and Support Claims) (page 6)

Court file number

PART 7(c): BANK ACCOUNTS, SAVINGS, SECURITIES AND PENSIONS

Show the items owned on the dates in each of the columns below by category, for example, cash, accounts in financial institutions, pensions, registered retirement or other savings plans, deposit receipts, any other savings, bonds, warrants, options, notes and other securities. Give your best estimate of the market value of the securities if the items were to be sold on the open market.

Category	INSTITUTION (including location)/ DESCRIPTION (including issuer and date)	Account number	Amount/Estimated Market Value		
			on date of marriage	on valuation date	today
85. TOTAL VALUE OF ACCOUNTS, SAVINGS, SECURITIES AND PENSIONS				**$**	

PART 7(d): LIFE AND DISABILITY INSURANCE

List all policies in existence on the dates in each of the columns below.

Company, Type & Policy No.	Owner	Beneficiary	Face Amount	Cash Surrender Value		
				on date of marriage	on valuation date	today
86. TOTAL CASH SURRENDER VALUE OF INSURANCE POLICIES					**$**	

PART 7(e): BUSINESS INTERESTS

Show any interest in an unincorporated business owned on the dates in each of the columns below. An interest in an incorporated business may be shown here or under "BANK ACCOUNTS, SAVINGS, SECURITIES, AND PENSIONS" in Part 7(c). Give your best estimate of the market value of your interest.

Name of Firm or Company	Interest	Estimated Market Value of YOUR Interest		
		on date of marriage	on valuation date	today
87. TOTAL VALUE OF BUSINESS INTERESTS			**$**	

Continued on next sheet →

FLR 13.1 (Rev. 04/03) (Français au verso)

Form 13.1: Financial Statement (Property and Support Claims) **(page 7)**

Court file number

PART 7(f): MONEY OWED TO YOU

Give details of all money that other persons owe to you on the dates in each of the columns below, whether because of business or from personal dealings. Include any court judgments in your favour, any estate money and any income tax refunds owed to you.

Details	Amount Owed to You		
	on date of marriage	on valuation date	today
88. TOTAL OF MONEY OWED TO YOU	**$**		

PART 7(g): OTHER PROPERTY

Show other property or assets owned on the dates in each of the columns below. Include property of any kind not listed above. Give your best estimate of market value.

Category	Details	Estimated Market Value of YOUR interest		
		on date of marriage	on valuation date	today
	89. TOTAL VALUE OF OTHER PROPERTY	**$**		
	90. VALUE OF ALL PROPERTY OWNED ON THE VALUATION DATE *(Add items* **[83]** *to* **[89]**.*)*		**$**	

PART 8: DEBTS AND OTHER LIABILITIES

Show your debts and other liabilities on the dates in each of the columns below. List them by category such as mortgages, charges, liens, notes, credit cards, and accounts payable. Don't forget to include:

- *any money owed to the Canada Customs and Revenue Agency;*
- *contingent liabilities such as guarantees or warranties given by you (but indicate that they are contingent); and*
- *any unpaid legal or professional bills as a result of this case.*

Category	Details	Amount Owing		
		on date of marriage	on valuation date	today
	91. TOTAL OF DEBTS AND OTHER LIABILITIES	**$**		

Continued on next sheet →

FLR 13.1 (Rev. 04/03) (Français au verso)

Form 13.1: Financial Statement (Property and Support Claims) **(page 8)**

Court file number

PART 9: PROPERTY, DEBTS AND OTHER LIABILITIES ON DATE OF MARRIAGE

Show by category the value of your property and your debts and other liabilities ***as of the date of your marriage****. DO NOT INCLUDE THE VALUE OF A MATRIMONIAL HOME THAT YOU OWNED ON THE DATE OF MARRIAGE IF THIS PROPERTY IS STILL A MATRIMONIAL HOME ON VALUATION DATE.*

Category and details	Value on date of marriage	
	Assets	Liabilities
Land		
General household items & vehicles		
Bank accounts, savings, securities & pensions		
Life & disability insurance		
Business interests		
Money owed to you		
Other property *(Specify.)*		
Debts and other liabilities *(Specify.)*		
TOTALS	**$**	**$**
92. NET VALUE OF PROPERTY OWNED ON DATE OF MARRIAGE *(From the total of the "Assets" column, subtract the total of the "Liabilities" column.)*	**$**	
93. VALUE OF ALL DEDUCTIONS *(Add items* **[91]** *and* **[92]**.*)*	**$**	

PART 10: EXCLUDED PROPERTY

Show by category the value of property owned on the valuation date that is excluded from the definition of "net family property" (such as gifts or inheritances received after marriage).

Category	Details	Value on valuation date
	94. TOTAL VALUE OF EXCLUDED PROPERTY	**$**

Continued on next sheet →

FLR 13.1 (Rev. 04/03) (Français au verso)

Form 13.1: Financial Statement (Property and Support Claims) (page 9)

Court file number

PART 11: DISPOSED-OF PROPERTY

Show by category the value of all property that you disposed of during the two years immediately preceding the making of this statement, or during the marriage, whichever period is shorter.

Category	Details	Value
	95. TOTAL VALUE OF DISPOSED-OF PROPERTY	**$**

PART 12: CALCULATION OF NET FAMILY PROPERTY

	Deductions	BALANCE
Value of all property owned on valuation date *(from item* **[90]** *above)*		**$**
Subtract value of all deductions *(from item* **[93]** *above)*	**$**	**$**
Subtract total value of excluded property *(from item* **[94]** *above)*	**$**	**$**
96. NET FAMILY PROPERTY		**$**

☐ I do not expect changes in my financial situation.

☐ I do expect changes in my financial situation as follows:

☐ I attach a proposed budget in the format of Part 4 of this form.

NOTE: As soon as you find out that the information in this financial statement is incorrect or incomplete, or there is a material change in your circumstances that affects or will affect the information in this financial statement, you MUST serve on every other party to this case and file with the court:

- ***a new financial statement with updated information, or***
- ***if changes are minor, an affidavit in Form 14A setting out the details of these changes.***

Sworn/Affirmed before me at ....
municipality

in ....
province, state or country

on .... *date*

____
Commissioner for taking affidavits
(Type or print name below if signature is illegible.)

____
Signature
(This form is to be signed in front of a lawyer, justice of the peace, notary public or commissioner for taking affidavits.)

FLR 13.1 (Rev. 04/03)

(Français au verso)

ONTARIO

Court File Number

____
(Name of court)

Family Law Rules, O.Reg. 114/99

Form 13B: Net Family Property Statement

at ____
Court office address

Applicant(s)

Full legal name & address for service — street & number, municipality, postal code, telephone & fax numbers and e-mail address (if any).	*Lawyer's name & address — street & number, municipality, postal code, telephone & fax numbers and e-mail address (if any).*

Respondent(s)

Full legal name & address for service — street & number, municipality, postal code, telephone & fax numbers and e-mail address (if any).	*Lawyer's name & address — street & number, municipality, postal code, telephone & fax numbers and e-mail address (if any).*

My name is *(full legal name)* ....

The valuation date for the following material is *(date)* ....

(Complete the tables by filling in the columns for both husband and wife, showing your assets, debts, etc., and those of your spouse.)

Table 1: Value of assets owned on valuation date
(List in the order of the categories in the financial statement.)

ITEM	HUSBAND	WIFE
1.	$	$
TOTAL 1		

Continued on next sheet

(Français au verso)

Court File Number

Form 13B: Net Family Property Statement (page 2)

Table 2: Value of debts and liabilities on valuation date *(List in the order of the categories in the financial statement.)*		
ITEM	**HUSBAND**	**WIFE**
	$	$
TOTAL 2		

Table 3: Net value of property (other than a matrimonial home) and debts on date of marriage *(List in the order of the categories in the financial statement.)*		
3(a) PROPERTY ITEM	**HUSBAND**	**WIFE**
	$	$
TOTAL OF PROPERTY ITEMS		
3(b) DEBIT ITEM		
TOTAL OF DEBIT ITEMS		
NET TOTAL 3 *[3(a) minus 3(b)]*		

Continued on next sheet

(Français au verso)

Court File Number

Form 13B: Net Family Property Statement (page 3)

Table 4: Value or property excluded under subsection 4(2) of the *Family Law Act* *(List in the order of the categories in the financial statement.)*		
ITEM	**HUSBAND**	**WIFE**
	$	**$**
TOTAL 4		

TOTAL 2 *(from page 2)*		
TOTAL 3 *(from page 2)*		
TOTAL 4 *(from above)*		
TOTAL 5 *([Total 2] + [Total 3] + [Total 4])*		

TOTAL 1 *(from page 1)*		
TOTAL 5 *(from above)*		
TOTAL 6: NET FAMILY PROPERTY *([Total 1] minus [Total 5])*		

Signature

Date of signature

CHAPTER 12

The Family Court of the Ontario Superior Court of Justice

The Family Court is a branch of the Ontario Superior Court of Justice, which operates in many, but not all, locations in Ontario. It is a single-level family court at the superior court level that has jurisdiction over all family law matters including:

- divorce,
- child support,
- support for spouses and common law partners,
- custody of and access to children,
- equalization of net family property,
- trust claims and claims for unjust enrichment,
- possession of the matrimonial home,
- adoption, and
- child protection.

The goal of the court is to deal with family problems in an integrated manner. Each Family Court site offers the following support services to litigants:

- a family law information centre,
- mediation services,
- legal support services (legal aid duty counsel),
- family law information meetings, and
- a supervised access and exchange centre.

This chapter

- sets out the locations of the Family Court,
- provides an overview of the procedure in the Family Court, and
- discusses the *Family Law Rules* and forms.

FAMILY COURT LOCATIONS

At the time of printing, the Family Court of the Superior Court of Justice operates in 18 of the province's 49 counties and judicial districts. In all other parts of the province, including the City of Toronto and the Regional Municipality of Peel, jurisdiction over family law matters continues to be divided between the Superior Court of Justice and the Ontario Court of Justice. Appendix B lists those provincial jurisdictions with the Family Court and those without. See chapter 16 for a discussion of the procedure in the Superior Court of Justice.

The province has committed itself to expanding the operation of the Family Court throughout the province. In addition, the federal government, as part of its child-centred family justice strategy, announced in December 2002, has pledged additional funding to the provinces to assist in the expansion of unified family courts such as the Family Court of the Superior Court of Justice.

OVERVIEW OF PROCEDURE IN THE FAMILY COURT

The procedure in the Family Court is governed by the *Family Law Rules*. The rules are written in plain language, and the forms under the rules are designed to be comprehensive and easy to use.

The Primary Objective

Rule 2(2) states that the "primary objective" of the *Family Law Rules* is to enable the court to deal with cases justly. This means

- ensuring that the procedure is fair to all parties,
- saving expense and time,
- dealing with the case in ways that are appropriate to its importance and complexity, and
- giving appropriate court resources to the case while taking account of the need to give resources to other cases.

Case Management

Case management is one of the key features of the *Family Law Rules*. Rule 2(5) requires the court to promote the primary objective, of dealing with cases justly, by active management of cases, which includes the following:

- at an early stage, identifying the issues, and separating and disposing of those issues that do not need full investigation and trial;
- encouraging and facilitating use of alternatives to the court process;
- helping the parties to settle all or part of the case;
- setting timetables or otherwise controlling the progress of the case;
- considering whether the likely benefits of taking a step justify the cost;
- dealing with as many aspects of the case as possible on the same occasion; and

- if appropriate, dealing with the case without parties and their lawyers needing to come to court, on the basis of written documents or by holding a telephone or video conference.

A case management judge is assigned to each case. The role of the case management judge is to

- generally supervise its progress,
- conduct case and settlement conferences,
- schedule a case or settlement conference if appropriate, and
- hear motions in the case.

Rule 17 provides for three types of case management conferences: a case conference, a settlement conference, and a trial management conference.

The purpose of these conferences is to define, narrow, or even settle the issues in dispute. The various types of conferences may be combined in appropriate circumstances. Under rule 14, except in cases of urgency or hardship, no motion may be brought before a case conference is held.

Under rule 39, all cases are placed on either a standard track or a fast track. Cases that involve divorce or property claims are standard track cases. All other cases are fast track cases.

fast vs standard

Fast track cases are assigned a first court date at the time the proceeding is commenced. On or before the first court date, the court clerk will review the file to make sure that the case is ready to proceed before a judge. A case management judge is assigned to the case before the first time the case comes to court.

Cases on the standard track are not assigned a court date at the time the proceeding is commenced. These cases do not come before a judge until a party requests a case conference or brings an urgent motion. A case management judge is assigned to the case at that time.

Rule 39 also sets timelines for the trial of family law cases. In both fast track and standard track cases, if a case has not been scheduled for trial within 200 days from the start of the case, the court sends a notice to the parties advising them that the case will be dismissed in 30 days if no steps are taken.

Steps in a Family Court Case

A Family Court case goes through the following steps:

1. *Application* — The case is started by the filing of an application. The party who files the application is the applicant. The other party is the respondent. The application sets out the issues that the court is being asked to resolve. If the application includes a claim for support and/or an equalization of net family property, the applicant must also file a financial statement. The application and any financial statement must be served on the respondent.
2. *Answer* — If the respondent wishes to defend the application, he or she must serve the applicant with an answer and file it with the court. If financial support or an equalization of net family property is claimed in the application, or if the respondent wishes to make such a claim, he or she must also serve and file a financial statement.

3. *First court date* — Fast track cases are given a first court date at the time the application is filed. If an answer has not been filed and the respondent does not appear at the first court date, the matter will proceed as an uncontested trial. If the respondent files an answer and/or appears at the first court date, the next step is a case conference.
4. *Case conference* — A case conference takes place after the first court date in fast track cases, and when either party requests one in standard track cases. The case conference is the first opportunity for the parties to discuss the case with a judge.
5. *Settlement conference* — A judge may schedule a settlement conference if he or she thinks it is necessary. The primary purpose of a settlement conference is to try to settle or narrow the issues in dispute.
6. *Trial management conference* — If the case does not settle, a judge may schedule a trial management conference if he or she thinks it is necessary. The purpose of a trial management conference is to continue to explore settlement possibilities, and, failing settlement, to make decisions affecting how the trial will proceed.
7. *Trial* — The trial judge will hear the evidence of the parties and their submissions as to the relevant law and then make final orders on any unresolved issues.

While the case is ongoing, either party may bring a motion to ask the court to make temporary orders to resolve certain issues before trial — for example, orders for interim custody and support. Only emergency or procedural motions may be brought before the case conference. Other motions may be brought after the case conference.

Figure 12.1 lists the principal rules that govern each of these steps.

THE FAMILY COURT RULES: A MORE DETAILED LOOK

There are 40 Family Court rules. For the most part, they are sequenced in the same order as the steps in a case. The forms required by the rules are numbered to correspond to the rule that governs the particular form. Some of the more important rules are discussed below.

Time: Rule 3

Rule 3 states how the number of days between two events is counted:

- The first day counted is the day after the first event, and the last day counted is the day of the second event.
    - For example, motion documents must be served at least four days before the motion date. The date of service is considered the first event and the date of the motion is considered the second event. If a motion is scheduled for Friday, November 7 and the motion documents are served on Monday, November 3, Tuesday is the first day counted, Wednesday is the second day, Thursday is the third day, and Friday is

FIGURE 12.1 STEPS IN A FAMILY COURT CASE

1. Application — rule 8
2. Answer — rule 10
3. First court date for fast track cases — rule 39(5)
4. Case conference — rule 17(4)
5. Settlement conference — rule 17(5)
6. Trial management conference — rule 17(6)
7. Trial — rule 23

important !!

the fourth day. Therefore, service on Monday is four days before the motion on Friday.

- If a rule or order gives less than seven days for something to be done, Saturdays, Sundays, and other days when court offices are closed do not count as days of the period.
- If the last day of a period of time under a rule or order falls on a day when court offices are closed, the period ends on the next day that they are open.

The rule also states that late filing of documents is not permitted without a court order or the written consent of the other party.

Where a Case Starts and Is To Be Heard: Rule 5

There are strict rules governing the place where a case can be started. A case must be started

- in the municipality where a party resides;
- if the case deals with custody or access, in the municipality where the child ordinarily resides; or
- in a municipality chosen by all parties, but only with the court's permission.

All steps in a case, other than enforcement of an order, are to take place where the case is started.

Service of Documents: Rule 6

Most court documents must be served on the other party. There are two levels of service under the *Family Law Rules* — special service and regular service.

Special service, which is dealt with in rule 6(3), is required for an application, a summons to witness, a notice of contempt motion, and any other document that can lead to imprisonment. Special service of a document is carried out by

- leaving a copy with the person to be served or, if the person is a corporation, by leaving a copy with an officer, director, or agent of the corporation, or with a person who appears to be managing a place of business of the corporation (if the person to be served is mentally incapable, a copy must also be left with the person's guardian; if the person is a child, a copy must also be left with the child's lawyer, if there is one);

- leaving a copy with the person's lawyer of record in the case, or with a lawyer who accepts service in writing on a copy of the document;
- mailing a copy to the person, together with an acknowledgment of service postcard, in which case service is not valid unless the return postcard, signed by the person, is filed with the court; or
- leaving a copy at the person's place of residence with anyone who appears to be an adult person resident at the same address and, on the same day, mailing another copy to the person at that address.

Regular service, which is dealt with in rule 6(2), applies to all other documents. Methods of regular service include

- mailing a copy to the person's lawyer or, if none, to the person;
- sending a copy by courier to the person's lawyer or, if none, to the person;
- depositing a copy at a **document exchange** to which the person's lawyer belongs; or
- faxing a copy to the person's lawyer or, if none, to the person.

document exchange
a subscription service in which law firms have access to a central facility to deliver and pick up documents, used primarily during postal strikes

substituted service
service using a method ordered by the court in circumstances when the usual methods of service provided by the court rules are not effective

Under rule 6(15), the court may order **substituted service**, using a method chosen by the court, if the party making the motion provides detailed evidence showing what steps have been taken to locate the person to be served and, if located, what steps have been taken to serve the person. The party making the motion must also show that the method of substituted service is likely to bring the document to the person's attention.

Under rule 6(16), the court may dispense with service if reasonable efforts to locate the person to be served have not been or would not be successful, and there is no method of substituted service that could reasonably be expected to bring the document to the person's attention.

Pursuant to rule 6(19), service of a document may be proved by

- an acceptance or admission of service, written by the person to be served or his or her lawyer,
- an affidavit of service (form 6B),
- a return postcard of the kind mentioned in rule 6(3)(c), or
- the date stamp on a copy of the document served by deposit at a document exchange.

Parties: Rule 7

The parties in a case before the Family Court are the applicant — the person who makes a claim — and the respondent — the person against whom a claim is made. All cases have a permanent case name and court file number. The person named as the applicant remains the applicant, even if the respondent later moves to vary a final order.

Starting a Case: Rule 8

All cases are started by filing an application. In fast track applications, the court clerk assigns a court date. The applicant is required to serve the application immediately on every other party, using special service.

Continuing Record: Rule 9

A person starting a case is required to prepare a continuing record of the case: this will become the court's permanent record of the case. The party must serve and file the continuing record. Once the continuing record is filed, the parties, under the supervision of the court clerk, are responsible for adding to it all documents that are filed in the case.

As the case progresses, parties are required to serve and file only documents that are not already in the continuing record.

Answering a Case: Rule 10

A respondent who wants to defend a case must serve and file an answer within 30 days (60 days if the respondent was served outside Canada or the United States). A respondent may include a claim against the applicant or any other person in his or her answer.

If a respondent does not serve and file an answer, or if an answer is struck out, the respondent is not entitled to notice of any step in the case, or to participate in the case in any way.

Financial Statements: Rule 13

Under rule 13(1), parties are required to serve and file the appropriate financial statement (form 13 or form 13.1) if an application, answer, reply, or notice of motion contains a claim for support, property, or exclusive possession, whether or not the matter is defended. The applicant must serve and file the financial statement with his or her application, and the respondent must serve and file his or her financial statement within the time for serving and filing his or her reply.[1]

Pursuant to rule 13(6), each party must make full and frank disclosure of the party's financial situation, and attach any documents to prove the party's income that the financial statement requires. Under rule 13(7), the court will not accept a financial statement for filing unless it includes copies of the party's income tax returns and notices of assessment for the three previous taxation years, a direction authorizing the Canada Customs and Revenue Agency to release copies of those documents to the court, or a sworn statement that the party is not required to file an income tax return because of the *Indian Act*. If the rules require the delivery of a financial statement, the court will not accept an application, answer, reply, notice of motion, or affidavit for filing without the financial statement.

A party who believes that the other party's financial statement does not contain enough information for a full understanding of that party's financial circumstances may ask for additional information. If the other party does not comply within seven

1 If the only claim is for child support in the table amount under the *Child Support Guidelines*, no financial statement is required by the applicant. However, the respondent must file a statement.

days, the dissatisfied party may apply to the court for an order that the other party give the information under rule 3(11). A party may question the other party on his or her financial statement under rule 20, but only after a request for additional information has been made.

The parties are required to update their financial statements as the case progresses. Under rules 13(12), (12.1), and (12.2), the parties must serve and file a new financial statement, or an affidavit that the information in the financial statement has not changed, before any case conference, motion, settlement conference, or trial. Rule 13(15) also requires the parties to immediately correct any information that has materially changed or that is discovered to be incorrect or incomplete.

Under rule 13(14), the parties to a property claim under part I of the *Family Law Act* must also serve and file a net family property statement before a settlement conference or trial.

Motions: Rule 14

A person may make a motion to the court for any of the following:

- a temporary order for a claim made in an application,
- directions on how to carry on the case, and
- a change in an order or agreement (including a final order).

Except in cases of urgency or hardship, motions are not permitted before a case conference is held.

Rules 14(9) and (10) set out the documents required on a motion. Most motions require a notice of motion (form 14) and affidavit (form 14A). However, if the motion is limited to procedural, uncomplicated, or unopposed matters, the party making the motion may use a motion form (form 14B) instead of a notice of motion and affidavit.

Most motions are made on notice to the other party. Pursuant to rule 14(11), the motion documents must be served on the other parties no later than four days before the motion date, and filed with the court no later than two days before the motion date. The party making the motion must also file a confirmation (form 14C) with the court no later than 2 p.m. two days before the motion date. Under rule 14(11.1), no documents for use on the motion may be filed after that time.

Under rule 14(12), a motion may be made without notice if

- the nature or circumstances of the motion make notice unnecessary or not reasonably possible;
- there is an immediate danger of a child's removal from Ontario, and the delay involved in serving a notice of motion would probably have serious consequences;
- there is an immediate danger to the health or safety of a child or of the party making the motion, and the delay involved in serving a notice of motion would probably have serious consequences; or
- service of a notice of motion would probably have serious consequences.

Under rule 14(14), any order made on a motion without notice must require the matter to come back before the court, and before the same judge if possible, within 14 days. It is to be served immediately on the other parties (rule 14(15)).

Pursuant to rule 14(21), if a party tries to delay the case, add to its costs, or in any other way tries to abuse the court's process by making numerous motions without merit, the court may order the party not to make any other motions in the case without the court's permission.

Motions To Change an Order or Agreement: Rule 15

Rule 15 sets out the procedure to vary an agreement or a final order such as a final custody or support order.

The notice of motion and supporting evidence must be served by special service, not regular service, and 30 days' notice (60 days' notice if the other party to be served resides outside Canada or the United States) is required.

Rule 15(7) sets out in detail the required contents of an affidavit on a motion to vary, including:

- the ordinary place of residence of the parties and the children;
- the name and birth date of each child to whom a proposed change relates;
- whether either party has married or begun living with another person;
- details of current custody and access arrangements;
- details of current support arrangements, including details of any unpaid support;
- details of the change asked for and details of the changed circumstances that are grounds for the change in the order or agreement;
- details of any efforts made to mediate or settle the issues and of any assessment report on custody or access;
- in a motion to change child support, the income and financial information required under the *Child Support Guidelines*;
- in a motion to change child support to an amount different from the table amount in the *Child Support Guidelines*, evidence to satisfy the court that it should make the requested order.

Under rule 15(12), a party asking for a change in child support may file a change of information form (form 15) with all required attachments instead of an affidavit.

Summary Judgment: Rule 16

motion for summary judgment
a motion for a final order without a trial

In any case other than a divorce,[2] either party may make a **motion for summary judgment** for a final order without a trial, after the respondent has served an answer or after the time for serving an answer has expired.

Under rule 16(4), a motion for summary judgment is to be supported by an affidavit or other evidence demonstrating that there is no genuine issue requiring a trial.

2 In a divorce case, the procedure provided in rule 36 for an uncontested divorce may be used.

Conferences: Rule 17

Rule 17 deals with the conferences that are at the heart of the case management system. Each contested case must have a case conference, and may also have a settlement conference and a trial management conference.

The purposes of a case conference, which are set out in rule 17(4), include:

- exploring the chances of settling the case,
- identifying the issues that are in dispute and those that are not in dispute,
- exploring ways to resolve the issues in dispute,
- ensuring disclosure of the relevant evidence,
- noting admissions that may simplify the case,
- setting the date for the next step in the case,
- if possible, having the parties agree to a specific timetable for the case, and
- organizing a settlement conference, or holding one if that is appropriate.

In a fast track case, the parties may be given a date for the case conference when they go to court for the first court date,[3] or a party may ask that the case conference be held at the same time as the first court date. In a standard track case, a case conference will be scheduled when either party requests one. Under rule 17(4.1), a party who asks for a case conference must serve and file a case conference notice (form 17).

The purposes of a settlement conference, which are set out in rule 17(5), include:

- exploring the chances of settling the case,
- settling or narrowing the issues in dispute,
- ensuring disclosure of the relevant evidence,
- noting admissions that may simplify the case,
- if possible, obtaining a view of how the court might decide the case,
- considering any other matter that may help bring a quick and just conclusion to the case,
- if the case is not settled, identifying the witnesses and other evidence to be presented at trial, estimating the time needed for trial, and scheduling the case for trial, and
- organizing a trial management conference, or holding one if that is appropriate.

Under rule 17(10), a case cannot be scheduled for trial unless a judge has conducted a settlement conference or has ordered that the case be scheduled for trial without a settlement conference. A judge who conducts a settlement conference on an issue will not be the judge who hears the issue at trial (see rule 17(24)).

3 In fast track cases, the first court date is set by the court when the application is filed.

The purposes of a trial management conference, which are set out in rule 17(6), include:

- exploring the chances of settling the case,
- arranging to receive an agreed statement of fact or evidence in written form, if appropriate,
- deciding how the trial will proceed,
- ensuring that the parties know what witnesses will testify and what other evidence will be presented at trial,
- estimating the time needed for a trial, and
- setting the trial date, if this has not already been done.

The various conferences may be combined on consent of the judge and the parties. Rule 17(8) allows the judge to make various orders at a conference, if notice has been served.

Under rule 17(13), the party requesting the conference is required to serve and file the appropriate **conference brief** no later than seven days before the date scheduled for the conference, and the other party is obliged to do so no later than four days before that date. The conference briefs are

- case conference brief (form 17A or form 17B),
- settlement conference brief (form 17C or form 17D), and
- trial management conference brief (form 17E).

conference brief
a case conference brief (form 17A or form 17B), a settlement conference brief (form 17C or form 17D), or a trial management conference brief (form 17E)

Under rule 17(21), case conference briefs and trial management conference briefs form part of the case's continuing record. Under rule 17(22), a settlement conference brief does not form part of the continuing record unless the court orders otherwise at the settlement conference. Under rule 17(14), each party must also file a confirmation (form 14C) no later than 2 p.m. two days before the date scheduled for the conference. No documents for use at the conference may be served or filed after this time.

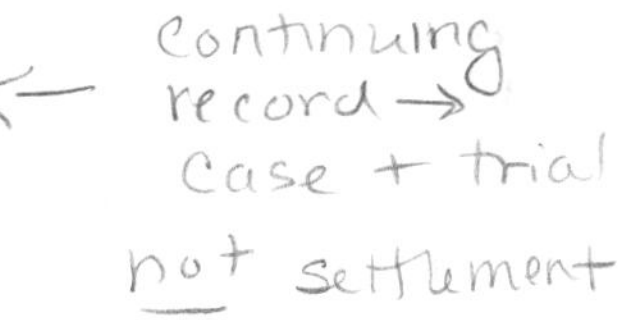

Pursuant to rule 17(15), the parties and their lawyers must attend each conference. If a conference is adjourned because a party is not prepared, has not served the required brief, has not made the required disclosure, or has otherwise not followed the rules under rule 17(18), that party will be ordered to pay costs.

Offers To Settle: Rule 18

A party may serve an offer to settle on any other party. Under rule 18(4), the offer is to be signed personally by the party making it and also by that party's lawyer, if there is one. Once an offer is made, under rule 18(5) it may be withdrawn by serving a notice of withdrawal at any time before the offer is accepted. An offer may also be time-limited. An offer that is not accepted within the time set out in the offer is considered to have been withdrawn under rule 18(6). An offer that has not expired or been withdrawn may be accepted by a party, even if the party has previously rejected the offer or made a counteroffer (see rule 18(10)). An offer expires and may not be accepted after the court begins to give a decision that disposes of a claim dealt with in the offer (rule 18(7)).

The terms of an offer are confidential; under rule 18(8), they may not be mentioned in any document filed in the continuing record and may not be mentioned to the judge hearing the claim dealt with in the offer.

Under rule 18(14), a party who makes an offer that is not accepted and who obtains an order that is as favourable as or more favourable than the offer is entitled to partial costs to the date the offer was made and full recovery of costs from the date it was made, as long as an offer relating to a motion was made at least one day before the motion date and an offer relating to a trial was made at least seven days before the trial.

Document Disclosure: Rule 19

If requested by the other party, a party must within 10 days give an affidavit listing every document that is relevant to any issue in the case and in the party's control, or available to the party on request.

Questioning a Witness and Disclosure: Rule 20

as of right
without needing the consent of the other party or an order of the court

Under rule 20(3), in a child protection case, a party is entitled, **as of right**, to obtain information from another party about any issue in the case. In all other cases, a party is entitled to obtain information only with the consent of the party or an order of the court (rule 20(4)).

Under rule 20(5), the court may make an order that a person be questioned under oath or disclose information by affidavit if

- it would be unfair to the party who wants the questioning or disclosure to carry on with the case without it,
- the information is not easily available by another method, or
- the questioning or disclosure will not cause unacceptable delay or undue expense.

The court may make an order that a person be questioned or disclose details about information in an affidavit or net family property statement.

Admission of Facts: Rule 22

A party may, at any time, serve a request to admit (form 22) on another party, asking the party to admit, for the purposes of the case only, that a fact is true or that a document is genuine. The other party served is deemed to admit that the fact is true or the document is genuine, unless he or she serves a response (form 22A) within 20 days.

Evidence and Trial: Rule 23

trial record
a document that assembles and organizes documents relevant to the trial to be used by the trial judge

Under rule 23(1), the applicant must serve and file a **trial record** at least 30 days before the start of the trial. A trial record must contain a table of contents and the following documents:

- the application, answer, and reply, if any;
- any agreed statement of facts;

- financial statements and net family property statements, if applicable, completed not more than 30 days before the record is served;
- any assessment report ordered by the court or obtained by consent of the parties;
- any temporary order relating to a matter still in dispute;
- any order relating to the trial;
- the relevant parts of any transcript on which the party intends to rely at trial; and
- any expert report on which the party intends to rely at trial.

Under rule 23(2), no later than seven days before the start of the trial, the respondent may serve, file, and add to the trial record any document not already in the record.

Under rule 23(3), a party who wants a witness to give evidence in court must serve a summons to witness (form 23) together with a witness fee of $50.

Pursuant to rule 23(23), a party who wants to call an expert witness at trial must serve and file the expert's report at least 14 days before the start of the trial.

Costs: Rule 24

There is a presumption that a successful party is entitled to costs at each step in the case. However, under rule 24(4), a successful party who has behaved unreasonably during a case may be deprived of all or part of the party's own costs or ordered to pay all or part of the unsuccessful party's costs. Under rule 24(10), the judge must decide who is entitled to costs and shall set the amount of the costs promptly after each step.

Orders: Rule 25

Under rule 25(2), the party in whose favour an order is made is required to prepare a draft of the order (form 25, 25A, 25B, 25C, or 25D). If that party does not have a lawyer or does not prepare the draft order within 10 days after the order is made, any other party may do so unless the court orders otherwise (rule 25(3)). If neither party has a lawyer, the clerk will prepare the order.

Pursuant to rule 25(4), the party who prepares an order is required to serve a draft, for approval of its form and content, on every other party who was in court or was represented when the order was made (including a child who has a lawyer). The order will then be signed by the judge who made it or by the clerk.[4] In accordance with rule 25(13), once the order is signed, the person who prepared the order is required to serve it on every other party, including a respondent who did not attend.

Case Management: Rule 39

All cases are placed on either a standard track or a fast track. Cases involving claims for divorce or property claims are standard track cases. All other cases are fast track cases.

4 Rules 25(5) to 25(7) set out the procedure for settling the contents of a disputed order.

In fast track cases, a case management judge is assigned to the case before the case comes to court. In standard track cases, a case management judge is assigned to the case when a party requests a case conference or brings an urgent motion.

Rule 39(9) sets out the functions of a case management judge. The case management judge assigned to a case

- generally supervises its progress,
- conducts the case conference and the settlement conference,
- on his or her own initiative, schedules a case conference or settlement conference at any time,
- hears motions in the case, when available to hear motions, and
- may, on motion, set aside an order of the clerk.

Rule 39 also sets timelines for the trial of family law cases. In both fast track and standard track cases, if a case has not been scheduled for trial within 200 days from the start of the case, the court sends a notice to the parties advising them that the case will be dismissed in 30 days if no steps are taken.

REFERENCES

Family Law Rules, O. Reg. 114/99.
Federal Child Support Guidelines, SOR/97-175.
Indian Act, RSC 1985, c. I-5.
Ontario *Child Support Guidelines*, O. Reg. 391/97.

REVIEW QUESTIONS

1. What is the primary objective of the *Family Law Rules*?
2. How is the court required under rule 2(5) to promote the primary objective?
3. What is the role of the case management judge?
4. What types of case management conferences are provided for under the *Family Law Rules*?
5. What types of cases are placed on the standard track? What types of cases are placed on the fast track?
6. What seven steps does a Family Court case go through?
7. In what municipality must a case be started?
8. When is special service of a document required? What are the methods of special service?
9. When is regular service of a document permitted? What are the methods of regular service?
10. How may service of a document be proved?
11. How are cases started under the *Family Law Rules*?
12. Who is responsible for maintaining the continuing record?
13. What must a respondent who wants to defend a case do?
14. When may a party make a motion? What documents are required on a motion?
15. What rule governs the procedure to vary an agreement or final order?
16. In what circumstances may a party apply for a summary judgment?
17. What cost consequences may flow from the making of an offer to settle?
18. Who is required to prepare a draft order?

CHAPTER 13

Divorce Procedure in the Family Court

A spouse who wishes to terminate his or her marriage must start a divorce proceeding. While seeking the divorce, the party may also ask the court to deal with issues of support and/or custody under the *Divorce Act* as well as property claims under the *Family Law Act*. If the parties have already settled these issues by way of a separation agreement, the applicant may ask the court to make an order that incorporates the terms of the parties' settlement, or the applicant may ask for a divorce only.

In chapter 5, we looked at the substantive law of divorce. In this chapter, we look at the procedure for obtaining a divorce in the Family Court of the Superior Court of Justice, including:

- an overview of divorce procedure,
- defended and undefended divorces, and
- the steps and documents required in a simple undefended divorce.

OVERVIEW OF DIVORCE PROCEDURE

Divorce procedure in the Family Court of the Superior Court of Ontario is governed by the *Family Law Rules* generally and by rule 36 specifically.

Starting a Divorce Case

Under rule 5, a divorce case should be started in the municipality where the applicant lives or, if the application claims custody or access, in the municipality where the children live.

Under rule 36(1), either spouse may start a divorce case by filing an application naming the other spouse as a respondent, or by filing a joint application with no respondent, using:

- form 8A if the applicant is asking for a divorce only or if the application is a joint application, and
- form 8 if the applicant is seeking other relief.

Pursuant to rule 7(3), the parties to a divorce case are the applicant and the respondent. If the divorce application claims that the respondent committed adultery with another person, under rule 36(3) that person does not need to be named.

In addition to the application, under rule 9 the applicant must prepare the continuing record of the case by completing a table of contents page. If the application includes a claim for support, property, or exclusive possession, the applicant must also serve and file a financial statement (form 13 or 13.1).[1]

Service of the Application

Under rule 8(5), the applicant must immediately serve the application on the respondent along with the table of contents of the continuing record (rule 9(1)). The applicant must use special service as defined in rule 6(3).

The applicant must then file the application and continuing record with the court, after adding the affidavit of service or other proof of service to the continuing record.

Defended Divorce

Under rule 10, a respondent who wants to defend a divorce case has 30 days if served in Canada or the United States (60 days if served elsewhere) to serve and file an answer (form 10). The answer may include a claim by the respondent against the applicant such as divorce, custody, support, or equalization of property.

The applicant then has the right, within 10 days, to serve and file a reply (form 10A) in response to any claim made by the respondent in the answer.

A divorce case is a standard track case[2] under rule 39. Accordingly, if the case is defended, the next step is a case conference, which will be scheduled by the court on the request of either party.

Undefended Divorce

Pursuant to rule 36(4), the court will not grant a divorce until the applicant files:

- a marriage certificate or marriage registration certificate, unless the application states that it is impractical to obtain a certificate and explains why; and
- a report on earlier divorce cases started by either spouse, issued under the *Central Registry of Divorce Proceedings Regulations* (Canada).[3]

Under rule 36(5), if the respondent does not defend the divorce, no court appearance is necessary, and the court decides the divorce case on the basis of affidavit evidence in form 36. Under rule 36(6), the applicant must also file:

- three copies of a draft divorce order (form 25A);
- a stamped envelope addressed to each party; and

1 See rule 13. No financial statement is required if the only additional claim is for child support in the table amount under the *Child Support Guidelines*.

2 As discussed in chapter 12, all cases in the Family Court are placed on either a fast track or a standard track.

3 The Central Registry of Divorce Proceedings (CRDP) prevents duplicate proceedings for divorce in different courts across Canada. Courts handling divorce proceedings submit a registration of divorce proceeding form to the CRDP, where it is recorded in a database. All divorce files are then checked to detect any duplication of proceedings. If there is no duplication, a clearance certificate is issued, which allows the case to proceed.

- if the divorce order contains a support order,
    - ❑ an extra copy of the order for filing with the director of the Family Responsibility Office, and
    - ❑ two copies of a draft support deduction order.

Pursuant to rule 36(7), the clerk reviews the document, prepares a certificate (form 36A), and presents the documents to a judge who may

- grant the divorce as set out in the draft order,
- have the clerk return the documents to the applicant to make any corrections that are necessary, or
- grant the divorce but make changes to the draft order, or refuse to grant the divorce, after giving the applicant a chance to file an additional affidavit or come to court to explain why the order should be made without change.

Divorce Certificate

Under the provisions of s. 12 of the *Divorce Act*, generally a divorce takes effect on the 31st day after the divorce judgment is granted.

Rule 36(8) requires the clerk to issue a divorce certificate (form 36B) on either party's request.

DEFENDED AND UNDEFENDED DIVORCES

As stated above, a divorce proceeding may be either defended (contested) or undefended (uncontested). Usually, an applicant knows before the divorce is started whether or not the case will be defended by his or her spouse.

A divorce will almost certainly be defended if the applicant claims not only a divorce but also custody and/or support and/or an equalization of net family property for the first time. A divorce is likely to be undefended if these issues were dealt with previously in a separation agreement or an action under the *Family Law Act*.

If the parties have settled these issues by way of a separation agreement, the applicant may ask the court to make an order that incorporates the terms of their settlement. Alternatively, the applicant may ask for a divorce only and continue to rely on the terms of the agreement.

STEPS IN A SIMPLE UNDEFENDED DIVORCE

Let's use the case of Brad and Jenny Pitts to illustrate the steps in a simple undefended divorce.

Our client, Jenny Pitts, is married to Brad Pitts. They separated on September 4, 2002, when Brad left Jenny for an old girlfriend named Gwyneth Paltry. On January 15, 2003, Jenny and Brad signed a separation agreement that settles all outstanding issues between them. They have agreed that Jenny will start a divorce case based on Brad's adultery, which Brad will not defend. Brad is willing to sign an affidavit admitting to the adultery.

Jenny was born on May 1, 1968 in Richmond Hill, Ontario, and Brad was born on April 6, 1965, also in Richmond Hill. They have lived in Richmond Hill all of their lives. They were married on June 6, 1993 in Thornhill, Ontario. It was Jenny's first marriage, but Brad was married briefly before to Lisa Cujo. That marriage ended in divorce on December 1, 1991.

Brad and Jenny have two children, Matthew Joseph, born on July 4, 1995, and Courtney Monica, born on February 14, 1997. They are living with Jenny at 4 Friendship Street, Richmond Hill, ON L3P 4N2. Brad moved in with Gwyneth at 15 Central Perk Place, Richmond Hill, ON L5K 1H3 when he left Jenny.

The separation agreement includes provisions as follows:

1. Jenny will have custody of the children, and Brad will have reasonable access.
2. Brad will pay child support, in accordance with the *Child Support Guidelines*, of $823 per month based on his annual income of $60,000.

Jenny does not want to incorporate any of the provisions in the divorce order. Assume that Jenny's application for divorce is being prepared on November 10, 2003.

Step 1: Get Supporting Documents

Before starting a divorce application for Jenny, you should have copies of the following documents:

- *Marriage certificate.* You must file the marriage certificate under rule 36(4), and it is helpful to have the certificate before you prepare the application to make sure that you name the parties properly.
- *Separation agreement.* It is helpful to have a copy of the agreement before you prepare the application to make sure that you have the correct details about the agreement (and you would have to attach a copy of the separation agreement to Jenny's affidavit if she wanted to incorporate any its provisions into the order).

As it turns out, Jenny has the original marriage certificate issued by the minister who performed the ceremony (see figure 13.1 on page 185). If Jenny did not have the marriage certificate, you would need to get a certificate of the registration of the marriage.

You may obtain a certified copy of a marriage certificate from the government of the jurisdiction in which the parties were married. If the parties were married in Ontario, as Jenny and Brad were, you order the certificate from the Office of the Registrar General in Thunder Bay. An application for the certificate is available at the court, or can be obtained online at the government of Ontario's Web site: www.gov.on.ca.

If Jenny and Brad had been married outside Ontario, you would also need a copy of the divorce certificate for Brad's divorce from Lisa Cujo, to file with the court in order to prove that his marriage to Jenny is valid.[4] You get a certificate of divorce from the court office of the court that granted the divorce.

---

4 Because Jenny and Brad were married in Ontario, you do not need Brad's certificate of divorce ending his marriage with Lisa. The Ontario courts are satisfied that an Ontario marriage licence would not have been issued without proof that Brad's earlier marriage was properly terminated.

Step 2: Complete the Forms

You must prepare three forms:

- an application,
- the continuing record, and
- the Central Divorce Registry form.

APPLICATION

The application used for a simple divorce is form 8A — Application (Divorce). Figure 13.2 on page 186 sets out Jenny's completed application.

PAGE 1

- Insert the name of the court — Ontario Superior Court of Justice Family Court — and the address of the appropriate court office. Under rule 5, Jenny's divorce should be commenced in Newmarket, the location of the court in York Region (where Richmond Hill is located). If you don't know the address of the court office, you can find it on the Web site for the Ministry of the Attorney General: www.attorneygeneral.jus.gov.on.ca. (Follow the links to Family Justice — Family Court Addresses.) The address of the Family Court in Newmarket is 50 Eagle Street West, Newmarket, ON L3Y 6B1.
- Insert the names and addresses of the applicant and the respondent. Use the names of the parties as they appear on the marriage certificate. Note that Jenny's full name is Jennifer Elizabeth Pitts,[5] and Brad's full name is Bradley David Pitts.
- Insert the names and addresses of the parties' lawyers, if any. In this case, Jenny is represented by your law firm, and Brad does not have a lawyer.

PAGE 2

- Insert the required information under the heading "Family History."
- Insert the required information under the heading "Previous Cases or Agreements." In this case, the parties have not been in a court case before, but they have made a written agreement. You must insert the date of the agreement: January 15, 2003. No terms of the agreement are in dispute.

PAGE 3

- *Claims*. In a simple divorce that is not a joint application, the applicant may claim a divorce only. In this case, complete the second frame only.
- *Supporting Facts*. Under the heading "Important Facts Supporting the Claim for Divorce," the applicant gives details of the grounds for divorce. Check the box next to the appropriate ground, and then provide the requested details.

In this case, Jenny can proceed on either the ground of separation or the ground of adultery, and has decided to proceed on the ground of adultery. As a result, you have to check the adultery box and provide details of the adultery. Under rule 36,

5 After the marriage, Jenny assumed Brad's surname.

you do not need to name the other person involved. If you do name another person, he or she will have to be served with the application.

If Jenny were to proceed on the ground of separation, you would check the separation box and fill in the appropriate dates. For the purposes of illustration, Jenny's application is completed for the grounds of both separation and adultery. However, Jenny would complete only the adultery section.

PAGE 4

- *Joint applications.* In a joint application for divorce, the top frame must be completed to set out details of the other orders that are being sought, and facts that support those claims. Since this is not a joint application, do not complete this frame.
- *Signatures.* Jenny must sign the application and date it. She should use her usual signature.
- *Lawyer's certificate.* Complete this part of the application by inserting the name of the applicant's lawyer and the name of the client. The lawyer must then sign the certificate.

CONTINUING RECORD

The continuing record is the court's record of all of the documents in the case. The general rule is that any document that is served and filed must be inserted in the continuing record. The applicant's law firm is responsible for the initial preparation of  the continuing record. The continuing record has a red front cover and three sections:

- *Table of contents.* The table of contents lists the documents, sets out the tab and page number where each document can be found, and names the party who filed the document. It is updated every time a document is added to the proceedings.
- *Endorsements.* The continuing record contains 10 or more blank pages for the judge to write endorsements, copies of all court orders, and any reasons for judgments.
- *Documents.* The continuing record contains all documents after they have been served and all affidavits of service.

The table of contents of Jenny's continuing record appears as figure 13.3 on page 190.

CENTRAL DIVORCE REGISTRY FORM

You must complete a Central Divorce Registry form and file it with the court so that the court can get a report from the Central Registry of Divorce Proceedings. This is a federal government form, which can be obtained from the government of Canada or the court office.

Step 3: File the Application

You or someone from your law firm must file Jenny's application with the court. You will need:

- the original and two copies of the application (the original for the court, one copy for the respondent, and one copy for your file);
- the original and two copies of the continuing record table of contents;
- the marriage certificate;
- the Central Divorce Registry form; and
- the court filing fee.

At the court, the court staff assigns a court file number to the case and puts a seal on the original application. The person filing the application must:

- write the court file number in the upper right-hand corner of the original and all copies of all of the forms, and
- fill in the date of filing of the application in the table of contents.

Step 4: Serve the Respondent

Your law firm must arrange to serve the respondent with a copy of the application and the table of contents of the continuing record. These documents must be served by special service as defined in rule 6(3). The person who serves the documents must then complete and swear an affidavit of service (form 6B).

If your firm's process server, Matt LeBlank, served the documents on Brad by personal service on November 28, 2003, the affidavit of service would be as set out in figure 13.4 on page 191.

Step 5: File the Application and Proof of Service

Once the application has been served, your law firm must arrange for someone to file the documents with the court. The person who files the documents also assembles the continuing record, files the original documents with the affidavit of service in the documents section of the continuing record, and inserts the table of contents page at the front of the continuing record.

Step 6: Complete the Affidavit and Divorce Order

Brad has 30 days to defend the divorce case by serving and filing an answer. Even though he and Jenny have agreed that the divorce will proceed on an undefended basis, the 30-day period must pass before the court will grant the divorce without a court appearance.

The court requires:

- an affidavit in form 36 sworn by Jenny,
- proof of the adultery (in this case, an affidavit in form 14A sworn by Brad), and
- a draft divorce order (form 25A).

Have a look at Jenny's affidavit, which appears as figure 13.5 on page 193. In particular, note the following:

- *Paragraph 5*. Jenny states that the legal basis for the divorce is that Brad "has committed adultery," but does not give any details of the adultery. An affidavit is a document that contains evidence sworn to under oath and should include only matters about which Jenny has personal knowledge. Jenny's only information about the adultery comes from what Brad has told her. All she can swear to is that Brad has admitted to her that the adultery has taken place. Under the law of evidence, a divorce cannot be granted solely on the basis of such an admission. What is required is an admission by Brad sworn to under oath.

- *Paragraph 5a.* When a divorce is sought on the ground of adultery, the court has a duty under s. 11 of the *Divorce Act* to satisfy itself that there has been no condonation or connivance on the part of the applicant. The information in this paragraph denying condonation or connivance constitutes "other information necessary for the court to grant the divorce" within the meaning of rule 36(5). (See chapter 5 for a more complete discussion of condonation and connivance.)

The court requires evidence of Brad's adultery. As stated above, Jenny cannot give that evidence because she does not have personal knowledge of the adultery. As a result, Jenny needs to file an affidavit from Brad in which he admits to the adultery under oath.

Brad's affidavit appears as figure 13.6 on page 197. Note that paragraph 2 contains Brad's sworn evidence that he has committed adultery. The paragraph starts with Brad's acknowledgment of his willingness to give this evidence even though he is not required by law to do so. This statement is included because of the provisions of s. 10 of the Ontario *Evidence Act*.[6]

Figure 13.7 on page 199 sets out a draft divorce order. Note that the judge's name and the date of the order are left blank on page 1 because you don't know when or by whom the application will be considered. The court will fill in this information. The date of signature on page 2 is left blank for the same reason.

Step 7: File the Documents with the Court

Under rules 36(5) and (6), you must file the following documents with the court:

- the original of Jenny's affidavit;
- the original of Brad's affidavit;
- three copies of the draft divorce order; and
- two stamped envelopes, one addressed to Jenny in care of your law firm, and the other addressed to Brad.

Be sure to keep copies of all documents for your file.

6 Section 10 reads as follows: "The parties to a proceeding instituted in consequence of adultery and the husbands and wives of such parties are competent to give evidence in such proceedings, but no witness in any such proceeding, whether a party to the suit or not, is liable to be asked or bound to answer any question tending to show that he or she is guilty of adultery, unless such witness has already given evidence in the same proceeding in disproof of his or her alleged adultery."

Step 8: Obtain the Divorce Order

The court clerk reviews the documents and presents them to a judge for review. If the judge is satisfied with the material, he or she will grant the divorce order. If the judge needs more information, the court will contact your law firm.

Step 9: Obtain a Certificate of Divorce

The divorce order will not take effect until the 31st day after the order is made. Either party can ask the court to issue a certificate of divorce as proof that the divorce has taken effect. The court clerk will check the file to make sure that the required time has passed and that neither party has appealed the order. There is a fee for the certificate.

REFERENCES

Divorce Act, RSC 1985, c. 3 (2d Supp.).
Evidence Act, RSO 1990, c. E.23.
Family Law Rules, O. Reg. 114/99.
Federal Child Support Guidelines, SOR/97-175.
Ontario *Child Support Guidelines*, O. Reg. 391/97.
www.attorneygeneral.jus.gov.on.ca (Ministry of Attorney General Web site).
www.gov.on.ca (Ontario government Web site).

REVIEW QUESTIONS

1. Generally speaking, where should a divorce case be started?
2. How may a spouse start a divorce case?
3. Who are the parties to a divorce case?
4. What must the applicant serve on the respondent? When? How?
5. If a respondent wants to defend a divorce case, what must he or she do? When?
6. What will the court do if the respondent does not defend the divorce?
7. Generally speaking, when does a divorce take effect?
8. When is a divorce likely to be defended? When is it likely to be undefended?
9. What forms must the applicant complete to start a divorce case?
10. What documents will the court require in order to grant a divorce in an undefended divorce case?

DRAFTING QUESTION

Jennifer Loped and Ben Affect were married for only a short time when they realized that they were totally incompatible. They have been separated since August 16, 2003, and Ben now wants to get a divorce. Jennifer, who kept her own surname following the marriage, was born in Newmarket on January 1, 1970, and Ben was born, also in Newmarket, on September 15, 1972. They have lived in Newmarket all of their lives and were married there on February 14, 2002. It was the first marriage for both of them. They have no children. Jennifer is now living at 123 Combs Drive, Newmarket, ON L3P 1J4. Ben is living at 215 Paltrow Court, Newmarket, ON L4X 2K6. Draft a divorce application to be signed by Ben.

FIGURE 13.1 JENNY'S AND BRAD'S MARRIAGE CERTIFICATE

Certificate of Marriage

This is to certify that, on the *sixth* day of *June* 19 *93*

at *Thornhill United Church* in the Province of Ontario

the marriage of *Jennifer Elizabeth Annistone* and

Bradley David Pitts was solemnized under marriage

Licence No. **C No. 322155**

issued on the *6th* day of *June* 19 *93*

Rev. Chandler Byng
Signature of person solemnizing marriage

Witnesses to marriage:

Ross Geller

Monica Geller

135 John Street, Thornhill, Ontario
Address

United Church
Clergy denomination

12345
Clergy registration certificate No.

FIGURE 13.2 JENNY'S APPLICATION

SEAL

ONTARIO SUPERIOR COURT OF JUSTICE FAMILY COURT

Court File Number

(Name of court)

at 50 Eagle Street West, Newmarket, ON L3Y 6B1

Court office address

Form 8A: Application (divorce) ☐ **Joint** ☒ **Simple**

Applicant

Full legal name & address for service — street & number, municipality, postal code, telephone & fax numbers and e-mail address (if any).	*Lawyer's name & address — street & number, municipality, postal code, telephone & fax numbers and e-mail address (if any).*
Jennifer Elizabeth Pitts 4 Friendship Street Richmond Hill, ON L3P 4N2	JoAnn Kurtz Barrister & Solicitor 123 College Street Toronto, ON M2K 1Y3 Tel: 416-555-1234 Fax: 416-555-1235

Respondent(s)

Full legal name & address for service — street & number, municipality, postal code, telephone & fax numbers and e-mail address (if any).	*Lawyer's name & address — street & number, municipality, postal code, telephone & fax numbers and e-mail address (if any).*
Bradley David Pitts 15 Central Perk Place Richmond Hill, ON L5K 1H3	

☐ **THIS CASE IS A JOINT APPLICATION FOR DIVORCE. THE DETAILS ARE SET OUT ON THE ATTACHED PAGES.** The application and affidavits in support of the application will be presented to a judge when the materials have been checked for completeness.

☒ **IN THIS CASE, THE APPLICANT IS CLAIMING DIVORCE ONLY.**

TO THE RESPONDENT(S): A COURT CASE FOR DIVORCE HAS BEEN STARTED AGAINST YOU IN THIS COURT. THE DETAILS ARE SET OUT ON THE ATTACHED PAGES.

THIS CASE IS ON THE STANDARD TRACK OF THE CASE MANAGEMENT SYSTEM. No court date has been set for this case but, if you have been served with a notice of motion, it has a court date and you or your lawyer should come to court for the motion. A case management judge will not be assigned until one of the parties asks the clerk of the court to schedule a case conference or until a notice of motion under subrule 14(5) is served before a case conference has been held. If, after 200 days, the case has not been scheduled for trial, the clerk of the court will send out a warning that the case will be dismissed in 30 days unless the parties file proof that the case has been settled or one of the parties asks for a case conference or a settlement conference.

IF YOU WANT TO OPPOSE ANY CLAIM IN THIS CASE, you or your lawyer must prepare an answer (Form 10 — a blank copy should be attached), serve a copy on the applicant and file a copy in the court office with an affidavit of service (Form 6B).

YOU HAVE ONLY 30 DAYS AFTER THIS APPLICATION IS SERVED ON YOU (60 DAYS IF THIS APPLICATION IS SERVED ON YOU OUTSIDE CANADA OR THE UNITED STATES) TO SERVE AND FILE AN ANSWER. IF YOU DO NOT, THE CASE WILL GO AHEAD WITHOUT YOU AND THE COURT MAY MAKE AN ORDER AND ENFORCE IT AGAINST YOU.

If you want to make a claim of your own, you or your lawyer must fill out the claim portion in the answer, serve a copy on the applicant and file a copy in the court office with an affidavit of service.

You should get legal advice about this case right away. If you cannot afford a lawyer, you may be able to get help from your local Legal Aid office. *(See your telephone directory under LEGAL AID).*

_______________ _______________

Date of issue *Clerk of the court*

FIGURE 13.2 CONTINUED

Form 8A: Application (divorce) (page 2) Court file number ________----________

FAMILY HISTORY

HUSBAND: Age: 38 Birthdate: April 6, 1965

Resident in *(municipality & province)* Richmond Hill, Ontario

since *(date)* April 6, 1965

Surname at birth: Pitts Surname just before marriage: Pitts

Divorced before? ☐ No. ☒ Yes. *(Place and date of previous divorce)* Toronto, Ontario — December 1, 1991

WIFE: Age: 35 Birthdate: May 1, 1968

Resident in *(municipality & province)* Richmond Hill, Ontario

since *(date)* May 1, 1968

Surname at birth: Annistone Surname just before marriage: Annistone

Divorced before? ☒ No. ☐ Yes. *(Place and date of previous divorce)* ________----________

RELATIONSHIP DATES:

☒ Married on *(date)* June 6, 1993 ☐ Started living together on *(date)*

☒ Separated on *(date)* September 4, 2002 ☐ Never lived together.

THE CHILD(REN):

List all children involved in this case, even if no claim is made for these children.

Full Legal Name	Age	Birthdate	Resident in *(municipality & province)*	Now Living with *(name of person and relationship to child)*
Matthew Joseph Pitts	8	July 4, 1995	Richmond Hill, ON	Jennifer Pitts, mother
Courtney Monica Pitts	6	February 14, 1997	Richmond Hill, ON	Jennifer Pitts, mother

PREVIOUS CASES OR AGREEMENTS

Have the parties or the children been in a court case before?

☒ No. ☐ Yes. *(Attach a summary of court cases — Form 8E.)*

Have the parties made a written agreement dealing with any matter involved in this case?

☐ No. ☒ Yes. *(Give date of agreement. Indicate which of its terms are in dispute. Attach an additional page if you need more space.)*

January 15, 2003. No terms of the agreement are in dispute.

FIGURE 13.2 CONTINUED

Form 8A: Application (divorce) (page 3) Court file number ______________

CLAIMS

USE THIS FRAME ONLY IF THIS CASE IS A JOINT APPLICATION FOR DIVORCE.

WE JOINTLY ASK THE COURT FOR THE FOLLOWING:

Claims under the *Divorce Act*

00 ☒ a divorce
01 ☐ spousal support
02 ☐ support for child(ren)
03 ☐ custody of child(ren)
04 ☐ access to child(ren)

Claims under the *Family Law Act* or *Children's Law Reform Act*

10 ☐ spousal support
11 ☐ support for child(ren)
12 ☐ custody of child(ren)
13 ☐ access to child(ren)
14 ☐ restraining/non-harassment order
15 ☐ indexing spousal support
16 ☐ declaration of parentage
17 ☐ guardianship over child's property

Claims relating to property

20 ☐ equalization of net family properties
21 ☐ exclusive possession of matrimonial home
22 ☐ exclusive possession of contents of matrimonial home
23 ☐ freezing assets
24 ☐ sale of family property

Other claims

30 ☐ costs
31 ☐ annulment of marriage
32 ☐ prejudgment interest
50 ☐ *(Other; specify.)*

USE THIS FRAME ONLY IF THE APPLICANT'S ONLY CLAIM IN THIS CASE IS FOR DIVORCE

I ASK THE COURT FOR:

00 ☒ a divorce

(Check if applicable.)
30 ☐ costs

IMPORTANT FACTS SUPPORTING THE CLAIM FOR DIVORCE

☒ **Separation:** The spouses have lived separate and apart since *(date)* September 4, 2002 and
☒ have not lived together again since that date in an unsuccessful attempt to reconcile.
☐ have lived together again during the following period(s) in an unsuccessful attempt to reconcile: *(Give dates.)*

☒ **Adultery:** *(Name of spouse)* Bradley David Pitts has committed adultery. *(Give details. It is not necessary to name any other person involved but, if you do name the other person, then you must serve this application on the other person.)*

The respondent has resided with another person as husband and wife at 15 Central Perk Place in Richmond Hill, Ontario from in or about September 2002 to the date of this application, and during that time has engaged in acts of sexual intercourse with her on numerous occasions .

☐ **Cruelty:** *(Name of spouse)* ______________ has treated *(name of spouse)* ______________ with physical or mental cruelty of such a kind as to make continued cohabitation intolerable. *(Give details.)*

FIGURE 13.2 CONCLUDED

Form 8A: Application (divorce) (page 4) Court file number ______________

USE THIS FRAME ONLY IF THIS CASE IS A JOINT APPLICATION FOR DIVORCE.

The details of the other order(s) that we jointly ask the court to make are as follows: *(Include any amounts of support and the names of the children for whom support, custody or access is to be ordered.)*

IMPORTANT FACTS SUPPORTING OUR CLAIM(S)

(Set out below the facts that form the legal basis for your claim(s). Attach an additional page if you need more space.)

Put a line through any blank space left on this page

In a joint application for divorce, there will be two signatures — one for each spouse. But in an application where the applicant's only claim is for divorce, you and your lawyer are the only ones who will sign and you should strike out the inappropriate zone for your spouse's signature and corresponding date.

_________________________	_________________________
Signature of applicant husband	*Date of signature*
_________________________	_________________________
Signature of applicant wife	*Date of signature*

LAWYER'S CERTIFICATE

My name is: JoAnn Kurtz
and I am the lawyer for *(name)* Jennifer Elizabeth Pitts in this divorce case.
I certify that I have complied with the requirements of section 9 of the *Divorce Act.*

_________________________	_________________________
Lawyer's signature	*Date of signature*

FIGURE 13.3 JENNY'S CONTINUING RECORD

ONTARIO

Court File Number:

Superior Court of Justice Family Court
50 Eagle Street West
Newmarket, ON L3Y 6B1

Applicant: Jennifer Elizabeth Pitts

Respondent: Bradley David Pitts

CUMULATIVE TABLE OF CONTENTS
(CONTINUING RECORD)
VOLUME 1

Document (*For an affidavit or transcript of evidence, indicate the name of the person who gave the affidavit or the evidence.*)	**Filed by** (*A = applicant or R = respondent*)	**Date of Document** (d, m, y)	**Date of Filing** (d, m, y)	**Tab/ Page**
Application	A	10/11/2003		1/ 1-4

FIGURE 13.4 MATT LEBLANK'S AFFIDAVIT OF SERVICE

Court File Number

ONTARIO SUPERIOR COURT OF JUSTICE FAMILY COURT
(Name of court)

Form 6B: Affidavit of service dated

at 50 Eagle Street West, Newmarket, ON L3Y 6B1
Court office address

Applicant(s)

Full legal name & address for service — street & number, municipality, postal code, telephone & fax and e-mail address (if any).	*Lawyer's name & address — street & number, municipality, postal code, telephone & fax numbers and e-mail address (if any).*
Jennifer Elizabeth Pitts 4 Friendship Street Richmond Hill, ON L3P 4N2	JoAnn Kurtz Barrister & Solicitor 123 College Street Toronto, ON M2K 1Y3 Tel: 416-555-1234 Fax: 416-555-1235

Respondent(s)

Full legal name & address for service — street & number, municipality, postal code, telephone & fax numbers and e-mail address (if any).	*Lawyer's name & address — street & number, municipality, postal code, telephone & fax numbers and e-mail address (if any).*
Bradley David Pitts 15 Central Perk Place Richmond Hill, ON L5K 1H3	

My name is *(full legal name)* Matt LeBlank

I live in *(municipality & province)* Toronto, Ontario

and I swear/affirm that the following is true:

1. On *(date)* November 28, 2003, I served *(name of person to be served)* Bradley David Pitts with the following document(s) in this case:

List the documents served.

Name of document	*Author (if applicable)*	*Date when document signed, issued, sworn, etc.*
Application	Jennifer Elizabeth Pitts	November 13, 2003
Continuing Record Table of Contents		

NOTE: You can leave out any part of this form that is not applicable.

2. I served the documents mentioned in paragraph 1 by,

Check one box only and go to indicated paragraph.

- ☒ special service. *(Go to paragraph 3 below if you used special service.)*
- ☐ mail. *(Go to paragraph 4 if you used mailed service.)*
- ☐ courier. *(Go to paragraph 5 if you used courier.)*
- ☐ deposit at a document exchange. *(Go to paragraph 6 if you used a document exchange.)*
- ☐ fax. *(Go to paragraph 7 if you used fax.)*
- ☐ substituted service or advertisement. *(Go to paragraph 8 if you used substituted service or advertisement.)*

3. I carried out special service of the document(s) on the person named in paragraph 1 at *(place or address)*

by:
- ☒ leaving a copy with the person.
- ☐ who is the *(office or position)* of the corporation named in paragraph 1.

FIGURE 13.4 CONCLUDED

Service dated ____________________ **(page 2)** Court file number ____________

☐ mailing a copy to the person together with a prepaid return postcard in Form 6 in an envelope bearing the sender's return address. This postcard, in which receipt of the document(s) is acknowledged, was returned and is attached to this affidavit.

☐ leaving a copy in a sealed envelope addressed to the person at the person's place of residence with *(name)* who provided me with identification to show that he/she was an adult person residing at the same address and by mailing another copy of the same document(s) on the same or following day to the person named in paragraph 1 at that place of residence.

☐ *(Other; specify. See rule 6 for details.)*

9. To serve the document(s), I had to travel 5 kilometres. My fee for service of the document(s) is $ $75.00 , including travel.

Sworn/Affirmed before me at ____________________ *Municipality* in ____________________ *province, state or country* on ____________ *date* ____________________ *Commssioner for taking affidavits (Type or print name below if signature is illegible.)*	*Signature* *(This form is to be signed in front of a lawyer, justice of the peace, notary public or commissioner for taking affidavits.)*

FIGURE 13.5 JENNY'S AFFIDAVIT

ONTARIO SUPERIOR COURT OF JUSTICE FAMILY COURT
(Name of court)

Form 36: Affidavit for Divorce

at 50 Eagle Street West, Newmarket, ON L3Y 6B1
Court office address

Applicant

Full legal name & address for service — street & number, municipality, postal code, telephone & fax numbers and e-mail address (if any).	*Lawyer's name & address — street & number, municipality, postal code, telephone & fax numbers and e-mail address (if any).*
Jennifer Elizabeth Pitts 4 Friendship Street Richmond Hill, ON L3P 4N2	JoAnn Kurtz Barrister & Solicitor 123 College Street Toronto, ON M2K 1Y3 Tel: 416-555-1234 Fax: 416-555-1235

Respondent(s)

Full legal name & address for service — street & number, municipality, postal code, telephone & fax numbers and e-mail address (if any).	*Lawyer's name & address — street & number, municipality, postal code, telephone & fax numbers and e-mail address (if any).*
Bradley David Pitts 15 Central Perk Place Richmond Hill, ON L5K 1H3	

My name is *(full legal name)* Jennifer Elizabeth Pitts

I live in *(municipality & province)* Richmond Hill, Ontario

and I swear/affirm that the following is true:

1. I am the applicant in this divorce case.
2. There is no chance of a reconciliation between the respondent and me.
3. All the information in the application in this case is correct, except: *(State any corrections or changes to the information in the application. Write "NONE" if there are no corrections or changes.)*

   NONE

4. ☒ The certificate or registration of my marriage to the respondent has been signed and sealed by the Registrar General of Ontario and
   - ☒ has been filed with the application.
   - ☐ is attached to this affidavit.

   ☐ The certificate of my marriage to the respondent was issued outside Ontario. It is called *(title of certificate)* ______________________.
   It was issued at *(place of issue)* ______________________
   on *(date)* ______________________ by *(name and title of person who issued certificate)* ______________________ and the information in it about my marriage is correct.

   ☐ I have not been able to get a certificate or registration of my marriage. I was married to the respondent on *(date)* ______________________ at *(place of marriage)* ______________________
   The marriage was performed by *(name and title)* ______________________
   who had the authority to perform marriages in that place.

5. The legal basis for the divorce is:
   ☐ that the respondent and I have been separated for at least one year. We separated on *(date)*
   ☒ *(Other. Specify.)*

   that the respondent has committed adultery. I have no personal knowledge of the adultery other than what the respondent has told me.

   5a. I have not condoned or connived at the respondent's adultery.

FIGURE 13.5 CONTINUED

Form 36: Affidavit for Divorce (page 2) Court file number ______________

6. I do not know about and I am not involved in any arrangement to make up or to hide evidence or to deceive the court in this divorce case.

Strike out the following paragraphs if they do not apply.

7. I do not want to make a claim for a division of property in this divorce case, even though I know that it may be legally impossible to make such a claim after the divorce.

8. I want the divorce order to include the following paragraph numbers of the attached consent, settlement, separation agreement or previous court order: *(List the numbers of the paragraphs that you want included in the divorce order.)*

9. There are *(number)* ___2___ children of the marriage. They are:

Full legal name of child	Birthdate (d,m,y)
Matthew Joseph Pitts	4 July 1995
Courtney Monica Pitts	14 February 1997

10. The custody and access arrangements for the child(ren) are as follows: *(Give summary.)*

I have custody of the children, and the respondent has reasonable access.

11. These are the arrangements that have been made for the support of the child(ren) of the marriage:

(a) The income of the party paying child support is $ ___60,000___ per year.

(b) The number of children for whom support is supposed to be paid is *(number)* ___2___

(c) The amount of support that should be paid according to the applicable table in the child support guidelines is $ ___823___ per month.

(d) The amount of child support actually being paid is $ ___823___ per month.
(NOTE:— *Where the dollar amounts in clauses (c) and (d) are different, you must fill out the frame on the next page. If the amounts in clauses (c) and (d) are the same, skip the frame and go directly to paragraph 12.*)

FIGURE 13.5 CONTINUED

Form 36: Affidavit for Divorce (page 3) Court file number ____________

(Paragraph 11 continued.)

Fill out the information in this frame only if the amounts in paragraphs 11(c) and 11(d) are different. If they are the same, go to paragraph 12.

(a) Child support is already covered by:

(i) ☐ a court order dated *(date)* ____________ that was made before the child support guidelines came into effect (before 1 May 1997). I attach a copy of the order

(ii) ☐ a domestic contract order dated *(date)* ____________ that was made before the child support guidelines came into effect (before 1 May 1997). I attach a copy of the contract

(iii) ☐ a court order or written agreement dated *(date)* ____________ made after the guidelines came into effect that has some direct or indirect benefits for the child(ren). I attach a copy.

(iv) ☐ a written consent between the parties dated *(date)* ____________ agreeing to the payment of an amount different from that set out in the guidelines.

(b) The child support clauses of this order or agreement require payment of $ ______per ____________in child support.

(c) These child support clauses ☐ are not indexed for any automatic cost-of-living increases.
☐ are indexed according to *(Give indexing formula)*

(d) These child support clauses ☐ have not been changed since the day the order or agreement was made.
☐ have been changed on *(Give dates and details of changes)*

(e) *(If you ticked off box (i) above, you can go to paragraph 12. If you ticked off boxes (ii), (iii) or (iv) above, then fill out the information after box of the corresponding number below. For example, if you ticked off box (iii) above, you would fill out the information alongside box (iii) below.)*

(ii) ☐ The amount being paid under this agreement is a fair and reasonable arrangement for the support of the child(ren) because: *(Give reasons.)*

(iii) ☐ The order or agreement directly or indirectly benefits the child(ren) because: *(Give details of benefits.)*

(iv) ☐ The amount to which the parties have consented is reasonable for the support of the child(ren) because: *(Give reasons.)*

FIGURE 13.5 CONCLUDED

Form 36: Affidavit for Divorce (page 4) Court file number ___________________

12. I am claiming costs in this case. The details of this claim are as follows: *(Give details.)*

N/A

13. The respondent's address last known to me is: *(Give address.)*

15 Central Perk Place
Richmond Hill, ON L5K 1H3

Put a line through any blank space left on this page.

Sworn/Affirmed before me at ______________________________
Municipality

in ______________________________
province, state or country

on ____________________ ______________________________
date *Commissioner for taking affidavits*
(Type or print name below if signature is illegible.)

____
Signature
(This form is to be signed in front of a lawyer, justice of the peace, notary public or commissioner for taking affidavits.)

FIGURE 13.6 BRAD'S AFFIDAVIT

ONTARIO SUPERIOR COURT OF JUSTICE FAMILY COURT
(Name of court)

Form 14A: Affidavit (General) dated ________

at 50 Eagle Street West, Newmarket, ON L3Y 6B1
Court office address

Applicant(s)

Full legal name & address for service — street & number, municipality, postal code, telephone & fax and e-mail address (if any).	*Lawyer's name & address — street & number, municipality, postal code, telephone & fax numbers and e-mail address (if any).*
Jennifer Elizabeth Pitts 4 Friendship Street Richmond Hill, ON L3P 4N2	JoAnn Kurtz Barrister & Solicitor 123 College Street Toronto, ON M2K 1Y3 Tel: 416-555-1234 Fax: 416-555-1235

Respondent(s)

Full legal name & address for service — street & number, municipality, postal code, telephone & fax numbers and e-mail address (if any).	*Lawyer's name & address — street & number, municipality, postal code, telephone & fax numbers and e-mail address (if any).*
Bradley David Pitts 15 Central Perk Place Richmond Hill, Ontario L5K 1H3	

My name is *(full legal name)* Bradley David Pitts

I live in *(municipality & province)* Richmond Hill, Ontario

and I swear/affirm that the following is true:

Set out the statements of fact in consecutively numbered paragraphs. Where possible, each numbered paragraph should consist of one complete sentence and be limited to a particular statement of fact. If you learned a fact from someone else, you must give that person's name and state that you believe that fact to be true.

1. I am the husband of the applicant.

2. The legal basis for the divorce is adultery. I am aware that I am not obliged to give evidence that I have committed adultery, but I am willing to give that evidence. I have been residing as husband and wife with Gwyneth Paltry at 15 Central Perk Place in Richmond Hill, Ontario since September 4, 2002, and I have engaged in sexual intercourse with her on numerous occasions.

3. The applicant has not condoned or connived at my adultery.

4. I do not know about and I am not involved in any arrangement to make up or to hide evidence or to deceive the court in this divorce case.

FIGURE 13.6 CONCLUDED

Form 14A: Affidavit (General) dated *(date)* ______________ (page 2) Court file number ______________

Put a line through any blank space left on this page.

Sworn/Affirmed before me at ______________ *Municipality* in ______________ *province, state or country* on ______________ ______________ *date* *Commssioner for taking affidavits* *(Type or print name below if signature is illegible.)*	______________ *Signature* *(This form is to be signed in front of a lawyer, justice of the peace, notary public or commissioner for taking affidavits.)*

FIGURE 13.7 DRAFT DIVORCE ORDER

SEAL

ONTARIO SUPERIOR COURT OF JUSTICE FAMILY COURT
(Name of court)

Court File Number

Form 25A: Divorce Order

at 50 Eagle Street West, Newmarket, ON L3Y 6B1
Court office address

Judge (print or type name)

Date of order

Applicant(s)

Full legal name & address for service — street & number, municipality, postal code, telephone & fax and e-mail address (if any).	*Lawyer's name & address — street & number, municipality, postal code, telephone & fax numbers and e-mail address (if any).*
Jennifer Elizabeth Pitts 4 Friendship Street Richmond Hill, ON L3P 4N2	JoAnn Kurtz Barrister & Solicitor 123 College Street Toronto, ON M2K 1Y3 Tel: 416-555-1234 Fax: 416-555-1235

Respondent(s)

Full legal name & address for service — street & number, municipality, postal code, telephone & fax numbers and e-mail address (if any).	*Lawyer's name & address — street & number, municipality, postal code, telephone & fax numbers and e-mail address (if any).*
Bradley David Pitts 15 Central Perk Place Richmond Hill, ON L5K 1H3	

The court considered an application of *(name)*
Jennifer Elizabeth Pitts

on *(date)*
The following persons were in court *(Give names of parties and lawyers in court. This paragraph may be struck out if the divorce is uncontested.)*

The court received evidence and considered submissions on behalf of *(name or names)*
Jennifer Elizabeth Pitts

THIS COURT ORDERS THAT:

1. *(full legal names of spouses)* Jennifer Elizabeth Pitts and Bradley David Pitts

If the court decides that the divorce should take effect earlier, replace "31" with the smaller number.

who were married at *(place)* Thornhill, Ontario

on *(date)* June 6, 1993

be divorced and that the divorce take effect 31 days after the date of this order.

(Add further paragraphs where the court orders other relief.)

FIGURE 13.7 CONCLUDED

Form 25A: Divorce Order (page 2) Court file number ______________

Put a line through any blank space left on this page. If additional space is needed, extra pages may be attached.

______________________ ______________________

Date of signature *Signature of judge or clerk of the court*

NOTE: *Neither spouse is free to remarry until this order takes effect, at which time you can get a* ***Certificate of Divorce*** *from the court office.*

CHAPTER 14

Support and Custody in the Family Court: A Fast Track Case and a Motion

A spouse who commences a divorce proceeding may ask the court to deal with questions of support and/or custody as part of the divorce case under the *Divorce Act*. All other parties must institute separate proceedings under the *Family Law Act* and the *Children's Law Reform Act*.

We looked at the substantive law of custody and access in chapter 6, spousal support in chapter 7, and child support in chapter 8. In this chapter, we look at the procedure in a support and custody case in the Family Court of the Superior Court of Justice, including:

- an overview of the procedure in a defended support and custody case,
- an examination of the documents required to start a support and custody case, and
- an examination of the steps and documents required to bring a motion for interim support and custody.

OVERVIEW OF PROCEDURE

The procedure in a support and custody case in the Family Court of the Superior Court of Justice is governed by the *Family Law Rules* generally. There is no specific rule governing these cases.

Starting a Support and Custody Case

Under rule 5, a custody case should generally be started in the municipality where the children live. Pursuant to rule 7, the parties to a support and/or custody case are the applicant and the respondent.

The applicant starts the case by filing an application in form 8 as required under rule 8(1). Under rule 13(1.1), the application must be accompanied by the appropriate financial statement, which is form 13 in a claim for support without a property claim. However, under rule 13(1.3) the applicant does not have to file a financial statement if the only claim for support is a claim for child support in the table amount under the *Child Support Guidelines*. Under rule 13(7), the applicant must attach to the financial statement copies of his or her income tax returns for the previous three years or, failing that, a direction to the Canada Customs and Revenue Agency authorizing disclosure of the applicant's tax information.

The applicant must also prepare the continuing record of the case in accordance with rule 9. The continuing record is the court's record of all documents in the case. The general rule is that any document that is served and filed must be put into the continuing record. The applicant's law firm is responsible for the initial preparation of the continuing record.

A claim for support and/or custody is a fast track case under rule 39(4). As a result, the court will set a first court date in accordance with rule 8(4), when the application is filed.

Service of the Application

The applicant must immediately serve the respondent with the application, financial statement, and table of contents of the continuing record, using special service as defined in rule 6(3).[1]

The applicant must then file the application, financial statement, and continuing record with the court, after adding the affidavit of service or other proof of service to the continuing record.

Subsequent Pleadings

Under rule 10, the respondent has 30 days if served in Canada or the United States (60 days if served elsewhere) to defend the case by serving and filing an answer (form 10) and financial statement (form 13).

If the respondent's answer makes a claim against the applicant under rule 10(6), the applicant may serve and file a reply (form 10A) within 10 days.

First Court Date and Case Conference

The court will schedule a first court date when the application is filed.

If the respondent does not serve and file an answer, the applicant may file an affidavit for an uncontested trial (form 23C) and ask the clerk to schedule the matter before a judge for a decision on the basis of the affidavit evidence.[2]

If the respondent serves and files an answer, the applicant may ask the clerk to schedule the case conference to be held at the same time as the first court date. The applicant must serve and file a case conference brief (form 17A) along with an updated continuing record table of contents no later than seven days before the case conference date.[3] Under rule 17(4), the applicant must confirm his or her attendance at

1 See rules 8(5), 9(1), and 13(1).

2 See rules 39(5) and 23(22).

3 If the applicant's financial statement is more than 30 days old, under rule 13(12) the applicant must update the financial statement by serving and filing either a new financial statement or an affidavit stating that the information in the financial statement has not changed.

the case conference by filing a confirmation (form 14C) no later than 2 p.m. two days before the conference date.

Other Conferences and Trial

If a case does not settle at the case conference, the judge may schedule another case conference, a settlement conference, and/or a trial management conference. If the case still does not settle, the court will schedule a trial at which a final order will be made concerning the issues.

Motion for Temporary Custody and Support

If a case does not settle, a final determination on the issues will not be made until the case comes to trial. Since it may be some time before the trial takes place, it is necessary to decide who will have custody of the children until the trial. In addition, one party may have a need for support for him- or herself and/or the children until a final decision is made. If the parties cannot agree on any of these issues, either of them may bring a motion for an order for temporary custody and/or support.

The *Family Court Rules* discourage parties from bringing motions before a case conference is held. Under rules 14(4.1) and (14.2), except in situations of urgency or hardship, no notice of motion or supporting evidence may be served and no motion may be heard before the case conference.

The **moving party** (the party who makes the motion) must get a date from the court office and complete a notice of motion (form 14) and an affidavit (form 14A). Pursuant to rule 14(11), the moving party must serve the notice of motion, affidavit, and an updated continuing record table of contents on the other party no later than four days before the motion date, and must file the documents with the court by no later than two days before the motion date. The moving party must also file a confirmation (form 14C) no later than 2 p.m. two days before the motion date.

moving party
the party who makes the motion

DOCUMENTS REQUIRED TO START A CUSTODY AND SUPPORT CASE

Let's use the case of Lucille Bell and her husband, Dizzy Arnaz, to illustrate the documents required in a custody and support case.

Our client, Lucille Bell, married Dizzy Arnaz on May 31, 1991, and the couple separated on July 4, 2003. It was the first marriage for both of them. Lucille was born on March 5, 1965, and Dizzy was born on June 11, 1963. They were both born in Ottawa and have lived there all of their lives.

Luci and Dizzy have two children: Rita Arnaz-Bell, born on August 30, 1993, and Ricky Arnaz-Bell, born on April 12, 1996. The children live with Lucille in the matrimonial home at 45 Lovett Court, Ottawa, ON K1V 9X4. Dizzy lives at 23 Leavit Place, Ottawa, ON K2W 8Y3.

Lucille has not worked outside the home since Rita's birth. Dizzy is employed as a high school teacher with the Ottawa-Carleton School Board and earns $65,000.

Lucille wants custody of the children, subject to reasonable access by Dizzy, and monthly child support in the amount of $879 (the table amount under the *Child Support Guidelines*). She also wants spousal support in the amount of $750 per month.

Assume that Lucille's application is prepared on November 17, 2003.

Application

The application used for a support and custody claim is form 8. Lucille's application appears as figure 14.1 on page 210.

PAGE 1

- Insert the name of the court — Ontario Superior Court of Justice Family Court — and the address of the appropriate court office. Under rule 5, Lucille's case should be commenced in Ottawa. The address of the Family Court in Ottawa is 161 Elgin Street, Ottawa, ON K2P 2K1.
- Insert the names and addresses of the parties.
- Insert the names and addresses of the parties' lawyers, if any. In this case, Lucille Bell is represented by your law firm, and Dizzy does not yet have a lawyer.
- The court will assign the first court date when the application is filed, so check the box indicating that a first court date is set.
- This case will be on the fast track of the case management system, so check that box.

PAGE 2

- This case includes a claim for support only. As a result, the required financial statement is form 13. Check the first box.

PAGE 3

- Insert the required information under the heading "Family History."
- Insert the date of marriage and the date of separation under the heading "Relationship Dates."
- Insert the names, birthdates, and living arrangements of the children under the heading "The Child(ren)."
- Under the heading "Previous Cases or Agreements," indicate that there have been none.

PAGE 4

This page sets out the applicant's claims.

- Lucille's claims for support are being made under the *Family Law Act*, and her claim for custody is being made under the *Children's Law Reform Act*. She is also claiming costs. Check boxes 10, 11, 13, 16, and 30. It is routine to ask to have spousal support payments indexed.
- Give details of the orders asked for. It is necessary to advise the court that Lucille is seeking custody of both children and to set out the amount of support that she is seeking for herself.

PAGE 5

This page sets out the facts on which Lucille relies in support of her claims. As you draft the allegations of fact, keep in mind the substantive law requirements for a valid **cause of action** for each of her claims.

cause of action
the basis for a legal action

- Lucille's claim for custody is based on the fact that she has always been the children's primary caregiver, the children have lived with her since the separation, and it is therefore in the children's best interests to remain in her custody.
- Lucille's claim for spousal support is based on her need and Dizzy's ability to pay.
- Child support will be determined in accordance with the table amounts in the *Child Support Guidelines*. The amount will be based on Dizzy's income, which should be disclosed by him in the financial statement he is required to file. The application gives information about Dizzy's income in case he does not file a financial statement.
- Lucille will sign and date the application.
- Because this is not a divorce case, no lawyer's certificate is required.

Financial Statement

Lucille must serve and file a financial statement in form 13 because of her claim for spousal support. She would not have to file a financial statement if she were claiming support for the children only in the table amount under the *Child Support Guidelines*.

See chapter 11 for an example of a completed financial statement.

Continuing Record Table of Contents

Under rule 9(7), Lucille must serve a copy of the continuing record table of contents when she serves the application and financial statement on Dizzy. The table of contents in this case appears as figure 14.2 at page 215.

STEPS AND DOCUMENTS IN A MOTION FOR TEMPORARY CUSTODY AND SUPPORT

Let's assume that Lucille Bell and Dizzy Arnaz attend the case conference and still cannot agree on the issues of support and custody pending the trial. Lucille decides to make a motion for temporary custody and support.

Step 1: Schedule the Motion

Contact the court office to get a date for the motion to be heard.

Step 2: Complete the Forms

You must prepare the following forms:

- a notice of motion,
- an affidavit,

- an updated continuing record table of contents, and
- if Lucille's financial statement is more than 30 days old, a new financial statement or an affidavit stating that the information in the financial statement has not changed.

NOTICE OF MOTION

The purpose of a notice of motion (form 14) is to inform the responding parties of the date and time of the motion and the orders that the moving party is asking the court to make.

- Insert the court file number in the upper right-hand corner.
- Insert the names and addresses of the parties and their lawyers.
- Insert the motion date obtained from the court.
- Check off the box indicating that you are serving an affidavit in support of the motion.
- List the additional documents from the continuing record being relied on (in this case, the financial statements of the parties).
- State the orders being requested on the motion (in this case, orders for temporary custody, temporary child support, and temporary spousal support).

Lucille's notice of motion appears as figure 14.3 on page 216.

AFFIDAVIT

The purpose of the affidavit (form 14A) is to provide the court with the evidence on which to make a decision on the motion. An affidavit is a statement of evidence sworn to under oath by the person making the affidavit.

Have a look at Lucille's affidavit, which appears as figure 14.4 on page 218 and sets out the following:

- *Parties' relationship.* Paragraph 1 states that Lucille and Dizzy were married and have now separated.
- *Information about the children.* Paragraphs 3 to 6 set out information about the children and the reasons why it would be in the best interests of the children for the moving party to be granted custody. Lucille is relying on the fact that she has always been the primary caregiver, that giving her custody would maintain the status quo, and that she is willing to encourage an ongoing relationship between the children and the respondent.
- *Information to support a claim for child support.* Paragraphs 2 and 7 provide information to support a claim for child support under the *Child Support Guidelines*. Lucille gives information about the number of children and the respondent's income.
- *Information to support her claim for spousal support.* In paragraphs 4 and 8, Lucille indicates that she needs support because she is not employed, has

not worked outside the home since Rita's birth, and proposes to continue to stay at home to care for the children. Dizzy earns $65,000 per year and is therefore able to pay support.

UPDATED TABLE OF CONTENTS

The continuing record table of contents must be updated to include the motion documents.

Step 3: Serve the Motion Documents

Pursuant to rule 14(10), Dizzy must be served with the following documents no later than four days before the scheduled motion date:

- a notice of motion,
- an affidavit,
- an updated financial statement if necessary, and
- an updated continuing record table of contents.

Dizzy may be served by regular service under rule 6 by:

- mailing a copy to Dizzy's lawyer or, if Dizzy has no lawyer, to Dizzy, in which case service is effective on the fifth day after mailing;
- sending a copy by courier to Dizzy's lawyer or, if Dizzy has no lawyer, to Dizzy, in which case service is effective on the day after the courier picks the documents up;
- depositing a copy at a document exchange to which Dizzy's lawyer belongs, in which case service is effective on the day after the document is date-stamped; or
- faxing a copy to Dizzy's lawyer or, if Dizzy has no lawyer, to Dizzy, in which case service must be carried out before 4 p.m. on a day when the court offices are open.

The person who serves the document must complete and swear an affidavit of service (form 6B).

Step 4: File the Motion Documents with the Court

No later than two days before the scheduled motion date, someone from your law firm must file the motion documents and the affidavit of service in the documents section of the continuing record. In addition, the continuing record table of contents must be updated.

Step 5: File a Confirmation with the Court

No later than 2 p.m. two days before the scheduled motion, your firm must file a confirmation (form 14C) with the court to let the court know that the moving party will be present for the motion.

Respondent

If Dizzy wants to present his own evidence to the court, he must swear an affidavit, serve it on Lucille, and file it with the court as soon as possible before the day of the motion, along with an updated financial statement, if necessary, and an updated continuing record table of contents. The responding party on a motion does not have to file a confirmation with the court.

Order

Under rule 25, the party in whose favour an order is made is required to prepare a draft of the order. An order reflecting Lucille's success on her motion appears as figure 14.5 on page 220.

REFERENCES

Children's Law Reform Act, RSO 1990, c. C.12.
Divorce Act, RSC 1985, c. 3 (2d Supp.).
Family Law Act, RSO 1990, c. F.3.
Family Law Rules, O. Reg. 114/99.
Federal Child Support Guidelines, SOR/97-175.
Ontario *Child Support Guidelines*, O. Reg. 391/97.

REVIEW QUESTIONS

1. Generally speaking, where should a custody case be started?
2. How is a custody case started?
3. What financial statement must be filed by an applicant if an application includes a claim for support without a property claim?
4. What documents must the applicant serve on the respondent? When? How?
5. What must the respondent do if he or she wishes to defend the case? When?
6. When does the court schedule a first court date?
7. What may the applicant do if the respondent does not defend the case?
8. What may the applicant do if the respondent defends the case?
9. What documents must the applicant serve and file before the case conference?
10. Why would a spouse make a motion for temporary custody and/or support?
11. What are the procedural requirements for a party to make a motion?

DRAFTING QUESTION

Monica and Chandler Byng were married on October 18, 1995 and separated on September 18, 2003. They were both born in Ottawa and have lived there all their lives. They have one child, a son named Joey Byng, who was born in Ottawa on December 22, 2000. Joey lives with Chandler in the matrimonial home at 25 Manhattan Avenue, Ottawa, ON K2S 8B3. Monica lives at 50 York Street, Ottawa, ON K3T 9C4. Chandler has not worked outside the home since Joey's birth. Monica works at a chef at the Central Perk Restaurant and earns $50,000 per year. Chandler has started a custody and support case in Ottawa, claiming custody of Joey, subject to reasonable access by Monica, and monthly child support in the amount of $429 (the table amount under the *Child Support Guidelines*). He has also claimed spousal support in the amount of $500 per month. The parties have attended a case conference, and Chandler now wants to make a motion for temporary custody, temporary child support in the amount of $429 per month, and temporary spousal support in the amount of $500 per month. Draft the notice of motion and affidavit.

FIGURE 14.1 LUCILLE'S APPLICATION

ONTARIO

SEAL

SUPERIOR COURT OF JUSTICE FAMILY COURT
(Name of court)

at 161 Elgin Street, Ottawa, ON K2P 2K1
Court office address

Court File Number

Family Law Rules, O. Reg. 114/99

Form 8: Application (General)

Applicant(s)

Full legal name & address for service – street & number, municipality, postal code, telephone & fax numbers and e-mail address (if any).	*Lawyer's name & address – street & number, municipality, postal code, telephone & fax numbers and e-mail address (if any).*
Lucille Bell 45 Lovett Court Ottawa, ON K1V 9X4	JoAnn Kurtz Barrister & Solicitor 123 College Street Ottawa, ON K3R 3L2 Tel: 613-555-1234 Fax: 613-555-2345

Respondent(s)

Full legal name & address for service – street & number, municipality, postal code, telephone & fax numbers and e-mail address (if any).	*Lawyer's name & address – street & number, municipality, postal code, telephone & fax numbers and e-mail address (if any).*
Dizzy Arnaz 23 Leavit Place Ottawa, ON K2W 8Y3	

TO THE RESPONDENT(S):

A COURT CASE HAS BEEN STARTED AGAINST YOU IN THIS COURT. THE DETAILS ARE SET OUT ON THE ATTACHED PAGES.

☒ **THE FIRST COURT DATE IS *(date)*** ______________ **AT** __________ ☐ a.m. ☐ p.m. or as soon as possible after that time, at: *(address)*

161 Elgin Street, Ottawa, ON K2P 2K1

NOTE: If this is a divorce case, no date will be set unless an Answer is filed. If you have also been served with a notice of motion, there may be an earlier court date and you or your lawyer should come to court for the motion.

☒ **THIS CASE IS ON THE FAST TRACK OF THE CASE MANAGEMENT SYSTEM.** A case management judge will be assigned by the time this case first comes before a judge.

☐ **THIS CASE IS ON THE STANDARD TRACK OF THE CASE MANAGEMENT SYSTEM. No court date has been set for this case** but, if you have been served with a notice of motion, it has a court date and you or your lawyer should come to court for the motion. A case management judge will not be assigned until one of the parties asks the clerk of the court to schedule a case conference or until a notice of motion under subrule 14(5) is served before a case conference has been held. If, after 200 days, the case has not been scheduled for trial, the clerk of the court will send out a warning that the case will be dismissed in 30 days unless the parties file proof that the case has been settled or one of the parties asks for a case conference or a settlement conference.

IF YOU WANT TO OPPOSE ANY CLAIM IN THIS CASE, you or your lawyer must prepare an Answer (Form 10 – a blank copy should be attached), serve a copy on the applicant(s) and file a copy in the court office with an Affidavit of Service (Form 6B). **YOU HAVE ONLY 30 DAYS AFTER THIS APPLICATION IS SERVED ON YOU (60 DAYS IF THIS APPLICATION IS SERVED ON YOU OUTSIDE CANADA OR THE UNITED STATES) TO SERVE AND FILE AN ANSWER. IF YOU DO NOT, THE CASE WILL GO AHEAD WITHOUT YOU AND THE COURT MAY MAKE AN ORDER AND ENFORCE IT AGAINST YOU.**

FIGURE 14.1 CONTINUED

Form 8: Application (General) **(page 2)**

Court File Number

Check the box of the paragraph that applies to your case

☒ This case includes a claim for support. It does not include a claim for property or exclusive possession of the matrimonial home and its contents. You **MUST** fill out a Financial Statement (Form 13 – a blank copy attached), serve a copy on the applicant(s) and file a copy in the court office with an Affidavit of Service even if you do not answer this case.

☐ This case includes a claim for property or exclusive possession of the matrimonial home and its contents. You **MUST** fill out a Financial Statement (Form 13.1 – a blank copy attached), serve a copy on the applicant(s) and file a copy in the court office with an Affidavit of Service even if you do not answer this case.

IF YOU WANT TO MAKE A CLAIM OF YOUR OWN, you or your lawyer must fill out the claim portion in the Answer, serve a copy on the applicant(s) and file a copy in the court office with an Affidavit of Service.

_ If you want to make a claim for support but do not want to make a claim for property or exclusive possession of the matrimonial home and its contents, you **MUST** fill out a Financial Statement (Form 13), serve a copy on the applicant(s) and file a copy in the court office.

_ However, if your only claim for support is for child support in the table amount specified under the Child Support Guidelines, you do not need to fill out, serve or file a Financial Statement.

_ If you want to make a claim for property or exclusive possession of the matrimonial home and its contents, whether or not it includes a claim for support, you **MUST** fill out a Financial Statement (Form 13.1, not Form 13), serve a copy on the applicant(s), and file a copy in the court office.

YOU SHOULD GET LEGAL ADVICE ABOUT THIS CASE RIGHT AWAY. If you cannot afford a lawyer, you may be able to get help from your local Legal Aid Ontario office. *(See your telephone directory under LEGAL AID.)*

Date of issue	*Clerk of the court*

FIGURE 14.1 CONTINUED

Form 8: Application (General) **(page 3)**

Court file number

FAMILY HISTORY

APPLICANT: Age: 38 Birthdate: *(d,m,y)* 5 March 1965

Resident in *(municipality & province)* Ottawa, Ontario

since *(date)* 5 March 1965

Surname at birth: Bell Surname just before marriage: Bell

Divorced before? ☒ No ☐ Yes *(Place and date of previous divorce)*

RESPONDENT: Age: 40 Birthdate: *(d,m,y)* 11 June 1963

Resident in *(municipality & province)* Ottawa, Ontario

since *(date)* 11 June 1963

Surname at birth: Arnaz Surname just before marriage: Arnaz

Divorced before? ☒ No ☐ Yes *(Place and date of previous divorce)*

RELATIONSHIP DATES:

☒ Married on *(date)* 31 May 1991 ☐ Started living together on *(date)*

☒ Separated on *(date)* 4 July 2003 ☐ Never lived together ☐ Still living together

THE CHILD(REN)

List all children involved in this case, even if no claim is made for these children.

Full legal name	Age	Birthdate *(d,m,y)*	Resident in *(municipality & province)*	Now Living With *(name of person and relationship to child)*
Rita Arnaz-Bell	10	30 August 1993	Ottawa, Ontario	Lucille Bell, mother
Ricky Arnaz-Bell	7	12 April 1996	Ottawa, Ontario	Lucille Bell, mother

PREVIOUS CASES OR AGREEMENTS

Have the parties or the children been in a court case before?

☒ No ☐ Yes *(Attach a Summary of Court Cases – Form 8E.)*

Have the parties made a written agreement dealing with any matter involved in this case?

☒ No ☐ Yes *(Give date of agreement. Indicate which of its terms are in dispute. Attach an additional page if you need more space.)*

FIGURE 14.1 CONTINUED

Form 8: Application (General) **(page 4)**

Court file number

CLAIM BY APPLICANT

I ASK THE COURT FOR THE FOLLOWING:
(Claims below include claims for temporary orders.)

Claims under the *Divorce Act* *(Check boxes in this column only if you are asking for a divorce and your case is in the Family Court of the Superior Court of Justice.)*	**Claims under the *Family Law Act* or *Children's Law Reform Act***	**Claims relating to property** *(Check boxes in this column only if your case is in the Family Court of the Superior Court of Justice.)*
00 ☐ a divorce 01 ☐ support for me 02 ☐ support for child(ren) – table amount 03 ☐ support for child(ren) - other than table amount 04 ☐ custody of child(ren) 05 ☐ access to child(ren)	10 ☒ support for me 11 ☒ support for child(ren) – table amount 12 ☐ support for child(ren) - other than table amount 13 ☒ custody of child(ren) 14 ☐ access to child(ren) 15 ☐ restraining/non-harassment order 16 ☒ indexing spousal support 17 ☐ indexing same-sex partner support 18 ☐ declaration of parentage 19 ☐ guardianship over child's property	20 ☐ equalization of net family properties 21 ☐ exclusive possession of matrimonial home 22 ☐ exclusive possession of contents of matrimonial home 23 ☐ freezing assets 24 ☐ sale of family property
Other claims 30 ☒ costs 31 ☐ annulment of marriage 32 ☐ prejudgment interest	50 ☐ Other *(Specify.)*	

Give details of the order that you want the court to make. *(Include any amounts of support (if known) and the names of the children for whom support, custody or access is claimed.)*

1. Custody of the children, Rita Arnaz-Bell, born 30 August 1993, and Ricky Arnaz-Bell, born 12 April 1996;

2. Support for the said children in the table amount in the Child Support Guidelines;

3. Spousal support in the amount of $750 per month;

4. Indexing of the spousal support order in accordance with s. 34(5) of the Family Law Act; and

5. Costs.

FIGURE 14.1 CONCLUDED

Form 8: **Application (General)** **(page 5)**

Court File Number

IMPORTANT FACTS SUPPORTING MY CLAIM FOR DIVORCE

☐ **Separation:** The spouses have lived separate and apart since *(date)* ______________ and

☐ have not lived together again since that date in an unsuccessful attempt to reconcile.

☐ have lived together again during the following period(s) in an unsuccessful attempt to reconcile: *(Give dates.)*

☐ **Adultery:** The respondent has committed adultery. *(Give details. It is not necessary to name any other person involved but, if you do name the other person, then you must serve this application on the other person.)*

☐ **Cruelty:** The respondent has treated the applicant with physical or mental cruelty of such a kind as to make continued cohabitation intolerable. *(Give details.)*

IMPORTANT FACTS SUPPORTING MY OTHER CLAIM(S)

(Set out below the facts that form the legal basis for your other claim(s). Attach an additional page if you need more space.)

1. The children have resided with the applicant since the separation, and the applicant has always been their primary caregiver. It would be in the best interests of the children to remain in the custody of the applicant.

2. The applicant is in need of spousal support from the respondent, and the respondent has the ability to pay such support.

3. The respondent is employed as a high school teacher with the Ottawa-Carleton School Board and earns $65,000 per year.

Put a line through any space left on this page. If additional space is needed, extra pages may be attached.

______________ ______________

Date of signature *Signature of applicant*

LAWYER'S CERTIFICATE

For divorce cases only

My name is: ______________

and I am the applicant's lawyer in this divorce case. I certify that I have complied with the requirements of section 9 of the *Divorce Act*.

______________ ______________

Date *Signature of Lawyer*

FIGURE 14.2 CONTINUING RECORD TABLE OF CONTENTS

ONTARIO

Court File Number:

Superior Court of Justice Family Court
161 Elgin Street
Ottawa, ON K2P 2K1

Applicant: Lucille Bell__________________

Respondent: Dizzy Arnaz___________________

CUMULATIVE TABLE OF CONTENTS (CONTINUING RECORD) VOLUME 1

Document (*For an affidavit or transcript of evidence, indicate the name of the person who gave the affidavit or the evidence.*)	**Filed by** (*A = applicant or R = respondent*)	**Date of Document** (d, m, y)	**Date of Filing** (d, m, y)	**Tab/ Page**
Application	A	17/11/2003		1/ 1-4
Financial Statement	A	17/11/2003		1/ 5-10

FIGURE 14.3 LUCILLE'S NOTICE OF MOTION

Court File Number

ONTARIO SUPERIOR COURT OF JUSTICE FAMILY COURT
(Name of court)

Form 14: Notice of Motion

at 161 Elgin Street, Ottawa, ON K2P 2K1
Court office address

Applicant(s)

Full legal name & address for service — street & number, municipality, postal code, telephone & fax and e-mail address (if any).	*Lawyer's name & address — street & number, municipality, postal code, telephone & fax numbers and e-mail address (if any).*
Lucille Bell 45 Lovett Court Ottawa, ON K1V 9X4	JoAnn Kurtz Barrister & Solicitor 123 College Street Ottawa, ON K3R 3L2 Tel: 613-555-1234 Fax: 613-555-2345

Respondent(s)

Full legal name & address for service — street & number, municipality, postal code, telephone & fax numbers and e-mail address (if any).	*Lawyer's name & address — street & number, municipality, postal code, telephone & fax numbers and e-mail address (if any).*
Dizzy Arnaz 23 Leavit Place Ottawa, ON K2W 8Y3	

The person making this motion or the person's lawyer must contact the clerk of the court by telephone or otherwise to choose a time and date when the court could hear this motion

TO THE PARTIES:
THE COURT WILL HEAR A MOTION on *(date)* ______________________
at ________ **a.m./p.m., or as soon as possible after that time at:** *(place of hearing)*

161 Elgin Street, Ottawa, ON K2P 2K1

This motion will be made by *(name of person making the motion)*

Lucille Bell

who will be asking the court for an order for the item(s) listed on the back of this notice.

☒ A copy of the affidavit(s) in support of this motion is served with this notice.
☐ A notice of a case conference is served with this notice to change an order.
If this material is missing, you should talk to the court office immediately.

The person making this motion is also relying on the following documents in the continuing record: *(List documents.)*

1. Financial statement of Lucille Bell sworn on (date)
2. Financial statement of Dizzy Arnaz sworn on (date)

If you want to oppose this motion or to give your own views, you should talk to your own lawyer and prepare your own affidavit, serve it on all other parties not later that 4 days before the date above and file it at the court office not later than 2 days before that date. Only written and affidavit evidence will be allowed at a motion unless the court gives permission for oral testimony. You may bring your lawyer to the motion.

IF YOU DO NOT COME TO THE MOTION, THE COURT MAY MAKE AN ORDER WITHOUT YOU AND ENFORCE IT AGAINST YOU.

____
Date of signature

____
Signature of person making this motion or of person's lawyer

JoAnn Kurtz
Barrister & Solicitor
123 College Street
Ottawa, ON K3R 3L2

Tel: 613-555-1234 Fax: 613-555-2345

Typed or printed name of person or of person's lawyer, address for service, telephone & fax number and e-mail address (if any)

NOTE TO PERSON MAKING THIS MOTION: *You MUST file a confirmation (Form 14C) not later than 2:00 p.m. on the day before the date set out above.*

If this is a motion to change past and future support payments under an order that has been assigned to a government agency, you must also serve this notice on that agency. If you do not, the agency can ask the court to set aside any order that you may get in this motion and can ask for costs against you.

FIGURE 14.3 CONCLUDED

State the order or orders requested on this motion.

1. An order for temporary custody of the children, Rita Arnaz-Bell, born on 30 August 1993, and Ricky Arnaz-Bell, born on 12 April 1996.
2. An order for temporary child support in accordance with the *Child Support Guidelines*.
3. An order for temporary spousal support in the amount of $750 per month.

FIGURE 14.4 LUCILLE'S AFFIDAVIT

Court File Number

ONTARIO SUPERIOR COURT OF JUSTICE FAMILY COURT
(Name of court)

Form 14A: Affidavit (General) dated
(date)

at 161 Elgin Street, Ottawa, ON K2P 2K1
Court office address

Applicant(s)

Full legal name & address for service — street & number, municipality, postal code, telephone & fax and e-mail address (if any).	*Lawyer's name & address — street & number, municipality, postal code, telephone & fax numbers and e-mail address (if any).*
Lucille Bell 45 Lovett Court Ottawa, ON K1V 9X4	JoAnn Kurtz Barrister & Solicitor 123 College Street Ottawa, ON K3R 3L2 Tel: 613-555-1234 Fax: 613-555-2345

Respondent(s)

Full legal name & address for service — street & number, municipality, postal code, telephone & fax numbers and e-mail address (if any).	*Lawyer's name & address — street & number, municipality, postal code, telephone & fax numbers and e-mail address (if any).*
Dizzy Arnaz 23 Leavit Place Ottawa, ON K2W 8Y3	

My name is *(full legal name)* Lucille Bell

I live in *(municipality & province)* Ottawa, Ontario

and I swear/affirm that the following is true:

Set out the statements of fact in consecutively numbered paragraphs. Where possible, each numbered paragraph should consist of one complete sentence and be limited to a particular statement of fact. If you learned a fact from someone else, you must give that person's name and state that you believe that fact to be true.

1. The respondent and I were married on May 31, 1991, and we separated on July 4, 2003.
2. We have two children – Rita Arnaz-Bell, born on August 30, 1993, and Ricky Arnaz-Bell, born on April 12, 1996.
3. The children have been residing with me since the separation in the matrimonial home at 45 Lovett Court in Ottawa.
4. I have always been the children's primary caregiver. I have stayed home with the children full time since Rita was born.
5. The children are well settled in the neighbourhood. They like their school and have many friends. If I am granted custody of the children, I would continue to reside with them in the matrimonial home and stay at home to look after them full time.
6. The children have a good relationship with their father, and I would like the children to see him as often as possible.
7. The respondent is employed as a high school teacher with the Ottawa-Carleton School Board and earns $65,000 per year. I am asking for support for the children in the amount of $879 per month as set out in the tables in the *Child Support Guidelines*.
8. I am also in need of support for myself, and the respondent has the ability to pay. I have no employment income, and my other income and expenses are set out in my financial statement filed in this application. I am asking for spousal support for myself in the amount of $750 per month.

FIGURE 14.4 CONCLUDED

Form 14A: Affidavit (General) dated *(date)* ______________ (page 2) Court file number ______________

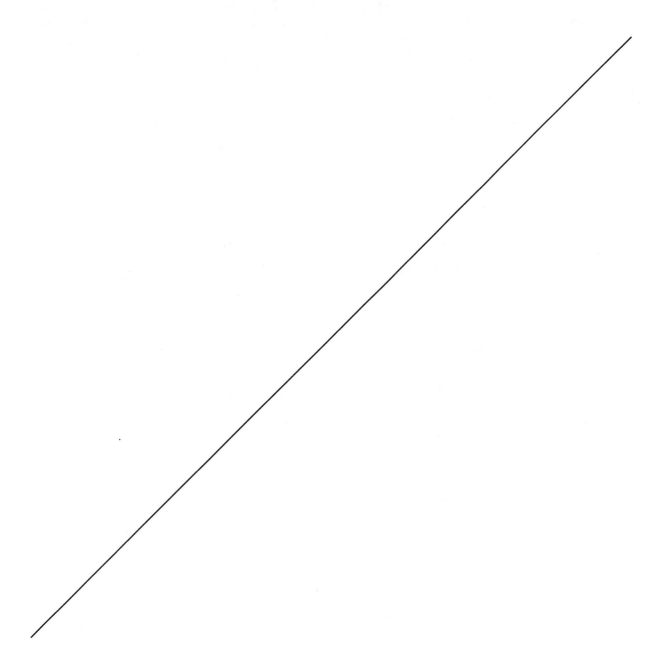

Put a line through any blank space left on this page.

Sworn/Affirmed before me at Ottawa
Municipality

in Ontario
province, state or country

on ______________
date

____
Commissioner for taking affidavits
(Type or print name below if signature is illegible.)

____
Signature
(This form is to be signed in front of a lawyer, justice of the peace, notary public or commissioner for taking affidavits.)

FIGURE 14.5 ORDER

SEAL

ONTARIO SUPERIOR COURT OF JUSTICE FAMILY COURT
(Name of court)

at 161 Elgin Street, Ottawa, ON K2P 2K1
Court office address

Court File Number
File Number

Form 25: Order (General)

☒ **Temporary**

☐ **Final**

Applicant(s)

Full legal name & address for service — street & number, municipality, postal code, telephone & fax numbers and e-mail address (if any).	*Lawyer's name & address — street & number, municipality, postal code, telephone & fax numbers and e-mail address (if any).*
Jennifer Elizabeth Pitts 4 Friendship Street Richmond Hill, ON L3P 4N2	JoAnn Kurtz Barrister & Solicitor 123 College Street Toronto, ON M2K 1Y3 Tel: 416-555-1234 Fax: 416-555-1235

Name of Judge
Judge (print or type name)

Date of Order
Date of order

Respondent(s)

Full legal name & address for service — street & number, municipality, postal code, telephone & fax numbers and e-mail address (if any).	*Lawyer's name & address — street & number, municipality, postal code, telephone & fax numbers and e-mail address (if any).*
Dizzy Arnaz 23 Leavit Place Ottawa, ON K2W 8Y3	

The court heard an application/motion made by *(name of person or persons)*

Lucille Bell

The following persons were in court *(names of parties and lawyers in court)*

JoAnn Kurtz, for Lucille Bell, and Dizzy Arnaz in person

The court received evidence and heard submissions on behalf of *(name or names)*

Lucille Bell and Dizzy Arnaz

THIS COURT ORDERS THAT:

1. The applicant, Lucille Bell, shall have temporary custody of the children, Rita Arnaz-Bell, born on August 30, 1993, and Ricky Arnaz-Bell, born on April 12, 1996.

2. The respondent, Dizzy Arnaz, shall have reasonable access to the said children.

3. The respondent shall pay temporary child support in accordance with the Child Support Guidelines in the amount of $879 per month.

4. The respondent shall pay temporary spousal support in the amount of $750 per month.

FIGURE 14.5 CONCLUDED

Form 25: Order (General) (page 2) Court file number __________

Put a line through any blank space left on this page. If additional space is needed, extra pages may be attached.

____________________	____________________
Date of signature	*Signature of judge or clerk of the court*

CHAPTER 15

Property Claims in the Family Court: A Standard Track Case and Conferences

Equalization of net family property (NFP) and other property claims are dealt with under the *Family Law Act*. A spouse may start a case dealing with property claims only, or may combine the property claims with claims for custody and/or support. A spouse may also include property claims in a divorce case.

We looked at the substantive law of property rights in chapter 9. In this chapter, we look at the procedure in a property case in the Family Court of the Superior Court of Justice, including:

- an overview of the procedure in a defended property case,
- an examination of the documents required to start a property case, and
- an examination of the steps and documents required to schedule a case conference.

OVERVIEW OF PROCEDURE

The procedure in a property case in the Family Court of the Superior Court of Justice is governed by the *Family Law Rules* generally. There is no specific rule that deals with property cases.

Starting a Property Case

Under rule 5, a property case should generally be started in the municipality where the applicant lives. If the case includes a claim for custody or access, the case should be started in the municipality where the children live.

In accordance with rule 8(1), the applicant starts the case by filing an application in form 8. The application must be accompanied by the required financial statements. Under rule 13(1.2), if the application includes a property claim or a claim for exclusive possession of the matrimonial home and its contents, the financial statement is to be in form 13.1. Under rule 13(7), the applicant must attach to the financial statement copies of his or her income tax returns for the previous three years or, failing that, a direction to the Canada Customs and Revenue Agency authorizing disclosure of the applicant's tax information. Under rule 13(14), the applicant must also serve and file a net family property statement (form 13B).

The applicant is also required by rule 9 to prepare the continuing record of the case. The continuing record is the court's record of all documents in the case. The general rule is that any document that is served and filed must be included in the continuing record. The continuing record has a red front cover and three sections:

- *Table of contents*. The table of contents lists the documents, sets out the tab and page number where each document can be found, and names the party who filed the document. It is updated every time a document is added to the proceedings.
- *Endorsements*. The continuing record contains 10 or more blank pages for the judge to write endorsements, copies of all court orders, and any reasons for judgments.
- *Documents*. The continuing record contains all documents after they have been served and all affidavits of service.

A property claim is a standard track case under rule 39(7). As a result, the court does not set a court date when the application is filed.

Service of the Application

The applicant must immediately serve the respondent with the application, financial statement, net family property statement, and table of contents of the continuing record, using special service as defined in rule 6(3).[1]

The applicant must then file the application, financial statement, net family property statement, and continuing record with the court, after adding the affidavit of service or other proof of service to the continuing record.

Subsequent Pleadings

Under rule 10, the respondent has 30 days if served in Canada or the United States (60 days if served elsewhere) to defend the case by serving and filing an answer (form 10), financial statement (form 13.1), and net family property statement (form 13B).

If the respondent's answer makes a claim against the applicant, the applicant may serve and file a reply (form 10A) within 10 days in accordance with rule 10(6).

Case Conference

There is no first court date in a standard track case. The first step in the case is a case conference, which the court schedules under rule 39(8)(c) when one of the parties requests it.

1 See rules 8(5), 9(1), and 13(1).

The applicant must serve and file a conference notice (form 17), a case conference brief (form 17A), and an updated continuing record table of contents no later than seven days before the case conference date.[2] Under rule 17(14), the applicant must confirm his or her attendance at the case conference by filing a confirmation (form 14C) no later than 2 p.m. two days before the conference date.

Other Conferences and Trial

If the case does not settle at the case conference, the judge may schedule another case conference, a settlement conference, and/or a trial management conference. If the case still does not settle, the court will schedule a trial at which a final order will be made concerning the issues.

DOCUMENTS REQUIRED TO START A PROPERTY CASE

Let's use the case of Frasier and Lilith Crane to illustrate the documents required in a property case.

Our client is Frasier Crane. He and Lilith were married on September 4, 1977, and separated on September 4, 2003, after they had a huge argument while planning their 25th anniversary party. They have no children, and both have successful careers as psychiatrists. Neither party is claiming support from the other, and they do not want a divorce at this time. The only issue between them is the equalization of their NFP. They have been unable to settle this issue because they cannot agree on the values of their respective medical practices, and Lilith will not agree to an independent evaluation.

Frasier was born on October 15, 1951 in Oshawa and Lilith (birth name Stern) was born on January 16, 1953, also in Oshawa. Frasier and Lilith have lived in Oshawa all their lives. It was the first marriage for both of them.

Frasier has moved to 25 Nervosa Place, Oshawa, ON L1H K5J, leaving Lilith in the matrimonial home at 933 Seattle Street, Oshawa, ON L2L K4J.

Assume that Frasier's application is prepared on December 1, 2003.

Application

The application used for an NFP equalization claim is form 8. Frasier's application appears as figure 15.1 on page 230.

PAGE 1

- Insert the name of the court — Ontario Superior Court of Justice Family Court — and the address of the appropriate court office. Under rule 5, Frasier's case should be commenced in Oshawa. The address of the Family Court in Oshawa is 33 King Street West, Oshawa, ON L1H 1A1.
- Insert the names and addresses of the parties.

2 If the applicant's financial statement and/or NFP statements are more than 30 days old, under rules 13(10) and (14) the applicant must update the statements by serving and filing either new statements or an affidavit stating that the information in the statements has not changed.

- Insert the names and addresses of the parties' lawyers if any. In this case, Frasier is represented by your law firm, and Lilith does not yet have a lawyer.
- This case will be on the standard track of the case management system, so check the appropriate box. Because this is a standard track case, no first court date is assigned.

PAGE 2

- This case includes a claim for property. As a result, the required financial statement is form 13.1. Check the second box.
- The form will be dated and signed when it is filed at the court.

PAGE 3

- Insert the required information under the heading "Family History."
- Insert the date of marriage and the date of separation under the heading "Relationship Dates."
- Under the heading "Previous Cases or Agreements," indicate that there have been none.

PAGE 4

This page sets out the applicant's claims.

- Frasier's claim for equalization of NFP is a property claim. He is also claiming costs. Therefore, check boxes 20 and 30.
- Give details of the orders asked for.

PAGE 5

This page sets out the facts on which Frasier relies in support of his claim for an equalization of NFP under the heading "Important Facts Supporting My Other Claims." When you draft the allegations of fact, you must keep in mind the substantive law requirements for a valid cause of action. As discussed in chapter 9, the right to an equalization of NFP applies to married spouses only. It arises when the parties separate and there is no reasonable prospect that they will resume cohabitation.

Frasier will have to sign and date the application. No lawyer's certification is required because this is not a divorce case.

Financial Statement

Frasier must serve and file a financial statement in form 13.1 and a net family property statement (form 13B). See chapter 11 for completed examples of these forms.

Continuing Record Table of Contents

Under rule 9(7), Frasier will have to serve a copy of the continuing record table of contents when he serves the application, financial statement, and net family property statement on Lilith. The table of contents appears as figure 15.2 on page 235.

STEPS AND DOCUMENTS REQUIRED FOR A CASE CONFERENCE

As discussed in chapter 12, all cases in the Family Court are case-managed, and the rules provide for three types of case management conferences:

- case conferences,
- settlement conferences, and
- trial management conferences.

The purpose of these conferences is to define, narrow, or even settle the issues in dispute.

Under rule 17, at least one case conference must be held in every defended case. The purposes of a case conference are to:

- identify the issues that are in dispute and separate them from those that are not in dispute;
- explore ways to resolve the issues that are in dispute or to settle the entire case;
- ensure that the parties disclose all relevant evidence;
- set a date for the next step in the case or, if possible, have the parties agree to a specific timetable for the steps in the case; and
- organize a settlement conference if necessary.

An application in which the applicant makes a property claim is a standard-track case under rule 39. In a standard track case, a case conference is scheduled when either party requests it. A case conference is the first opportunity for the parties to meet with a judge to review the case.

When Frasier wants to schedule a case conference, you must take the steps set out below.

Step 1: Schedule the Conference

Contact the court office to get a date and time for the case conference.

Step 2: Prepare the Necessary Documents

You will need the following documents for a case conference:

- a conference notice (form 17);
- a case conference brief (form 17A);
- if the statements are more than 30 days old, an updated financial statement and net family property statement or an affidavit stating that the information in the statements has not changed; and
- an updated continuing record table of contents.

CONFERENCE NOTICE

The purpose of this document is to notify the opposing party of the date and time of the case conference that you have scheduled.

Frasier's conference notice appears as figure 15.3 on page 236.

CASE CONFERENCE BRIEF

The case conference brief (form 17A) is a lengthy document designed to provide the court and the opposing party with detailed information about the case and the filing party's view of the issues in the case. Frasier's case conference brief appears as figure 15.4 on page 237.

- The first page identifies the parties and date of the case conference.
- *Part 1: Family Facts.* This part sets out facts about the parties' relationship.
- *Part 2: Issues.* This part provides information on the issues that have been settled and the issues that have not been settled.
- *Part 3: Issues for This Case Conference.* This part sets out the party's view of the issues and important facts for the case conference. In this case, the outstanding issue is the valuation of the two medical practices.
- *Part 4: Financial Information.* This part asks for additional financial information in cases of child support.
- *Part 5: Procedural Issues.* This part asks for the party's views on procedural issues. In this case, Frasier would like an order for the valuation of the two medical practices.
- The form must be signed and dated by both the party and the party's lawyer.

CONTINUING RECORD TABLE OF CONTENTS

You must update the continuing record table of contents by adding the case conference notice, the case conference brief, and any updated financial statements or affidavits you are serving and filing.

Step 3: Serve the Documents

The person who has requested the case conference must serve the conference notice, case conference brief, updated financial statements or affidavit, if required, and updated table of contents at least seven days before the case conference. Regular service under rule 6(2) may be used.

Step 4: File the Documents with the Court

The person who serves the documents must complete an affidavit of service (form 6B). The original documents and affidavit of service must be filed with the court no later than seven days before the case conference along with the continuing record table of contents, updated to include the affidavit of service.

No brief or other document for use at the conference may be served on the other party or filed with the court after 2 p.m. two days before the conference.

Step 5: File a Confirmation with the Court

No later than 2 p.m. two days before the case conference, each party must file a confirmation (form 14C) confirming that he or she will attend the conference.

REFERENCES

Divorce Act, RSC 1985, c. 3 (2d Supp.).

Family Law Act, RSO 1990, c. F.3.

Family Law Rules, O. Reg. 114/99.

REVIEW QUESTIONS

1. Generally speaking, where should a property case be started?
2. How is a property case started?
3. What financial statement must be filed by an applicant if an application includes a property claim?
4. What documents must the applicant serve on the respondent? When? How?
5. What must the respondent do if he or she wishes to defend the case? By when?
6. When does the court schedule a first court date?
7. Who schedules a case conference? When?
8. What documents must the applicant serve for the case conference?

FIGURE 15.1 FRASIER'S APPLICATION

ONTARIO

SEAL

SUPERIOR COURT OF JUSTICE FAMILY COURT
(Name of court)

at 33 King Street West, Oshawa, ON L1H 1A1
Court office address

Court File Number

Family Law Rules, O. Reg. 114/99
Form 8: Application (General)

Applicant(s)

Full legal name & address for service – street & number, municipality, postal code, telephone & fax numbers and e-mail address (if any).	*Lawyer's name & address – street & number, municipality, postal code, telephone & fax numbers and e-mail address (if any).*
Frasier Crane 25 Nervosa Place Oshawa, ON L1H K5J	JoAnn Kurtz 123 College Street Oshawa, ON L2J 2B2 Tel: 905-555-1234 Fax: 905-555-1235

Respondent(s)

Full legal name & address for service – street & number, municipality, postal code, telephone & fax numbers and e-mail address (if any).	*Lawyer's name & address – street & number, municipality, postal code, telephone & fax numbers and e-mail address (if any).*
Lilith Crane 933 Seattle Street Oshawa, ON L2L K4J	

TO THE RESPONDENT(S):

A COURT CASE HAS BEEN STARTED AGAINST YOU IN THIS COURT. THE DETAILS ARE SET OUT ON THE ATTACHED PAGES.

☐ **THE FIRST COURT DATE IS *(date)*** ______ **AT** ______ ☐ a.m. ☐ p.m. or as soon as possible after that time, at: *(address)*

NOTE: If this is a divorce case, no date will be set unless an Answer is filed. If you have also been served with a notice of motion, there may be an earlier court date and you or your lawyer should come to court for the motion.

☐ **THIS CASE IS ON THE FAST TRACK OF THE CASE MANAGEMENT SYSTEM.** A case management judge will be assigned by the time this case first comes before a judge.

☒ **THIS CASE IS ON THE STANDARD TRACK OF THE CASE MANAGEMENT SYSTEM. No court date has been set for this case** but, if you have been served with a notice of motion, it has a court date and you or your lawyer should come to court for the motion. A case management judge will not be assigned until one of the parties asks the clerk of the court to schedule a case conference or until a notice of motion under subrule 14(5) is served before a case conference has been held. If, after 200 days, the case has not been scheduled for trial, the clerk of the court will send out a warning that the case will be dismissed in 30 days unless the parties file proof that the case has been settled or one of the parties asks for a case conference or a settlement conference.

IF YOU WANT TO OPPOSE ANY CLAIM IN THIS CASE, you or your lawyer must prepare an Answer (Form 10 – a blank copy should be attached), serve a copy on the applicant(s) and file a copy in the court office with an Affidavit of Service (Form 6B). **YOU HAVE ONLY 30 DAYS AFTER THIS APPLICATION IS SERVED ON YOU (60 DAYS IF THIS APPLICATION IS SERVED ON YOU OUTSIDE CANADA OR THE UNITED STATES) TO SERVE AND FILE AN ANSWER. IF YOU DO NOT, THE CASE WILL GO AHEAD WITHOUT YOU AND THE COURT MAY MAKE AN ORDER AND ENFORCE IT AGAINST YOU.**

FIGURE 15.1 CONTINUED

Form 8: Application (General) **(page 2)**

Court File Number

Check the box of the paragraph that applies to your case

☐ This case includes a claim for support. It does not include a claim for property or exclusive possession of the matrimonial home and its contents. You **MUST** fill out a Financial Statement (Form 13 – a blank copy attached), serve a copy on the applicant(s) and file a copy in the court office with an Affidavit of Service even if you do not answer this case.

☒ This case includes a claim for property or exclusive possession of the matrimonial home and its contents. You **MUST** fill out a Financial Statement (Form 13.1 – a blank copy attached), serve a copy on the applicant(s) and file a copy in the court office with an Affidavit of Service even if you do not answer this case.

IF YOU WANT TO MAKE A CLAIM OF YOUR OWN, you or your lawyer must fill out the claim portion in the Answer, serve a copy on the applicant(s) and file a copy in the court office with an Affidavit of Service.

_ If you want to make a claim for support but do not want to make a claim for property or exclusive possession of the matrimonial home and its contents, you **MUST** fill out a Financial Statement (Form 13), serve a copy on the applicant(s) and file a copy in the court office.

_ However, if your only claim for support is for child support in the table amount specified under the Child Support Guidelines, you do not need to fill out, serve or file a Financial Statement.

_ If you want to make a claim for property or exclusive possession of the matrimonial home and its contents, whether or not it includes a claim for support, you **MUST** fill out a Financial Statement (Form 13.1, not Form 13), serve a copy on the applicant(s), and file a copy in the court office.

YOU SHOULD GET LEGAL ADVICE ABOUT THIS CASE RIGHT AWAY. If you cannot afford a lawyer, you may be able to get help from your local Legal Aid Ontario office. *(See your telephone directory under LEGAL AID.)*

______________________	______________________
Date of issue	*Clerk of the court*

FIGURE 15.1 CONTINUED

Form 8: Application (General) **(page 3)**

Court file number

FAMILY HISTORY

APPLICANT: Age: 52 Birthdate: *(d,m,y)* 15 October 1951

Resident in *(municipality & province)* Oshawa, Ontario

since *(date)* 15 October 1951

Surname at birth: Crane Surname just before marriage: Crane

Divorced before? ☒ No ☐ Yes *(Place and date of previous divorce)*

RESPONDENT: Age: 50 Birthdate: *(d,m,y)* 16 January 1953

Resident in *(municipality & province)* Oshawa, Ontario

since *(date)* 16 January 1953

Surname at birth: Stern Surname just before marriage: Stern

Divorced before? ☒ No ☐ Yes *(Place and date of previous divorce)*

RELATIONSHIP DATES:

☒ Married on *(date)* September 4, 1977 ☐ Started living together on *(date)*

☒ Separated on *(date)* September 4, 2003 ☐ Never lived together ☐ Still living together

THE CHILD(REN)

List all children involved in this case, even if no claim is made for these children.

Full legal name	**Age**	**Birthdate** *(d,m,y)*	**Resident in** *(municipality & province)*	**Now Living With** *(name of person and relationship to child)*

PREVIOUS CASES OR AGREEMENTS

Have the parties or the children been in a court case before?

☒ No ☐ Yes *(Attach a Summary of Court Cases – Form 8E.)*

Have the parties made a written agreement dealing with any matter involved in this case?

☒ No ☐ Yes *(Give date of agreement. Indicate which of its terms are in dispute. Attach an additional page if you need more space.)*

FIGURE 15.1 CONTINUED

Form 8: Application (General) **(page 4)** Court file number

CLAIM BY APPLICANT

I ASK THE COURT FOR THE FOLLOWING:
(Claims below include claims for temporary orders.)

Claims under the *Divorce Act* *(Check boxes in this column only if you are asking for a divorce and your case is in the Family Court of the Superior Court of Justice.)*	**Claims under the *Family Law Act* or *Children's Law Reform Act***	**Claims relating to property** *(Check boxes in this column only if your case is in the Family Court of the Superior Court of Justice.)*
00 ☐ a divorce 01 ☐ support for me 02 ☐ support for child(ren) – table amount 03 ☐ support for child(ren) - other than table amount 04 ☐ custody of child(ren) 05 ☐ access to child(ren)	10 ☐ support for me 11 ☐ support for child(ren) – table amount 12 ☐ support for child(ren) - other than table amount 13 ☐ custody of child(ren) 14 ☐ access to child(ren) 15 ☐ restraining/non-harassment order 16 ☐ indexing spousal support 17 ☐ indexing same-sex partner support 18 ☐ declaration of parentage 19 ☐ guardianship over child's property	20 ☒ equalization of net family properties 21 ☐ exclusive possession of matrimonial home 22 ☐ exclusive possession of contents of matrimonial home 23 ☐ freezing assets 24 ☐ sale of family property
Other claims 30 ☒ costs 31 ☐ annulment of marriage 32 ☐ prejudgment interest	50 ☐ Other *(Specify.)*	

Give details of the order that you want the court to make. *(Include any amounts of support (if known) and the names of the children for whom support, custody or access is claimed.)*

1. An equalization of the net family property of the parties pursuant to s. 5 of the Family Law Act, RSO 1990, c. F.3.

FIGURE 15.1 CONCLUDED

Form 8: **Application (General)** **(page 5)**

Court File Number

IMPORTANT FACTS SUPPORTING MY CLAIM FOR DIVORCE

☐ **Separation:** The spouses have lived separate and apart since *(date)* ______________________ and

☐ have not lived together again since that date in an unsuccessful attempt to reconcile.

☐ have lived together again during the following period(s) in an unsuccessful attempt to reconcile: *(Give dates.)*

☐ **Adultery:** The respondent has committed adultery. *(Give details. It is not necessary to name any other person involved but, if you do name the other person, then you must serve this application on the other person.)*

☐ **Cruelty:** The respondent has treated the applicant with physical or mental cruelty of such a kind as to make continued cohabitation intolerable. *(Give details.)*

IMPORTANT FACTS SUPPORTING MY OTHER CLAIM(S)

(Set out below the facts that form the legal basis for your other claim(s). Attach an additional page if you need more space.)

1. The parties were married on September 4, 1977 and separated on September 4, 2003. There is no reasonable prospect that they will resume cohabitation. The applicant therefore seeks an equalization of the net family property of the parties.

Put a line through any space left on this page. If additional space is needed, extra pages may be attached.

______________________ ______________________

Date of signature *Signature of applicant*

LAWYER'S CERTIFICATE

For divorce cases only

My name is: ______________________

and I am the applicant's lawyer in this divorce case. I certify that I have complied with the requirements of section 9 of the *Divorce Act.*

______________________ ______________________

Date *Signature of Lawyer*

FIGURE 15.2 CONTINUING RECORD TABLE OF CONTENTS

ONTARIO

Court File Number:

Superior Court of Justice Family Court
33 King Street West
Oshawa, ON L1H 1A1

Applicant: Frasier Crane

Respondent: Lilith Crane

CUMULATIVE TABLE OF CONTENTS
(CONTINUING RECORD)
VOLUME 1

Document *(For an affidavit or transcript of evidence, indicate the name of the person who gave the affidavit or the evidence.)*	**Filed by** *(A = applicant or R = respondent)*	**Date of Document** (d, m, y)	**Date of Filing** (d, m, y)	**Tab/ Page**
Application	A	01/12/2003		1/ 1-4
Financial Statement	A	01/12/2003		1/ 5-10
Net Family Property Statement	A	01/12/2003		1/11-13

FIGURE 15.3 FRASIER'S CONFERENCE NOTICE

ONTARIO SUPERIOR COURT OF JUSTICE FAMILY COURT
(Name of court)

Court File Number

Form 17
Conference
Notice

at 33 King Street West, Oshawa, ON L1H 1A1
Court office address

Applicant(s)

Full legal name & address for service — street & number, municipality, postal code, telephone & fax numbers and e-mail address (if any).	*Lawyer's name & address — street & number, municipality, postal code, telephone & fax numbers and e-mail address (if any).*
Frasier Crane 25 Nervosa Place Oshawa, ON L1H K5J	JoAnn Kurtz 123 College Street Tel: 905-555-1234 Toronto, ON L2J 2B2 Fax: 905-555-1235

Respondent(s)

Full legal name & address for service — street & number, municipality, postal code, telephone & fax numbers and e-mail address (if any).	*Lawyer's name & address — street & number, municipality, postal code, telephone & fax numbers and e-mail address (if any).*
Lilith Crane 933 Seattle Street Oshawa, ON L2L K4J	

Name & address of Children's Lawyer's agent (street & number, municipality, postal code, telephone & fax numbers and e-mail address (if any)) and name of person represented.

TO: *(name of party or parties or lawyer(s))* Lilith Crane

A ☒ **CASE CONFERENCE** ☐ **SETTLEMENT CONFERENCE** ☐ **TRIAL MANAGEMENT CONFERENCE**

WILL BE HELD at *(place of conference)* 33 King Street West, Oshawa, ON L1H 1A1

at ________ **a.m./p.m. on** *(date)* ________

The conference has been arranged at the request of

☒ the applicant ☐ the respondent
☐ the case management judge ☐ *(Other; specify.)* ________

to deal with the following issues:

1. equalization of net family property

You must participate at that time and date by

☒ coming to court at the address set out above.
☐ video-conference or telephone at *(location of video terminal or telephone)* ________

as agreed under arrangements already made by *(name of person)* ________ for video/telephone conferencing.

IF YOU DO NOT PARTICIPATE AS SET OUT ABOVE, THE CASE MAY GO ON WITHOUT YOU OR THE COURT MAY DISMISS THE CASE.

________ *Date of signature*

________ *Signature of clerk of the court*

NOTE: *The party requesting the conference (or, if the conference is not requested by a party, the applicant) must serve and file a case conference brief (Form 17A or 17B), settlement conference brief (Form 17C or 17D) or trial management conference brief (Form 17E) not later than seven days before the date scheduled for the conference. The other party must serve and file a brief not later than four days before the conference date. Each party must also file a confirmation (Form 14C) not later than 2 p.m. two days before the conference.*

FIGURE 15.4 FRASIER'S CASE CONFERENCE BRIEF

ONTARIO

Court File Number

SUPERIOR COURT OF JUSTICE FAMILY COURT
(Name of court)

at 33 King Street West, Oshawa, ON L1H 1A1
Court office address

Family Law Rules, O. Reg. 114/99
Form 17A:
Case Conference Brief- General

Name of party filing this brief	Date of case conference
Frasier Crane	

Applicant(s)

Full legal name & address for service — street & number, municipality, postal code, telephone & fax numbers and e-mail address (if any).	*Lawyer's name & address — street & number, municipality, postal code, telephone & fax numbers and e-mail address (if any).*
Frasier Crane 25 Nervosa Place Oshawa, ON L1H K5J	JoAnn Kurtz Barrister & Solicitor 123 College Street Oshawa, ON L2J 2B2 Tel: 905-555-1234 Fax: 905-555-1235

Respondent(s)

Full legal name & address for service — street & number, municipality, postal code, telephone & fax numbers and e-mail address (if any).	*Lawyer's name & address — street & number, municipality, postal code, telephone & fax numbers and e-mail address (if any).*
Lilith Crane 933 Seattle Street Oshawa, ON L2L K4J	

Name & address of Children's Lawyer's agent (street & number, municipality, postal code, telephone & fax numbers and e-mail address (if any)) and name of person represented.

PART 1: FAMILY FACTS

1. **APPLICANT:** Age: 52 Birthdate: 15 October 1951
2. **RESPONDENT:** Age: 50 Birthdate: 16 January 1953
3. **RELATIONSHIP DATES:**

☒ Married on *(date)* 4 September 1977 ☐ Started living together on *(date)*

☒ Separated on *(date)* 4 September 2003 ☐ Never lived together.

☐ Other *(Explain.)*

4. The basic information about the child(ren) is as follows:

Child's full legal name	Age	Birthdate *(d,m,y)*	Grade/Year and school	Now living with

FIGURE 15.4 CONTINUED

Form 17A: Case Conference Brief - General (page 2)

Court File Number

PART 2: ISSUES

5. What are the issues in this case that HAVE been settled:

☐ child custody ☐ spousal support ☐ ownership of property
☐ access ☐ same-sex partner support ☐ possession of home
☐ restraining order ☐ child support ☐ equalization of net family property
☐ Other *(Specify.)*

6. What are the issues in this case that have NOT yet been settled:

☐ child custody ☐ spousal support ☐ ownership of property
☐ access ☐ same-sex partner support ☐ possession of home
☐ restraining order ☐ child support ☒ equalization of net family property *(Attach Net Family Property Statement, Form 13B)*
☐ Other *(Specify.)*

7. If child or spousal or same-sex partner support is an issue, give the income of the parties:

Applicant: $ ________ per year for the year 20____

Respondent: $ ________ per year for the year 20____

8. Have you explored any ways to settle the issues that are still in dispute in this case?

☒ No. ☐ Yes. *(Give details)*

9. Have any of the issues that have been settled been turned into a court order or a written agreement?

☒ No.
☐ Yes. ☐ an order dated ________
☐ a written agreement that is attached.

10. Have the parents attended a family law or parenting education session?

☒ No. (Should they attend one? No)
☐ Yes. *(Give details.)*

PART 3: ISSUES FOR THIS CASE CONFERENCE

11. What are the issues for this case conference? What are the important facts for this case conference?

Issues: The valuation of the respective medical practices of both parties.

Facts: Both the applicant and the respondent carry on well-established, successful psychiatric practices in the City of Oshawa.

FIGURE 15.4 CONTINUED

Form 17A: **Case Conference Brief - General** **(page 3)**

Court File Number

12. What is your proposal to resolve these issues?

That an independent evaluator be agreed upon or appointed to set a value on the medical practices of the parties.

13. Do you want the court to make a temporary or final order at the case conference about any of these issues?

☐ No. ☒ Yes. *(Give details)*

That an independent evaluator be appointed to set a value on the medical practices of the parties.

PART 4: FINANCIAL INFORMATION

NOTE: *If a claim for support has been made in this case, you must serve and file a new financial statement (Form 13 or 13.1), if it is different from the one filed in the continuing record or if the one in the continuing record is more than 30 days old. If there are minor changes but no major changes in your financial statement, you can serve and file an affidavit with details of the changes instead of a new financial statement. If you have not yet filed a financial statement in the continuing record, you must do it now.*

The page/tab number of the financial statement in the continuing record is ____________

14. If a claim is being made for child support and a claim is made for special expenses under the child support guidelines, give details of those expenses or attach additional information.

15. If a claim is made for child support and you claim that the Child Support Guidelines table amount should not be ordered, briefly outline the reasons here or attach an additional page.

FIGURE 15.4 CONCLUDED

Form 17A: **Case Conference Brief - General** **(page 4)**

Court File Number

PART 5: PROCEDURAL ISSUES

16. If custody or access issues are not yet settled:

(a) Is a custody or access assessment needed?

☐ No. ☐ Yes. *(Give names of possible assessors.)*

(b) Does a child or a parent under 18 years of age need legal representation from the Office of the Children's Lawyer?

☐ No. ☐ Yes. *(Give details and reasons.)*

17. Does any party need an order for the disclosure of documents, the questioning of witnesses, a property valuation or any other matter in this case?

☐ No. ☒ Yes. *(Give details.)*

That an independent evaluator be appointed to set a value of the medical practices of the parties.

18. Are any other procedural orders needed?

☒ No. ☐ Yes. *(Give details.)*

19. Have all the persons who should be parties in this case been added as parties?

☒ Yes. ☐ No. *(Who needs to be added?)*

20. Are there any other issues that should be reviewed at the case conference?

☒ No. ☐ Yes. *(Give details)*

Date of party's signature	*Signature of party*
Date of lawyer's signature	*Signature of party's lawyer*

CHAPTER 16

Proceedings in the Superior Court of Justice

The single-level Family Court of the Superior Court of Justice operates in many, but not all, locations in Ontario (see appendix B). In those areas where the Family Court of the Superior Court of Justice does not operate, including the City of Toronto and the Regional Municipality of Peel, jurisdiction over family law matters continues to be divided between the Superior Court of Justice and the Ontario Court of Justice. In those locations, cases that include divorce or property claims must be brought before the Superior Court of Justice, while cases that involve only custody and/or support claims may be brought before either the Superior Court of Justice or the Ontario Court of Justice.

The procedure in family law matters in the Ontario Court of Justice is governed by the *Family Law Rules*.

This chapter examines procedure in the Superior Court of Justice, including:

- a general overview of procedure,
- the documents required in an uncontested divorce, and
- the procedure in an uncontested divorce.

OVERVIEW OF PROCEDURE IN THE SUPERIOR COURT OF JUSTICE

Procedure in the Superior Court of Justice is governed by the *Rules of Civil Procedure*. The *Family Law Rules* do not apply. In addition to the general rules, rule 69 governs divorce proceedings, and rule 70 governs other family law proceedings.

Commencement of Proceedings

Rule 14 governs the commencement of proceedings. There are two types of proceedings in the Superior Court of Justice: actions and applications. Actions, other than divorce actions, are commenced by statement of claim (form 14A). Divorce actions are commenced by petition for divorce (form 69A or 69B). Applications are commenced by notice of application (form 14E).

A party seeking a divorce must commence a divorce action, and can also claim in the petition relief under the *Family Law Act* and/or the *Children's Law Reform*

Act. A party who is not seeking a divorce and is making claims under the *Family Law Act* and/or the *Children's Law Reform Act* only may proceed by way of either action or application.

The parties to the various proceedings are as follows:

- action: plaintiff and defendant;
- divorce action: petitioner and respondent; and
- application: applicant and respondent.

Financial Statements

Whatever the form of proceeding, financial statements are required if the proceeding includes claims for support or property. Rule 69.14 deals with financial statements in divorce proceedings, and rule 70.04 deals with financial statements in other family law proceedings. See chapter 11 for a more complete discussion of financial statements.

Pleadings in an Action

A family law action follows the same procedure as any action. Under rule 14.08, the plaintiff must serve the defendant with the statement of claim within six months after it is issued. The statement of claim must be served personally or by an alternative to personal service under rule 16.

Under rule 18, a defendant who wishes to defend the action has 20 days if the defendant was served in Ontario (40 days if served elsewhere in Canada or in the United States, and 60 days if served anywhere else) to serve and file a statement of defence (form 18A).

In accordance with rule 25.04, the plaintiff may then deliver a reply (form 25A) within 10 days.

A defendant who wishes to assert a claim against the plaintiff must deliver a statement of defence and counterclaim (form 27A) within the time for delivery of a statement of defence. The plaintiff defends a counterclaim by serving and filing a reply and defence to counterclaim (form 27C) within 20 days. Under rule 27, the defendant may then deliver a reply to defence to counterclaim (form 27D) within 10 days.

Pleadings in a Divorce Action

Under rule 69.05, the petitioner must serve the respondent with the petition for divorce within six months after it is issued. The petition must be served personally, by acceptance of service by the respondent's lawyer, or by mail with an acknowledgment of receipt card. If the petition is served personally, under rule 69.04 it must be served by someone other than the petitioner.

Under rule 69.07, a respondent who wishes to dispute the petitioner's claim but seeks no separate relief may defend the action by serving and filing an answer (form 69D) within 20 days if the respondent was served in Ontario (40 days if served elsewhere in Canada or the United States, and 60 days if served anywhere else).

In accordance with rule 69.08, the petitioner may then serve and file a reply (form 69E) within 10 days.

Under rules 69.09 and 69.10, a respondent who wishes to assert a claim against the petitioner must serve and file an answer and counterpetition (form 69F) within the time limit for delivery of an answer. The answer responds to the petitioner's allegations in the petition, and the counterpetition contains the respondent's claims against the petitioner.

Under rule 69.12, the petitioner then has 20 days in which to serve and file a reply and answer to counterpetition (form 69H). The reply responds to the answer, and the answer to counterpetition responds to the claims made in the counterpetition.

The respondent may then serve and file a reply to answer to counterpetition (form 69I) pursuant to rule 69.13 within 10 days if it is necessary to respond to the petitioner's allegations in the answer to counterpetition.

Pleadings in an Application

When a proceeding is brought by way of application, the applicant gets a hearing date from the registrar of the court. The applicant must serve the notice of application and supporting affidavits at least 10 days before the hearing date if the notice is served in Ontario (20 days if served outside Ontario).The notice of application with proof of service must be filed with the court at least 4 days before the hearing, and the affidavits must be filed with the court at least two days before the hearing (see rules 38.06 and 39.01).

Under rule 38.07(1), a respondent who wishes to defend an application must serve and file a notice of appearance (form 38A) as soon as possible. The respondent must serve and file any affidavits being relied upon at least two days before the hearing.

Before the hearing, both parties are required to serve and file a record and factum under rule 38.09.

If there are serious issues in dispute, the judge at the hearing is likely to direct a trial of the issues, in which case the proceeding becomes very similar to an action commenced by statement of claim.

Motions

Motions on procedural matters or for interim relief may be brought at any time after the proceedings are commenced. Motions are governed by rule 37.

Discovery

Under rule 30, the parties are required to disclose to each other all documents relating to any matter in issue in the action that are or have been in their possession, control, or power by serving an affidavit of documents (form 30A).

Rule 31 gives parties the right to examine each other for discovery under oath, either orally or in writing. The purpose of the examination for discovery is to allow the parties to obtain more information about each other's cases before trial.

Offers To Settle

A party who wishes to settle may serve an offer to settle (form 49A) on the other party. An offer to settle may be withdrawn at any time before acceptance. A party wishing to accept an offer serves an acceptance of offer (form 49C). Under rule 49, a party who makes an offer at least seven days before the trial that is not accepted and who obtains an order that is as favourable as or more favourable than the offer is entitled to partial costs to the date the offer was made, and to full recovery of costs from the date it was made.

Pre-Trial Procedures

Any time after the completion of the pleading stage, a party who is ready for trial may set the action down for trial by serving and filing a trial record. Sixty days after the action is set down, or on the consent of the other party, the registrar will place the action on the trial list under rule 48.

After the action has been set down for trial, either party may request a pre-trial conference at which the parties and their lawyers meet with a judge to consider the possibility of settlement or, failing that, ways in which to shorten and simplify the trial.

Trial

A matter that does not settle proceeds to trial. The trial judge hears the evidence of the parties and their submissions as to the relevant law and then makes final orders about any unresolved issues.

DOCUMENTS AND PROCEDURE IN AN UNCONTESTED DIVORCE

Let's revisit the case of Brad and Jenny Pitts from chapter 13 (who now live in Toronto) to see how their divorce would proceed in the Superior Court of Justice.

Our client, Jenny Pitts, is married to Brad Pitts. The couple separated on September 4, 2002, when Brad left Jenny for an old girlfriend named Gwyneth Paltry. On January 15, 2003, Jenny and Brad signed a separation agreement that settles all outstanding issues between them. They have agreed that Jenny will start a divorce case based on Brad's adultery, which Brad will not defend. Brad is willing to sign an affidavit admitting to the adultery.

Jenny was born on May 1, 1968 in Toronto, Ontario, and Brad was born on April 6, 1965. They have lived in Toronto all of their lives. They were married on June 6, 1993 in Thornhill, Ontario. It was Jenny's first marriage, but Brad was married briefly before to Lisa Cujo. That marriage ended in divorce on December 1, 1991.

Brad and Jenny have two children, Matthew Joseph, born on July 4, 1995, and Courtney Monica, born on February 14, 1997. They are living with Jenny at 4 Friendship Street, Toronto, ON M3P 4N2. The children attend Father LeBlanc School, where Matthew is in grade 3 and Courtney is in grade 1.

Brad moved in with Gwyneth at 15 Central Perk Place, Toronto, ON M5K 1H3 when he left Jenny.

The separation agreement includes provisions as follows:

1. Jenny will have custody of the children, and Brad will have reasonable access.
2. Brad will pay child support, in accordance with the *Child Support Guidelines*, of $823 per month based on his annual income of $60,000.

Jenny does not want to incorporate any of the provisions in the divorce judgment. Assume that Jenny's petition for divorce is being prepared on November 10, 2003.

Overview of Procedure in an Uncontested Divorce

When the time for delivery of an answer has passed, the petitioner will note the respondent in default and move for default judgment pursuant to rule 69.19. The motion is generally determined on the basis of affidavit evidence, but the petitioner may examine witnesses at the hearing of the motion instead or in addition to the affidavit evidence.

The motion for judgment will not be heard until a marriage certificate or a certificate of the registration of the marriage has been filed with the court, unless the petition stated that it is impossible to obtain a certificate. In addition, the motion will not be heard until the court has received a certificate or report with respect to prior pending proceedings commenced by either spouse.[1]

Step 1: Get Supporting Documents

Before starting a divorce action for Jenny, you should have copies of the following documents:

- *Marriage certificate.* You must file the marriage certificate under rule 36(4), and it is helpful to have the certificate before you prepare the application to make sure that you name the parties properly.
- *Separation agreement.* It is helpful to have a copy of the agreement before you prepare the application to make sure that you have the correct details about the agreement (and you would have to attach a copy of the separation agreement to Jenny's affidavit if she wanted to incorporate any its provisions into the order).

As it turns out, Jenny has the original marriage certificate issued by the minister who performed the ceremony (see figure 13.1 on page 185). If Jenny did not have the marriage certificate, you would need to get a certificate of the registration of the marriage.

You may obtain a certified copy of a marriage certificate from the government of the jurisdiction in which the parties were married. If the parties were married in Ontario, as Jenny and Brad were, you order the certificate from the Office of the Registrar General in Thunder Bay. An application for the certificate is available at the court, or can be obtained online at the government of Ontario's Web site: www.gov.on.ca.

If Jenny and Brad had been married outside Ontario, you would also need a copy of the divorce certificate for Brad's divorce from Lisa Cujo, to file with the court in order to prove that his marriage to Jenny is valid. You get a certificate of divorce from the court office of the court that granted the divorce.

Step 2: Prepare the Petition for Divorce

Jenny's petition for divorce is in form 69A, which appears as figure 16.1 on page 254.

TITLE OF PROCEEDING

Insert the names of the parties. The petitioner is the person bringing the action. The other spouse is the respondent. The parties should be identified in the title of

1 See rule 69.18. Also see chapter 13 for a discussion of the Central Registry of Divorce Proceedings.

the proceeding as "husband" and "wife" in addition to their formal designation as "petitioner" and "respondent."

Be sure to use the names of the parties as they appear in the marriage certificate. Note that Jenny's full name is Jennifer Elizabeth Pitts, and Brad's full name is Bradley David Pitts.

Pursuant to rule 69.03(4), it is not necessary in the case of adultery to set out the name of the other person alleged to have been involved.

COURT AND SERVICE INFORMATION

Insert the address of the court office where the petition is being issued. The registrar of the court will insert the date when the petition is issued.

Insert the name and address of each respondent.

CLAIM

State everything you want the court to include in the judgment. Every divorce petition includes a claim for divorce. Additional claims under the *Divorce Act* might include claims for custody or access and support. If you are claiming support, rule 69.03(7) requires you to set out the nature and amount of the relief claimed and the amount for each dependant.[2]

If the parties have entered into a separation agreement, the petitioner may either seek to have terms of the separation agreement incorporated into the divorce judgment or seek no additional relief and continue to rely on the separation agreement. If the petitioner is claiming relief in accordance with the separation agreement, refer to the agreement by date and paragraph number, and set out the provisions of each paragraph to be incorporated in full.

Additional claims may be made under the *Family Law Act* and/or the *Children's Law Reform Act*. For example, if custody, access, or support has been claimed under the *Divorce Act*, it is prudent to seek the same relief pursuant to the *Family Law Act* and/or *Children's Law Reform Act* in the event that a divorce is not granted. Claims may also be made for equalization of net family property (NFP) and exclusive possession of the matrimonial home.

In our case, Jenny is seeking a divorce only.

GROUNDS FOR DIVORCE

Form 69A has material preprinted for each of the three possible grounds:

- *Separation*. Set out the date on which the parties separated. If the parties resumed cohabitation for any period, set out the relevant dates. If not, state "none."
- *Adultery*. Set out the particulars of the adultery alleged. Even though it is not necessary to name the other person involved, you should include the person's name, if you know it, when providing particulars.
- *Cruelty*. Set out the particulars of the alleged cruelty.

2 It is unnecessary to include a specific amount for child support. Instead, state it to be in accordance with the *Child Support Guidelines*.

Complete only the portion of the petition that sets out the ground on which your client is relying. In our case, the petitioner is relying on Brad's adultery with Gwyneth Paltry.

RECONCILIATION

In paragraph 4, set out the particulars of any efforts to reconcile. If no efforts have been made, state "none."

DETAILS OF MARRIAGE

Set out the details of the parties' marriage, previous marital status, and birth. Use the information from the marriage certificate if you have it.

MARRIAGE CERTIFICATE INFORMATION

State whether a marriage certificate:

- is being filed with the court when the petition is issued,
- will be filed before trial, or
- cannot be filed.

Note that the form distinguishes between a certificate of the marriage and a certificate of the registration of the marriage. A certificate of the marriage is the original certificate completed by the person who performed the marriage ceremony. A certificate of the registration of the marriage is the document obtained from the registrar general. In our case, Jenny has a certificate of the marriage completed by Rev. Chandler Byng.

RESIDENCE

Information about the residence of the parties is required to establish the jurisdiction of the Ontario courts. In paragraphs 18 and 19, set out the municipality and province of residence. You can state that a party has resided there since birth, if that is the case. If not, insert a specific date.

CHILDREN

It is necessary to provide information about any children of the marriage, even if no claim is being made for custody, child support, or access to the children.

- *Paragraph 22*. Give the name, birth date, school, and grade for each child. State the person with whom each child lives (referring to the parties as husband or wife) and the length of time the child has lived there. Also state the municipality and province where the children ordinarily reside. In our case, both children have lived with Jenny since birth in Toronto.
- *Paragraph 23(a)*. Complete this paragraph only if the petitioner is seeking a custody order, in which case the paragraph should agree with the claim on page 2 of the petition. In our case, Jenny is not seeking a custody order, so this paragraph is left blank.
- *Paragraph 23(b)*. Complete this paragraph if the petitioner is not seeking a custody or access order. Jenny is not seeking an order because she is

content to rely on the provisions of a separation agreement. The form does not contain a statement to that effect, so it must be added.

- *Paragraph 23(c)*. Complete this paragraph only if the petitioner is seeking an order for access. In our case, no order is being sought, so paragraph 23(c) is struck out.
- *Paragraph 24*. Set out details of the existing access arrangements and whether or not they are satisfactory.
- *Paragraph 25*. Complete this paragraph only if a custody or access order is being sought. In our case, no order is being sought, so this paragraph is left blank.
- *Paragraph 26*. Set out any material change in the circumstances of the spouses that is expected to affect the children. In our case, there is no material change.
- *Paragraph 27*. Set out the details of the existing arrangements for support of the children and whether or not those arrangements are being honoured. Complete paragraph 27(c) only if the petitioner is seeking a support order. In our case, the petitioner is not seeking a support order, so paragraph 27(c) is struck out.
- *Paragraph 28*. State whether or not the educational needs of the children are being met. In our case, they are.

OTHER COURT PROCEEDINGS

If there have been other court proceedings between the parties, set out the name of the court, the court file number, the kind of order the court was asked to make, and what order, if any, the court made. If the proceeding is not yet completed, give its current status. In our case, there are no other proceedings.

DOMESTIC CONTRACTS AND FINANCIAL ARRANGEMENTS

Set out the date and nature of any domestic contract between the parties, and indicate whether the contract is now in effect. If support payments are not being paid in full, state the amount that has not been paid. In our case, there is a separation agreement, dated January 15, 2003, that is in effect.

COLLUSION, CONDONATION, AND CONNIVANCE

As discussed in chapter 5, collusion, condonation, and connivance are bars to the granting of a divorce.

Collusion is an agreement or conspiracy for the purpose of subverting the administration of justice, including an agreement to fabricate or suppress evidence or to deceive the court. Collusion is an absolute bar to a divorce whether the divorce is brought on a fault or a no-fault ground.

Connivance and condonation apply only to divorces on fault grounds. Connivance takes place when a petitioner encourages his or her spouse to commit a matrimonial offence so that the petitioner has grounds for divorce. Condonation takes place when the petitioner forgives a matrimonial offence. Neither connivance nor condonation are absolute bars to a divorce. The court may grant a divorce notwithstanding either condonation or connivance if the court believes that the public interest would be better served by granting the divorce.

It is necessary to complete paragraph 31, which deals with collusion, in all divorces. Complete paragraph 32, which deals with condonation and connivance, only if the divorce is sought on one of the fault grounds. This paragraph should be struck out if the divorce is sought on the ground of separation only.

Since Jenny's petition is sought on the grounds of adultery, both paragraphs must be completed.

MATTERS OTHER THAN DIVORCE AND CUSTODY

This portion of the petition must be completed if the petitioner is seeking any relief other than a divorce or custody — for example, if the petitioner is seeking support and/or an equalization of NFP. If such claims have been made, the petitioner must set out in separate, consecutively numbered paragraphs the material facts on which the petitioner relies in support of those claims.

TRIAL

You must insert the place where the petitioner proposes that the trial be held. The place of trial is governed by rule 69.17. The petitioner may name any place in Ontario. However, if the petition claims custody of or access to a child ordinarily resident in Ontario, the place of trial must be in the county in which the child ordinarily resides.

DECLARATION OF PETITIONER

The petitioner must sign the petition, declaring the statements to be true to the best of his or her knowledge, information, and belief. The petitioner should use his or her usual signature.

STATEMENT OF SOLICITOR

The petitioner's lawyer must sign the petition, so complete this part of the petition by inserting the name of the petitioner's lawyer. Also insert the lawyer's firm name, address, and telephone and fax numbers.

BACKSHEET

Complete a backsheet, including an acknowledgment of service, which will be completed by the respondent and the process server when the petition is served. The backsheet for Jenny's petition appears as figure 16.2 on page 260.

Step 3: Issue the Petition

You or someone from your law firm must go to the local registrar's office to have the petition issued. You will need:

- the original and one copy of the petition,
- the marriage certificate,[3] and
- the court fee.

---

3 Although the marriage certificate can be filed later, it is best to file it when the petition is issued.

In this case, no financial statement is required because no claim is being made for support and/or equalization of NFP.

The registrar will assign a court file number to the action, put a seal on the petition, date it, and sign it. The registrar will give you the original petition and keep a copy for the court file.

STEP 4: SERVE THE PETITION

Your law firm must arrange to serve the respondent with a copy of the petition. Under rule 69.04, the petition must be served personally, by acceptance of service by the respondent's solicitor, or by mail with an acknowledgment of receipt card. If the petition is served personally, it must be served by someone other than the petitioner. The person who effects service must ask the respondent to complete and sign the acknowledgment of service on the back of the petition, and sign as witness to the respondent's signature or record the respondent's refusal to sign. The person who effects service should also complete an affidavit of service.

Pursuant to rule 69.05, the petition must be served within six months after it is issued.

Step 5: Prepare Documents for Default Judgment

You may apply for default judgment after the time for delivery of an answer has expired.

You will need the following documents to get a default judgment:

- a motion record including:
  - ❑ a table of contents;
  - ❑ a combined requisition to note default and notice of motion for judgment (form 60Q);
  - ❑ the petitioner's affidavit (form 69R);
  - ❑ the respondent's affidavit, if any (form 69S);
  - ❑ a copy of the petition for divorce;
  - ❑ a copy of financial statements, if any;
  - ❑ a blue backsheet; and
- a draft judgment (form 69T).

The motion record table of contents for Jenny's affidavit appears as figure 16.3 on page 261. Jenny's form 69Q appears as figure 16.4 on p. 262.

PETITIONER'S AFFIDAVIT

Rule 69.19(2) sets out the requirements for the contents of the petitioner's affidavit, which is to be in form 69R. Jenny's affidavit appears as figure 16.5 on page 263.

- Because the marriage certificate is not signed and sealed by the registrar general of Ontario, paragraph 3 of the affidavit sets out the title of the certificate, its date and place of issue, and the name and office of the person who issued it. It also states that the certificate contains the correct particulars of the marriage. This information satisfies the requirements of rule 69.19(2)(c).

- Paragraph 4 of the affidavit must set out particulars of the grounds for divorce. However, Jenny has no personal knowledge of the adultery.
- Paragraph 5 addresses the issue of collusion. The wording comes from rule 69.19(2)(f).
- Paragraph 6 address the issues of condonation and connivance and is required under rule 69.12(2)(g) because Jenny is relying on Brad's adultery.
- Paragraph 7 is required under rule 69.19(2)(j). It is customary to address the issue of support in the affidavit as well.
- It is customary to address the issue of costs, whether or not a claim is made.
- Paragraph 10 is required under rule 69.19(2)(n).

RESPONDENT'S AFFIDAVIT

Jenny will require an affidavit from Brad to provide proof of his adultery. Jenny cannot give evidence on this point because she does not have personal knowledge of the adultery. Brad must admit to his adultery under oath.

Rule 69.19(3) sets out the requirements for the contents of the respondent's affidavit, which is to be in form 69S. Brad's affidavit appears as figure 16.6 on page 265.

- Paragraph 1 is required by rule 69.19(3)(a).
- Paragraphs 2, 3, 5, and 6 are required by rule 69.19(3)(d).
- The wording of paragraph 4 is determined by rule 69.19(3)(c). After stating his willingness to give evidence of his adultery, Brad goes on to give the evidence.
- Paragraph 7 is required by rule 69.19(3)(e).
- Paragraph 8 is required by rule 69.19(3)(b).

DRAFT JUDGMENT

Jenny's draft judgment appears as figure 16.7 on page 267.

The court will insert the name of the judge and the date of the judgment at the top of the judgment. It will also insert a date 31 days after the date of the judgment in paragraph 1.

Step 6: File the Documents with the Court

You must file the following documents with the court:

- the motion record,
- the original petition and proof of service,
- four copies of the draft judgment, and
- a stamped envelope addressed to each party.

Step 7: Obtain the Divorce Judgment

The registrar presents the documents to a judge. If judgment is granted on the motion in accordance with the draft judgment, the registrar signs and enters the judgment and mails a copy of it in each envelope provided.

Step 8: Obtain a Certificate of Divorce

The divorce does not take effect until the 31st day after the divorce judgment is granted. Either party may apply to the court under rule 69.22 for a certificate of divorce as proof that the divorce has taken effect.

You will require the following documents:

- a requisition (see figure 16.8 on page 268),
- an affidavit (see figure 16.9 on page 269) stating that
  - ❑ no appeal from the divorce is pending, or any such appeal has been abandoned or dismissed, and
  - ❑ no order has been made extending the time for appealing from the divorce, or if any such order has been made, the extended time has expired without an appeal being taken;
- a copy of the divorce judgment as entered; and
- a draft certificate in form 69V (see figure 16.10 on page 270).

The registrar will search the court records and will issue the certificate if it is ascertained that there is no indication the affidavit is incorrect.

REFERENCES

Children's Law Reform Act, RSO 1990, c. C.12.
Divorce Act, RSC 1985, c. 3 (2d Supp.).
Family Law Act, RSO 1990, c. F.3.
Family Law Rules, O. Reg. 114/99.
Rules of Civil Procedure, RRO 1990, reg. 194.

REVIEW QUESTIONS

1. What rule governs divorce proceedings in the Superior Court of Justice?
2. What rule governs other family law proceedings in the Superior Court of Justice?
3. Name the parties to an action, a divorce action, and an application.
4. How is a divorce action commenced?
5. What must the petitioner serve on the respondent? How? By when?
6. What must a respondent do if he or she wishes to dispute the petitioner's claim? By when?
7. What may the petitioner then do?
8. What must a respondent do if he or she wishes to assert a claim against the petitioner? By when?
9. Name all the pleadings that may then be filed. By whom? By when?
10. What may a petitioner do if the respondent does not defend the divorce action?
11. Who may obtain a certificate of divorce from the court? How? When?

DRAFTING QUESTION

Jennifer Loped and Ben Affect were married for only a short time when they realized that they were totally incompatible. They have been separated since August 16, 2003, and Ben now wants a divorce. Jennifer, who kept her own surname following the marriage, was born in Toronto on January 1, 1970, and Ben was born, also in Toronto, on September 15, 1972. They have lived in Toronto all their lives, and were married there on February 14, 2002. It was the first marriage for both of them. They have no children. Jennifer is now living at 123 Combs Drive, Toronto, ON M3P 1J4. Ben is living at 215 Paltrow Court, Toronto, ON M4X 2K6. Draft a divorce petition to be signed by Ben.

FIGURE 16.1 JENNY'S PETITION FOR DIVORCE

Court File No.

ONTARIO

SUPERIOR COURT OF JUSTICE

BETWEEN:

JENNIFER ELIZABETH PITTS

Petitioner
(Wife)

and

BRADLEY DAVID PITTS

Respondent
(Husband)

PETITION FOR DIVORCE

TO THE RESPONDENT

A LEGAL PROCEEDING FOR DIVORCE HAS BEEN COMMENCED AGAINST YOU by the petitioner. The claim made against you appears on the following pages.

IF YOU WISH TO DEFEND THIS PROCEEDING, you or an Ontario lawyer acting for you must prepare an answer in form 69D prescribed by the *Rules of Civil Procedure*, serve it on the petitioner's lawyer or, where the petitioner does not have a lawyer, serve it on the petitioner, and file it, with proof of service, in this court office, WITHIN TWENTY DAYS after this petition is served on you, if you are served in Ontario.

If you are served in another province or territory of Canada or in the United States of America, the period for serving and filing your answer is forty days. If you are served outside Canada and the United States of America, the period is sixty days.

Instead of serving and filing an answer, you may serve and file a notice of intent to defend in form 69J prescribed by the *Rules of Civil Procedure*. This will entitle you to ten more days within which to serve and file your answer.

If this petition for divorce contains a claim for support or division of property, you must serve and file a financial statement in form 69K prescribed by the *Rules of Civil Procedure* within the time set out above for serving and filing your answer, whether or not you wish to defend this proceeding. If you serve and file an answer, your financial statement must accompany your answer.

IF YOU FAIL TO SERVE AND FILE AN ANSWER, A DIVORCE MAY BE GRANTED IN YOUR ABSENCE AND WITHOUT FURTHER NOTICE TO YOU, JUDGMENT MAY BE GRANTED AGAINST YOU ON ANY OTHER CLAIM IN THIS PETITION AND YOU MAY LOSE YOUR RIGHT TO SUPPORT OR DIVISION OF PROPERTY.

FIGURE 16.1 CONTINUED

If you wish to defend this proceeding but are unable to pay legal fees, legal aid may be available to you by contacting a local Legal Aid office.

NEITHER SPOUSE IS FREE TO REMARRY until a divorce has been granted and has taken effect. Once a divorce has taken effect, you may obtain a certificate of divorce from this court office.

Date:

Issued by: ______________________
Local Registrar

Address of court office:

393 University Avenue
Toronto, ON M5G 1E6

TO: BRADLEY DAVID PITTS

15 Central Perk Place

Toronto, ON M5K 1H3

Claim

1. The petitioner claims:

(a) a divorce;
(b) under the *Divorce Act* (Canada),
(i)
(ii)
(iii)

(c) under the *Family Law Act*,
(i)
(ii)
(iii)

GROUNDS FOR DIVORCE — SEPARATION

2. (a) The spouses have lived separate and apart since . The spouses have resumed cohabitation during the following periods in an unsuccessful attempt at reconciliation:

Date(s) of cohabitation

GROUNDS FOR DIVORCE — ADULTERY

2. (b) The respondent spouse has committed adultery. Particulars are as follows:

The respondent has resided with Gwyneth Paltry as husband and wife at 15 Central Perk Place in Toronto, Ontario from in or about September 2002 to the date of this petition, and during that time has engaged in acts of sexual intercourse with her on numerous occasions.

FIGURE 16.1 CONTINUED

GROUNDS FOR DIVORCE — CRUELTY

2. (c) The respondent has treated the petitioner with physical or mental cruelty of such a kind as to render intolerable the continued cohabitation of the spouses. Particulars are as follows:

RECONCILIATION

3. There is no possibility of reconciliation of the spouses.

4. The following efforts to reconcile have been made: None

DETAILS OF MARRIAGE

5. Date of marriage: June 6, 1993
6. Place of marriage (municipality and province, state or country): Thornhill, Ontario
7. Wife's surname immediately before marriage: Annistone
8. Wife's surname at birth: Annistone
9. Husband's surname immediately before marriage: Pitts
10. Husband's surname? at birth: Pitts
11. Marital status of husband at time of marriage? (never married, divorced or widower): divorced
12. Marital status of wife at time of marriage? (never married, divorced or widow): never married
13. Wife's birthplace (province, state or country): Ontario
14. Wife's birth date: May 1, 1968
15. Husband's birthplace (province, state or country): Ontario
16. Husband's birth date: April 6, 1965

17. (a) ☒ A certificate of ☒ the marriage
☐ the registration of the marriage
of the spouses has been filed with the court.

(b) ☐ It is impossible to obtain a certificate of the marriage or its registration because:

(c) ☐ A certificate of the marriage or its registration will be filed before this action is set down for trial or a motion is made for judgment.

RESIDENCE

18. The petitioner has resided in Toronto, Ontario since birth.
19. The respondent has resided in Toronto, Ontario since birth.
20. The respondent's current address is: 15 Central Perk Place, Toronto, ON M5K 1H3

FIGURE 16.1 CONTINUED

21. The
☒ petitioner
☒ respondent has habitually resided in Ontario for at least one year immediately preceding the commencement of this proceeding.

CHILDREN

22. The following are all the living children of the marriage as defined by the *Divorce Act* (Canada):

Full Name	Birth Date	School and grade or year	Person with whom child lives and length of time child has lived there
Matthew Joseph Pitts	July 4, 1995	Father LeBlank School, Grade 3	Wife, since birth
Courtney Monica Pitts	February 14, 1997	Father LeBlank School, Grade 1	Wife, since birth

The children ordinarily reside in Toronto, Ontario.

23. (a) The petitioner seeks an order for custody or joint custody of the following children on the following terms:

Name of Child — Terms of the Order

The respondent
☐ agrees
☐ does not agree with the above terms.

(b) The petitioner is not seeking an order for custody and
☐ is content that a previous order for custody continue in force
☐ is attempting to obtain an order for custody in another proceeding full particulars of which are as follows:

X is content to rely on the provisions in a separation agreement between the parties dated January 15, 2003, by which the wife has custody of the children and the husband has reasonable access.

(c) ~~The petitioner seeks an order for access (visiting arrangements) and is content that the respondent have an order for custody of the following children on the following terms:~~

~~Name of Child~~ — ~~Terms of the Order~~

FIGURE 16.1 CONTINUED

~~The respondent~~

☐ ~~agrees~~

☐ ~~does not agree with the above terms.~~

24.(a) The following are the existing visiting arrangements (access) for the spouse who does not have the children living with him or her: The husband has reasonable access to the children.

(b) The existing visiting arrangements (access) are satisfactory/~~not satisfactory~~.

25. The order sought in paragraph 23 is in the best interests of the children for the following reasons: N/A

26. The following material changes in the circumstances of the spouses are expected to affect the children, their custody and the visiting arrangements (access) in the future: None

27. (a) The existing arrangements between the spouses for support for the children are as follows:

Amount paid	Time period (weekly, monthly, etc.)	Paid by (husband or wife)	Paid for (name of child)
$823	monthly	husband	Matthew and Courtney

(b) The existing support arrangements ☒ are being honoured ☐ are not being honoured.

~~(c) The petitioner proposes that the support arrangements for the children should be as follows:~~

~~Amount to be paid~~	~~Time period (weekly, monthly, etc.)~~	~~To be paid by (husband or wife)~~	~~To be paid by (name of child)~~

28. The educational needs of the children

☒ are being met ☐ are not being met.

OTHER COURT PROCEEDINGS

29. The following are all other court proceedings with reference to the marriage or any child of the marriage: None

FIGURE 16.1 CONCLUDED

DOMESTIC CONTRACTS AND FINANCIAL ARRANGEMENTS

30. The spouses have entered into the following domestic contracts and other written or oral financial arrangements:

Date	Nature of Contract or arrangement	Status
January 15, 2002	Separation Agreement	In effect

COLLUSION, CONDONATION AND CONNIVANCE

31. There has been no collusion in relation to this divorce proceeding.

32. There has been no condonation of or connivance at the grounds for divorce in this proceeding.

MATTERS OTHER THAN DIVORCE AND CUSTODY

33. The grounds for the relief sought in paragraph 1, other than a divorce or custody, are as follows:

TRIAL

34. The petitioner proposes that if there is a trial in this action, it be held at: Toronto

DECLARATION OF PETITIONER

35. I have read and understand this petition for divorce. The statements in it are true, to the best of my knowledge, information and belief.

Date: November , 2003

____

Jennifer Elizabeth Pitts

STATEMENT OF SOLICITOR

36. I, JoAnn Kurtz, solicitor for the petitioner, certify to this court that I have complied with the requirements of section 9 of the *Divorce Act* (Canada).

Date: November , 2003

____

JoAnn Kurtz
Barrister & Solicitor
123 College Street
Toronto, ON M5N 2X1

Tel: 416-555-1234
Fax: 416-555-1235

FIGURE 16.2 BACKSHEET FOR JENNY'S PETITION

PITTS v. PITTS

ACKNOWLEDGEMENT OF SERVICE

I, Bradley David Pitts, am the respondent named in this petition. I acknowledge receipt of a copy of this petition. My address for service of documents in this divorce proceeding is

Date ____________ Signature or respondent ________________

Signature of witness ________________

I, , served this petition personally on the respondent.

( ) The respondent completed and signed the acknowledgment of service above in my presence and I signed it as witness.

( ) The respondent declined to complete and sign the acknowledgment of service.

Signature ________________

ONTARIO
SUPERIOR COURT OF JUSTICE

Proceeding commenced at Toronto

PETITION FOR DIVORCE

JoAnn Kurtz
Barrister & Solicitor
123 College Street
Toronto, ON M5N 2X1

Tel: 416-555-1234
Fax: 416-555-1235

FIGURE 16.3 MOTION RECORD TABLE OF CONTENTS

Court File No.

ONTARIO
SUPERIOR COURT OF JUSTICE

B E T W E E N:

JENNIFER ELIZABETH PITTS

Petitioner/Wife

and

BRADLEY DAVID PITTS

Respondent/Husband

MOTION RECORD
TABLE OF CONTENTS

Page No.

JoAnn Kurtz
Barrister & Solicitor
123 College Street
Toronto, ON M5N 2X1

Tel: 416-555-1234
Fax: 416-555-1235

Solicitor for the petitioner

FIGURE 16.4 JENNY'S FORM 69Q

Court File No.

ONTARIO

SUPERIOR COURT OF JUSTICE

B E T W E E N:

JENNIFER ELIZABETH PITTS

Petitioner

Wife

and

BRADLEY DAVID PITTS

Respondent

Husband

REQUISITION

TO THE REGISTRAR

I require you to note the respondent Bradley David Pitt in default in this action on the ground that he or she has not filed an answer within the prescribed time. The petition has been filed with proof of service.

NOTICE OF MOTION

The motion is for default judgment in accordance with the petition.

The grounds for the motion are that the respondent has not filed an answer and has been noted in default.

The following documentary evidence will be relied on:

1. the petition
2. the certificate of marriage or of the registration of marriage filed in this action
3. the affidavit of the petitioner dated *(insert date)*
4. the affidavit of the respondent dated (*insert date*)

JoAnn Kurtz
Barrister & Solicitor
123 College Street
Toronto, ON M5N 2X1
Telephone: 416-555-1234

FIGURE 16.5 JENNY'S AFFIDAVIT

Court File No.

ONTARIO
SUPERIOR COURT OF JUSTICE

B E T W E E N:

JENNIFER ELIZABETH PITTS

Petitioner/Wife

and

BRADLEY DAVID PITTS

Respondent/Husband

AFFIDAVIT OF JENNIFER ELIZABETH PITTS

I, JENNIFER ELIZABETH PITTS of the City of Toronto in the Province of Ontario, the petitioner in this action, MAKE OATH AND SAY:

1. There is no possibility of the reconciliation of the spouses because I do not wish to resume cohabitation with the respondent.

2. All the information in the petition in this action is correct with the following exceptions: none.

3. The certificate of marriage was issued on June 6, 1993 at Thornhill, Ontario by Chandler Byng, a minister of the United Church of Canada. A copy of the certificate was filed with the court. I confirm that this certificate sets out the correct particulars of my marriage to the respondent.

4. The ground for divorce is adultery. I have no personal knowledge of the respondent's adultery other than what the respondent has told me.

5. There has been no agreement, conspiracy, understanding, or arrangement to which I am directly or indirectly a party for the purpose of subverting the administration of justice, fabricating or suppressing evidence, or deceiving the court.

6. I have not condoned or connived at the respondent's adultery.

FIGURE 16.5 CONCLUDED

7. The issues relating to division of property between the respondent and me have been resolved to our mutual satisfaction by a separation agreement in writing dated January 15, 2003. I therefore do not claim a division of property, and I am aware that if I do not make a claim for division of property at this time, I may be barred from making such a claim after the divorce.

8. I do not claim support from the respondent. I am aware that if I do not make a claim for support at this time, I may be barred from making such a claim after the divorce

9. I do not claim costs in this action.

10. The respondent currently resides at 15 Central Perk Place, Toronto, ON M5K 1H3. This is the address at which the respondent was served with a copy of the petition, and I believe that the respondent may be served at the same address with a copy of the divorce judgment.

SWORN before me at the)
City of Toronto in the)
Province of Ontario on)
(*month, day, year*)) ______________________

Jennifer Elizabeth Pitts

A commissioner, etc.

FIGURE 16.6 BRAD'S AFFIDAVIT

Court File No.

ONTARIO
SUPERIOR COURT OF JUSTICE

B E T W E E N:

JENNIFER ELIZABETH PITTS

Petitioner/Wife

and

BRADLEY DAVID PITTS

Respondent/Husband

AFFIDAVIT OF BRADLEY DAVID PITTS

I, BRADLEY DAVID PITTS of the City of Toronto in the Province of Ontario, the responent in this action, MAKE OATH AND SAY:

1. I am the husband of the petitioner.

2. There is no possibility of the reconciliation of the spouses because I do not wish to resume cohabitation with the petitioner.

3. All the information in the petition in this action is correct with the following exceptions: none.

4. The ground for divorce is adultery. I am aware that I am not obliged to give evidence that I have committed adultery, but I am willing to give that evidence. Since on or about September 4, 2002 I have been residing with Gwyneth Paltry as husband and wife at 15 Central Perk Place in Toronto, Ontario, and during that time have engaged in acts of sexual intercourse with her on numerous occasions.

5. There has been no agreement, conspiracy, understanding, or arrangement to which I am directly or indirectly a party for the purpose of subverting the administration of justice, fabricating or suppressing evidence, or deceiving the court.

6. The petitioner has not condoned or connived at my adultery.

FIGURE 16.6 CONCLUDED

7. The issues relating to division of property between the petitioner and me have been resolved to our mutual satisfaction by separation agreement in writing dated January 15, 2003. I therefore do not claim a division of property, and I am aware that if I do not make a claim for division of property at this time, I may be barred from making such a claim after the divorce.

8. I may be served with the divorce judgment at 15 Central Perk Place, Toronto, ON M5K 1H3.

SWORN before me at the)
City of Toronto in the)
Province of Ontario on)
(*month, day, year*)) ________________________

Bradley David Pitts

A commissioner, etc.

FIGURE 16.7 DIVORCE JUDGMENT

Court File No.

ONTARIO
SUPERIOR COURT OF JUSTICE

THE HONOURABLE)
)

BETWEEN:

JENNIFER ELIZABETH PITTS

Petitioner/Wife

and

BRADLEY DAVID PITTS

Respondent/Husband

DIVORCE JUDGMENT

THIS MOTION made by the petitioner for judgment for divorce was heard this day at Toronto. The respondent did not defend this action although properly served with the petition as appears from the affidavit of service filed.

ON READING the petition, the notice of motion for judgment, the affidavit dated (*month, day, year*) of the petitioner and the affidavit dated (*month, day, year*) of the respondent filed in support of the motion,

1. THIS COURT ORDERS AND ADJUDGES that Jennifer Elizabeth Pitts and David Bradley Pitts, who were married at Thornhill, Ontario on June 6, 1993, are divorced and that the divorce takes effect on .

____
Local Registrar

FIGURE 16.8 REQUISITION

Court File No.

ONTARIO

SUPERIOR COURT OF JUSTICE

B E T W E E N:

JENNIFER ELIZABETH PITTS

Petitioner/Wife

and

BRADLEY DAVID PITTS

Respondent/Husband

REQUISITION

TO THE REGISTRAR

- I require you to issue a certificate of divorce in the above proceedings commenced at Toronto.
- Affidavit attached.
- Copy of divorce judgment as issued attached.

I HAVE SEARCHED THE COURT RECORDS PURSUANT TO RULE 69.22(C) AND HAVE ASCERTAINED THAT THERE IS NO INDICATION THAT THE AFFIDAVIT FILED IS INCORRECT.

Date ______________________ ______________________
LOCAL REGISTRAR

JoAnn Kurtz
Barrister & Solicitor
123 College Street
Toronto, ON M5N 2X1

Tel: 416-555-1234
Fax: 416-555-1235

FIGURE 16.9 JENNY'S AFFIDAVIT

Court File No.

ONTARIO
SUPERIOR COURT OF JUSTICE

B E T W E E N:

JENNIFER ELIZABETH PITTS

Petitioner/Wife

and

BRADLEY DAVID PITTS

Respondent/Husband

AFFIDAVIT OF JENNIFER ELIZABETH PITTS

I, JENNIFER ELIZABETH PITTS of the City of Toronto in the Province of Ontario, the petitioner in this action, MAKE OATH AND SAY:

1. I am the petitioner in this proceeding.

2. No appeal from the divorce is pending.

3. No order has been made extending the time for appealing from the divorce.

SWORN before me at the)
City of Toronto in the)
Province of Ontario on)
(*month, day, year*))

____
Jennifer Elizabeth Pitts

A commissioner, etc.

FIGURE 16.10 DRAFT CERTIFICATE OF DIVORCE

Court File No.

ONTARIO

SUPERIOR COURT OF JUSTICE

CERTIFICATE OF DIVORCE

This is to certify that the marriage of

JENNIFER ELIZABETH PITTS and BRADLEY DAVID PITTS, which was solemnized at Thornhill, Ontario on June 6, 1993, was dissolved by a Judgment of this Court which became effective on (*month, day, year*).

Date ______________________________ *Local Registrar*

Local registrar

At

Toronto

CHAPTER 17

Enforcement of Orders and Agreements

In previous chapters, we looked at the law and procedures that apply when seeking various family law orders or negotiating family law settlements. In this chapter, we look at how these orders and settlements are enforced.

This chapter discusses enforcement of:

- support orders,
- support provisions in separation agreements, and
- custody orders and agreements.

ENFORCEMENT OF SUPPORT ORDERS

Historically, support orders were enforced in the same manner as any other order for the payment of money. A party who was owed money under a support order had to collect the arrears by way of garnishment or writ of seizure and sale. Over time, additional enforcement remedies were made available through the Family Court. However, enforcement of an order remained the responsibility of the party to whom support was payable under the order.

By the mid 1980s, approximately 85 percent of all family support orders were in default, and the Ontario government enacted the *Support and Custody Order Enforcement Act* to govern the enforcement of support orders. That statute was replaced in 1992 by the *Family Support Plan Act*, which was in turn replaced by the *Family Responsibility and Support Arrears Enforcement Act, 1996*, which came into force on May 12, 1997. Under these statutes, the government, rather than the party to whom support is payable, is ordinarily responsible for the collection and enforcement of support orders.[1]

1 These programs have not been completely successful. In his 2002-2003 annual report, the Ontario ombudsman noted that the Family Responsibility Office "has consistently generated the second highest number of complaints" to his office, with an increase in complaints in 2002-2003 over previous years. According to the report, $1.3 billion in support arrears were owing in Ontario as of the end of December 2002.

Overview of the Family Responsibility and Support Arrears Enforcement Act, 1996

Under the *Family Responsibility and Support Arrears Enforcement Act, 1996*, all Ontario support orders are sent to the Family Responsibility Office for collection. The party who is required to make the support payments (the payor) does not make support payments directly to the party who is entitled to support under the order (the recipient). Instead, all payments are made to the Family Responsibility Office, which in turn makes payment to the recipient. The main enforcement tool under the Act is the **support deduction order**, which allows the Family Responsibility Office to arrange for support payments to be deducted automatically from the payor's income sources, such as salaries or pensions. If support is not paid, the Family Responsibility Office has the power to take additional enforcement actions against the payor.

support deduction order
an order made under the *Family Responsibility and Support Arrears Enforcement Act, 1996*, which allows the Family Responsibility Office to arrange for support payments to be deducted automatically from the payor's income sources

The Act allows the parties to opt out of enforcement by the Family Responsibility Office, unless the court orders otherwise. Both the payor and the recipient must complete a notice of withdrawal form. If the parties opt out of the Act, the payor makes support payments directly to the recipient. If payments are not made, the recipient may enforce the support order. Parties who have opted out of the Act may opt back in by written notice signed by either the payor or the recipient.

Support Orders under the Act

Under s. 9(1) of the Act, every support order made by an Ontario court must state in its operative part that "unless the order is withdrawn from the Director's office, it shall be enforced by the Director and that amounts owing under the order shall be paid to the Director, who shall pay them to the person to whom they are owed."[2]

Under s. 10(1), every Ontario court that makes a support order must also make a support deduction order. A support deduction order allows the director to require the payor's income source to deduct support payments from the payor's income. Section 1(1) of the Act defines an income source as "an individual, corporation or other entity that owes or makes any payment, whether periodically or in a lump sum, to or on behalf of a payor."

Under s. 12(1), the clerk or registrar of the court that makes the support order is required to file a copy of the support order and the support deduction order with the Family Responsibility Office promptly after it is made. Section 11(2) requires the court, before making a support deduction order, to make inquiries of the parties about the payor's income sources. (The court fulfills this requirement by requiring the parties to complete and file a support deduction information form when an application for support is filed.)

Information for the Family Responsibility Office

When the Family Responsibility Office receives the support order and support deduction order from the court, it sends the recipient a filing package, which includes the following:

2 "Director" means the director of the Family Responsibility Office.

- *Support filing form.* This form provides information about the recipient and the court order (see figure 17.1 on page 280).
- *Registration for direct deposit form.* This form authorizes the Family Responsibility Office to deposit payments directly to the recipient's bank (see figure 17.2 on page 281).
- *Payor information form.* This form provides information about the payor (see figure 17.3 on page 282).
- *Statement of arrears form.* This form, which must be sworn to under oath, is required for the Family Responsibility Office to begin collecting any arrears owed under the order (see figure 17.4 on page 285).

The court also sends a payor information form to the payor for completion and return.

Enforcement of the Support Deduction Order

If the payor information form or support deduction information form shows the payor's employer or other income source, the Family Responsibility Office sends a support deduction notice to the income source, notifying the income source that it is obligated to deduct support payments from the payor's income and forward the deducted amounts to the Family Responsibility Office. A copy of the notice is also sent to the payor.

Under s. 22(1) of the Act, an income source that receives a support deduction notice is required to deduct from the money the income source owes to the payor the amount of support owed by the payor or any other amount that is set out in the notice, and to pay that amount to the Family Responsibility Office. Under s. 22(2), the income source must make the first payment to the Family Responsibility Office not later than the payor's first payday that falls at least 14 days after service of the notice.

Section 23 of the Act states that the maximum amount that can be deducted by an income source is 50 percent of the *net amount* owed by the income source to the payor. The "net amount" is defined in s. 23(5) as the total amount owing by the income source to the payor after deducting:

- income tax,
- Canada Pension Plan,
- employment insurance,
- union dues, and
- such other deductions as may be prescribed by the regulations.

Will and Grace separated, and Will obtained an order granting him custody of their son Jack, child support in the amount of $625 per month, and spousal support in the amount of $500 per month, for total support payable of $1,125 per month.

Grace teaches interior design at Ontario University. Her salary is $78,000 per year, and she is paid $3,000 every two weeks. The following amounts are deducted from her salary:

- Income tax $714.97
- Canada Pension Plan $144.35
- Employment insurance $63.91
- Union dues $9.00
- Parking $18.00
- Pension $176.94
- Payroll savings plan $200.00

Grace's total deductions are $1,327.17, leaving her with take-home pay of $1,672.83.

The Family Responsibility Office serves Ontario University with a support deduction notice. Ontario University must now deduct from Grace's pay and send to the Family Responsibility Office the amount of the support payment up to a maximum of 50 percent of her net amount.

Under the Act, not all of Grace's deductions are used in calculating her net amount: only income tax, Canada Pension Plan, employment insurance, and union dues (totalling $932.23) are deducted. Accordingly, while Grace's take-home pay is only $1,672.83, her net amount under the Act is $2,067.77, 50 percent of which is $1,033.89.

Accordingly, Ontario University is required to deduct $1,033.89 from Grace's first paycheque of each month and send it to the Family Responsibility Office. The university must deduct the balance of $91.11 in support from her second paycheque in the month. No further deductions are required until the following month.

Until the income source starts to make the deductions, the payor is required to make support payments directly to the Family Responsibility Office pursuant to s. 22(3) of the Act.

Under s. 25, if there is an interruption of payments by an income source to the payor — for example, if the payor is fired or laid off — both the income source and the payor must notify the Family Responsibility Office in writing within 10 days. If payments are resumed, both the payor and the income source must notify the Family Responsibility office within 10 days. If the payor instead becomes entitled to income from another income source, the payor must notify the director of the new income source within 10 days.

Under s. 26(7), an income source who fails to make the necessary deductions after receiving a support deduction notice is liable to pay to the Family Responsibility Office the amount it should have deducted. It may also be guilty of an offence pursuant to s. 51(2).

A payor who believes that too much money is being deducted under the support deduction order because of a mistake of fact may bring a motion to the court under s. 27(1). The support deduction order itself can be varied only by order of the court, and then only if the support order to which it relates is varied pursuant to s. 27(7). The court also has the discretion to suspend the operation of a support deduction order, but only if:

- it would be unconscionable, having regard to all of the circumstances, to have the support obligation paid by way of support deduction; or
- the parties to the support order agree that they do not want support deduction to apply, and the court requires the payor to post security (see s. 28).

Other Enforcement Procedures

The director of the Family Responsibility Office has the duty to enforce support orders pursuant to s. 5(1) and, pursuant to s. 6(1), the power to use, in addition to the support deduction order, any other enforcement mechanism whether or not expressly provided for in the Act.

The following additional enforcement mechanisms are expressly provided for in the Act when a support order filed with the Family Responsibility Office is in default:

- *Suspension of driver's licence.* The director may suspend the payor's driver's licence unless, within 30 days of receiving a first notice of a driver's licence suspension, the payor
    - ❑ makes an arrangement satisfactory to the director to comply with the order and pay the arrears,
    - ❑ obtains an order that the director refrain from directing suspension of the licence and the payor applies to vary the terms of the support order, or
    - ❑ pays all the arrears (see ss. 34–37).
- *Filing of financial statement.* The director may request that the payor complete and file a financial statement with proof of income (see s. 40).
- *Default hearing.* The director may require the payor to deliver a financial statement and proof of income, and to appear before the court to explain his or her default. The court has the power to make a variety of orders — for example, that the payor make payments toward the arrears or be jailed for up to 90 days (see s. 41).
- *Registration of the support order against land.* The director may register the support order in the proper land registry office as a charge against the payor's land that can be enforced by sale of the property (see s. 42).
- *Registration under the* Personal Property Security Act. The director can register the arrears under the *Personal Property Security Act* as a lien or charge on any interest in all the personal property that the payor owns or holds in Ontario at the time of registration, or acquires afterward (see s. 43).
- *Garnishment of joint accounts.* The director may issue a notice of garnishment to a bank or other financial institution to seize up to 50 percent of the funds held by the payor in a joint bank account (see s. 45).
- *Seizing lottery winnings.* The Ontario Lottery Corporation is required to deduct arrears from any lottery prize of $1,000 or more (see s. 46).
- *Reporting to consumer reporting agencies.* The director may report the payor's default to credit-rating bureaus (see s. 47).

- *Restraining order*. The court may make an order restraining the disposition or wasting of assets that my hinder or defeat the enforcement of a support order or support deduction order (see s. 48).
- *Arrest of absconding payor*. The court may issue a warrant for a payor's arrest to be brought before the court, if the court is satisfied that the payor is about to leave Ontario and there are reasonable grounds to believe that the payor intends to evade payment of the arrears (see s. 49).

When a support order filed with the Family Responsibility Office is in default, the director may also use the following enforcement mechanisms, which are not expressly provided for in the Act:

- *Writ of seizure and sale*. The director may issue and file a writ of seizure and sale for arrears under rule 28 of the *Family Law Rules*.
- *Garnishment*. The director may use the garnishment procedure under rule 29 of the *Family Law Rules* to intercept money owing to the payor, such as wages, pensions, bank accounts, rents, and funds from federal sources, such as income tax refunds, employment insurance benefits, or GST refunds.
- *Reporting payor to private collection agencies*. If no payment has been received in over six months, the director may refer a case to its enhanced collection agency project, under which a private collection agent attempts to collect the arrears.
- *Suspend a passport or other federal licence*. The director may ask the federal government to suspend a passport or other federal licence, such as a pilot's licence.

Enforcement Remedies Available to the Individual Recipient

If the parties withdraw their support order from the Family Responsibility Office, it is up to the recipient to take steps to enforce the order.

The following remedies are available to a support recipient under the Act:

- registration of the support order against land under s. 42,
- registration under the *Personal Property Security Act* pursuant to s. 43,
- a restraining order under s. 48, and
- a warrant for the arrest of an absconding payor under s. 49.

The following remedies are available to a support recipient under the *Family Law Rules*:

- a request for a financial statement under rule 27(1),
- a request for a statement of income from an income source of the payor under rule 27(7),
- a financial examination of the payor under rule 27(11),
- a writ of seizure and sale under rule 28,
- garnishment under rule 29,

- a default hearing under rule 30, and
- the appointment of a receiver under rule 26(3).

ENFORCEMENT OF SUPPORT PROVISIONS IN DOMESTIC CONTRACTS

The support provisions in a domestic contract can be enforced in the same way as any other contract: by suing for breach of contract if payments are not made.

In addition, under s. 35 of the *Family Law Act*, either party to a domestic contract may file the contract with the court. The support provision in the contract may then be enforced as if it were an order of the court.

ENFORCEMENT OF CUSTODY ORDERS AND AGREEMENTS

A custody order or agreement requires the ongoing cooperation of the parties whether they share custody or one party has custody and the other access. Underlying the order is an assumption that custodial parents will make children available to access parents, and that access parents will return children to the custodial parents at the end of their access periods. However, sometimes that does not happen, in which case there are a number of enforcement remedies available.

Contempt Proceedings

An order, other than an order for payment of money, may be enforced by contempt proceedings. Contempt involves a willful refusal to comply with the provisions of the order.

In the Family Court of the Superior Court of Justice and the Ontario Court of Justice, contempt proceedings are governed by rule 31 of the *Family Law Rules*.[3] A notice of contempt motion must be served by special service. If the court finds a person in contempt, it may order, among other things, that the person

- be imprisoned,
- pay a fine, and
- pay an amount to another party as a penalty.

Under the Children's Law Reform Act

Under s. 36 of the *Children's Law Reform Act*, a court may direct the sheriff or the police force to locate, apprehend, and deliver a child to the person lawfully entitled to custody or access, if the court is satisfied that someone is unlawfully withholding the child from that person, or is likely to remove the child from Ontario contrary to a separation agreement or court order.

3 In the Superior Court of Justice, contempt proceedings are governed by rule 60 of the *Rules of Civil Procedure*.

Section 37 gives the court the power to make orders with respect to property, support payments, and passports in order to prevent a party from unlawfully removing a child from Ontario. The court may order the party to

- transfer property to a trustee;
- make support payments to a trustee;
- post a bond; or
- deliver the party's passport, the child's passport, and any other travel documents to the court.

Section 38 gives the Ontario Court of Justice powers to punish willful contempt of custody or access orders by fine or imprisonment or both.

Under s. 39, the court may make orders requiring any person or public body to provide the court with particulars of the address of the respondent, where the court is of the opinion that the information is necessary for the purpose of bringing a custody or access application or enforcing a custody or access order.

Under the Divorce Act

Pursuant to s. 20 of the *Divorce Act*, a custody or access order has legal effect throughout Canada, and may be registered in any court in a province and enforced as an order of that court.

Under the Criminal Code

Abduction of a child by his or her parent or guardian is a crime under ss. 282 and 283 of the *Criminal Code*. It is an offence for a parent or guardian to take or keep a child with the intent to deprive another parent of the child, whether or not there is a custody order or agreement.

It is a defence to the charge if the parent or guardian takes the child with the consent of the other parent or guardian or takes or keeps the child in order to protect the child from imminent danger or harm.

REFERENCES

Children's Law Reform Act, RSO 1990, c. C.12.
Criminal Code, RSC 1985, c. C-46.
Divorce Act, RSC 1985, c. 3 (2d Supp.).
Family Law Act, RSO 1990, c. F.3.
Family Law Rules, O. Reg. 114/99.
Family Responsibility and Support Arrears Enforcement Act, 1996, SO 1996, c. 31.
Personal Property Security Act, RSO 1990, c. P.10.
Rules of Civil Procedure, RRO 1990, reg. 194.

REVIEW QUESTIONS

1. What statute governs the enforcement of support orders in Ontario?
2. To whom is a support payor required to make support payments?
3. How and when may the parties to a support order opt out of enforcement by the Family Responsibility Office?
4. What must every support order made by an Ontario court include?
5. What must an Ontario court do when making a support order?
6. What action must be taken by the clerk or registrar of the court that makes a support order?
7. What is included in the Family Responsibility Office filing package?
8. What is a support deduction notice?
9. What is the responsibility of an income source that receives a support deduction notice?
10. What is the maximum amount that can be deducted by an income source?
11. What must be done if there is an interruption of payments by an income source to the payor? When? By whom?
12. What is the liability of an income source who fails to make the necessary deductions after receiving a support deduction notice?
13. What action may a payor take if he or she believes that too much money is being deducted under a support deduction order because of a mistake in fact?
14. In addition to the support deduction notice, what enforcement mechanisms are available to the Family Responsibility Office?
15. What enforcement mechanisms are available to an individual support recipient?
16. How may the support provisions in a domestic contract be enforced?
17. What are contempt proceedings? How are they used to enforce custody orders?
18. What provisions for the enforcement of custody orders and agreements are found in the *Children's Law Reform Act*?
19. How may the *Criminal Code* be used to enforce a custody order?

FIGURE 17.1 SUPPORT FILING FORM

Ministry of Community, Family and Children's Services

Family Responsibility Office
P.O. Box 220
Downsview ON M3M A3A

Support Filing Form

Language Preferred: ☐ English ☐ French

Case Number		
Last Name	First Name	Middle Initial
Address: Street Number and Name / Apartment Number	Lot, Concession or Township	
City / Town	Province	Postal Code
Home Telephone Number Area code ( ) ________	Date of Birth: Day / Month / Year ____ / ____ / ____	Social Insurance Number ______ - ______ - ______
Employer:		
Work Telephone Number Area code ( ) ________		
Last Name of Person Owing Support	First Name	Middle Initial

My Support Provisions are contained in a *(check one)*

☐ Court Order ☐ Separation Agreement ☐ Marriage Contract

☐ Cohabitation Agreement ☐ Paternity Agreement Date ______ / ______ / ______
Day Month Year

(Agreement / Contract must be filed with the Ontario Court of Justice or Superior Court of Justice Family Court)

Are you claiming spousal support for yourself? ☐ Yes ☐ No

Are you claiming support for the child(ren) named in the order / agreement? ☐ Yes ☐ No

If yes, list the name(s) of the child(ren) you are claiming support for *(use additional sheet if required)*

Last Name, First Name, Initial(s)	**Date of Birth Day / Month / Year**	**Sex**
		☐ Male ☐ Female
		☐ Male ☐ Female
		☐ Male ☐ Female
		☐ Male ☐ Female

Do you currently receive or have you applied for ☐ Family Benefits ☐ General Welfare ☐ No

Do you have another case filed with the Family Responsibility Office? If yes, please provide the name that the case is filed under and the case number.

Name case is filed under	**Case Number**

You must sign this form in order for the Family Responsibility Office to enforce the support terms of your order/ agreement / contract.

Signature ____________ Date ____________

FRO-005E (12/2002)

Page 2 of 10

FIGURE 17.2 REGISTRATION FOR DIRECT DEPOSIT FORM

Ministry of Community, Family and Children's Services

Family Responsibility Office
P.O. Box 220
Downsview ON M3M A3A

Registration for Direct Deposit

Case Number

When the Family Responsibility Office receives a support payment that is owed to you, these funds will be sent by DIRECT DEPOSIT to the bank of your choice. To ensure that you receive your money quickly, the following information must be provided. Incorrect information could result in your payment being sent to the wrong account.

Instructions

If you wish to have your support payments deposited into your **CHEQUING ACCOUNT, COMPLETE SECTION 'A'** and **ATTACH A BLANK PERSONAL CHEQUE** with **'VOID'** written on it.

If, however, you wish to designate your **SAVINGS ACCOUNT**, complete **SECTION "A"**, take this form to your bank and ask them to complete **SECTION "B"** – Banking Data.

DO NOT FORGET TO SIGN THE BOTTOM OF THE FORM AUTHORIZING THE DIRECT DEPOSIT SERVICE

Important notes about changing bank accounts

If your account number changed, or if you wish to have your support payments deposited to a different account, you must complete a new DIRECT DEPOSIT FORM and return it to the Family Responsibility Office. After the changes have been processed, your support payments will be sent to your new account. **DO NOT CLOSE YOUR OLD ACCOUNT UNTIL YOU RECEIVE YOUR FIRST PAYMENT TO THE NEW ACCOUNT.**

SECTION "A" – Support Recipient Information **PLEASE PRINT CLEARLY**

Last Name	First Name	Middle Initial
Address: Street Number and Name / Apartment Number	Lot, Concession or Township	
City / Town	Province	Postal Code
Telephone number where you can be reached during the day Area Code ( )		

NOTE: If attaching a VOID cheque, please tape the cheque over the Banking Information in Section "B"

SECTION "B" – Banking Information *To be completed by your bank if you are not attaching a VOID Cheque*

Branch Number	Institution Number	Account number
Name of Financial Institution		Place Bank Stamp
Branch		
Branch Address		
Bank Official's Signature and Position		Date

Until further notice, I authorize the direct deposit of my support payments to the account and financial institution designated in this form.

Signature of Recipient

Date

FRO-005E (12/2002)

Page 3 of 10

FIGURE 17.3 PAYOR INFORMATION FORM

Ministry of Community, Family and Children's Services

Family Responsibility Office
P.O. Box 220
Downsview ON M3M A3A

Payor Information Form
Information for Recipient to Complete

Page 1 of 3

Case Number

Payor's Last Name	Payor's First Name	Initial	☐ Male ☐ Female

Payor's Address: Street Number and Name / Apartment Number	Lot, Concession or Township

City / Town	Province	Postal Code

Home Telephone Number
Area code (   ) ______________

Payor's Previous Address: Street Number and Name / Apartment Number	Lot, Concession or Township

City / Town	Province	Postal Code

Payor lived at this address
from ______ / ______ / ______ to ______ / ______ / ______
Day Month Year Day Month Year

Does Payor use any other name(s)? If so, what name(s)?

Does the Payor have a Driver's Licence? ☐ Yes ☐ No ☐ Unknown	If Payor has Driver's Licence, Licence Number______________ Prov. __________

Social Insurance Number *(This may be found on payor's tax return or your tax return* ________ - ________ - ________	Payor's Date of Birth: Day / Month / Year _____ / _____ / _____
Payor's mother's name before marriage	Payor's Health Insurance Number

Payor's Marital Status:
☐ Single ☐ Married ☐ Divorced ☐ Separated ☐ Cohabiting

Income Information

Indicate if Payor self-employed:
☐ Yes ☐ No If yes, give details of employment________________________
(e.g. Sole Owner, Partner, Family Business)

Payor's Current Employer / Income Source

Payor's Position	Date Started: Day / Month / Year _____ / _____ / _____

Employer's Address: Street Number and Name	Unit/Suite Number

City / Town	Province	Postal Code

Employer's Telephone Number
Area code (   )

Payor's Previous Employer / Income Source

Payor's Position	Date Started: Day / Month / Year _____ / _____ / _____

Employer's Address: Street Number and Name	Unit/Suite Number

City / Town	Province	Postal Code

Employer's Telephone Number
Area code (   )

FRO-005E (12/2002) Page 4 of 10

FIGURE 17.3 CONTINUED

Payor Information Form

Information for Recipient to Complete

Page 2 of 3

Case Number

Property Information

Does the payor own / lease / rent a car, truck, boat, snowmobile, farm equipment or recreational vehicle?

1.	Vehicle Type	Model	Year	Colour	
	Licence Plate number	Serial number	☐ Rent	☐ Own	☐Lease
2.	Vehicle Type	Model	Year	Colour	
	Licence Plate number	Serial number	☐ Rent	☐ Own	☐Lease

Does the Payor own *(alone or jointly with another person / company)* a house, cottage, farm, land, apartment building, office or investment property either in or outside of Canada?

1.	Type of Property		
	Address: Street Number and Name / Apartment Number		Lot, Concession or Township
	City / Town	Province	Postal Code
	What is / are the name(s) of the person(s) / company who also own this property?		
2.	Type of Property		
	Address: Street Number and Name / Apartment Number		Lot, Concession or Township
	City / Town	Province	Postal Code
	What is / are the name(s) of the person(s) / company who also own this property?		

Please attach additional information on a separate sheet of paper.

Other Information

Do you have the name and addresses of any of the payor's relatives or friends who may help us locate the payor if required?

1.	Name	Relationship to Payor
	Address: Street Number & Name / Apartment Number / City / Province / Postal Code	Telephone Number Area code ( )
2.	Name	Relationship to Payor
	Address: Street Number & Name / Apartment Number / City / Province / Postal Code	Telephone Number Area code ( )

Does the Payor belong to any professional or community groups, associations, clubs, unions that may help us to locate the payor, if required? *(Provide name of organization, address and telephone number if possible.)*

FRO-005E (12/2002) Page 5 of 10

FIGURE 17.3 CONCLUDED

Payor Information Form

Information for Recipient to Complete

Page 3 of 3

Case Number

Does the Payor have other sources of income? *(e.g. Workers' Compensation, Employment Insurance Benefit, Disability Insurance, Pension Income).* If YES, provide as much detail as possible, including claim numbers if known.

Please attach additional information *(e.g. Business cards, business contacts), on separate sheet of paper.*

Does Payor frequently travel outside of Canada?

If yes, for ☐ Business ☐ Pleasure Passport Number ______________________

Does Payor have any Federal Licences? *(e.g. Pilot Licence, Transport Licence)*

Type of Licence: ______________________ Licence Number ______________________

Physical Description of Payor *(This information is required if we need to serve the Payor with Court Documents.)*
If possible, include a current photograph of the payor. Please attach the photograph to a separate sheet of paper and write the payor's name, date the photograph was taken and your case number.

Height	Weight	Build	Eye Colour	Eye Glasses ☐ Yes ☐ No

Hair Colour	Skin Colour	Distinguishing Marks or Features (eg. Tattoos)

Financial Information

Does the Payor have any Credit Cards?

Card Type	Account Number
Card Type	Account Number

Where does the Payor Bank?

1.	Name of Financial Institution	Account Number
	Address	
2.	Name of Financial Institution	Account Number
	Address	

List any other assets you are aware of. *(e.g. Stocks, Bonds, Term Deposits, Life Insurance, Investment Certificates, RRSP)*
If you require more space, please attach a separate sheet of paper

Type of Asset	Location	Account / Policy / Serial Number

FRO-005E (12/2002) Page 6 of 10

FIGURE 17.4 STATEMENT OF ARREARS FORM

Ministry of Community, Family and Children's Services

Family Responsibility Office
P.O. Box 220
Downsview ON M3M A3A

Statement of Arrears

Case Number

Support Recipient's Name
Payor's Name

1. I am the support recipient under the following:

Order

Date of Order ________ Court ________ Court File Number ________

Agreement filed with the Court

Date of Agreement ________ Court Agreement Filed With ________ Court File Number ________

2. The following amounts due under the order / agreement have not been paid. *(If you need more space, complete "Schedule A".)*

Check if applicable. ☐ See "Schedule A" attached

Date Payment Due Day/Month/Year	Amount Due	Date Paid Day/Month/Year	Amount Paid	Arrears

If you are entitled to interest on your support, *you must calculate the interest amount.* **Attach a copy of your calculations.**

If you are entitled to a COLA adjustment to your support, *you must include the adjustment in the amount due.* **Attach a copy of your calculations.**

Total Arrears $ ________ **(a)**

Total Interest to date (if any) $ ________ **(b)** **Applicable interest rate used** ________ %

My arrears as at ________ (Date) TOTAL $ ________ **(c)** **(Add A and B)**

You must sign this form in the presence of a lawyer, justice of the peace, notary public or commissioner for taking affidavits

Sworn before me at the ________ of ________ in

the ________ of ________

this ________ day of ________ , 20 ________

________ Signature of a commissioner, etc.

________ Signature of Support Recipient

FIGURE 17.4 CONCLUDED

Ministry of Community, Family and Children's Services

Family Responsibility Office
P.O. Box 220
Downsview ON M3M A3A

Schedule "A"
To Statement of Arrears Form

Case Number

Date Payment Due Day/Month/Year	Amount Due	Date Paid Day/Month/Year	Amount Paid	Arrears

Enter amount onto Statement of Arrears Form.

FRO-005E (12/2002) Page 10 of 10

CHAPTER 18

Variation and Indexing of Orders

A custody or access order, whether made under the *Divorce Act* or the *Family Law Act*, is never final. It is always subject to variation if the circumstances of the parties and/or the children change. Orders for spousal[1] and child support under both the *Divorce Act* and the *Family Law Act* may also be varied by the court if there has been a change in circumstances of any of the parties. In addition, orders for spousal support may be indexed to the cost of living.

In this chapter we will look at:

- variation of custody orders,
- variation of spousal support orders,
- variation of child support orders,
- procedure on a variation application, and
- indexing of spousal support.

VARIATION OF CUSTODY ORDERS

Custody orders under both the *Divorce Act* and the *Family Law Act* may be varied. A custody order made under the *Divorce Act* must be varied under the *Divorce Act*. A custody order made under the *Family Law Act* must be varied under the *Family Law Act*.

Variation Under the Divorce Act

Variation of custody (and support) orders is dealt with under s. 17 of the Act.

A variation proceeding may be commenced by either or both former spouses or by any other person, although a person other than a former spouse requires leave of the court. The court has the power to vary, rescind, or suspend a custody order or any provision thereof. The court may include in a variation order any provisions that could be included in a custody order.

1 In this chapter, the term "spouse" and related terms are used with respect to support payments under both the *Divorce Act* and the *Family Law Act*. When referring to support payments under the *Divorce Act*, the term includes only a husband or wife in a valid marriage. When referring to support payments under the *Family Law Act*, the term may also include parties of the same or opposite sex who are cohabiting.

Section 17(5) sets out the factors the court is to consider in a variation proceeding. It states that before the court makes a variation order, the court must satisfy itself that there has been a change in the condition, means, needs, or other circumstances of the child that occurred since the making of the custody order. The section also states that, in making the variation order, the court must take into consideration only the best interests of the child as determined by reference to that change.

As when making a custody order, the court is not to take into consideration the past conduct of any person unless the conduct is relevant to the ability of that person to act as a parent of the child. The court is also directed to give effect to the principle that a child of the marriage should have as much contact with each former spouse as is consistent with the best interests of the child. For that purpose, where the variation order would grant custody of the child to a person who does not currently have custody, the court is directed to take into consideration the willingness of the person seeking custody to facilitate that contact.

Variation Under the Children's Law Reform Act

Variation of custody orders is dealt with under s. 29. According to that section, a court must not make an order that varies a custody or access order unless there has been a material change in circumstances that affects or is likely to affect the best interests of the child.

Principles Applied in Varying Custody Orders

While the language of the statutes differs, a court will apply the same principles whether a case is decided under the *Children's Law Reform Act* or the *Divorce Act*.

Under either statute, the party applying to vary the original order must show that there has been a *material change* in circumstances since the original order was made that affects the best interests of the child. If this threshold test is met, then the court will consider whether a variation in the existing order is necessary to meet the best interests of the child under these changed circumstances.

A variation application is not an appeal. It is not designed to correct an error made by the trial judge. Rather, it is assumed that the original order was correctly made.

VARIATION OF SPOUSAL SUPPORT ORDERS

Support orders under both the *Divorce Act* and the *Family Law Act* may be varied. Under s. 17(4.1) of the *Divorce Act*, the court must be satisfied that there has been a change in the condition, means, needs, or other circumstances of either former spouse since the making of the spousal support order. Under s. 37(2) of the *Family Law Act*, the court must be satisfied that there has been a material change in the dependant's or respondent's circumstances, or that evidence not available on the previous hearing has become available.

VARIATION OF CHILD SUPPORT ORDERS

Both the *Divorce Act* (in s.17.1) and the *Family Law Act* (in s. 37) provide for variation of child support orders in the event of a change of circumstances as provided for in the *Child Support Guidelines*.

Section 14 of the guidelines sets out the changes in circumstances that would justify a variation:

- if child support was previously determined in accordance with the tables, any change in circumstances that would result in a different child support order; or
- if child support was previously determined without reference to the tables, any change in the condition, means, needs, or other circumstances of either parent or spouse or of any child who is entitled to support.

PROCEDURE ON A VARIATION APPLICATION

A variation application in the Ontario Superior Court of Justice Family Court is governed by the *Family Law Rules*. A variation application in the Superior Court of Justice is governed by the *Rules of Civil Procedure*.

Variation Under the Family Law Rules

Rule 15 governs variation proceedings, which are called "motions to change an order or agreement."

A variation proceeding is brought by way of a motion in the proceeding in which the order was made. Under rule 15(1), notice of motion must be served by special service at least 30 days before the motion is to be heard if the party to be served resides in Canada or the United States, and 60 days if the party resides elsewhere.

According to rule 15(3), rule 5 governs where the case is to be started as if the motion were a new case.

Rule 15(7) sets out requirements for the contents of an affidavit in support of a motion to vary. The affidavit must set out:

- the place where the parties and the children ordinarily reside;
- the name and birth date of each child to whom a proposed change relates;
- whether a party has married or begun to live with another person;
- details of current custody and access arrangements;
- details of current support arrangements, including details of any unpaid support;
- details of the variation asked for and of the changed circumstances that are grounds for the variation;
- details of any efforts made to mediate or settle the issues and of any assessment report on custody or access;
- in a motion to vary child support, the income and financial information required under s. 21 of the *Child Support Guidelines*; and
- in a motion to vary child support to an amount different from the *Child Support Guidelines* table amount, evidence to satisfy the court that it should make the order asked for.

If the existing order is in the continuing record, the affidavit should say so. If not, a copy of the existing order must be attached to the affidavit as an exhibit.

Under rule 15(13), the court has the power to direct a trial if it is of the opinion that the issues cannot be properly dealt with on a motion.

Variation Under the Rules of Civil Procedure

Rule 69.24 governs variation of a final custody order or spousal support order made under the *Divorce Act*. Rule 69.24.1 governs variation of a child support order. A proceeding to vary a final order is brought by way of a notice of application. Rule 70.08.1 governs variation of a final custody order under the *Children's Law Reform Act* and a final spousal support order under the *Family Law Act*. Rule 70.08.2 governs variation of a final child support order under the *Family Law Act*. These rules state that the relevant provisions of rule 69 apply.

INDEXING SPOUSAL SUPPORT

The amount of spousal support, whether set by order or agreement, is determined on the basis of the recipient's need and the payor's ability to pay. The need of the recipient is calculated on the basis of his or her expenses at the time the order is made or agreement entered into.

If the cost of living goes up after the support amount is set, the recipient's expenses will also go up. Over time, the support payment will no longer be adequate to meet the needs of the recipient.

Historically, a recipient whose support payments became inadequate as a result of inflation would have to bring a proceeding to vary the support order or separation agreement based on a change in circumstances. These applications were expensive, and the recipient would have to wait until the inflationary change was large enough to constitute a "material" change in circumstances.

Now, courts have the power to order that spousal support orders be "indexed" to changes in the cost of living so that they rise automatically. It is also customary for support payments in separation agreements to be similarly indexed. The clauses that provide for indexing are called "cost of living adjustment (COLA) clauses."

Measuring Inflation

The government of Canada, through its central statistical agency, Statistics Canada, maintains statistics to track changes in consumer prices and thus measure changes in the cost of living and the rate of inflation.

The consumer price index (CPI) is an indicator of the changes in consumer prices. It is obtained by comparing, over a period of time, the cost of selected goods and services. This "basket" of goods is priced at 100 as at a specific date, which acts as the time base or base period of the index. The current CPI time base or base period is 1986. It is standard practice when quoting an index level to note the base year.

The same basket of goods is then priced every month, and the increase (or, rarely, decrease) in prices compared with that base period cost of 100 can be measured.

If the cost of the basket of goods in the first year after the base year is 125, the increase is 25 points. The percentage change over the base year is

$$\frac{25}{100} = 25\%$$

If the cost of the basket of goods goes up to 150 in the second year, the percentage change for that year over the base year is another 25/100 or another 25 percent. The total change in the two years since the base year is 50 points, for a total percentage change from the base year of 50 percent.

What is the percentage change between the prices at the end of the first year and the end of the second year?

Absolute change in CPI:

CPI year 2 of 150 – CPI year 1 of 125 = 25 points

Percentage change in CPI:

$$\frac{\text{Absolute change 25}}{\text{CPI year 1 of 125}} = 20\%$$

Statistics Canada maintains a number of different consumer price indexes for different items and locations. For example, there is a CPI for all items for Canada, and a CPI for all items for the City of Toronto. The CPI is published monthly and is available at the Statistics Canada Web site at www.statcan.ca.

Power To Index Spousal Support

Spousal support may be indexed in the following circumstances:

- *A new order under the* Family Law Act. Section 34(5) of the Act gives the court the power to order that periodic support payments be indexed to the cost of living at the time the support order is made.
- *An existing order under the* Family Law Act. Sections 38 and 39 of the Act give the court the power to index a support order that was not indexed at the time it was made. Indexing in this situation is not automatic. Pursuant to s. 38(3), the court has discretion to refuse to index the support payments, although the presumption is in favour of indexing.
- *Orders under the* Divorce Act. While the *Divorce Act* does not contain a provision specifically authorizing indexing, the Supreme Court of Canada in *Richardson v. Richardson* held that the court has power to order indexing under the Act.
- *New domestic contracts.* The parties may agree in a domestic contract to index support payments. If they do so, the parties may fashion their own rules for indexing, which are binding on both parties.
- *Existing domestic contracts.* A domestic contract that is silent on the issue of indexing may be filed with the Ontario Court of Justice under s. 35 of the *Family Law Act*. It is then treated as if it were a court order for the purposes

of indexing under s. 38 of the Act. A domestic contract that bars variation of spousal support generally, or indexing specifically, may not be indexed.[2]

How Indexing Works

All indexing formulas, whether in support orders or separation agreements, have the following ingredients in common:

1. *Payment change date.* This is the date on which the amount of the payment changes. The change occurs at regular intervals, usually annually.
2. *Indexing factor.* This is a method of measuring the change in the cost of living together with a formula for increasing payments in proportion to increases in the cost of living.

The CPI is the most commonly used indexing factor. Another common way to index support payments is to tie them to increases in the payor's income.

Indexing Under the Family Law Act

In order to determine the payment change date and the indexing factor, it is necessary to follow the instructions in ss. 34(5) and (6) of the Act, which read as follows:

> (5) In an order made under clause (1)(a), other than an order for the support of a child, the court may provide that the amount payable shall be increased annually on the order's anniversary date by the indexing factor, as defined in subsection (6), for November of the previous year.
>
> (6) The indexing factor for a given month is the percentage change in the Consumer Price Index for Canada for prices of all items since the same month of the previous year, as published by Statistics Canada.

Section 34(5) tells us that the payment change date is the "anniversary date" of the order. The relevant date is the day the order was made as indicated on the face of the order.

Section 34(6) tells us that the indexing factor is the change in the CPI over a one-year period *ending* in the month of November in the year before the anniversary date.

Assume that a court made an order on April 7, 2002, with support payments of $1,000. The CPI All Items — Canada for November 2001 is 120, and for November 2002 is 125. Calculate the increase in support in 2003.

Payment change date
The anniversary of the order: April 7, 2003

Indexing factor
Section 34(5) directs us to use the indexing factor for "November of the previous year" — in other words, November of the year before the payment change date, or November 2002.

2 See s. 35(4).

The indexing factor for November 2002 is defined in s. 34(6) to be the percentage change in the CPI "since the same month of the previous year," or November 2001. Accordingly, we are directed to measure the percentage change in the CPI between November 2001 and November 2002.

To calculate the increase in CPI and the increase in the amount payable, use the following formula:

$$\frac{\text{CPI end of period}}{\text{CPI beginning of period}} \times \text{Current support amount} = \text{New support amount}$$

$$\frac{\text{CPI November 2002 of 125}}{\text{CPI November 2001 of 120}} \times \$1{,}000 = \$1{,}041.67$$

$1,041.67 is the increased amount of support to be paid on the first payment *after* the anniversary date. Note that payment in the increased amount is not necessarily due on the anniversary date, since the date on which payment is due is not necessarily the day on which the order was made.

For the next anniversary date, the increase would be calculated as follows, assuming that CPI All Items — Canada for November 2003 is 131.

Payment change date
The next anniversary of the order: April 7, 2004

Indexing factor
Use the indexing factor for November 2003:

$$\frac{\text{CPI November 2003 of 131}}{\text{CPI November 2002 of 125}} \times \$1{,}041.67 = \$1{,}091.67$$

Indexing Under Domestic Contracts

It is not unusual for domestic contracts to include a provision for the indexing of spousal support. An example of an indexing clause is as follows (assuming that the husband is paying spousal support and the agreement was signed in 2002):

15.0 COST OF LIVING CLAUSE

15.1 (a) The amount of spousal support payable pursuant to paragraph __ of this agreement will change at one-year intervals in accordance with the All Items Consumer Price Index for the City of Toronto with base year 1986 equal to 100, as provided by Statistics Canada.

(b) This change in amount will occur on the first day of June of each year in which support is payable, starting with June 1, 2003 [*the next following year*]. This change will be equal to 100 percent of the percentage change in the Consumer Price Index:

(i) for the June 2003 change, in the period from the month of execution of this agreement to April 2003 and

(ii) for each subsequent change, in the 12-month period from the previous April to the April of the year of the current change.

15.2(a) In case of an increase in support payments, if in any such year the husband's income for the December to December period before the proposed increase in support payments does not increase at the same or greater percentage than the percentage increase in the cost of living calculated in paragraph 15.1, at the husband's option the increase in support payments will be equal to this percentage increase in the husband's income, so calculated.

(b) For the purpose of paragraph 15.2(a), income means income as defined in the *Income Tax Act*, without reduction of employment expenses or gross up for dividends.

(c) If the husband chooses to rely on paragraph 15.2(a), he will, no later than May 1, produce to the wife a copy of his income tax return for the two immediately preceding years, which will form the basis of the calculation of his percentage increase in income.

This indexing clause gives the payor husband the choice of two methods for calculating the increase in payments, and the right to choose the method most advantageous to him.

The first method uses the CPI[3] to determine the indexing factor and a payment change date chosen by the parties (although it may not be the anniversary of the date on which the contract was signed).

In the first year, the indexing factor requires measurement of the CPI from the date of execution of the agreement to April of the year on which the first change occurs, and thereafter from April to April. This provision "catches" increases in the cost of living from the time the agreement is signed.

June 1 is picked as the payment change date even though that is not the anniversary date of the agreement. This date gives the parties enough time to obtain the CPI figures for the April to April interval used to determine the indexing factor. The date also allows the payor to file his income tax return (due by April 30), calculate the increase in taxable income, and decide whether he wants to pay increased support based on the increase in income or the increase in CPI.

Here's how the first CPI increase would be calculated:

Assume that the contract was executed on March 1, 2002, the payment is $1,000 per month, and the CPI for March 2002 is 120 and for April 2003 is 127.

Payment change date
As specified in the agreement: June 1, 2003

Indexing factor
The change in CPI between March 2002 and April 2003:

3 Note that the agreement uses the CPI for Toronto, not the CPI for Canada, as is used in the *Family Law Act*. Remember to use the appropriate CPI figures when doing your indexing calculations.

$$\frac{\text{CPI April 2003 of 127}}{\text{CPI March 2003 of 120}} \times \$1{,}000 = \$1{,}058.33$$

As of June 1, 2003 the payments will increase from $1,000 to $1,058.33.

Here's how the second CPI increase would be calculated:

Assume that the CPI for April 2004 is 131.

Payment change date
As specified in the agreement: June 1, 2004

Indexing factor
The change in CPI between April 2003 and April 2004:

$$\frac{\text{CPI April 2004 of 131}}{\text{CPI April 2003 of 127}} \times \$1{,}058.33 = \$1{,}091.66$$

As of June 1, 2004, the payments will increase from $1,058.33 to $1,091.66.

Before making the increased payment in either year, the husband in this example will want to see whether his income has increased as much as the CPI in order to choose the least expensive mode of calculation.

For the June 2003 increase, use the husband's income reported for the taxation years 2002 and 2001. On April 30, 2003, the payor will have just filed his income tax return for the 2002 taxation year, so the 2002 taxation year information is the most current information available in June 2003.

Assume that the payor's 2001 income was $60,000 and his 2002 income was $72,000.

Payment change date
As specified in the agreement: June 1, 2003

Indexing factor
Percentage change in income from taxation year 2001 to taxation year 2002:

$$\frac{\text{2002 income of \$72,000}}{\text{2001 income of \$60,000}} \times \$1{,}000 = \$1{,}200.00$$

Clearly, the payor will elect to use the CPI increase and pay $1,058.33 rather than base the change in payments on the increase in income, which would result in a payment of $1,200.00.

REFERENCES

Children's Law Reform Act, RSO 1990, c. C.12.
Divorce Act, RSC 1985, c. 3 (2d Supp.).
Family Law Act, RSO 1990, c. F.3.
Family Law Rules, O. Reg. 114/99.
Ontario *Child Support Guidelines*, O. Reg. 391/97.
Richardson v. Richardson, [1987] 1 SCR 857.
Rules of Civil Procedure, RRO 1990, reg. 194.
www.statcan.ca (Statistics Canada Web site).

REVIEW QUESTIONS

1. What section of the *Divorce Act* deals with variation of custody orders?
2. Under the *Divorce Act*, what factors must the court consider on a proceeding to vary a custody order?
3. What section of the *Children's Law Reform Act* governs variation of custody orders?
4. What must a party show when applying to vary a custody order?
5. How is a variation application different from an appeal?
6. What section of the *Divorce Act* deals with variation of spousal support orders?
7. What section of the *Family Law Act* deals with variation of spousal support orders?
8. Under s.14 of the *Child Support Guidelines*, what changes in circumstances justify a variation in a child support order?
9. What rule governs variation proceedings in the Superior Court of Justice Family Court?
10. What is a cost of living adjustment (COLA) clause?
11. What is the consumer price index?
12. In what circumstances may spousal support be indexed?
13. What is the "payment change date" in an indexing formula?
14. What is the "indexing factor" in an indexing formula?
15. What is the indexing factor under the *Family Law Act*?

DISCUSSION QUESTION

A support order was made on June 19, 2002. The order provides as follows:

> "The husband shall pay to the wife for her support the sum of $1,000 per month commencing on the first day of July 2002 and on the first day of every month thereafter."

The order also contains a provision by which it is indexed under the *Family Law Act*.

Assume the following CPI data:

2001:	JAN-101	FEB-101	MAR-101	APR-102	MAY-102	JUN-102
	JUL-103	AUG-103	SEP-103	OCT-103	NOV-104	DEC-105
2002:	JAN-105	FEB-105	MAR-105	APR-106	MAY-106	JUN-106
	JUL-107	AUG-107	SEP-107	OCT-107	NOV-108	DEC-109

When will the first increase of the order take effect? What will the new support payment be?

APPENDIX A

Family Law and Same-Sex Couples

On June 10, 2003, the Ontario Court of Appeal in *Halpern v. Canada (Attorney General)* ruled that the common law definition of marriage as "the voluntary union for life of one man and one woman to the exclusion of all others" is contrary to the *Canadian Charter of Rights and Freedoms*. Courts in British Columbia and Quebec had already made similar rulings. Shortly after *Halpern*, the federal government announced that it would be proposing legislation to change the common law definition of marriage to allow for same-sex marriage. However, as of the date of this book's publication, the federal government has not done this. As a result, there is currently no settled definition of marriage.

In addition, neither the federal *Divorce Act* nor the Ontario *Family Law Act* has been amended to address issues arising out of the breakdown of same-sex marriages.

This appendix reviews the current state of family law as it relates to same-sex couples, including the law of:

- annulment,
- divorce,
- custody and access,
- spousal support,
- child support,
- property rights, and
- domestic contracts.

ANNULMENT

An annulment, as discussed in chapter 4, is a judgment that declares that a marriage is void. It is a common law remedy — in other words, all of the law in this area comes from case decisions. There is no legislation that deals with the matter.

As of the date of this book's publication, the courts have not yet been called upon to address the issue of annulment of a same-sex marriage.

DIVORCE

As of the date of this book's publication, the *Divorce Act* has not been amended to address the issue of same-sex marriages. The definition of a "spouse" under the Act is "either of a man or woman who are married to each other." Until the legislation is amended, or a court extends the definition of spouse to include same-sex couples, a same-sex couple who marries may be unable to obtain a divorce.

CUSTODY AND ACCESS

Custody and access are dealt with in both the federal *Divorce Act* and the provincial *Children's Law Reform Act*.

Under the Divorce Act

The definition of a "spouse" under the *Divorce* Act is "either of a man or woman who are married to each other." Until the definition of spouse is amended or interpreted to extend to same-sex couples, custody and access issues between married same-sex parents, who may be unable to institute divorce proceedings, cannot be dealt with under the *Divorce Act*.

Under the Children's Law Reform Act

Until same-sex married couples are given the right to institute proceedings under the *Divorce Act*, child custody and access issues between same-sex couples, whether married or cohabiting, will have to be dealt with under the *Children's Law Reform Act*.

The *Children's Law Reform Act* focuses on the nature of the relationship between parents and children rather than on the relationship between the parents, and as a result is fairly neutral on the issue of same-sex relationships.

Section 1 of the Act states that "a person is the child of his or her natural parents and his or her status as their child is independent of whether the child is born within or outside marriage." The section also states that "where an adoption order has been made ... the child is the child of the adopting parents as if they were the natural parents." Section 21 states that a parent of a child or any other person may apply to the court for an order respecting custody of or access to the child.

As a result, both members of a same-sex couple who have children, whether the couple is married or cohabiting, have standing as parties in any custody or access application.

SPOUSAL SUPPORT

Spousal support is dealt with in both the federal *Divorce Act* and the provincial *Family Law Act*.

Under the Divorce Act

The definition of a "spouse" under the *Divorce* Act is "either of a man or woman who are married to each other." Until the definition of spouse is amended or interpreted to extend to same-sex couples, support issues between married same-sex couples, who may be unable to institute divorce proceedings, cannot be dealt with under the *Divorce Act*.

Under the Family Law Act

Until same-sex married couples are given the right to institute proceedings under the *Divorce Act*, support issues between same-sex couples, whether married or cohabiting, will have to be dealt with under the *Family Law Act*.

As originally drafted, the *Family Law Act* conferred support rights only on spouses. With respect to support issues, a spouse is defined to be

- either of a man or woman who are married to each other;
- either of a man or woman who have entered into a void or voidable marriage in good faith on the part of the person asserting the claim for support;
- either of a man or woman who are not married to each other and have cohabited
    - continuously for a period of not less than three years or
    - in a relationship of some permanence, if they are the natural or adoptive parents of a child.

The *Family Law Act* was amended in 1999 to make provision for the support of same-sex partners as well. A same-sex partner is defined in s. 29 to be either of two persons of the same sex who have cohabited

- continuously for a period of not less than three years or
- in a relationship of some permanence, if they are the natural or adoptive parents of a child.

The purpose of the amendment was to treat unmarried same-sex couples in the same way as unmarried couples of the opposite sex. The amendment did not contemplate the possibility of same-sex marriage, nor has the Act been further amended to deal with same-sex marriages.

The right to support arises as soon as a party satisfies the definition of a same-sex partner. As with spouses of the opposite sex, support is decided on the basis of the need of the same-sex partner applying for support and the ability of the other same-sex partner to pay.

Tax Treatment of Support Orders for Same-Sex Partners

Under the *Income Tax Act*, periodic support payments paid pursuant to a court order or separation agreement for a common law partner are taxable as income in the hands of the receiving partner and are deductible from the paying partner's income. A common law partner is defined to include a person of the same sex with whom the taxpayer has lived and had a relationship with for at least 12 continuous months.

CHILD SUPPORT

Child support is dealt with in both the federal *Divorce Act* and the provincial *Family Law Act*.

Under the Divorce Act

The definition of a "spouse" under the *Divorce* Act is "either of a man or woman who are married to each other." Until the definition of spouse is amended or interpreted to extend to same-sex couples, child support issues between married same-sex couples, who may be unable to institute divorce proceedings, cannot be dealt with under the *Divorce Act*.

Under the Family Law Act

Until same-sex married couples are given the right to institute proceedings under the *Divorce Act*, child support issues between same-sex couples, whether married or cohabiting, will have to be dealt with under the *Family Law Act*.

The child support provisions of the *Family Law Act* focus on the relationship between the parents and their children rather than on the relationship between the parents, and as a result, are no different for same-sex couples than for couples of the opposite sex.

PROPERTY RIGHTS

The *Family Law Act* gives separating spouses the right to seek a division of their property in accordance with a formula set out in the Act. However, the property provisions of the Act apply only to "spouses" as defined in the Act. Under s. 1(1), a "spouse" means either of a man and woman who are married to each other, or have gone through a marriage that is voidable or void, in good faith on the part of the person asserting a right to property. Accordingly, the provisions do not apply to either same-sex couples or couples of the opposite sex who are simply cohabiting, nor do they apply to same-sex married couples.

As stated above under the heading "Spousal Support," the *Family Law Act* was amended in 1999 to make provision for the support of same-sex partners. The purpose of the amendment was to treat unmarried same-sex couples in the same way as unmarried couples of the opposite sex. The amendment did not contemplate the possibility of same-sex marriage, nor has the Act been further amended to deal with same-sex marriages.

Because the equalization provisions of the Act do not apply to either married or unmarried same-sex couples, their property is divided based on common law principles of property ownership and equitable principles of trust.

DOMESTIC CONTRACTS

Separation agreements and other domestic contracts are dealt with in part IV of the *Family Law Act*. Section 53 of the Act allows two person of the same sex who are cohabiting or intend to cohabit and who are not married to each other to enter into a cohabitation agreement; and s. 54 allows two persons of the same sex who cohabited and are living separate and apart to enter into a separation agreement. However, s. 52, which deals with marriage contracts, has not been amended to address the issue of same-sex marriages, and allows only a man and a woman who are married to each other or intend to marry to enter into a marriage contract.

APPENDIX B

Judicial Districts and Counties

FAMILY COURT JURISDICTIONS

1. Durham Regional Municipality — Oshawa
2. Frontenac County — Kingston
3. Haliburton County — Minden
4. Hamilton-Wentworth Regional Municipality — Hamilton
5. Lanark County — Perth
6. Leeds and Grenville Counties — Brockville
7. Lennox and Addington Counties — Napanee
8. Middlesex County — London
9. Muskoka District Municipality — Bracebridge, Huntsville
10. Niagara Regional Municipality — St. Catharines
11. Northumberland County — Cobourg
12. Ottawa
13. Peterborough County — Peterborough
14. Prescott and Russell Counties — L'Orignal
15. Simcoe County — Barrie
16. Stormount, Dundas, and Glengarry Counties — Cornwall
17. Victoria County — Lindsay
18. York Regional Municipality

NON-FAMILY COURT JURISDICTIONS

1. Algoma District — Sault Ste. Marie
2. Brant County — Brantford

3. Bruce County — Walkerton
4. Chatham-Kent Municipality — Chatham
5. Cochrane District — Timmins
6. Dufferin County — Orangeville
7. Elgin County — St. Thomas
8. Essex County — Windsor
9. Grey County — Owen Sound
10. Haldimond County — Cayuga
11. Halton Regional Municipality — Milton
12. Hastings County — Belleville
13. Huron County — Goderich
14. Kenora District — Kenora
15. Lambton County — Sarnia
16. Manitoulin District — Gore Bay
17. Nipissing District — North Bay
18. Norfolk County — Simcoe
19. Oxford County — Woodstock
20. Parry Sound District — Parry Sound
21. Peel Regional Municipality — Brampton
22. Perth County — Stratford
23. Prince Edward County — Picton
24. Rainy River District
25. Renfrew County — Pembroke
26. Sudbury Regional Municipality — Sudbury
27. Thunder Bay District — Thunder Bay
28. Timiskaming District — Haileybury
29. Toronto
30. Waterloo Regional Municipality — Kitchener
31. Wellington County — Guelph

APPENDIX C

Family Law Legislation

DIVORCE ACT

RSC 1985, c. 3 (2d Supp.)

CONTENTS

SHORT TITLE

Short title

1. This Act may be cited as the *Divorce Act*.

INTERPRETATION

Definitions

2(1) In this Act,

"age of majority," in respect of a child, means the age of majority as determined by the laws of the province where the child ordinarily resides, or, if the child ordinarily resides outside of Canada, eighteen years of age;

"appellate court," in respect of an appeal from a court, means the court exercising appellate jurisdiction with respect to that appeal;

"applicable guidelines" means

(a) where both spouses or former spouses are ordinarily resident in the same province at the time an application for a child support order or a variation order in respect of a child support order is made, or the amount of a child support order is to be recalculated pursuant to section 25.1, and that province has been designated by an order made under subsection (5), the laws of the province specified in the order, and

(b) in any other case, the Federal Child Support Guidelines;

"child of the marriage" means a child of two spouses or former spouses who, at the material time,

(a) is under the age of majority and who has not withdrawn from their charge, or

(b) is the age of majority or over and under their charge but unable, by reason of illness, disability or other cause, to withdraw from their charge or to obtain the necessaries of life;

"child support order" means an order made under subsection 15.1(1);

"corollary relief proceeding" means a proceeding in a court in which either or both former spouses seek a child support order, a spousal support order or a custody order;

"court," in respect of a province, means

(a) for the Province of Ontario, the Superior Court of Justice,

(a.1) for the Province of Prince Edward Island or Newfoundland, the trial division of the Supreme Court of the Province,

(b) for the Province of Quebec, the Superior Court,

(c) for the Provinces of Nova Scotia and British Columbia, the Supreme Court of the Province,

(d) for the Province of New Brunswick, Manitoba, Saskatchewan or Alberta, the Court of Queen's Bench for the Province, and

(e) for Yukon or the Northwest Territories, the Supreme Court, and in Nunavut, the Nunavut Court of Justice,

and includes such other court in the province the judges of which are appointed by the Governor General as is designated by the Lieutenant Governor in Council of the province as a court for the purposes of this Act;

"custody" includes care, upbringing and any other incident of custody;

"custody order" means an order made under subsection 16(1);

"divorce proceeding" means a proceeding in a court in which either or both spouses seek a divorce alone or together with a child support order, a spousal support order or a custody order;

"Federal Child Support Guidelines" means the guidelines made under section 26.1;

"provincial child support service" means any service, agency or body designated in an agreement with a province under subsection 25.1(1);

"spousal support order" means an order made under subsection 15.2(1);

"spouse" means either of a man or woman who are married to each other;

"support order" means a child support order or a spousal support order;

"variation order" means an order made under subsection 17(1);

"variation proceeding" means a proceeding in a court in which either or both former spouses seek a variation order.

Child of the marriage

(2) For the purposes of the definition "child of the marriage" in subsection (1), a child of two spouses or former spouses includes

(a) any child for whom they both stand in the place of parents; and

(b) any child of whom one is the parent and for whom the other stands in the place of a parent.

Term not restrictive

(3) The use of the term "application" to describe a proceeding under this Act in a court shall not be construed as limiting the name under which and the form and manner in which that proceeding may be taken in that court, and the name, manner and form of the proceeding in that court shall be such as is provided for by the rules regulating the practice and procedure in that court.

Idem

(4) The use in section 21.1 of the terms "affidavit" and "pleadings" to describe documents shall not be construed as limiting the name that may be used to refer to those documents in a court and the form of those documents, and the name and form of the documents shall be such as is provided for by the rules regulating the practice and procedure in that court.

Provincial child support guidelines

(5) The Governor in Council may, by order, designate a province for the purposes of the definition "applicable guidelines" in subsection (1) if the laws of the province establish comprehensive guidelines for the determination of child support that deal with the matters referred to in section 26.1. The order shall specify the laws of the province that constitute the guidelines of the province.

Amendments included

(6) The guidelines of a province referred to in subsection (5) include any amendments made to them from time to time.

JURISDICTION

Jurisdiction in divorce proceedings

3(1) A court in a province has jurisdiction to hear and determine a divorce proceeding if either spouse has been ordinarily resident in the province for at least one year immediately preceding the commencement of the proceeding.

Jurisdiction where two proceedings commenced on different days

(2) Where divorce proceedings between the same spouses are pending in two courts that would otherwise have jurisdiction under subsection (1) and were commenced on different days and the proceeding that was commenced first is not discontinued within thirty days after it was commenced, the court in which a divorce proceeding was commenced first has exclusive jurisdiction to hear and determine any divorce proceeding then pending between the spouses and the second divorce proceeding shall be deemed to be discontinued.

Jurisdiction where two proceedings commenced on same day

(3) Where divorce proceedings between the same spouses are pending in two courts that would otherwise have jurisdiction under subsection (1) and were commenced on the same day and neither proceeding is discontinued within thirty days after it was commenced, the Federal Court has exclusive jurisdiction to hear and determine any divorce proceeding then pending between the spouses and the divorce proceedings in those courts shall be transferred to the Federal Court on the direction of that Court.

Jurisdiction in corollary relief proceedings

4(1) A court in a province has jurisdiction to hear and determine a corollary relief proceeding if

(a) either former spouse is ordinarily resident in the province at the commencement of the proceeding; or

(b) both former spouses accept the jurisdiction of the court.

Jurisdiction where two proceedings commenced on different days

(2) Where corollary relief proceedings between the same former spouses and in respect of the same matter are pending in two courts that would otherwise have jurisdiction under subsection (1) and were commenced on different days and the proceeding that was commenced first is not discontinued within thirty days after it was commenced, the court in which a corollary relief proceeding was commenced first has exclusive jurisdiction to hear and determine any corollary relief proceeding then pending between the former spouses in respect of that matter and the second corollary relief proceeding shall be deemed to be discontinued.

Jurisdiction where two proceedings commenced on same day

(3) Where proceedings between the same former spouses and in respect of the same matter are pending in two courts that would otherwise have jurisdiction under subsection (1) and were commenced on the same day and neither proceeding is discontinued within thirty days after it was commenced, the Federal Court has exclusive jurisdiction to hear and determine any corollary relief proceeding then pending between the former spouses in respect of that matter and the corollary relief proceedings in those courts shall be transferred to the Federal Court on the direction of that Court.

Jurisdiction in variation proceedings

5(1) A court in a province has jurisdiction to hear and determine a variation proceeding if

(a) either former spouse is ordinarily resident in the province at the commencement of the proceeding; or

(b) both former spouses accept the jurisdiction of the court.

Jurisdiction where two proceedings commenced on different days

(2) Where variation proceedings between the same former spouses and in respect of the same matter are pending in two courts that would otherwise have jurisdiction under subsection (1) and were commenced on different days and the proceeding that was commenced first is not discontinued within thirty days after it was commenced, the court in which a variation proceeding was commenced first has exclusive jurisdiction to hear and determine any variation proceeding then pending between the former spouses in respect of that matter and the second variation proceeding shall be deemed to be discontinued.

Jurisdiction where two proceedings commenced on same day

(3) Where variation proceedings between the same former spouses and in respect of the same matter are pending in two courts that would otherwise have jurisdiction under subsection (1) and were commenced on the same day and neither proceeding is discontinued within thirty days after it was commenced, the Federal Court has exclusive jurisdiction to hear and determine any variation proceeding then pending between the former spouses in respect of that matter and the variation proceedings in those courts shall be transferred to the Federal Court on the direction of that Court.

Transfer of divorce proceeding where custody application

6(1) Where an application for an order under section 16 is made in a divorce proceeding to a court in a province and is opposed and the child of the marriage in respect of whom the order is sought is most substantially connected with another province, the court may, on application by a spouse or on its own motion, transfer the divorce proceeding to a court in that other province.

Transfer of corollary relief proceeding where custody application

(2) Where an application for an order under section 16 is made in a corollary relief proceeding to a court in a province and is opposed and the child of the marriage in respect of whom the order is sought is most substantially connected with another province, the court may, on application by a former spouse or on its own motion, transfer the corollary relief proceeding to a court in that other province.

Transfer of variation proceeding where custody application

(3) Where an application for a variation order in respect of a custody order is made in a variation proceeding to a court in a province and is opposed and the child of the marriage

in respect of whom the variation order is sought is most substantially connected with another province, the court may, on application by a former spouse or on its own motion, transfer the variation proceeding to a court in that other province.

Exclusive jurisdiction

(4) Notwithstanding sections 3 to 5, a court in a province to which a proceeding is transferred under this section has exclusive jurisdiction to hear and determine the proceeding.

Exercise of jurisdiction by judge

7. The jurisdiction conferred on a court by this Act to grant a divorce shall be exercised only by a judge of the court without a jury.

DIVORCE

Divorce

8(1) A court of competent jurisdiction may, on application by either or both spouses, grant a divorce to the spouse or spouses on the ground that there has been a breakdown of their marriage.

Breakdown of marriage

(2) Breakdown of a marriage is established only if

(a) the spouses have lived separate and apart for at least one year immediately preceding the determination of the divorce proceeding and were living separate and apart at the commencement of the proceeding; or

(b) the spouse against whom the divorce proceeding is brought has, since celebration of the marriage,

(i) committed adultery, or

(ii) treated the other spouse with physical or mental cruelty of such a kind as to render intolerable the continued cohabitation of the spouses.

Calculation of period of separation

(3) For the purposes of paragraph (2)(a),

(a) spouses shall be deemed to have lived separate and apart for any period during which they lived apart and either of them had the intention to live separate and apart from the other; and

(b) a period during which spouses have lived separate and apart shall not be considered to have been interrupted or terminated

(i) by reason only that either spouse has become incapable of forming or having an intention to continue to live separate and apart or of continuing to live separate and apart of the spouse's own volition, if it appears to the court that the separation would probably have continued if the spouse had not become so incapable, or

(ii) by reason only that the spouses have resumed cohabitation during a period of, or periods totalling, not more than ninety days with reconciliation as its primary purpose.

Duty of legal adviser

9(1) It is the duty of every barrister, solicitor, lawyer or advocate who undertakes to act on behalf of a spouse in a divorce proceeding

(a) to draw to the attention of the spouse the provisions of this Act that have as their object the reconciliation of spouses, and

(b) to discuss with the spouse the possibility of the reconciliation of the spouses and to inform the spouse of the marriage counselling or guidance facilities known to him or her that might be able to assist the spouses to achieve a reconciliation,

unless the circumstances of the case are of such a nature that it would clearly not be appropriate to do so.

Idem

(2) It is the duty of every barrister, solicitor, lawyer or advocate who undertakes to act on behalf of a spouse in a divorce proceeding to discuss with the spouse the advisability of negotiating the matters that may be the subject of a support order or a custody order and to inform the spouse of the mediation facilities known to him or her that might be able to assist the spouses in negotiating those matters.

Certification

(3) Every document presented to a court by a barrister, solicitor, lawyer or advocate that formally commences a divorce proceeding shall contain a statement by him or her certifying that he or she has complied with this section.

Duty of court — reconciliation

10(1) In a divorce proceeding, it is the duty of the court, before considering the evidence, to satisfy itself that there is no possibility of the reconciliation of the spouses, unless the circumstances of the case are of such a nature that it would clearly not be appropriate to do so.

Adjournment

(2) Where at any stage in a divorce proceeding it appears to the court from the nature of the case, the evidence or the attitude of either or both spouses that there is a possibility of the reconciliation of the spouses, the court shall

(a) adjourn the proceeding to afford the spouses an opportunity to achieve a reconciliation; and

(b) with the consent of the spouses or in the discretion of the court, nominate

(i) a person with experience or training in marriage counselling or guidance, or

(ii) in special circumstances, some other suitable person,

to assist the spouses to achieve a reconciliation.

Resumption

(3) Where fourteen days have elapsed from the date of any adjournment under subsection (2), the court shall resume the proceeding on the application of either or both spouses.

Nominee not competent or compellable

(4) No person nominated by a court under this section to assist spouses to achieve a reconciliation is competent or compellable in any legal proceedings to disclose any admission or communication made to that person in his or her capacity as a nominee of the court for that purpose.

Evidence not admissible

(5) Evidence of anything said or of any admission or communication made in the course of assisting spouses to achieve a reconciliation is not admissible in any legal proceedings.

Duty of court — bars

11(1) In a divorce proceeding, it is the duty of the court

(a) to satisfy itself that there has been no collusion in relation to the application for a divorce and to dismiss the application if it finds that there was collusion in presenting it;

(b) to satisfy itself that reasonable arrangements have been made for the support of any children of the marriage, having regard to the applicable guidelines, and, if such arrangements have not been made, to stay the granting of the divorce until such arrangements are made; and

(c) where a divorce is sought in circumstances described in paragraph 8(2)(b), to satisfy itself that there has been no condonation or connivance on the part of the spouse bringing the proceeding, and to dismiss the application for a divorce if that spouse has condoned or connived at the act or conduct complained of unless, in the opinion of the court, the public interest would be better served by granting the divorce.

Revival

(2) Any act or conduct that has been condoned is not capable of being revived so as to constitute a circumstance described in paragraph 8(2)(b).

Condonation

(3) For the purposes of this section, a continuation or resumption of cohabitation during a period of, or periods totalling, not more than ninety days with reconciliation as its primary purpose shall not be considered to constitute condonation.

Definition of "collusion"

(4) In this section, "collusion" means an agreement or conspiracy to which an applicant for a divorce is either directly or indirectly a party for the purpose of subverting the administration of justice, and includes any agreement, understanding or arrangement to fabricate or suppress evidence or to deceive the court, but does not include an agreement

to the extent that it provides for separation between the parties, financial support, division of property or the custody of any child of the marriage.

Effective date generally

12(1) Subject to this section, a divorce takes effect on the thirty-first day after the day on which the judgment granting the divorce is rendered.

Special circumstances

(2) Where, on or after rendering a judgment granting a divorce,

(a) the court is of the opinion that by reason of special circumstances the divorce should take effect earlier than the thirty-first day after the day on which the judgment is rendered, and

(b) the spouses agree and undertake that no appeal from the judgment will be taken, or any appeal from the judgment that was taken has been abandoned,

the court may order that the divorce takes effect at such earlier time as it considers appropriate.

Effective date where appeal

(3) A divorce in respect of which an appeal is pending at the end of the period referred to in subsection (1), unless voided on appeal, takes effect on the expiration of the time fixed by law for instituting an appeal from the decision on that appeal or any subsequent appeal, if no appeal has been instituted within that time.

Certain extensions to be counted

(4) For the purposes of subsection (3), the time fixed by law for instituting an appeal from a decision on an appeal includes any extension thereof fixed pursuant to law before the expiration of that time or fixed thereafter on an application instituted before the expiration of that time.

No late extensions of time for appeal

(5) Notwithstanding any other law, the time fixed by law for instituting an appeal from a decision referred to in subsection (3) may not be extended after the expiration of that time, except on an application instituted before the expiration of that time.

Effective date where decision of Supreme Court of Canada

(6) A divorce in respect of which an appeal has been taken to the Supreme Court of Canada, unless voided on the appeal, takes effect on the day on which the judgment on the appeal is rendered.

Certificate of divorce

(7) Where a divorce takes effect in accordance with this section, a judge or officer of the court that rendered the judgment granting the divorce or, where that judgment has been appealed, of the appellate court that rendered the judgment on the final appeal, shall, on request, issue to any person a certificate that a divorce granted under this Act dissolved the marriage of the specified persons effective as of a specified date.

Conclusive proof

(8) A certificate referred to in subsection (7), or a certified copy thereof, is conclusive proof of the facts so certified without proof of the signature or authority of the person appearing to have signed the certificate.

Legal effect throughout Canada

13. On taking effect, a divorce granted under this Act has legal effect throughout Canada.

Marriage dissolved

14. On taking effect, a divorce granted under this Act dissolves the marriage of the spouses.

COROLLARY RELIEF

Interpretation

Definition of "spouse"

15. In sections 15.1 to 16, "spouse" has the meaning assigned by subsection 2(1), and includes a former spouse.

Child Support Orders

Child support order

15.1(1) A court of competent jurisdiction may, on application by either or both spouses, make an order requiring a spouse to pay for the support of any or all children of the marriage.

Interim order

(2) Where an application is made under subsection (1), the court may, on application by either or both spouses, make an interim order requiring a spouse to pay for the support of any or all children of the marriage, pending the determination of the application under subsection (1).

Guidelines apply

(3) A court making an order under subsection (1) or an interim order under subsection (2) shall do so in accordance with the applicable guidelines.

Terms and conditions

(4) The court may make an order under subsection (1) or an interim order under subsection (2) for a definite or indefinite period or until a specified event occurs, and may impose terms, conditions or restrictions in connection with the order or interim order as it thinks fit and just.

Court may take agreement, etc., into account

(5) Notwithstanding subsection (3), a court may award an amount that is different from the amount that would be determined in accordance with the applicable guidelines if the court is satisfied

(a) that special provisions in an order, a judgment or a written agreement respecting the financial obligations of the spouses, or the division or transfer of their property, directly or indirectly benefit a child, or that special provisions have otherwise been made for the benefit of a child; and

(b) that the application of the applicable guidelines would result in an amount of child support that is inequitable given those special provisions.

Reasons

(6) Where the court awards, pursuant to subsection (5), an amount that is different from the amount that would be determined in accordance with the applicable guidelines, the court shall record its reasons for having done so.

Consent orders

(7) Notwithstanding subsection (3), a court may award an amount that is different from the amount that would be determined in accordance with the applicable guidelines on the consent of both spouses if it is satisfied that reasonable arrangements have been made for the support of the child to whom the order relates.

Reasonable arrangements

(8) For the purposes of subsection (7), in determining whether reasonable arrangements have been made for the support of a child, the court shall have regard to the applicable guidelines. However, the court shall not consider the arrangements to be unreasonable solely because the amount of support agreed to is not the same as the amount that would otherwise have been determined in accordance with the applicable guidelines.

Spousal Support Orders

Spousal support order

15.2(1) A court of competent jurisdiction may, on application by either or both spouses, make an order requiring a spouse to secure or pay, or to secure and pay, such lump sum or periodic sums, or such lump sum and periodic sums, as the court thinks reasonable for the support of the other spouse.

Interim order

(2) Where an application is made under subsection (1), the court may, on application by either or both spouses, make an interim order requiring a spouse to secure or pay, or to secure and pay, such lump sum or periodic sums, or such lump sum and periodic sums, as

the court thinks reasonable for the support of the other spouse, pending the determination of the application under subsection (1).

Terms and conditions

(3) The court may make an order under subsection (1) or an interim order under subsection (2) for a definite or indefinite period or until a specified event occurs, and may impose terms, conditions or restrictions in connection with the order as it thinks fit and just.

Factors

(4) In making an order under subsection (1) or an interim order under subsection (2), the court shall take into consideration the condition, means, needs and other circumstances of each spouse, including

(a) the length of time the spouses cohabited;

(b) the functions performed by each spouse during cohabitation; and

(c) any order, agreement or arrangement relating to support of either spouse.

Spousal misconduct

(5) In making an order under subsection (1) or an interim order under subsection (2), the court shall not take into consideration any misconduct of a spouse in relation to the marriage.

Objectives of spousal support order

(6) An order made under subsection (1) or an interim order under subsection (2) that provides for the support of a spouse should

(a) recognize any economic advantages or disadvantages to the spouses arising from the marriage or its breakdown;

(b) apportion between the spouses any financial consequences arising from the care of any child of the marriage over and above any obligation for the support of any child of the marriage;

(c) relieve any economic hardship of the spouses arising from the breakdown of the marriage; and

(d) in so far as practicable, promote the economic self-sufficiency of each spouse within a reasonable period of time.

Priority

Priority to child support

15.3(1) Where a court is considering an application for a child support order and an application for a spousal support order, the court shall give priority to child support in determining the applications.

Reasons

(2) Where, as a result of giving priority to child support, the court is unable to make a spousal support order or the court makes a spousal support order in an amount that is less than it otherwise would have been, the court shall record its reasons for having done so.

Consequences of reduction or termination of child support order

(3) Where, as a result of giving priority to child support, a spousal support order was not made, or the amount of a spousal support order is less than it otherwise would have been, any subsequent reduction or termination of that child support constitutes a change of circumstances for the purposes of applying for a spousal support order, or a variation order in respect of the spousal support order, as the case may be.

Custody Orders

Order for custody

16(1) A court of competent jurisdiction may, on application by either or both spouses or by any other person, make an order respecting the custody of or the access to, or the custody of and access to, any or all children of the marriage.

Interim order for custody

(2) Where an application is made under subsection (1), the court may, on application by either or both spouses or by any other person, make an interim order respecting the custody

of or the access to, or the custody of and access to, any or all children of the marriage pending determination of the application under subsection (1).

Application by other person

(3) A person, other than a spouse, may not make an application under subsection (1) or (2) without leave of the court.

Joint custody or access

(4) The court may make an order under this section granting custody of, or access to, any or all children of the marriage to any one or more persons.

Access

(5) Unless the court orders otherwise, a spouse who is granted access to a child of the marriage has the right to make inquiries, and to be given information, as to the health, education and welfare of the child.

Terms and conditions

(6) The court may make an order under this section for a definite or indefinite period or until the happening of a specified event and may impose such other terms, conditions or restrictions in connection therewith as it thinks fit and just.

Order respecting change of residence

(7) Without limiting the generality of subsection (6), the court may include in an order under this section a term requiring any person who has custody of a child of the marriage and who intends to change the place of residence of that child to notify, at least thirty days before the change or within such other period before the change as the court may specify, any person who is granted access to that child of the change, the time at which the change will be made and the new place of residence of the child.

Factors

(8) In making an order under this section, the court shall take into consideration only the best interests of the child of the marriage as determined by reference to the condition, means, needs and other circumstances of the child.

Past conduct

(9) In making an order under this section, the court shall not take into consideration the past conduct of any person unless the conduct is relevant to the ability of that person to act as a parent of a child.

Maximum contact

(10) In making an order under this section, the court shall give effect to the principle that a child of the marriage should have as much contact with each spouse as is consistent with the best interests of the child and, for that purpose, shall take into consideration the willingness of the person for whom custody is sought to facilitate such contact.

Variation, Rescission or Suspension of Orders

Order for variation, rescission or suspension

17(1) A court of competent jurisdiction may make an order varying, rescinding or suspending, prospectively or retroactively,

(a) a support order or any provision thereof on application by either or both former spouses; or

(b) a custody order or any provision thereof on application by either or both former spouses or by any other person.

Application by other person

(2) A person, other than a former spouse, may not make an application under paragraph (1)(b) without leave of the court.

Terms and conditions

(3) The court may include in a variation order any provision that under this Act could have been included in the order in respect of which the variation order is sought.

Factors for child support order

(4) Before the court makes a variation order in respect of a child support order, the court shall satisfy itself that a change of circumstances as provided for in the applicable

guidelines has occurred since the making of the child support order or the last variation order made in respect of that order.

Factors for spousal support order

(4.1) Before the court makes a variation order in respect of a spousal support order, the court shall satisfy itself that a change in the condition, means, needs or other circumstances of either former spouse has occurred since the making of the spousal support order or the last variation order made in respect of that order, and, in making the variation order, the court shall take that change into consideration.

Factors for custody order

(5) Before the court makes a variation order in respect of a custody order, the court shall satisfy itself that there has been a change in the condition, means, needs or other circumstances of the child of the marriage occurring since the making of the custody order or the last variation order made in respect of that order, as the case may be, and, in making the variation order, the court shall take into consideration only the best interests of the child as determined by reference to that change.

Conduct

(6) In making a variation order, the court shall not take into consideration any conduct that under this Act could not have been considered in making the order in respect of which the variation order is sought.

Guidelines apply

(6.1) A court making a variation order in respect of a child support order shall do so in accordance with the applicable guidelines.

Court may take agreement, etc., into account

(6.2) Notwithstanding subsection (6.1), in making a variation order in respect of a child support order, a court may award an amount that is different from the amount that would be determined in accordance with the applicable guidelines if the court is satisfied

(a) that special provisions in an order, a judgment or a written agreement respecting the financial obligations of the spouses, or the division or transfer of their property, directly or indirectly benefit a child, or that special provisions have otherwise been made for the benefit of a child; and

(b) that the application of the applicable guidelines would result in an amount of child support that is inequitable given those special provisions.

Reasons

(6.3) Where the court awards, pursuant to subsection (6.2), an amount that is different from the amount that would be determined in accordance with the applicable guidelines, the court shall record its reasons for having done so.

Consent orders

(6.4) Notwithstanding subsection (6.1), a court may award an amount that is different from the amount that would be determined in accordance with the applicable guidelines on the consent of both spouses if it is satisfied that reasonable arrangements have been made for the support of the child to whom the order relates.

Reasonable arrangements

(6.5) For the purposes of subsection (6.4), in determining whether reasonable arrangements have been made for the support of a child, the court shall have regard to the applicable guidelines. However, the court shall not consider the arrangements to be unreasonable solely because the amount of support agreed to is not the same as the amount that would otherwise have been determined in accordance with the applicable guidelines.

Objectives of variation order varying spousal support order

(7) A variation order varying a spousal support order should

(a) recognize any economic advantages or disadvantages to the former spouses arising from the marriage or its breakdown;

(b) apportion between the former spouses any financial consequences arising from the care of any child of the marriage over and above any obligation for the support of any child of the marriage;

(c) relieve any economic hardship of the former spouses arising from the breakdown of the marriage; and

(d) in so far as practicable, promote the economic self-sufficiency of each former spouse within a reasonable period of time.

OBJECTIVES OF VARIATION ORDER VARYING ORDER FOR SUPPORT OF CHILD

Maximum contact

(9) In making a variation order varying a custody order, the court shall give effect to the principle that a child of the marriage should have as much contact with each former spouse as is consistent with the best interests of the child and, for that purpose, where the variation order would grant custody of the child to a person who does not currently have custody, the court shall take into consideration the willingness of that person to facilitate such contact.

Limitation

(10) Notwithstanding subsection (1), where a spousal support order provides for support for a definite period or until a specified event occurs, a court may not, on an application instituted after the expiration of that period or the occurrence of the event, make a variation order for the purpose of resuming that support unless the court is satisfied that

(a) a variation order is necessary to relieve economic hardship arising from a change described in subsection (4.1) that is related to the marriage; and

(b) the changed circumstances, had they existed at the time of the making of the spousal support order or the last variation order made in respect of that order, as the case may be, would likely have resulted in a different order.

Copy of order

(11) Where a court makes a variation order in respect of a support order or a custody order made by another court, it shall send a copy of the variation order, certified by a judge or officer of the court, to that other court.

Variation order by affidavit, etc.

17.1 Where both former spouses are ordinarily resident in different provinces, a court of competent jurisdiction may, in accordance with any applicable rules of the court, make a variation order pursuant to subsection 17(1) on the basis of the submissions of the former spouses, whether presented orally before the court or by means of affidavits or any means of telecommunication, if both former spouses consent thereto.

Provisional Orders

Definitions

18(1) In this section and section 19,

"Attorney General," in respect of a province, means

(a) for Yukon, the member of the Executive Council of Yukon designated by the Commissioner of Yukon,

(b) for the Northwest Territories, the member of the Council of the Northwest Territories designated by the Commissioner of the Northwest Territories,

(b.1) for Nunavut, the member of the Executive Council of Nunavut designated by the Commissioner of Nunavut, and

(c) for the other provinces, the Attorney General of the province, and includes any person authorized in writing by the member or Attorney General to act for the member or Attorney General in the performance of a function under this section or section 19;

"provisional order" means an order made pursuant to subsection (2).

Provisional order

(2) Notwithstanding paragraph 5(1)(a) and subsection 17(1), where an application is made to a court in a province for a variation order in respect of a support order and

(a) the respondent in the application is ordinarily resident in another province and has not accepted the jurisdiction of the court, or both former spouses have not consented to the application of section 17.1 in respect of the matter, and

(b) in the circumstances of the case, the court is satisfied that the issues can be adequately determined by proceeding under this section and section 19, the court shall make a variation order with or without notice to and in the absence of the respondent, but such order is provisional only and has no legal effect until it is confirmed in a proceeding under section 19 and, where so confirmed, it has legal effect in accordance with the terms of the order confirming it.

Transmission

(3) Where a court in a province makes a provisional order, it shall send to the Attorney General for the province

(a) three copies of the provisional order certified by a judge or officer of the court;

(b) a certified or sworn document setting out or summarizing the evidence given to the court; and

(c) a statement giving any available information respecting the identification, location, income and assets of the respondent.

Idem

(4) On receipt of the documents referred to in subsection (3), the Attorney General shall send the documents to the Attorney General for the province in which the respondent is ordinarily resident.

Further evidence

(5) Where, during a proceeding under section 19, a court in a province remits the matter back for further evidence to the court that made the provisional order, the court that made the order shall, after giving notice to the applicant, receive further evidence.

Transmission

(6) Where evidence is received under subsection (5), the court that received the evidence shall forward to the court that remitted the matter back a certified or sworn document setting out or summarizing the evidence, together with such recommendations as the court that received the evidence considers appropriate.

Transmission

19(1) On receipt of any documents sent pursuant to subsection 18(4), the Attorney General for the province in which the respondent is ordinarily resident shall send the documents to a court in the province.

Procedure

(2) Subject to subsection (3), where documents have been sent to a court pursuant to subsection (1), the court shall serve on the respondent a copy of the documents and a notice of a hearing respecting confirmation of the provisional order and shall proceed with the hearing, in the absence of the applicant, taking into consideration the certified or sworn document setting out or summarizing the evidence given to the court that made the provisional order.

Return to Attorney General

(3) Where documents have been sent to a court pursuant to subsection (1) and the respondent apparently is outside the province and is not likely to return, the court shall send the documents to the Attorney General for that province, together with any available information respecting the location and circumstances of the respondent.

Idem

(4) On receipt of any documents and information sent pursuant to subsection (3), the Attorney General shall send the documents and information to the Attorney General for the province of the court that made the provisional order.

Right of respondent

(5) In a proceeding under this section, the respondent may raise any matter that might have been raised before the court that made the provisional order.

Further evidence

(6) Where, in a proceeding under this section, the respondent satisfies the court that for the purpose of taking further evidence or for any other purpose it is necessary to remit the matter back to the court that made the provisional order, the court may so remit the matter and adjourn the proceeding for that purpose.

Order of confirmation or refusal

(7) Subject to subsection (7.1), at the conclusion of a proceeding under this section, the court shall make an order

(a) confirming the provisional order without variation;

(b) confirming the provisional order with variation; or

(c) refusing confirmation of the provisional order.

Guidelines apply

(7.1) A court making an order under subsection (7) in respect of a child support order shall do so in accordance with the applicable guidelines.

Further evidence

(8) The court, before making an order confirming the provisional order with variation or an order refusing confirmation of the provisional order, shall decide whether to remit the matter back for further evidence to the court that made the provisional order.

Interim order for support of children

(9) Where a court remits a matter pursuant to this section in relation to a child support order, the court may, pending the making of an order under subsection (7), make an interim order in accordance with the applicable guidelines requiring a spouse to pay for the support of any or all children of the marriage.

Interim order for support of spouse

(9.1) Where a court remits a matter pursuant to this section in relation to a spousal support order, the court may make an interim order requiring a spouse to secure or pay, or to secure and pay, such lump sum or periodic sums, or such lump sum and periodic sums, as the court thinks reasonable for the support of the other spouse, pending the making of an order under subsection (7).

Terms and conditions

(10) The court may make an order under subsection (9) or (9.1) for a definite or indefinite period or until a specified event occurs, and may impose terms, conditions or restrictions in connection with the order as it thinks fit and just.

Provisions applicable

(11) Subsections 17(4), (4.1) and (6) to (7) apply, with such modifications as the circumstances require, in respect of an order made under subsection (9) or (9.1) as if it were a variation order referred to in those subsections.

Report and filing

(12) On making an order under subsection (7), the court in a province shall

(a) send a copy of the order, certified by a judge or officer of the court, to the Attorney General for that province, to the court that made the provisional order and, where that court is not the court that made the support order in respect of which the provisional order was made, to the court that made the support order;

(b) where an order is made confirming the provisional order with or without variation, file the order in the court; and

(c) where an order is made confirming the provisional order with variation or refusing confirmation of the provisional order, give written reasons to the Attorney General for that province and to the court that made the provisional order.

Definition of "court"

20(1) In this section, "court," in respect of a province, has the meaning assigned by subsection 2(1) and includes such other court having jurisdiction in the province as is designated by the Lieutenant Governor in Council of the province as a court for the purposes of this section.

Legal effect throughout Canada

(2) Subject to subsection 18(2), an order made under any of sections 15.1 to 17 or subsection 19(7), (9) or (9.1) has legal effect throughout Canada.

Enforcement

(3) An order that has legal effect throughout Canada pursuant to subsection (2) may be

(a) registered in any court in a province and enforced in like manner as an order of that court; or

(b) enforced in a province in any other manner provided for by the laws of that province, including its laws respecting reciprocal enforcement between the province and a jurisdiction outside Canada.

Variation of orders

(4) Notwithstanding subsection (3), a court may only vary an order that has legal effect throughout Canada pursuant to subsection (2) in accordance with this Act.

Assignment of order

20.1(1) A support order may be assigned to

(a) any minister of the Crown for Canada designated by the Governor in Council;

(b) any minister of the Crown for a province, or any agency in a province, designated by the Lieutenant Governor in Council of the province;

(c) any member of the Legislative Assembly of Yukon, or any agency in Yukon, designated by the Commissioner of Yukon;

(d) any member of the Council of the Northwest Territories, or any agency in the Northwest Territories, designated by the Commissioner of the Northwest Territories; or

(e) any member of the Legislative Assembly of Nunavut, or any agency in Nunavut, designated by the Commissioner of Nunavut.

Rights

(2) A minister, member or agency referred to in subsection (1) to whom an order is assigned is entitled to the payments due under the order, and has the same right to be notified of, and to participate in, proceedings under this Act to vary, rescind, suspend or enforce the order as the person who would otherwise be entitled to the payments.

APPEALS

Appeal to appellate court

21(1) Subject to subsections (2) and (3), an appeal lies to the appellate court from any judgment or order, whether final or interim, rendered or made by a court under this Act.

Restriction on divorce appeals

(2) No appeal lies from a judgment granting a divorce on or after the day on which the divorce takes effect.

Restriction on order appeals

(3) No appeal lies from an order made under this Act more than thirty days after the day on which the order was made.

Extension

(4) An appellate court or a judge thereof may, on special grounds, either before or after the expiration of the time fixed by subsection (3) for instituting an appeal, by order extend that time.

Powers of appellate court

(5) The appellate court may

(a) dismiss the appeal; or

(b) allow the appeal and

(i) render the judgment or make the order that ought to have been rendered or made, including such order or such further or other order as it deems just, or

(ii) order a new hearing where it deems it necessary to do so to correct a substantial wrong or miscarriage of justice.

Procedure on appeals

(6) Except as otherwise provided by this Act or the rules or regulations, an appeal under this section shall be asserted, heard and decided according to the ordinary procedure governing appeals to the appellate court from the court rendering the judgment or making the order being appealed.

GENERAL

Definition of "spouse"

21.1(1) In this section, "spouse" has the meaning assigned by subsection 2(1) and includes a former spouse.

Affidavit re removal of barriers to religious remarriage

(2) In any proceedings under this Act, a spouse (in this section referred to as the "deponent") may serve on the other spouse and file with the court an affidavit indicating

(a) that the other spouse is the spouse of the deponent;

(b) the date and place of the marriage, and the official character of the person who solemnized the marriage;

(c) the nature of any barriers to the remarriage of the deponent within the deponent's religion the removal of which is within the other spouse's control;

(d) where there are any barriers to the remarriage of the other spouse within the other spouse's religion the removal of which is within the deponent's control, that the deponent

(i) has removed those barriers, and the date and circumstances of that removal, or

(ii) has signified a willingness to remove those barriers, and the date and circumstances of that signification;

(e) that the deponent has, in writing, requested the other spouse to remove all of the barriers to the remarriage of the deponent within the deponent's religion the removal of which is within the other spouse's control;

(f) the date of the request described in paragraph (e); and

(g) that the other spouse, despite the request described in paragraph (e), has failed to remove all of the barriers referred to in that paragraph.

Powers of court where barriers not removed

(3) Where a spouse who has been served with an affidavit under subsection (2) does not

(a) within fifteen days after that affidavit is filed with the court or within such longer period as the court allows, serve on the deponent and file with the court an affidavit indicating that all of the barriers referred to in paragraph (2)(e) have been removed, and

(b) satisfy the court, in any additional manner that the court may require, that all of the barriers referred to in paragraph (2)(e) have been removed,

the court may, subject to any terms that the court considers appropriate,

(c) dismiss any application filed by that spouse under this Act, and

(d) strike out any other pleadings and affidavits filed by that spouse under this Act.

Special case

(4) Without limiting the generality of the court's discretion under subsection (3), the court may refuse to exercise its powers under paragraphs (3)(c) and (d) where a spouse who has been served with an affidavit under subsection (2)

(a) within fifteen days after that affidavit is filed with the court or within such longer period as the court allows, serves on the deponent and files with the court an affidavit indicating genuine grounds of a religious or conscientious nature for refusing to remove the barriers referred to in paragraph (2)(e); and

(b) satisfies the court, in any additional manner that the court may require, that the spouse has genuine grounds of a religious or conscientious nature for refusing to remove the barriers referred to in paragraph (2)(e).

Affidavits

(5) For the purposes of this section, an affidavit filed with the court by a spouse must, in order to be valid, indicate the date on which it was served on the other spouse.

Where section does not apply

(6) This section does not apply where the power to remove the barrier to religious remarriage lies with a religious body or official.

Recognition of foreign divorce

22(1) A divorce granted, on or after the coming into force of this Act, pursuant to a law of a country or subdivision of a country other than Canada by a tribunal or other authority having jurisdiction to do so shall be recognized for all purposes of determining the marital status in Canada of any person, if either former spouse was ordinarily resident in that country or subdivision for at least one year immediately preceding the commencement of proceedings for the divorce.

Idem

(2) A divorce granted, after July 1, 1968, pursuant to a law of a country or subdivision of a country other than Canada by a tribunal or other authority having jurisdiction to do so, on the basis of the domicile of the wife in that country or subdivision determined as if she were unmarried and, if she was a minor, as if she had attained the age of majority, shall be recognized for all purposes of determining the marital status in Canada of any person.

Other recognition rules preserved

(3) Nothing in this section abrogates or derogates from any other rule of law respecting the recognition of divorces granted otherwise than under this Act.

Provincial laws of evidence

23(1) Subject to this or any other Act of Parliament, the laws of evidence of the province in which any proceedings under this Act are taken, including the laws of proof of service of any document, apply to such proceedings.

Presumption

(2) For the purposes of this section, where any proceedings are transferred to the Federal Court under subsection 3(3) or 5(3), the proceedings shall be deemed to have been taken in the province specified in the direction of the Court to be the province with which both spouses or former spouses, as the case may be, are or have been most substantially connected.

Proof of signature or office

24. A document offered in a proceeding under this Act that purports to be certified or sworn by a judge or an officer of a court shall, unless the contrary is proved, be proof of the appointment, signature or authority of the judge or officer and, in the case of a document purporting to be sworn, of the appointment, signature or authority of the person before whom the document purports to be sworn.

Definition of "competent authority"

25(1) In this section, "competent authority," in respect of a court, or appellate court, in a province means the body, person or group of persons ordinarily competent under the laws of that province to make rules regulating the practice and procedure in that court.

Rules

(2) Subject to subsection (3), the competent authority may make rules applicable to any proceedings under this Act in a court, or appellate court, in a province, including, without limiting the generality of the foregoing, rules

(a) regulating the practice and procedure in the court, including the addition of persons as parties to the proceedings;

(b) respecting the conduct and disposition of any proceedings under this Act without an oral hearing;

(b.1) respecting the application of section 17.1 in respect of proceedings for a variation order;

(c) regulating the sittings of the court;

(d) respecting the fixing and awarding of costs;

(e) prescribing and regulating the duties of officers of the court;

(f) respecting the transfer of proceedings under this Act to or from the court; and

(g) prescribing and regulating any other matter considered expedient to attain the ends of justice and carry into effect the purposes and provisions of this Act.

Exercise of power

(3) The power to make rules for a court or appellate court conferred by subsection (2) on a competent authority shall be exercised in the like manner and subject to the like terms and conditions, if any, as the power to make rules for that court conferred on that authority by the laws of the province.

Not statutory instruments

(4) Rules made pursuant to this section by a competent authority that is not a judicial or quasi-judicial body shall be deemed not to be statutory instruments within the meaning and for the purposes of the Statutory Instruments Act.

Agreements with provinces

25.1(1) With the approval of the Governor in Council, the Minister of Justice may, on behalf of the Government of Canada, enter into an agreement with a province authorizing a provincial child support service designated in the agreement to

(a) assist courts in the province in the determination of the amount of child support; and

(b) recalculate, at regular intervals, in accordance with the applicable guidelines, the amount of child support orders on the basis of updated income information.

Effect of recalculation

(2) Subject to subsection (5), the amount of a child support order as recalculated pursuant to this section shall for all purposes be deemed to be the amount payable under the child support order.

Liability

(3) The former spouse against whom a child support order was made becomes liable to pay the amount as recalculated pursuant to this section thirty-one days after both former spouses to whom the order relates are notified of the recalculation in the manner provided for in the agreement authorizing the recalculation.

Right to vary

(4) Where either or both former spouses to whom a child support order relates do not agree with the amount of the order as recalculated pursuant to this section, either former spouse may, within thirty days after both former spouses are notified of the recalculation in the manner provided for in the agreement authorizing the recalculation, apply to a court of competent jurisdiction for an order under subsection 17(1).

Effect of application

(5) Where an application is made under subsection (4), the operation of subsection (3) is suspended pending the determination of the application, and the child support order continues in effect.

Withdrawal of application

(6) Where an application made under subsection (4) is withdrawn before the determination of the application, the former spouse against whom the order was made becomes liable to pay the amount as recalculated pursuant to this section on the day on which the former spouse would have become liable had the application not been made.

Regulations

26(1) The Governor in Council may make regulations for carrying the purposes and provisions of this Act into effect and, without limiting the generality of the foregoing, may make regulations

(a) respecting the establishment and operation of a central registry of divorce proceedings in Canada; and

(b) providing for uniformity in the rules made pursuant to section 25.

Regulations prevail

(2) Any regulations made pursuant to subsection (1) to provide for uniformity in the rules prevail over those rules.

Guidelines

26.1(1) The Governor in Council may establish guidelines respecting the making of orders for child support, including, but without limiting the generality of the foregoing, guidelines

(a) respecting the way in which the amount of an order for child support is to be determined;

(b) respecting the circumstances in which discretion may be exercised in the making of an order for child support;

(c) authorizing a court to require that the amount payable under an order for child support be paid in periodic payments, in a lump sum or in a lump sum and periodic payments;

(d) authorizing a court to require that the amount payable under an order for child support be paid or secured, or paid and secured, in the manner specified in the order;

(e) respecting the circumstances that give rise to the making of a variation order in respect of a child support order;

(f) respecting the determination of income for the purposes of the application of the guidelines;

(g) authorizing a court to impute income for the purposes of the application of the guidelines; and

(h) respecting the production of income information and providing for sanctions when that information is not provided.

Principle

(2) The guidelines shall be based on the principle that spouses have a joint financial obligation to maintain the children of the marriage in accordance with their relative abilities to contribute to the performance of that obligation.

Definition of "order for child support"

(3) In subsection (1), "order for child support" means

(a) an order or interim order made under section 15.1;

(b) a variation order in respect of a child support order; or

(c) an order or an interim order made under section 19.

Fees

27(1) The Governor in Council may, by order, authorize the Minister of Justice to prescribe a fee to be paid by any person to whom a service is provided under this Act or the regulations.

Agreements

(2) The Minister of Justice may, with the approval of the Governor in Council, enter into an agreement with the government of any province respecting the collection and remittance of any fees prescribed pursuant to subsection (1).

Review and report

28. The Minister of Justice shall undertake a comprehensive review of the provisions and operation of the Federal Child Support Guidelines and the determination of child support under this Act and shall cause a report on the review to be laid before each House of Parliament within five years after the coming into force of this section.

Children's Law Reform Act

RSO 1990, c. C.12

CONTENTS

PART IV
Amendments

PART I
EQUAL STATUS OF CHILDREN

Rule of parentage

1(1) Subject to subsection (2), for all purposes of the law of Ontario a person is the child of his or her natural parents and his or her status as their child is independent of whether the child is born within or outside marriage.

Exception for adopted children

(2) Where an adoption order has been made, section 158 or 159 of the *Child and Family Services Act* applies and the child is the child of the adopting parents as if they were the natural parents.

Kindred relationships

(3) The parent and child relationships as determined under subsections (1) and (2) shall be followed in the determination of other kindred relationships flowing therefrom.

Common law distinction of legitimacy abolished

(4) Any distinction at common law between the status of children born in wedlock and born out of wedlock is abolished and the relationship of parent and child and kindred relationships flowing therefrom shall be determined for the purposes of the common law in accordance with this section.

Rule of construction

2(1) For the purposes of construing any instrument, Act or regulation, unless the contrary intention appears, a reference to a person or group or class of persons described in terms of relationship by blood or marriage to another person shall be construed to refer to or include a person who comes within the description by reason of the relationship of parent and child as determined under section 1.

Application

(2) Subsection (1) applies to,

(a) any Act of the Legislature or any regulation, order or by-law made under an Act of the Legislature enacted or made before, on or after the 31st day of March, 1978; and

(b) any instrument made on or after the 31st day of March, 1978.

PART II
ESTABLISHMENT OF PARENTAGE

Court under ss. 4 to 7

3. The court having jurisdiction for the purposes of sections 4 to 7 is,

(a) the Family Court, in the areas where it has jurisdiction under subsection 21.1(4) of the *Courts of Justice Act*;

(b) the Superior Court of Justice, in the rest of Ontario.

Paternity and maternity declarations

4(1) Any person having an interest may apply to a court for a declaration that a male person is recognized in law to be the father of a child or that a female person is the mother of a child.

Declaration of paternity recognized at law

(2) Where the court finds that a presumption of paternity exists under section 8 and unless it is established, on the balance of probabilities, that the presumed father is not the father of the child, the court shall make a declaratory order confirming that the paternity is recognized in law.

Declaration of maternity

(3) Where the court finds on the balance of probabilities that the relationship of mother and child has been established, the court may make a declaratory order to that effect.

Idem

(4) Subject to sections 6 and 7, an order made under this section shall be recognized for all purposes.

Application for declaration of paternity where no presumption

5(1) Where there is no person recognized in law under section 8 to be the father of a child, any person may apply to the court for a declaration that a male person is his or her father, or any male person may apply to the court for a declaration that a person is his child.

Limitation

(2) An application shall not be made under subsection (1) unless both the persons whose relationship is sought to be established are living.

Declaratory order

(3) Where the court finds on the balance of probabilities that the relationship of father and child has been established, the court may make a declaratory order to that effect and, subject to sections 6 and 7, the order shall be recognized for all purposes.

Reopening on new evidence

6. Where a declaration has been made under section 4 or 5 and evidence becomes available that was not available at the previous hearing, the court may, upon application, discharge or vary the order and make such other orders or directions as are ancillary thereto.

Appeal

7. An appeal lies from an order under section 4 or 5 or a decision under section 6 in accordance with the rules of the court.

Presumption of paternity

8(1) Unless the contrary is proven on a balance of probabilities, there is a presumption that a male person is, and he shall be recognized in law to be, the father of a child in any one of the following circumstances:

1. The person is married to the mother of the child at the time of the birth of the child.
2. The person was married to the mother of the child by a marriage that was terminated by death or judgment of nullity within 300 days before the birth of the child or by divorce where the decree *nisi* was granted within 300 days before the birth of the child.
3. The person marries the mother of the child after the birth of the child and acknowledges that he is the natural father.
4. The person was cohabiting with the mother of the child in a relationship of some permanence at the time of the birth of the child or the child is born within 300 days after they ceased to cohabit.
5. The person has certified the child's birth, as the child's father, under the *Vital Statistics Act* or a similar Act in another jurisdiction in Canada.
6. The person has been found or recognized in his lifetime by a court of competent jurisdiction in Canada to be the father of the child.

Where marriage void

(2) For the purpose of subsection (1), where a man and woman go through a form of marriage with each other, in good faith, that is void and cohabit, they shall be deemed to be married during the time they cohabit and the marriage shall be deemed to be terminated when they cease to cohabit.

Conflicting presumptions

(3) Where circumstances exist that give rise to a presumption or presumptions of paternity by more than one father under subsection (1), no presumption shall be made as to paternity and no person is recognized in law to be the father.

Admissibility in evidence of acknowledgment against interest

9. A written acknowledgment of parentage that is admitted in evidence in any civil proceeding against the interest of the person making the acknowledgment is proof, in the absence of evidence to the contrary, of the fact.

Approved blood tests

10(1) Upon the application of a party in a civil proceeding in which the court is called upon to determine the parentage of a child, the court may give the party leave to obtain blood tests of such persons as are named in the order granting leave and to submit the results in evidence.

Conditions attached

(2) Leave under subsection (1) may be given subject to such terms and conditions as the court thinks proper.

Inference from refusal

(3) Where leave is given under subsection (1) and a person named therein refuses to submit to the blood test, the court may draw such inferences as it thinks appropriate.

Consent to procedure

(4) The *Health Care Consent Act, 1996* applies to the blood test as if it were treatment under that Act.

Regulations for blood tests

11. The Lieutenant Governor in Council may make regulations governing blood tests for which leave is given by a court under section 10 including, without limiting the generality of the foregoing,

(a) the method of taking blood samples and the handling, transportation and storage thereof;

(b) the conditions under which a blood sample may be tested;

(c) designating persons or facilities or classes thereof who are authorized to conduct blood tests for the purposes of section 10;

(d) prescribing procedures respecting the admission of reports of blood tests in evidence;

(e) prescribing forms for the purpose of section 10 and this section and providing for their use.

Statutory declaration of parentage

12(1) A person may file in the office of the Registrar General a statutory declaration, in the form prescribed by the regulations, affirming that he or she is the father or mother, as the case may be, of a child.

Idem

(2) Two persons may file in the office of the Registrar General a statutory declaration, in the form prescribed by the regulations, jointly affirming that they are the father and mother of a child.

Copies of statutory declarations under *Vital Statistics Act*

13. Upon application and upon payment of the fee prescribed under the *Vital Statistics Act*, any person who has an interest, furnishes substantially accurate particulars and satisfies the Registrar General as to the reason for requiring it may obtain from the Registrar General a certified copy of a statutory declaration filed under section 12.

Filing of court decisions respecting parentage

14(1) Every registrar or clerk of a court in Ontario shall furnish the Registrar General with a statement in the form prescribed by the regulations respecting each order or judgment of the court that confirms or makes a finding of parentage.

Inspection by public

(2) Upon application and upon payment of the fee prescribed under the *Vital Statistics Act*, any person may inspect a statement respecting an order or judgment filed under subsection (1) and obtain a certified copy thereof from the Registrar General.

Certified copies as evidence

15. A certificate certifying a copy of a document to be a true copy, obtained under section 12, 13 or 14, purporting to be signed by the Registrar General or Deputy Registrar General or on which the signature of either is lithographed, printed or stamped is, without proof of the office or signature of the Registrar General or Deputy Registrar General, receivable in evidence as proof, in the absence of evidence to the contrary, of the filing and contents of the document for all purposes in any action or proceeding.

Duties of Registrar General

16. Nothing in this Act shall be construed to require the Registrar General to amend a registration showing parentage other than in recognition of an order made under section 4, 5 or 6.

Regulations for forms

17. The Lieutenant Governor in Council may make regulations prescribing forms for the purposes of this Part.

PART III
CUSTODY, ACCESS AND GUARDIANSHIP

Interpretation

Definitions, Part III

18(1) In this Part,

"court" means the Ontario Court of Justice, the Family Court or the Superior Court of Justice;

"extra-provincial order" means an order, or that part of an order, of an extra-provincial tribunal that grants to a person custody of or access to a child;

"extra-provincial tribunal" means a court or tribunal outside Ontario that has jurisdiction to grant to a person custody of or access to a child;

"separation agreement" means an agreement that is a valid separation agreement under Part IV of the *Family Law Act.*

Child

(2) A reference in this Part to a child is a reference to the child while a minor.

Purposes, Part III

19. The purposes of this Part are,

(a) to ensure that applications to the courts in respect of custody of, incidents of custody of, access to and guardianship for children will be determined on the basis of the best interests of the children;

(b) to recognize that the concurrent exercise of jurisdiction by judicial tribunals of more than one province, territory or state in respect of the custody of the same child ought to be avoided, and to make provision so that the courts of Ontario will, unless there are exceptional circumstances, refrain from exercising or decline jurisdiction in cases where it is more appropriate for the matter to be determined by a tribunal having jurisdiction in another place with which the child has a closer connection;

(c) to discourage the abduction of children as an alternative to the determination of custody rights by due process; and

(d) to provide for the more effective enforcement of custody and access orders and for the recognition and enforcement of custody and access orders made outside Ontario.

Custody and Access

Father and mother entitled to custody

20(1) Except as otherwise provided in this Part, the father and the mother of a child are equally entitled to custody of the child.

Rights and responsibilities

(2) A person entitled to custody of a child has the rights and responsibilities of a parent in respect of the person of the child and must exercise those rights and responsibilities in the best interests of the child.

Authority to act

(3) Where more than one person is entitled to custody of a child, any one of them may exercise the rights and accept the responsibilities of a parent on behalf of them in respect of the child.

Where parents separate

(4) Where the parents of a child live separate and apart and the child lives with one of them with the consent, implied consent or acquiescence of the other of them, the right of the other to exercise the entitlement of custody and the incidents of custody, but not the entitlement to access, is suspended until a separation agreement or order otherwise provides.

Access

(5) The entitlement to access to a child includes the right to visit with and be visited by the child and the same right as a parent to make inquiries and to be given information as to the health, education and welfare of the child.

Marriage of child

(6) The entitlement to custody of or access to a child terminates on the marriage of the child.

Entitlement subject to agreement or order

(7) Any entitlement to custody or access or incidents of custody under this section is subject to alteration by an order of the court or by separation agreement.

Application for custody or access

21. A parent of a child or any other person may apply to a court for an order respecting custody of or access to the child or determining any aspect of the incidents of custody of the child.

Jurisdiction

22(1) A court shall only exercise its jurisdiction to make an order for custody of or access to a child where,

(a) the child is habitually resident in Ontario at the commencement of the application for the order;

(b) although the child is not habitually resident in Ontario, the court is satisfied,

(i) that the child is physically present in Ontario at the commencement of the application for the order,

(ii) that substantial evidence concerning the best interests of the child is available in Ontario,

(iii) that no application for custody of or access to the child is pending before an extra-provincial tribunal in another place where the child is habitually resident,

(iv) that no extra-provincial order in respect of custody of or access to the child has been recognized by a court in Ontario,

(v) that the child has a real and substantial connection with Ontario, and

(vi) that, on the balance of convenience, it is appropriate for jurisdiction to be exercised in Ontario.

Habitual residence

(2) A child is habitually resident in the place where he or she resided,

(a) with both parents;

(b) where the parents are living separate and apart, with one parent under a separation agreement or with the consent, implied consent or acquiescence of the other or under a court order; or

(c) with a person other than a parent on a permanent basis for a significant period of time,

whichever last occurred.

Abduction

(3) The removal or withholding of a child without the consent of the person having custody of the child does not alter the habitual residence of the child unless there has been acquiescence or undue delay in commencing due process by the person from whom the child is removed or withheld.

Serious harm to child

23. Despite sections 22 and 41, a court may exercise its jurisdiction to make or to vary an order in respect of the custody of or access to a child where,

(a) the child is physically present in Ontario; and

(b) the court is satisfied that the child would, on the balance of probabilities, suffer serious harm if,

(i) the child remains in the custody of the person legally entitled to custody of the child,

(ii) the child is returned to the custody of the person legally entitled to custody of the child, or

(iii) the child is removed from Ontario.

Merits of application for custody or access

24(1) The merits of an application under this Part in respect of custody of or access to a child shall be determined on the basis of the best interests of the child.

Best interests of child

(2) In determining the best interests of a child for the purposes of an application under this Part in respect of custody of or access to a child, a court shall consider all the needs and circumstances of the child including,

(a) the love, affection and emotional ties between the child and,

(i) each person entitled to or claiming custody of or access to the child,

(ii) other members of the child's family who reside with the child, and

(iii) persons involved in the care and upbringing of the child;

(b) the views and preferences of the child, where such views and preferences can reasonably be ascertained;

(c) the length of time the child has lived in a stable home environment;

(d) the ability and willingness of each person applying for custody of the child to provide the child with guidance and education, the necessaries of life and any special needs of the child;

(e) any plans proposed for the care and upbringing of the child;

(f) the permanence and stability of the family unit with which it is proposed that the child will live; and

(g) the relationship by blood or through an adoption order between the child and each person who is a party to the application.

Past conduct

(3) The past conduct of a person is not relevant to a determination of an application under this Part in respect of custody of or access to a child unless the conduct is relevant to the ability of the person to act as a parent of a child.

Declining jurisdiction

25. A court having jurisdiction under this Part in respect of custody or access may decline to exercise its jurisdiction where it is of the opinion that it is more appropriate for jurisdiction to be exercised outside Ontario.

Delay

26(1) Where an application under this Part in respect of custody of or access to a child has not been heard within six months after the commencement of the proceedings, the clerk or local registrar of the court shall list the application for the court and give notice to the parties of the date and time when and the place where the court will fix a date for the hearing of the application.

Directions

(2) At a hearing of a matter listed by the clerk or local registrar in accordance with subsection (1), the court by order may fix a date for the hearing of the application and may give such directions in respect of the proceedings and make such order in respect of the costs of the proceedings as the court considers appropriate.

Early date

(3) Where the court fixes a date under subsection (2), the court shall fix the earliest date that, in the opinion of the court, is compatible with a just disposition of the application.

Effect of divorce proceedings

27. Where an action for divorce is commenced under the *Divorce Act* (Canada), any application under this Part in respect of custody of or access to a child that has not been determined is stayed except by leave of the court.

Custody and Access – Orders

Powers of court

28. The court to which an application is made under section 21,

(a) by order may grant the custody of or access to the child to one or more persons;

(b) by order may determine any aspect of the incidents of the right to custody or access; and

(c) may make such additional order as the court considers necessary and proper in the circumstances.

Order varying an order

29. A court shall not make an order under this Part that varies an order in respect of custody or access made by a court in Ontario unless there has been a material change in circumstances that affects or is likely to affect the best interests of the child.

Custody and Access – Assistance to Court

Assessment of needs of child

30(1) The court before which an application is brought in respect of custody of or access to a child, by order, may appoint a person who has technical or professional skill to assess and report to the court on the needs of the child and the ability and willingness of the parties or any of them to satisfy the needs of the child.

When order may be made

(2) An order may be made under subsection (1) on or before the hearing of the application in respect of custody of or access to the child and with or without a request by a party to the application.

Agreement by parties

(3) The court shall, if possible, appoint a person agreed upon by the parties, but if the parties do not agree the court shall choose and appoint the person.

Consent to act

(4) The court shall not appoint a person under subsection (1) unless the person has consented to make the assessment and to report to the court within the period of time specified by the court.

Attendance for assessment

(5) In an order under subsection (1), the court may require the parties, the child and any other person who has been given notice of the proposed order, or any of them, to attend for assessment by the person appointed by the order.

Refusal to attend

(6) Where a person ordered under this section to attend for assessment refuses to attend or to undergo the assessment, the court may draw such inferences in respect of the ability and willingness of any person to satisfy the needs of the child as the court considers appropriate.

Report

(7) The person appointed under subsection (1) shall file his or her report with the clerk or local registrar of the court.

Copies of report

(8) The clerk or local registrar of the court shall give a copy of the report to each of the parties and to counsel, if any, representing the child.

Admissibility of report

(9) The report mentioned in subsection (7) is admissible in evidence in the application.

Assessor may be witness

(10) Any of the parties, and counsel, if any, representing the child, may require the person appointed under subsection (1) to attend as a witness at the hearing of the application.

Directions

(11) Upon motion, the court by order may give such directions in respect of the assessment as the court considers appropriate.

Fees and expenses

(12) The court shall require the parties to pay the fees and expenses of the person appointed under subsection (1).

Idem, proportions or amounts

(13) The court shall specify in the order the proportions or amounts of the fees and expenses that the court requires each party to pay.

Idem, serious financial hardship

(14) The court may relieve a party from responsibility for payment of any of the fees and expenses of the person appointed under subsection (1) where the court is satisfied that payment would cause serious financial hardship to the party.

Other expert evidence

(15) The appointment of a person under subsection (1) does not prevent the parties or counsel representing the child from submitting other expert evidence as to the needs of the child and the ability and willingness of the parties or any of them to satisfy the needs of the child.

Mediation

31(1) Upon an application for custody of or access to a child, the court, at the request of the parties, by order may appoint a person selected by the parties to mediate any matter specified in the order.

Consent to act

(2) The court shall not appoint a person under subsection (1) unless the person,

(a) has consented to act as mediator; and

(b) has agreed to file a report with the court within the period of time specified by the court.

Duty of mediator

(3) It is the duty of a mediator to confer with the parties and endeavour to obtain an agreement in respect of the matter.

Form of report

(4) Before entering into mediation on the matter, the parties shall decide whether,

(a) the mediator is to file a full report on the mediation, including anything that the mediator considers relevant to the matter in mediation; or

(b) the mediator is to file a report that either sets out the agreement reached by the parties or states only that the parties did not reach agreement on the matter.

Filing of report

(5) The mediator shall file his or her report with the clerk or local registrar of the court in the form decided upon by the parties under subsection (4).

Copies of report

(6) The clerk or local registrar of the court shall give a copy of the report to each of the parties and to counsel, if any, representing the child.

Admissions made in the course of mediation

(7) Where the parties have decided that the mediator's report is to be in the form described in clause (4)(b), evidence of anything said or of any admission or communication made in the course of the mediation is not admissible in any proceeding except with the consent of all parties to the proceeding in which the order was made under subsection (1).

Fees and expenses

(8) The court shall require the parties to pay the fees and expenses of the mediator.

Idem, proportions or amounts

(9) The court shall specify in the order the proportions or amounts of the fees and expenses that the court requires each party to pay.

Idem, serious financial hardship

(10) The court may relieve a party from responsibility for payment of any of the fees and expenses of the mediator where the court is satisfied that payment would cause serious financial hardship to the party.

Further evidence from outside Ontario

32(1) Where a court is of the opinion that it is necessary to receive further evidence from a place outside Ontario before making a decision, the court may send to the Attorney General, Minister of Justice or similar officer of the place outside Ontario such supporting material as may be necessary together with a request,

(a) that the Attorney General, Minister of Justice or similar officer take such action as may be necessary in order to require a named person to attend before the proper tribunal in that place and produce or give evidence in respect of the subject-matter of the application; and

(b) that the Attorney General, Minister of Justice or similar officer or the tribunal send to the court a certified copy of the evidence produced or given before the tribunal.

Cost of obtaining evidence

(2) A court that acts under subsection (1) may assess the cost of so acting against one or more of the parties to the application or may deal with such cost as costs in the cause.

Request from outside Ontario for further evidence

33(1) Where the Attorney General receives from an extra-provincial tribunal a request similar to that referred to in section 32 and such supporting material as may be necessary, it is the duty of the Attorney General to refer the request and the material to the proper court.

Obtaining evidence

(2) A court to which a request is referred by the Attorney General under subsection (1) shall require the person named in the request to attend before the court and produce or give evidence in accordance with the request.

Custody and Access – Enforcement

Supervision of custody or access

34(1) Where an order is made for custody of or access to a child, a court may give such directions as it considers appropriate for the supervision of the custody or access by a person, a children's aid society or other body.

Consent to act

(2) A court shall not direct a person, a children's aid society or other body to supervise custody or access as mentioned in subsection (1) unless the person, society or body has consented to act as supervisor.

Order restraining harassment

35(1) On application, a court may make an interim or final order restraining a person from molesting, annoying or harassing the applicant or children in the applicant's lawful custody and may require the person to enter into the recognizance or post the bond that the court considers appropriate.

Offence

(2) A person who contravenes a restraining order is guilty of an offence and on conviction is liable to either or both a fine of $5,000 and imprisonment for a term of not more than three months for a first offence and not more than two years for a subsequent offence.

Note: On a day to be named by proclamation of the Lieutenant Governor, subsection (2) is repealed by the Statutes of Ontario, 2000, chapter 33, subsection 21(1). See: 2000, c. 33, ss. 21(1), 23.

Note: Despite the repeal of subsection (2), any prosecution begun under that subsection before its repeal shall continue as if it were still in force. See: 2000, c. 33, s. 21(3).

Arrest without warrant

(3) A police officer may arrest without warrant a person the police officer believes on reasonable and probable grounds to have contravened a restraining order.

Existing orders

(4) Subsections (2) and (3) also apply in respect of contraventions, committed after those subsections come into force, of restraining orders made under a predecessor of this section.

Note: On a day to be named by proclamation of the Lieutenant Governor, section 35 is repealed by the Statutes of Ontario, 2000, chapter 33, subsection 21(2). See: 2000, c. 33, ss. 21(2), 23.

Note: Despite the repeal of section 35, any proceeding begun under that section before its repeal shall continue as if section 35 were still in force, and any order made under section 35, after its repeal, remains in force until it terminates by its own terms or is rescinded or terminated by a court. See: 2000, c. 33, s. 21(4).

Order where child unlawfully withheld

36(1) Where a court is satisfied upon application by a person in whose favour an order has been made for custody of or access to a child that there are reasonable and probable grounds for believing that any person is unlawfully withholding the child from the applicant, the court by order may authorize the applicant or someone on his or her behalf to apprehend the child for the purpose of giving effect to the rights of the applicant to custody or access, as the case may be.

Order to locate and take child

(2) Where a court is satisfied upon application that there are reasonable and probable grounds for believing,

(a) that any person is unlawfully withholding a child from a person entitled to custody of or access to the child;

(b) that a person who is prohibited by court order or separation agreement from removing a child from Ontario proposes to remove the child or have the child removed from Ontario; or

(c) that a person who is entitled to access to a child proposes to remove the child or to have the child removed from Ontario and that the child is not likely to return,

the court by order may direct a police force, having jurisdiction in any area where it appears to the court that the child may be, to locate, apprehend and deliver the child to the person named in the order.

Application without notice

(3) An order may be made under subsection (2) upon an application without notice where the court is satisfied that it is necessary that action be taken without delay.

Duty to act

(4) The police force directed to act by an order under subsection (2) shall do all things reasonably able to be done to locate, apprehend and deliver the child in accordance with the order.

Entry and search

(5) For the purpose of locating and apprehending a child in accordance with an order under subsection (2), a member of a police force may enter and search any place where he or she has reasonable and probable grounds for believing that the child may be with such assistance and such force as are reasonable in the circumstances.

Time

(6) An entry or a search referred to in subsection (5) shall be made only between 6 a.m. and 9 p.m. standard time unless the court, in the order, authorizes entry and search at another time.

Expiration of order

(7) An order made under subsection (2) shall name a date on which it expires, which shall be a date not later than six months after it is made unless the court is satisfied that a longer period of time is necessary in the circumstances.

When application may be made

(8) An application under subsection (1) or (2) may be made in an application for custody or access or at any other time.

COURT ORDERS, REMOVAL AND RETURN OF CHILDREN

To prevent unlawful removal of child

37(1) Where a court, upon application, is satisfied upon reasonable and probable grounds that a person prohibited by court order or separation agreement from removing a child from Ontario proposes to remove the child from Ontario, the court in order to prevent the removal of the child from Ontario may make an order under subsection (3).

To ensure return of child

(2) Where a court, upon application, is satisfied upon reasonable and probable grounds that a person entitled to access to a child proposes to remove the child from Ontario and is not likely to return the child to Ontario, the court in order to secure the prompt, safe return of the child to Ontario may make an order under subsection (3).

Order by court

(3) An order mentioned in subsection (1) or (2) may require a person to do any one or more of the following:

1. Transfer specific property to a named trustee to be held subject to the terms and conditions specified in the order.
2. Where payments have been ordered for the support of the child, make the payments to a specified trustee subject to the terms and conditions specified in the order.
3. Post a bond, with or without sureties, payable to the applicant in such amount as the court considers appropriate.
4. Deliver the person's passport, the child's passport and any other travel documents of either of them that the court may specify to the court or to an individual or body specified by the court.

Idem, Ontario Court of Justice

(4) The Ontario Court of Justice shall not make an order under paragraph 1 of subsection (3).

Terms and conditions

(5) In an order under paragraph 1 of subsection (3), the court may specify terms and conditions for the return or the disposition of the property as the court considers appropriate.

Safekeeping

(6) A court or an individual or body specified by the court in an order under paragraph 4 of subsection (3) shall hold a passport or travel document delivered in accordance with the order in safekeeping in accordance with any directions set out in the order.

Directions

(7) In an order under subsection (3), a court may give such directions in respect of the safekeeping of the property, payments, passports or travel documents as the court considers appropriate.

Contempt of orders of Ontario Court of Justice

38(1) In addition to its powers in respect of contempt, the Ontario Court of Justice may punish by fine or imprisonment, or both, any wilful contempt of or resistance to its process or orders in respect of custody of or access to a child, but the fine shall not in any case exceed $5,000 nor shall the imprisonment exceed ninety days.

Conditions of imprisonment

(2) An order for imprisonment under subsection (1) may be made conditional upon default in the performance of a condition set out in the order and may provide for the imprisonment to be served intermittently.

Information as to address

39(1) Where, upon application to a court, it appears to the court that,

(a) for the purpose of bringing an application in respect of custody or access under this Part; or

(b) for the purpose of the enforcement of an order for custody or access,

the proposed applicant or person in whose favour the order is made has need to learn or confirm the whereabouts of the proposed respondent or person against whom the order referred to in clause (b) is made, the court may order any person or public body to provide the court with such particulars of the address of the proposed respondent or person against whom the order referred to in clause (b) is made as are contained in the records in the custody of the person or body, and the person or body shall give the court such particulars as are contained in the records and the court may then give the particulars to such person or persons as the court considers appropriate.

Exception

(2) A court shall not make an order on an application under subsection (1) where it appears to the court that the purpose of the application is to enable the applicant to identify or to obtain particulars as to the identity of a person who has custody of a child, rather than to learn or confirm the whereabouts of the proposed respondent or the enforcement of an order for custody or access.

Compliance with order

(3) The giving of information in accordance with an order under subsection (1) shall be deemed for all purposes not to be a contravention of any Act or regulation or any common law rule of confidentiality.

Section binds Crown

(4) This section binds the Crown in right of Ontario.

Custody and Access – Extra-Provincial Matters

Interim powers of court

40. Upon application, a court,

(a) that is satisfied that a child has been wrongfully removed to or is being wrongfully retained in Ontario; or

(b) that may not exercise jurisdiction under section 22 or that has declined jurisdiction under section 25 or 42,

may do any one or more of the following:

1. Make such interim order in respect of the custody or access as the court considers is in the best interests of the child.
2. Stay the application subject to,
   i. the condition that a party to the application promptly commence a similar proceeding before an extra-provincial tribunal, or
   ii. such other conditions as the court considers appropriate.
3. Order a party to return the child to such place as the court considers appropriate and, in the discretion of the court, order payment of the cost of the reasonable travel and other expenses of the child and any parties to or witnesses at the hearing of the application.

Enforcement of extra-provincial orders

41(1) Upon application by any person in whose favour an order for the custody of or access to a child has been made by an extra-provincial tribunal, a court shall recognize the order unless the court is satisfied,

(a) that the respondent was not given reasonable notice of the commencement of the proceeding in which the order was made;

(b) that the respondent was not given an opportunity to be heard by the extra-provincial tribunal before the order was made;

(c) that the law of the place in which the order was made did not require the extra-provincial tribunal to have regard for the best interests of the child;

(d) that the order of the extra-provincial tribunal is contrary to public policy in Ontario; or

(e) that, in accordance with section 22, the extra-provincial tribunal would not have jurisdiction if it were a court in Ontario.

Effect of recognition of order

(2) An order made by an extra-provincial tribunal that is recognized by a court shall be deemed to be an order of the court and enforceable as such.

Conflicting orders

(3) A court presented with conflicting orders made by extra-provincial tribunals for the custody of or access to a child that, but for the conflict, would be recognized and enforced by the court under subsection (1) shall recognize and enforce the order that appears to the court to be most in accord with the best interests of the child.

Further orders

(4) A court that has recognized an extra-provincial order may make such further orders under this Part as the court considers necessary to give effect to the order.

Superseding order, material change in circumstances

42(1) Upon application, a court by order may supersede an extra-provincial order in respect of custody of or access to a child where the court is satisfied that there has been a material change in circumstances that affects or is likely to affect the best interests of the child and,

(a) the child is habitually resident in Ontario at the commencement of the application for the order; or

(b) although the child is not habitually resident in Ontario, the court is satisfied,

(i) that the child is physically present in Ontario at the commencement of the application for the order,

(ii) that the child no longer has a real and substantial connection with the place where the extra-provincial order was made,

(iii) that substantial evidence concerning the best interests of the child is available in Ontario,

(iv) that the child has a real and substantial connection with Ontario, and

(v) that, on the balance of convenience, it is appropriate for jurisdiction to be exercised in Ontario.

Declining jurisdiction

(2) A court may decline to exercise its jurisdiction under this section where it is of the opinion that it is more appropriate for jurisdiction to be exercised outside Ontario.

Superseding order, serious harm

43. Upon application, a court by order may supersede an extra-provincial order in respect of custody of or access to a child if the court is satisfied that the child would, on the balance of probability, suffer serious harm if,

(a) the child remains in the custody of the person legally entitled to custody of the child;

(b) the child is returned to the custody of the person entitled to custody of the child; or

(c) the child is removed from Ontario.

True copy of extra-provincial order

44. A copy of an extra-provincial order certified as a true copy by a judge, other presiding officer or registrar of the tribunal that made the order or by a person charged with keeping the orders of the tribunal is proof, in the absence of evidence to the contrary, of the making of the order, the content of the order and the appointment and signature of the judge, presiding officer, registrar or other person.

Court may take notice of foreign law

45. For the purposes of an application under this Part, a court may take notice, without requiring formal proof, of the law of a jurisdiction outside Ontario and of a decision of an extra-provincial tribunal.

CONVENTION ON CIVIL ASPECTS OF INTERNATIONAL CHILD ABDUCTION

Definition

46(1) In this section,

"convention" means the Convention on the Civil Aspects of International Child Abduction, set out in the Schedule to this section.

Convention in force

(2) On, from and after the 1st day of December, 1983, except as provided in subsection (3), the convention is in force in Ontario and the provisions thereof are law in Ontario.

Crown, legal costs under convention

(3) The Crown is not bound to assume any costs resulting under the convention from the participation of legal counsel or advisers or from court proceedings except in accordance with the *Legal Aid Services Act, 1998.*

Central Authority

(4) The Ministry of the Attorney General shall be the Central Authority for Ontario for the purpose of the convention.

Application to court

(5) An application may be made to a court in pursuance of a right or an obligation under the convention.

Request to ratify convention

(6) The Attorney General shall request the Government of Canada to submit a declaration to the Ministry of Foreign Affairs of the Kingdom of the Netherlands, declaring that the convention extends to Ontario.

Regulations

(7) The Lieutenant Governor in Council may make such regulations as the Lieutenant Governor in Council considers necessary to carry out the intent and purpose of this section.

Conflict

(8) Where there is a conflict between this section and any other enactment, this section prevails. ...

Guardianship

Appointment of guardian

47(1) Upon application by a child's parent or by any other person, on notice to the Children's Lawyer, a court may appoint a guardian of the child's property.

Responsibility of guardian

(2) A guardian of the property of a child has charge of and is responsible for the care and management of the property of the child.

PARENTS AND JOINT GUARDIANS

Parents as guardians

48(1) As between themselves and subject to any court order or any agreement between them, the parents of a child are equally entitled to be appointed by a court as guardians of the property of the child.

Parent and other person

(2) As between a parent of a child and a person who is not a parent of the child, the parent has a preferential entitlement to be appointed by a court as a guardian of the property of the child.

More than one guardian

(3) A court may appoint more than one guardian of the property of a child.

Guardians jointly responsible

(4) Where more than one guardian is appointed of the property of a child, the guardians are jointly responsible for the care and management of the property of the child.

Criteria

49. In deciding an application for the appointment of a guardian of the property of a child, the court shall consider all the circumstances, including,

(a) the ability of the applicant to manage the property of the child;

(b) the merits of the plan proposed by the applicant for the care and management of the property of the child; and

(c) the views and preferences of the child, where such views and preferences can reasonably be ascertained.

Effect of appointment

50. The appointment of a guardian by a court under this Part has effect in all parts of Ontario.

Payment of debt due to child if no guardian

51(1) If no guardian of a child's property has been appointed, a person who is under a duty to pay money or deliver personal property to the child discharges that duty, to the extent of the amount paid or the value of the personal property delivered, subject to subsection (1.1), by paying money or delivering personal property to,

(a) the child, if the child has a legal obligation to support another person;
(b) a parent with whom the child resides; or
(c) a person who has lawful custody of the child.

Same

(1.1) The total of the amount of money paid and the value of personal property delivered under subsection (1) shall not exceed the prescribed amount or, if no amount is prescribed, $10,000.

Money payable under judgment

(2) Subsection (1) does not apply in respect of money payable under a judgment or order of a court.

Receipt for payment

(3) A receipt or discharge for money or personal property not in excess of the amount or value set out in subsection (1) received for a child by a parent with whom the child resides or a person who has lawful custody of the child has the same validity as if a court had appointed the parent or the person as a guardian of the property of the child.

Responsibility for money or property

(4) A parent with whom a child resides or a person who has lawful custody of a child who receives and holds money or personal property referred to in subsection (1) has the responsibility of a guardian for the care and management of the money or personal property.

Regulations

(5) The Lieutenant Governor in Council may, by regulation, prescribe an amount for the purpose of subsection (1.1).

Accounts

52. A guardian of the property of a child may be required to account or may voluntarily pass the accounts in respect of the care and management of the property of the child in the same manner as a trustee under a will may be required to account or may pass the accounts in respect of the trusteeship.

Transfer of property to child

53. A guardian of the property of a child shall transfer to the child all property of the child in the care of the guardian when the child attains the age of eighteen years.

Management fees and expenses

54. A guardian of the property of a child is entitled to payment of a reasonable amount for fees for and expenses of management of the property of the child.

Bond by guardian

55(1) A court that appoints a guardian of the property of a child shall require the guardian to post a bond, with or without sureties, payable to the child in such amount as the court considers appropriate in respect of the care and management of the property of the child.

Where parent appointed guardian

(2) Subsection (1) does not apply where the court appoints a parent of a child as guardian of the property of the child and the court is of the opinion that it is appropriate not to require the parent to post a bond.

Where child has support obligation

56. Upon application by a child who has a legal obligation to support another person, the court that appointed a guardian of the property of the child or a co-ordinate court by order shall end the guardianship for the child.

REMOVAL AND RESIGNATION OF GUARDIAN

Removal

57(1) A guardian of the property of a child may be removed by a court for the same reasons for which a trustee may be removed.

Resignation

(2) A guardian of the property of a child, with the permission of a court, may resign as guardian upon such conditions as the court considers appropriate.

Notice to Estate Registrar for Ontario

58. A notice of every application to a court for appointment of a guardian of the property of a child shall be transmitted by the clerk or local registrar of the court to the Estate Registrar for Ontario.

Disposition of Property

Court order re property of child

59(1) Upon application by a child's parent or by any other person, on notice to the Children's Lawyer, the Superior Court of Justice by order may require or approve, or both,

(a) the disposition or encumbrance of all or part of the interest of the child in land;

(b) the sale of the interest of the child in personal property; or

(c) the payment of all or part of any money belonging to the child or of the income from any property belonging to the child, or both.

Criteria

(2) An order shall be made under subsection (1) only where the Court is of the opinion that the disposition, encumbrance, sale or payment is necessary or proper for the support or education of the child or will substantially benefit the child.

Conditions

(3) An order under subsection (1) may be made subject to such conditions as the Court considers appropriate.

Limitation

(4) The Court shall not require or approve a disposition or encumbrance of the interest of a child in land contrary to a term of the instrument by which the child acquired the interest.

Execution of documents

(5) The Court, where it makes an order under subsection (1), may order that the child or another person named in the order execute any documents necessary to carry out the disposition, encumbrance, sale or payment.

Directions

(6) The Court by order may give such directions as it considers necessary for the carrying out of an order made under subsection (1).

Validity of documents

(7) Every document executed in accordance with an order under this section is as effectual as if the child by whom it was executed was eighteen years of age or, if executed by another person in accordance with the order, as if the child had executed it and had been eighteen years of age at the time.

Liability

(8) No person incurs or shall be deemed to incur liability by making a payment in accordance with an order under clause (1)(c).

Order for maintenance where power of appointment in favour of children

60(1) Upon application by or with the consent of a person who has an estate for life in property with power to devise or appoint the property to one or more of his or her children, the Superior Court of Justice may order that such part of the proceeds of the property as the Court considers proper be used for the support, education or benefit of one or more of the children.

Idem

(2) An order may be made under subsection (1) whether or not,

(a) there is a gift over in the event that there are no children to take under the power; or

(b) any person could dispose of the property in the event that there are no children to take under the power.

Testamentary Custody and Guardianship

APPOINTMENTS BY WILL

Custody

61(1) A person entitled to custody of a child may appoint by will one or more persons to have custody of the child after the death of the appointor.

Guardianship

(2) A guardian of the property of a child may appoint by will one or more persons to be guardians of the property of the child after the death of the appointor.

Appointment by minor

(3) An unmarried parent who is a minor may make an appointment mentioned in subsection (1) or (2) by a written appointment signed by the parent.

Limitation

(4) An appointment under subsection (1), (2) or (3) is effective only,

(a) if the appointor is the only person entitled to custody of the child or who is the guardian of the property of the child, as the case requires, on the day immediately before the appointment is to take effect; or

(b) if the appointor and any other person entitled to custody of the child or who is the guardian of the property of the child, as the case requires, die at the same time or in circumstances that render it uncertain which survived the other.

Where more than one appointment

(5) Where two or more persons are appointed to have custody of or to be guardians of the property of a child by appointors who die as mentioned in clause (4)(b), only the appointments of the persons appointed by both or all of the appointors are effective.

Consent of appointee

(6) No appointment under subsection (1), (2) or (3) is effective without the consent of the person appointed.

Expiration of appointment

(7) An appointment under subsection (1), (2) or (3) for custody of a child or guardianship of the property of a child expires ninety days after the appointment becomes effective or, where the appointee applies under this Part for custody of the child or guardianship of the property of the child within the ninety-day period, when the application is disposed of.

Application or order under ss.21, 47

(8) An appointment under this section does not apply to prevent an application for or the making of an order under section 21 or 47.

Application

(9) This section applies in respect of,

(a) any will made on or after the 1st day of October, 1982; and

(b) any will made before the 1st day of October, 1982, if the testator is living on that day.

Procedure

PROCEDURE, GENERAL

Joinder of proceedings

62(1) An application under this Part may be made in the same proceeding and in the same manner as an application under the *Family Law Act*, or in another proceeding.

Nature of order

(2) An application under this Part may be an original application or for the variance of an order previously given or to supersede an order of an extra-provincial tribunal.

Parties

(3) The parties to an application under this Part in respect of a child shall include,

(a) the mother and the father of the child;

(b) a person who has demonstrated a settled intention to treat the child as a child of his or her family;

(c) a person who had the actual care and upbringing of the child immediately before the application; and

(d) any other person whose presence as a party is necessary to determine the matters in issue.

Combining of applications

(4) Where, in an application under this Part, it appears to the court that it is necessary or desirable in the best interests of the child to have other matters first or simultaneously determined, the court may direct that the application stand over until such other proceedings are brought or determined as the court considers appropriate, subject to section 26.

Where identity of father not known

(5) Where there is no presumption of paternity and the identity of the father is not known or is not reasonably capable of being ascertained, the court may order substituted service or may dispense with service of documents upon the father in the proceeding.

Application or response by minor

63(1) A minor who is a parent may make an application under this Part without a next friend and may respond without a litigation guardian.

Consent by minor

(2) A consent in respect of a matter provided for by this Part is not invalid by reason only that the person giving the consent is a minor.

Child entitled to be heard

64(1) In considering an application under this Part, a court where possible shall take into consideration the views and preferences of the child to the extent that the child is able to express them.

Interview by court

(2) The court may interview the child to determine the views and preferences of the child.

Recording

(3) The interview shall be recorded.

Counsel

(4) The child is entitled to be advised by and to have his or her counsel, if any, present during the interview.

Where child is sixteen or more years old

65. Nothing in this Part abrogates the right of a child of sixteen or more years of age to withdraw from parental control.

All proceedings in one court

66. Except as otherwise provided, where an application is made to a court under this Part, no person who is a party to the proceeding shall make an application under this Part to any other court in respect of a matter in issue in the proceeding, but the court may order that the proceeding be transferred to a court having other jurisdiction where, in the opinion of the court, the court having other jurisdiction is more appropriate to determine the matters in issue that should be determined at the same time.

CONSENT AND DOMESTIC CONTRACTS

Consent orders

67(1) Upon the consent of the parties in an application under this Part, the court may make any order that the court is otherwise empowered to make by this Part, subject to the duty of the court to have regard to the best interests of the child.

Incorporation of contract in order

(2) Any matter provided for in this Part and in a domestic contract as defined in the *Family Law Act* may be incorporated in an order made under this Part.

Part subject to contracts

68. Where a domestic contract as defined in the *Family Law Act* makes provision in respect of a matter that is provided for in this Part, the contract prevails except as otherwise provided in Part IV of the *Family Law Act*.

Jurisdiction of Superior Court of Justice

69. This Part does not deprive the Superior Court of Justice of its *parens patriae* jurisdiction.

70. REPEALED: 2001, c. 9, Sched. B, s. 4(6).

WHERE TO APPLY FOR INTERIM ORDERS AND VARIATIONS

Place of application for interim order

71(1) An application for an interim order shall be made to the court in which the original proceeding was taken.

Place of application to vary order

(2) An application under this Part to vary an order may be made to the court in which the original proceeding was taken or to a co-ordinate court in another part of Ontario.

Interim order

72. In a proceeding under this Part, the court may make such interim order as the court considers appropriate.

Appeal from Ontario Court of Justice

73. An appeal from an order of the Ontario Court of Justice under this Part lies to the Superior Court of Justice.

Order effective pending appeal

74. An order under this Part is effective even if an appeal is taken from the order, unless the court that made the order or the court to which the appeal is taken orders otherwise.

Rule of construction, guardianship of person and property

75(1) For the purposes of construing any instrument, Act or regulation, unless the contrary intention appears, a reference to a guardian with respect to the person of a child shall be construed to refer to custody of the child and a reference to a guardian with respect to property of a child shall be construed to refer to guardianship of the property of the child.

Application

(2) Subsection (1) applies to any instrument, any Act of the Legislature or any regulation, order or by-law made under an Act of the Legislature enacted or made before, on or after the 1st day of October, 1982.

76. REPEALED.

PART IV
AMENDMENTS

Amendment to s. 20

77. Section 20 is amended by adding the following subsection:

Duty of separated parents

(4a) Where the parents of a child live separate and apart and the child is in the custody of one of them and the other is entitled to access under the terms of a separation agreement or order, each shall, in the best interests of the child, encourage and support the child's continuing parent-child relationship with the other.

Amendment to s. 24

78(1) Subsection 24(1) is amended by inserting after "application" in the first line "or motion."

Same

(2) Subsections 24(2) and (3) are repealed and the following substituted:

Best interests of child

(2) In determining the best interests of a child for the purpose of an application or motion under this Part in respect of custody of or access to a child, a court shall consider all the child's needs and circumstances, including,

(a) the love, affection and emotional ties between the child and,

(i) each person seeking custody or access,

(ii) other members of the child's family residing with him or her, and

(iii) persons involved in the child's care and upbringing;

(b) the child's views and preferences, if they can reasonably be ascertained;

(c) the length of time the child has lived in a stable home environment;

(d) the ability of each person seeking custody or access to act as a parent;

(e) the ability and willingness of each person seeking custody to provide the child with guidance, education and necessities of life and to meet any special needs of the child;

(f) any plans proposed for the child's care and upbringing;

(g) the permanence and stability of the family unit with which it is proposed that the child will live; and

(h) the relationship, by blood or through an adoption order, between the child and each person who is a party to the application or motion.

Domestic violence to be considered

(3) In assessing a person's ability to act as a parent, the court shall consider the fact that the person has at any time committed violence against his or her spouse, same-sex partner or child, against his or her child's parent or against another member of the person's household.

Definitions

(3.1) In subsection (3),

"same-sex partner" means either of two persons of the same sex who live together in a conjugal relationship outside marriage;

"spouse" means,

(a) a spouse as defined in section 1 of the Family Law Act, or

(b) either of two persons of the opposite sex who live together in a conjugal relationship outside marriage

Restrictions on consideration of other past conduct

(4) Other than the conduct referred to in subsection (3), a person's past conduct may be considered only if the court is satisfied that it is relevant to the person's ability to act as a parent.

Amendment to the Act

79. This Act is amended by adding the following section:

Application to fix times or days of access

28a(1) If an order in respect of access to a child provides for a person's access to the child without specifying times or days, a party to the order may apply to the court that made it to vary it by specifying times or days.

Order

(2) The court may vary the order by specifying the times or days agreed to by the parties, or the times or days the court considers appropriate if the parties do not agree.

Separation agreements

(3) Subsection (1) also applies, with necessary modifications, in respect of a separation agreement under section 54 of the Family Law Act *or a predecessor of that section that provides for a person's access to a child without specifying times or days.*

Exception

(4) Subsection (1) does not apply in respect of orders made under the Divorce Act *(Canada) or a predecessor of that Act.*

Amendment to s. 29

80. Section 29 is amended by adding the following subsection:

Exception

(2) Subsection (1) does not apply in respect of orders made under subsection 28a(2) (fixing times or days of access) or 34a(2) or (6) (access enforcement, etc.).

Amendment to s. 30

81. Subsection 30(14) is repealed and the following substituted:

Idem, serious financial hardship

(14) The court may require one party to pay all the fees and expenses of the person appointed under subsection (1) if the court is satisfied that payment would cause the other party or parties serious financial hardship.

Amendment to s. 31

82. Subsection 31(10) is repealed and the following substituted:

Idem, serious financial hardship

(10) The court may require one party to pay all the mediator's fees and expenses if the court is satisfied that payment would cause the other party or parties serious financial hardship.

Amendment to the Act

83. This Act is further amended by adding the following section:

MOTIONS RE RIGHT OF ACCESS

Motion to enforce right of access

34a(1) A person in whose favour an order has been made for access to a child at specific times or on specific days and who claims that a person in whose favour an order has been made for custody of the child has wrongfully denied him or her access to the child may make a motion for relief under subsection (2) to the court that made the access order.

Order for relief

(2) If the court is satisfied that the responding party wrongfully denied the moving party access to the child, the court may, by order,

(a) require the responding party to give the moving party compensatory access to the child for the period agreed to by the parties, or for the period the court considers appropriate if the parties do not agree;

(b) require supervision as described in section 34;

(c) require the responding party to reimburse the moving party for any reasonable expenses actually incurred as a result of the wrongful denial of access;

(d) appoint a mediator in accordance with section 31 as if the motion were an application for access.

Period of compensatory access

(3) A period of compensatory access shall not be longer than the period of access that was wrongfully denied.

What constitutes wrongful denial of access

(4) A denial of access is wrongful unless it is justified by a legitimate reason such as one of the following:

1. *The responding party believed on reasonable grounds that the child might suffer physical or emotional harm if the right of access were exercised.*
2. *The responding party believed on reasonable grounds that he or she might suffer physical harm if the right of access were exercised.*
3. *The responding party believed on reasonable grounds that the moving party was impaired by alcohol or a drug at the time of access.*
4. *The moving party failed to present himself or herself to exercise the right of access within one hour of the time specified in the order or the time otherwise agreed on by the parties.*
5. *The responding party believed on reasonable grounds that the child was suffering from an illness of such a nature that it was not appropriate in the circumstances that the right of access be exercised.*
6. *The moving party did not satisfy written conditions concerning access that were agreed to by the parties or that form part of the order for access.*
7. *On numerous occasions during the preceding year, the moving party had, without reasonable notice and excuse, failed to exercise the right of access.*
8. *The moving party had informed the responding party that he or she would not seek to exercise the right of access on the occasion in question.*

Motion re failure to exercise of right of access, etc.

(5) A person in whose favour an order has been made for custody of a child and who claims that a person in whose favour an order has been made for access to the child has, without reasonable notice and excuse, failed to exercise the right of access or to return the

child as the order requires, may make a motion for relief under subsection (6) to the court that made the access order.

Order for relief

(6) If the court is satisfied that the responding party, without reasonable notice and excuse, failed to exercise the right of access or to return the child as the order requires, the court may, by order,

(a) require supervision as described in section 34;

(b) require the responding party to reimburse the moving party for any reasonable expenses actually incurred as a result of the failure to exercise the right of access or to return the child as the order requires;

(c) appoint a mediator in accordance with section 31 as if the motion were an application for access.

Speedy hearing

(7) A motion under subsection (1) or (5) shall be heard within ten days after it has been served.

Limitation

(8) A motion under subsection (1) or (5) shall not be made more than thirty days after the alleged wrongful denial or failure.

Oral evidence only

(9) The motion shall be determined on the basis of oral evidence only, unless the court gives leave to file an affidavit.

Scope of evidence at hearing limited

(10) At the hearing of the motion, unless the court orders otherwise, evidence shall be admitted only if it is directly related to,

(a) the alleged wrongful denial of access or failure to exercise the right of access or return the child as the order requires; or

(b) the responding party's reasons for the denial or failure.

Separation agreement may be filed with court

(11) A person who is a party to a separation agreement made under section 54 of the Family Law Act *or a predecessor of that section may file the agreement with the clerk of the Ontario Court (Provincial Division) or of the Unified Family Court, together with the person's affidavit stating that the agreement is in effect and has not been set aside or varied by a court or agreement.*

Note: Subsection (11) is amended by the Statutes of Ontario, 2001, chapter 9, Schedule B, subsection 4 (8) by striking out "Ontario Court (Provincial Division)" and substituting "Ontario Court of Justice." See: 2001, c. 9, Sched. B, s. 4(8).

Note: Subsection (11) is amended by the Statutes of Ontario, 2001, chapter 9, Schedule B, subsection 4 (9) by striking out "Unified Family Court" and substituting "Family Court." See: 2001, c. 9, Sched. B, s. 4(9).

Effect of filing

(12) When a separation agreement providing for access to a child at specific times or on specific days is filed in this manner, subsections (1) and (5) apply as if the agreement were an order of the court where it is filed.

Motions made in bad faith

(13) If the court is satisfied that a person has made a motion under subsection (1) or (5) in bad faith, the court may prohibit him or her from making further motions without leave of the court.

Idem

(14) Subsections (1) and (5) do not apply in respect of orders made under the Divorce Act *(Canada) or a predecessor of that Act.*

Application

(15) Subsections (1) and (5) do not apply in respect of a denial of access or a failure to exercise a right of access or to return a child as the order or agreement requires that takes place before the day this section comes into force.

Amendment to s. 35

84. Subsection 35(1) is repealed and the following substituted:

Order restraining harassment

(1) On application, a court may make an interim or final order restraining a person from molesting, annoying or harassing the applicant or children in the applicant's lawful custody, or from communicating with the applicant or children, except as the order provides, and may require the person to enter into the recognizance that the court considers appropriate.

Coming into force of ss. 77-84

85. Sections 77 to 84 do not come into force until a day to be named by proclamation of the Lieutenant Governor.

Family Law Act

RSO 1990, c. F.3

CONTENTS

PREAMBLE

Whereas it is desirable to encourage and strengthen the role of the family; and whereas for that purpose it is necessary to recognize the equal position of spouses as individuals within marriage and to recognize marriage as a form of partnership; and whereas in support of such recognition it is necessary to provide in law for the orderly and equitable settlement of the affairs of the spouses upon the breakdown of the partnership, and to provide for other mutual obligations in family relationships, including the equitable sharing by parents of responsibility for their children;

Therefore, Her Majesty, by and with the advice and consent of the Legislative Assembly of the Province of Ontario, enacts as follows:

Definitions

1(1) In this Act,

"child" includes a person whom a parent has demonstrated a settled intention to treat as a child of his or her family, except under an arrangement where the child is placed for valuable consideration in a foster home by a person having lawful custody;

"child support guidelines" means the guidelines established by the regulations made under subsections 69(2) and (3);

"cohabit" means to live together in a conjugal relationship, whether within or outside marriage;

"court" means the Ontario Court (Provincial Division), the Unified Family Court or the Ontario Court (General Division);

"domestic contract" means a domestic contract as defined in Part IV (Domestic Contracts);

"parent" includes a person who has demonstrated a settled intention to treat a child as a child of his or her family, except under an arrangement where the child is placed for valuable consideration in a foster home by a person having lawful custody;

"paternity agreement" means a paternity agreement as defined in Part IV (Domestic Contracts);

"spouse" means either of a man and woman who,

(a) are married to each other, or

(b) have together entered into a marriage that is voidable or void, in good faith on the part of a person relying on this clause to assert any right.

Polygamous marriages

(2) In the definition of "spouse," a reference to marriage includes a marriage that is actually or potentially polygamous, if it was celebrated in a jurisdiction whose system of law recognizes it as valid.

PROCEDURAL AND OTHER MISCELLANEOUS MATTERS

Staying application

2(1) If, in an application under this Act, it appears to the court that for the appropriate determination of the spouses' affairs it is necessary or desirable to have other matters determined first or simultaneously, the court may stay the application until another proceeding is brought or determined as the court considers appropriate.

All proceedings in one court

(2) Except as this Act provides otherwise, no person who is a party to an application under this Act shall make another application under this Act to another court, but the court may order that the proceeding be transferred to a court having other jurisdiction where, in the first court's opinion, the other court is more appropriate to determine the matters in issue that should be determined at the same time.

Applications in Ontario Court (General Division)

(3) In the Ontario Court (General Division), an application under this Act may be made by action or application.

Statement re removal of barriers to remarriage

(4) A party to an application under section 7 (net family property), 10 (questions of title between spouses), 33 (support), 34 (powers of court) or 37 (variation) may serve on the

other party and file with the court a statement, verified by oath or statutory declaration, indicating that,

(a) the author of the statement has removed all barriers that are within his or her control and that would prevent the other spouse's remarriage within that spouse's faith; and

(b) the other party has not done so, despite a request.

Idem

(5) Within ten days after service of the statement, or within such longer period as the court allows, the party served with a statement under subsection (4) shall serve on the other party and file with the court a statement, verified by oath or statutory declaration, indicating that the author of the statement has removed all barriers that are within his or her control and that would prevent the other spouse's remarriage within that spouse's faith.

Dismissal, etc.

(6) When a party fails to comply with subsection (5),

(a) if the party is an applicant, the proceeding may be dismissed;

(b) if the party is a respondent, the defence may be struck out.

Exception

(7) Subsections (5) and (6) do not apply to a party who does not claim costs or other relief in the proceeding.

Extension of times

(8) The court may, on motion, extend a time prescribed by this Act if it is satisfied that,

(a) there are apparent grounds for relief;

(b) relief is unavailable because of delay that has been incurred in good faith; and

(c) no person will suffer substantial prejudice by reason of the delay.

Incorporation of contract in order

(9) A provision of a domestic contract in respect of a matter that is dealt with in this Act may be incorporated in an order made under this Act.

Act subject to contracts

(10) A domestic contract dealing with a matter that is also dealt with in this Act prevails unless this Act provides otherwise.

Registration of orders

(11) An order made under this Act that affects real property does not affect the acquisition of an interest in the real property by a person acting in good faith without notice of the order, unless the order is registered in the proper land registry office.

Mediation

3(1) In an application under this Act, the court may, on motion, appoint a person whom the parties have selected to mediate any matter that the court specifies.

Consent to act

(2) The court shall appoint only a person who,

(a) has consented to act as mediator; and

(b) has agreed to file a report with the court within the period of time specified by the court.

Duty of mediator

(3) The mediator shall confer with the parties, and with the children if the mediator considers it appropriate to do so, and shall endeavour to obtain an agreement between the parties.

Full or limited report

(4) Before entering into mediation, the parties shall decide whether,

(a) the mediator is to file a full report on the mediation, including anything that he or she considers relevant; or

(b) the mediator is to file a limited report that sets out only the agreement reached by the parties or states only that the parties did not reach agreement.

Filing and copies of report

(5) The mediator shall file with the clerk or registrar of the court a full or limited report, as the parties have decided, and shall give a copy to each of the parties.

Admissions, etc., in the course of mediation

(6) If the parties have decided that the mediator is to file a limited report, no evidence of anything said or of any admission or communication made in the course of the mediation is admissible in any proceeding, except with the consent of all parties to the proceeding in which the mediator was appointed.

Fees and expenses

(7) The court shall require the parties to pay the mediator's fees and expenses and shall specify in the order the proportions or amounts of the fees and expenses that each party is required to pay.

Idem, serious financial hardship

(8) The court may require one party to pay all the mediator's fees and expenses if the court is satisfied that payment would cause the other party or parties serious financial hardship.

PART I
FAMILY PROPERTY

Definitions

4(1) In this Part,

"court" means a court as defined in subsection 1(1), but does not include the Ontario Court (Provincial Division);

"matrimonial home" means a matrimonial home under section 18 and includes property that is a matrimonial home under that section at the valuation date;

"net family property" means the value of all the property, except property described in subsection (2), that a spouse owns on the valuation date, after deducting,

(a) the spouse's debts and other liabilities, and

(b) the value of property, other than a matrimonial home, that the spouse owned on the date of the marriage, after deducting the spouse's debts and other liabilities, calculated as of the date of the marriage;

"property" means any interest, present or future, vested or contingent, in real or personal property and includes,

(a) property over which a spouse has, alone or in conjunction with another person, a power of appointment exercisable in favour of himself or herself,

(b) property disposed of by a spouse but over which the spouse has, alone or in conjunction with another person, a power to revoke the disposition or a power to consume or dispose of the property, and

(c) in the case of a spouse's rights under a pension plan that have vested, the spouse's interest in the plan including contributions made by other persons;

"valuation date" means the earliest of the following dates:

1. The date the spouses separate and there is no reasonable prospect that they will resume cohabitation.
2. The date a divorce is granted.
3. The date the marriage is declared a nullity.
4. The date one of the spouses commences an application based on subsection 5(3) (improvident depletion) that is subsequently granted.
5. The date before the date on which one of the spouses dies leaving the other spouse surviving.

Excluded property

(2) The value of the following property that a spouse owns on the valuation date does not form part of the spouse's net family property:

1. Property, other than a matrimonial home, that was acquired by gift or inheritance from a third person after the date of the marriage.
2. Income from property referred to in paragraph 1, if the donor or testator has expressly stated that it is to be excluded from the spouse's net family property.

3. Damages or a right to damages for personal injuries, nervous shock, mental distress or loss of guidance, care and companionship, or the part of a settlement that represents those damages.
4. Proceeds or a right to proceeds of a policy of life insurance, as defined in the *Insurance Act*, that are payable on the death of the life insured.
5. Property, other than a matrimonial home, into which property referred to in paragraphs 1 to 4 can be traced.
6. Property that the spouses have agreed by a domestic contract is not to be included in the spouse's net family property.

Onus of proof re deductions and exclusions

(3) The onus of proving a deduction under the definition of "net family property" or an exclusion under subsection (2) is on the person claiming it.

Close of business

(4) When this section requires that a value be calculated as of a given date, it shall be calculated as of close of business on that date.

Net family property not to be less than zero

(5) If a spouse's net family property as calculated under subsections (1), (2) and (4) is less than zero, it shall be deemed to be equal to zero.

EQUALIZATION OF NET FAMILY PROPERTIES

Divorce, etc.

5(1) When a divorce is granted or a marriage is declared a nullity, or when the spouses are separated and there is no reasonable prospect that they will resume cohabitation, the spouse whose net family property is the lesser of the two net family properties is entitled to one-half the difference between them.

Death of spouse

(2) When a spouse dies, if the net family property of the deceased spouse exceeds the net family property of the surviving spouse, the surviving spouse is entitled to one-half the difference between them.

Improvident depletion of spouse's net family property

(3) When spouses are cohabiting, if there is a serious danger that one spouse may improvidently deplete his or her net family property, the other spouse may on an application under section 7 have the difference between the net family properties divided as if the spouses were separated and there were no reasonable prospect that they would resume cohabitation.

No further division

(4) After the court has made an order for division based on subsection (3), neither spouse may make a further application under section 7 in respect of their marriage.

Idem

(5) Subsection (4) applies even though the spouses continue to cohabit, unless a domestic contract between the spouses provides otherwise.

Variation of share

(6) The court may award a spouse an amount that is more or less than half the difference between the net family properties if the court is of the opinion that equalizing the net family properties would be unconscionable, having regard to,

(a) a spouse's failure to disclose to the other spouse debts or other liabilities existing at the date of the marriage;

(b) the fact that debts or other liabilities claimed in reduction of a spouse's net family property were incurred recklessly or in bad faith;

(c) the part of a spouse's net family property that consists of gifts made by the other spouse;

(d) a spouse's intentional or reckless depletion of his or her net family property;

(e) the fact that the amount a spouse would otherwise receive under subsection (1), (2) or (3) is disproportionately large in relation to a period of cohabitation that is less than five years;

(f) the fact that one spouse has incurred a disproportionately larger amount of debts or other liabilities than the other spouse for the support of the family;

(g) a written agreement between the spouses that is not a domestic contract; or

(h) any other circumstance relating to the acquisition, disposition, preservation, maintenance or improvement of property.

Purpose

(7) The purpose of this section is to recognize that child care, household management and financial provision are the joint responsibilities of the spouses and that inherent in the marital relationship there is equal contribution, whether financial or otherwise, by the spouses to the assumption of these responsibilities, entitling each spouse to the equalization of the net family properties, subject only to the equitable considerations set out in subsection (6).

ELECTION

Spouse's will

6(1) When a spouse dies leaving a will, the surviving spouse shall elect to take under the will or to receive the entitlement under section 5.

Spouse's intestacy

(2) When a spouse dies intestate, the surviving spouse shall elect to receive the entitlement under Part II of the *Succession Law Reform Act* or to receive the entitlement under section 5.

Spouse's partial intestacy

(3) When a spouse dies testate as to some property and intestate as to other property, the surviving spouse shall elect to take under the will and to receive the entitlement under Part II of the *Succession Law Reform Act*, or to receive the entitlement under section 5.

Property outside estate

(4) A surviving spouse who elects to take under the will or to receive the entitlement under Part II of the *Succession Law Reform Act*, or both in the case of a partial intestacy, shall also receive the other property to which he or she is entitled because of the first spouse's death.

Gifts by will

(5) The surviving spouse shall receive the gifts made to him or her in the deceased spouse's will in addition to the entitlement under section 5 if the will expressly provides for that result.

Insurance, etc.

(6) Where a surviving spouse,

(a) is the beneficiary,

(i) of a policy of life insurance, as defined in the *Insurance Act*, that was taken out on the life of the deceased spouse and owned by the deceased spouse or was taken out on the lives of a group of which he or she was a member, or

(ii) of a lump sum payment provided under a pension or similar plan on the death of the deceased spouse; and

(b) elects or has elected to receive the entitlement under section 5,

the payment under the policy or plan shall be credited against the surviving spouse's entitlement under section 5, unless a written designation by the deceased spouse provides that the surviving spouse shall receive payment under the policy or plan in addition to the entitlement under section 5.

Idem

(7) If a surviving spouse,

(a) elects or has elected to receive the entitlement under section 5; and

(b) receives payment under a life insurance policy or a lump sum payment provided under a pension or similar plan that is in excess of the entitlement under section 5,

and there is no written designation by the deceased spouse described in subsection (6), the deceased spouse's personal representative may recover the excess amount from the surviving spouse.

Effect of election to receive entitlement under s. 5

(8) When a surviving spouse elects to receive the entitlement under section 5, the gifts made to him or her in the deceased spouse's will are revoked and the will shall be interpreted as if the surviving spouse had died before the other, unless the will expressly provides that the gifts are in addition to the entitlement under section 5.

Idem

(9) When a surviving spouse elects to receive the entitlement under section 5, the spouse shall be deemed to have disclaimed the entitlement under Part II of the *Succession Law Reform Act*.

Manner of making election

(10) The surviving spouse's election shall be in the form prescribed by the regulations made under this Act and shall be filed in the office of the Estate Registrar for Ontario within six months after the first spouse's death.

Deemed election

(11) If the surviving spouse does not file the election within that time, he or she shall be deemed to have elected to take under the will or to receive the entitlement under the *Succession Law Reform Act*, or both, as the case may be, unless the court, on application, orders otherwise.

Priority of spouse's entitlement

(12) The spouse's entitlement under section 5 has priority over,

(a) the gifts made in the deceased spouse's will, if any, subject to subsection (13);

(b) a person's right to a share of the estate under Part II (Intestate Succession) of the *Succession Law Reform Act*;

(c) an order made against the estate under Part V (Support of Dependants) of the *Succession Law Reform Act*, except an order in favour of a child of the deceased spouse.

Exception

(13) The spouse's entitlement under section 5 does not have priority over a gift by will made in accordance with a contract that the deceased spouse entered into in good faith and for valuable consideration, except to the extent that the value of the gift, in the court's opinion, exceeds the consideration.

Distribution within six months of death restricted

(14) No distribution shall be made in the administration of a deceased spouse's estate within six months of the spouse's death, unless,

(a) the surviving spouse gives written consent to the distribution; or

(b) the court authorizes the distribution.

Idem, notice of application

(15) No distribution shall be made in the administration of a deceased spouse's death after the personal representative has received notice of an application under this Part, unless,

(a) the applicant gives written consent to the distribution; or

(b) the court authorizes the distribution.

Extension of limitation period

(16) If the court extends the time for a spouse's application based on subsection 5(2), any property of the deceased spouse that is distributed before the date of the order and without notice of the application shall not be brought into the calculation of the deceased spouse's net family property.

Exception

(17) Subsections (14) and (15) do not prohibit reasonable advances to dependants of the deceased spouse for their support.

Definition

(18) In subsection (17),

"dependant" has the same meaning as in Part V of the *Succession Law Reform Act*.

Liability of personal representative

(19) If the personal representative makes a distribution that contravenes subsection (14) or (15), the court makes an order against the estate under this Part and the undistributed portion

of the estate is not sufficient to satisfy the order, the personal representative is personally liable to the applicant for the amount that was distributed or the amount that is required to satisfy the order, whichever is less.

Order suspending administration

(20) On motion by the surviving spouse, the court may make an order suspending the administration of the deceased spouse's estate for the time and to the extent that the court decides.

Application to court

7(1) The court may, on the application of a spouse, former spouse or deceased spouse's personal representative, determine any matter respecting the spouses' entitlement under section 5.

Personal action; estates

(2) Entitlement under subsections 5(1), (2) and (3) is personal as between the spouses but,

(a) an application based on subsection 5(1) or (3) and commenced before a spouse's death may be continued by or against the deceased spouse's estate; and

(b) an application based on subsection 5(2) may be made by or against a deceased spouse's estate.

Limitation

(3) An application based on subsection 5(1) or (2) shall not be brought after the earliest of,

(a) two years after the day the marriage is terminated by divorce or judgment of nullity;

(b) six years after the day the spouses separate and there is no reasonable prospect that they will resume cohabitation;

(c) six months after the first spouse's death.

Statement of property

8. In an application under section 7, each party shall serve on the other and file with the court, in the manner and form prescribed by the rules of the court, a statement verified by oath or statutory declaration disclosing particulars of,

(a) the party's property and debts and other liabilities,

(i) as of the date of the marriage,

(ii) as of the valuation date, and

(iii) as of the date of the statement;

(b) the deductions that the party claims under the definition of "net family property";

(c) the exclusions that the party claims under subsection 4(2); and

(d) all property that the party disposed of during the two years immediately preceding the making of the statement, or during the marriage, whichever period is shorter.

Powers of court

9(1) In an application under section 7, the court may order,

(a) that one spouse pay to the other spouse the amount to which the court finds that spouse to be entitled under this Part;

(b) that security, including a charge on property, be given for the performance of an obligation imposed by the order;

(c) that, if necessary to avoid hardship, an amount referred to in clause (a) be paid in instalments during a period not exceeding ten years or that payment of all or part of the amount be delayed for a period not exceeding ten years; and

(d) that, if appropriate to satisfy an obligation imposed by the order,

(i) property be transferred to or in trust for or vested in a spouse, whether absolutely, for life or for a term of years, or

(ii) any property be partitioned or sold.

Financial information, inspections

(2) The court may, at the time of making an order for instalment or delayed payments or on motion at a later time, order that the spouse who has the obligation to make payments shall,

(a) furnish the other spouse with specified financial information, which may include periodic financial statements; and

(b) permit inspections of specified property of the spouse by or on behalf of the other spouse, as the court directs.

Variation

(3) If the court is satisfied that there has been a material change in the circumstances of the spouse who has the obligation to make instalment or delayed payments, the court may, on motion, vary the order, but shall not vary the amount to which the court found the spouse to be entitled under this Part.

Ten-year period

(4) Subsections (3) and 2(8) (extension of times) do not permit the postponement of payment beyond the ten-year period mentioned in clause (1)(c).

Determination of questions of title between spouses

10(1) A person may apply to the court for the determination of a question between that person and his or her spouse or former spouse as to the ownership or right to possession of particular property, other than a question arising out of an equalization of net family properties under section 5, and the court may,

(a) declare the ownership or right to possession;

(b) if the property has been disposed of, order payment in compensation for the interest of either party;

(c) order that the property be partitioned or sold for the purpose of realizing the interests in it; and

(d) order that either or both spouses give security, including a charge on property, for the performance of an obligation imposed by the order,

and may make ancillary orders or give ancillary directions.

Estates

(2) An application based on subsection (1) may be made by or continued against the estate of a deceased spouse.

Operating business or farm

11(1) An order made under section 9 or 10 shall not be made so as to require or result in the sale of an operating business or farm or so as to seriously impair its operation, unless there is no reasonable alternative method of satisfying the award.

Idem

(2) To comply with subsection (1), the court may,

(a) order that one spouse pay to the other a share of the profits from the business or farm; and

(b) if the business or farm is incorporated, order that one spouse transfer or have the corporation issue to the other shares in the corporation.

Orders for preservation

12. In an application under section 7 or 10, if the court considers it necessary for the protection of the other spouse's interests under this Part, the court may make an interim or final order,

(a) restraining the depletion of a spouse's property; and

(b) for the possession, delivering up, safekeeping and preservation of the property.

Variation and realization of security

13. If the court has ordered security or charged a property with security for the performance of an obligation under this Part, the court may, on motion,

(a) vary or discharge the order; or

(b) on notice to all persons having an interest in the property, direct its sale for the purpose of realizing the security or charge.

Presumptions

14. The rule of law applying a presumption of a resulting trust shall be applied in questions of the ownership of property between husband and wife, as if they were not married, except that,

(a) the fact that property is held in the name of spouses as joint tenants is proof, in the absence of evidence to the contrary, that the spouses are intended to own the property as joint tenants; and

(b) money on deposit in the name of both spouses shall be deemed to be in the name of the spouses as joint tenants for the purposes of clause (a).

Conflict of laws

15. The property rights of spouses arising out of the marital relationship are governed by the internal law of the place where both spouses had their last common habitual residence or, if there is no place where the spouses had a common habitual residence, by the law of Ontario.

Application of Part

16(1) This Part applies to property owned by spouses,

(a) whether they were married before or after the 1st day of March, 1986; and

(b) whether the property was acquired before or after that day.

Application of s. 14

(2) Section 14 applies whether the event giving rise to the presumption occurred before or after the 1st day of March, 1986.

PART II
MATRIMONIAL HOME

Definitions

17. In this Part,

"court" means a court as defined in subsection 1(1) but does not include the Ontario Court (Provincial Division);

"property" means real or personal property.

Matrimonial home

18(1) Every property in which a person has an interest and that is or, if the spouses have separated, was at the time of separation ordinarily occupied by the person and his or her spouse as their family residence is their matrimonial home.

Ownership of shares

(2) The ownership of a share or shares, or of an interest in a share or shares, of a corporation entitling the owner to occupy a housing unit owned by the corporation shall be deemed to be an interest in the unit for the purposes of subsection (1).

Residence on farmland, etc.

(3) If property that includes a matrimonial home is normally used for a purpose other than residential, the matrimonial home is only the part of the property that may reasonably be regarded as necessary to the use and enjoyment of the residence.

Possession of matrimonial home

19(1) Both spouses have an equal right to possession of a matrimonial home.

Idem

(2) When only one of the spouses has an interest in a matrimonial home, the other spouse's right of possession,

(a) is personal as against the first spouse; and

(b) ends when they cease to be spouses, unless a separation agreement or court order provides otherwise.

Designation of matrimonial home

20(1) One or both spouses may designate property owned by one or both of them as a matrimonial home, in the form prescribed by the regulations made under this Act.

Contiguous property

(2) The designation may include property that is described in the designation and is contiguous to the matrimonial home.

Registration

(3) The designation may be registered in the proper land registry office.

Effect of designation by both spouses

(4) On the registration of a designation made by both spouses, any other property that is a matrimonial home under section 18 but is not designated by both spouses ceases to be a matrimonial home.

Effect of designation by one spouse

(5) On the registration of a designation made by one spouse only, any other property that is a matrimonial home under section 18 remains a matrimonial home.

Cancellation of designation

(6) The designation of a matrimonial home is cancelled, and the property ceases to be a matrimonial home, on the registration or deposit of,

(a) a cancellation, executed by the person or persons who made the original designation, in the form prescribed by the regulations made under this Act;

(b) a decree absolute of divorce or judgment of nullity;

(c) an order under clause 23(e) cancelling the designation; or

(d) proof of death of one of the spouses.

Revival of other matrimonial homes

(7) When a designation of a matrimonial home made by both spouses is cancelled, section 18 applies again in respect of other property that is a matrimonial home.

Alienation of matrimonial home

21(1) No spouse shall dispose of or encumber an interest in a matrimonial home unless,

(a) the other spouse joins in the instrument or consents to the transaction;

(b) the other spouse has released all rights under this Part by a separation agreement;

(c) a court order has authorized the transaction or has released the property from the application of this Part; or

(d) the property is not designated by both spouses as a matrimonial home and a designation of another property as a matrimonial home, made by both spouses, is registered and not cancelled.

Setting aside transaction

(2) If a spouse disposes of or encumbers an interest in a matrimonial home in contravention of subsection (1), the transaction may be set aside on an application under section 23, unless the person holding the interest or encumbrance at the time of the application acquired it for value, in good faith and without notice, at the time of acquiring it or making an agreement to acquire it, that the property was a matrimonial home.

Proof that property not a matrimonial home

(3) For the purpose of subsection (2), a statement by the person making the disposition or encumbrance,

(a) verifying that he or she is not, or was not, a spouse at the time of the disposition or encumbrance;

(b) verifying that the person is a spouse who is not separated from his or her spouse and that the property is not ordinarily occupied by the spouses as their family residence;

(c) verifying that the person is a spouse who is separated from his or her spouse and that the property was not ordinarily occupied by the spouses, at the time of their separation, as their family residence;

(d) where the property is not designated by both spouses as a matrimonial home, verifying that a designation of another property as a matrimonial home, made by both spouses, is registered and not cancelled; or

(e) verifying that the other spouse has released all rights under this Part by a separation agreement,

shall, unless the person to whom the disposition or encumbrance is made had notice to the contrary, be deemed to be sufficient proof that the property is not a matrimonial home.

Idem, attorney's personal knowledge

(4) The statement shall be deemed to be sufficient proof that the property is not a matrimonial home if it is made by the attorney of the person making the disposition or encumbrance, on the basis of the attorney's personal knowledge.

Liens arising by operation of law

(5) This section does not apply to the acquisition of an interest in property by operation of law or to the acquisition of a lien under section 48 of the *Legal Aid Services Act, 1998*.

Right of redemption and to notice

22(1) When a person proceeds to realize upon a lien, encumbrance or execution or exercises a forfeiture against property that is a matrimonial home, the spouse who has a right of possession under section 19 has the same right of redemption or relief against forfeiture as the other spouse and is entitled to the same notice respecting the claim and its enforcement or realization.

Service of notice

(2) A notice to which a spouse is entitled under subsection (1) shall be deemed to be sufficiently given if served or given personally or by registered mail addressed to the spouse at his or her usual or last known address or, if none, the address of the matrimonial home, and, if notice is served or given by mail, the service shall be deemed to have been made on the fifth day after the day of mailing.

Idem: power of sale

(3) When a person exercises a power of sale against property that is a matrimonial home, sections 33 and 34 of the *Mortgages Act* apply and subsection (2) does not apply.

Payments by spouse

(4) If a spouse makes a payment in exercise of the right conferred by subsection (1), the payment shall be applied in satisfaction of the claim giving rise to the lien, encumbrance, execution or forfeiture.

Realization may continue in spouse's absence

(5) Despite any other Act, when a person who proceeds to realize upon a lien, encumbrance or execution or exercises a forfeiture does not have sufficient particulars of a spouse for the purpose and there is no response to a notice given under subsection (2) or under section 33 of the *Mortgages Act*, the realization or exercise of forfeiture may continue in the absence and without regard to the interest of the spouse and the spouse's rights under this section end on the completion of the realization or forfeiture.

Powers of court respecting alienation

23. The court may, on the application of a spouse or person having an interest in property, by order,

(a) determine whether or not the property is a matrimonial home and, if so, its extent;

(b) authorize the disposition or encumbrance of the matrimonial home if the court finds that the spouse whose consent is required,

(i) cannot be found or is not available,

(ii) is not capable of giving or withholding consent, or

(iii) is unreasonably withholding consent,

subject to any conditions, including provision of other comparable accommodation or payment in place of it, that the court considers appropriate;

(c) dispense with a notice required to be given under section 22;

(d) direct the setting aside of a transaction disposing of or encumbering an interest in the matrimonial home contrary to subsection 21(1) and the revesting of the interest or any part of it on the conditions that the court considers appropriate; and

(e) cancel a designation made under section 20 if the property is not a matrimonial home.

Order for possession of matrimonial home

24(1) Regardless of the ownership of a matrimonial home and its contents, and despite section 19 (spouse's right of possession), the court may on application, by order,

(a) provide for the delivering up, safekeeping and preservation of the matrimonial home and its contents;

(b) direct that one spouse be given exclusive possession of the matrimonial home or part of it for the period that the court directs and release other property that is a matrimonial home from the application of this Part;

(c) direct a spouse to whom exclusive possession of the matrimonial home is given to make periodic payments to the other spouse;

(d) direct that the contents of the matrimonial home, or any part of them,

(i) remain in the home for the use of the spouse given possession, or

(ii) be removed from the home for the use of a spouse or child;

(e) order a spouse to pay for all or part of the repair and maintenance of the matrimonial home and of other liabilities arising in respect of it, or to make periodic payments to the other spouse for those purposes;

(f) authorize the disposition or encumbrance of a spouse's interest in the matrimonial home, subject to the other spouse's right of exclusive possession as ordered; and

(g) where a false statement is made under subsection 21(3), direct,

(i) the person who made the false statement, or

(ii) a person who knew at the time he or she acquired an interest in the property that the statement was false and afterwards conveyed the interest,

to substitute other real property for the matrimonial home, or direct the person to set aside money or security to stand in place of it, subject to any conditions that the court considers appropriate.

Temporary or interim order

(2) The court may, on motion, make a temporary or interim order under clause (1)(a), (b), (c), (d) or (e).

Order for exclusive possession: criteria

(3) In determining whether to make an order for exclusive possession, the court shall consider,

(a) the best interests of the children affected;

(b) any existing orders under Part I (Family Property) and any existing support orders;

(c) the financial position of both spouses;

(d) any written agreement between the parties;

(e) the availability of other suitable and affordable accommodation; and

(f) any violence committed by a spouse against the other spouse or the children.

Best interests of child

(4) In determining the best interests of a child, the court shall consider,

(a) the possible disruptive effects on the child of a move to other accommodation; and

(b) the child's views and preferences, if they can reasonably be ascertained.

Offence

(5) A person who contravenes an order for exclusive possession is guilty of an offence and upon conviction is liable,

(a) in the case of a first offence, to a fine of not more than $5,000 or to imprisonment for a term of not more than three months, or to both; and

(b) in the case of a second or subsequent offence, to a fine of not more than $10,000 or to imprisonment for a term of not more than two years, or to both.

Arrest without warrant

(6) A police officer may arrest without warrant a person the police officer believes on reasonable and probable grounds to have contravened an order for exclusive possession.

Existing orders

(7) Subsections (5) and (6) also apply in respect of contraventions, committed on or after the 1st day of March, 1986, of orders for exclusive possession made under Part III of the *Family Law Reform Act*, being chapter 152 of the Revised Statutes of Ontario, 1980.

VARIATION

Possessory order

25(1) On the application of a person named in an order made under clause 24(1)(a), (b), (c), (d) or (e) or his or her personal representative, if the court is satisfied that there has been a material change in circumstances, the court may discharge, vary or suspend the order.

Conditions

(2) On the motion of a person who is subject to conditions imposed in an order made under clause 23(b) or (d) or 24(1)(g), or his or her personal representative, if the court is

satisfied that the conditions are no longer appropriate, the court may discharge, vary or suspend them.

Existing orders

(3) Subsections (1) and (2) also apply to orders made under the corresponding provisions of Part III of the *Family Law Reform Act*, being chapter 152 of the Revised Statutes of Ontario, 1980.

SPOUSE WITHOUT INTEREST IN MATRIMONIAL HOME

Joint tenancy with third person

26(1) If a spouse dies owning an interest in a matrimonial home as a joint tenant with a third person and not with the other spouse, the joint tenancy shall be deemed to have been severed immediately before the time of death.

Sixty-day period after spouse's death

(2) Despite clauses 19(2)(a) and (b) (termination of spouse's right of possession), a spouse who has no interest in a matrimonial home but is occupying it at the time of the other spouse's death, whether under an order for exclusive possession or otherwise, is entitled to retain possession against the spouse's estate, rent free, for sixty days after the spouse's death.

Registration of order

27. Orders made under this Part or under Part III of the *Family Law Reform Act*, being chapter 152 of the Revised Statutes of Ontario, 1980 are registrable against land under the *Registry Act* and the *Land Titles Act*.

Application of Part

28(1) This Part applies to matrimonial homes that are situated in Ontario.

Idem

(2) This Part applies,

(a) whether the spouses were married before or after the 1st day of March, 1986; and

(b) whether the matrimonial home was acquired before or after that day.

PART III
SUPPORT OBLIGATIONS

Definitions

29. In this Part,

"dependant" means a person to whom another has an obligation to provide support under this Part;

"same-sex partner" means either of two persons of the same sex who have cohabited,

(a) continuously for a period of not less than three years, or

(b) in a relationship of some permanence, if they are the natural or adoptive parents of a child;

"spouse" means a spouse as defined in subsection 1(1), and in addition includes either of a man and woman who are not married to each other and have cohabited,

(a) continuously for a period of not less than three years, or

(b) in a relationship of some permanence, if they are the natural or adoptive parents of a child.

Obligation of spouses and same-sex partners for support

30. Every spouse and every same-sex partner has an obligation to provide support for himself or herself and for the other spouse or same-sex partner, in accordance with need, to the extent that he or she is capable of doing so.

Obligation of parent to support child

31(1) Every parent has an obligation to provide support for his or her unmarried child who is a minor or is enrolled in a full time program of education, to the extent that the parent is capable of doing so.

Idem

(2) The obligation under subsection (1) does not extend to a child who is sixteen years of age or older and has withdrawn from parental control.

Obligation of child to support parent

32. Every child who is not a minor has an obligation to provide support, in accordance with need, for his or her parent who has cared for or provided support for the child, to the extent that the child is capable of doing so.

Order for support

33(1) A court may, on application, order a person to provide support for his or her dependants and determine the amount of support.

Applicants

(2) An application for an order for the support of a dependant may be made by the dependant or the dependant's parent.

Note: On a day to be named by proclamation of the Lieutenant Governor, section 33 is amended by the Statutes of Ontario, 2002, chapter 24, Schedule B, section 37 by adding the following subsection:

Same

(2.1) The Limitations Act, 2002 *applies to an application made by the dependant's parent or by an agency referred to in subsection (3) as if it were made by the dependant himself or herself.*

See: 2002, c. 24, Sched. B, ss. 37, 51.

Same

(3) An application for an order for the support of a dependant who is the respondent's spouse, same-sex partner or child may also be made by one of the following agencies,

(a) the Ministry of Community and Social Services in the name of the Minister;

(b) a municipality, excluding a lower-tier municipality in a regional municipality;

(c) a district social services administration board under the *District Social Services Administration Boards Act*;

(d) a band approved under section 15 of the *General Welfare Assistance Act*; or

(e) a delivery agent under the *Ontario Works Act, 1997*,

if the agency is providing or has provided a benefit under the *Family Benefits Act,* assistance under the *General Welfare Assistance Act* or the *Ontario Works Act, 1997* or income support under the *Ontario Disability Support Program Act, 1997* in respect of the dependant's support, or if an application for such a benefit or assistance has been made to the agency by or on behalf of the dependant.

Setting aside domestic contract

(4) The court may set aside a provision for support or a waiver of the right to support in a domestic contract or paternity agreement and may determine and order support in an application under subsection (1) although the contract or agreement contains an express provision excluding the application of this section,

(a) if the provision for support or the waiver of the right to support results in unconscionable circumstances;

(b) if the provision for support is in favour of or the waiver is by or on behalf of a dependant who qualifies for an allowance for support out of public money; or

(c) if there is default in the payment of support under the contract or agreement at the time the application is made.

Adding party

(5) In an application the court may, on a respondent's motion, add as a party another person who may have an obligation to provide support to the same dependant.

Idem

(6) In an action in the Ontario Court (General Division), the defendant may add as a third party another person who may have an obligation to provide support to the same dependant.

Purposes of order for support of child

(7) An order for the support of a child should,

(a) recognize that each parent has an obligation to provide support for the child;

(b) apportion the obligation according to the child support guidelines.

Purposes of order for support of spouse or same-sex partner

(8) An order for the support of a spouse or same-sex partner should,

(a) recognize the spouse's or same-sex partner's contribution to the relationship and the economic consequences of the relationship for the spouse or same-sex partner;

(b) share the economic burden of child support equitably;

(c) make fair provision to assist the spouse or same-sex partner to become able to contribute to his or her own support; and

(d) relieve financial hardship, if this has not been done by orders under Parts I (Family Property) and II (Matrimonial Home).

Determination of amount for support of spouses, same-sex partners, parents

(9) In determining the amount and duration, if any, of support for a spouse, same-sex partner or parent in relation to need, the court shall consider all the circumstances of the parties, including,

(a) the dependant's and respondent's current assets and means;

(b) the assets and means that the dependant and respondent are likely to have in the future;

(c) the dependant's capacity to contribute to his or her own support;

(d) the respondent's capacity to provide support;

(e) the dependant's and respondent's age and physical and mental health;

(f) the dependant's needs, in determining which the court shall have regard to the accustomed standard of living while the parties resided together;

(g) the measures available for the dependant to become able to provide for his or her own support and the length of time and cost involved to enable the dependant to take those measures;

(h) any legal obligation of the respondent or dependant to provide support for another person;

(i) the desirability of the dependant or respondent remaining at home to care for a child;

(j) a contribution by the dependant to the realization of the respondent's career potential;

(k) REPEALED.

(l) if the dependant is a spouse or same-sex partner,

(i) the length of time the dependant and respondent cohabited,

(ii) the effect on the spouse's or same-sex partner's earning capacity of the responsibilities assumed during cohabitation,

(iii) whether the spouse or same-sex partner has undertaken the care of a child who is of the age of eighteen years or over and unable by reason of illness, disability or other cause to withdraw from the charge of his or her parents,

(iv) whether the spouse or same-sex partner has undertaken to assist in the continuation of a program of education for a child eighteen years of age or over who is unable for that reason to withdraw from the charge of his or her parents,

(v) in the case of a spouse, any housekeeping, child care or other domestic service performed by the spouse for the family, as if the spouse were devoting the time spent in performing that service in remunerative employment and were contributing the earnings to the family's support,

(v.1) in the case of a same-sex partner, any housekeeping, child care or other domestic service performed by the same-sex partner for the respondent or the respondent's family, as if the same-sex partner were devoting the time spent in performing that service in remunerative employment and were contributing the earnings to the support of the respondent or the respondent's family,

(vi) the effect on the spouse's or same-sex partner's earnings and career development of the responsibility of caring for a child; and

(m) any other legal right of the dependant to support, other than out of public money.

Conduct

(10) The obligation to provide support for a spouse or same-sex partner exists without regard to the conduct of either spouse or same-sex partner, but the court may in determining the amount of support have regard to a course of conduct that is so unconscionable as to constitute an obvious and gross repudiation of the relationship.

Application of child support guidelines

(11) A court making an order for the support of a child shall do so in accordance with the child support guidelines.

Exception: special provisions

(12) Despite subsection (11), a court may award an amount that is different from the amount that would be determined in accordance with the child support guidelines if the court is satisfied,

(a) that special provisions in an order or a written agreement respecting the financial obligations of the parents, or the division or transfer of their property, directly or indirectly benefit a child, or that special provisions have otherwise been made for the benefit of a child; and

(b) that the application of the child support guidelines would result in an amount of child support that is inequitable given those special provisions.

Reasons

(13) Where the court awards, under subsection (12), an amount that is different from the amount that would be determined in accordance with the child support guidelines, the court shall record its reasons for doing so.

Exception: consent orders

(14) Despite subsection (11), a court may award an amount that is different from the amount that would be determined in accordance with the child support guidelines on the consent of both parents if the court is satisfied that,

(a) reasonable arrangements have been made for the support of the child to whom the order relates; and

(b) where support for the child is payable out of public money, the arrangements do not provide for an amount less than the amount that would be determined in accordance with the child support guidelines.

Reasonable arrangements

(15) For the purposes of clause (14)(a), in determining whether reasonable arrangements have been made for the support of a child,

(a) the court shall have regard to the child support guidelines; and

(b) the court shall not consider the arrangements to be unreasonable solely because the amount of support agreed to is not the same as the amount that would otherwise have been determined in accordance with the child support guidelines.

Powers of court

34(1) In an application under section 33, the court may make an interim or final order,

(a) requiring that an amount be paid periodically, whether annually or otherwise and whether for an indefinite or limited period, or until the happening of a specified event;

(b) requiring that a lump sum be paid or held in trust;

(c) requiring that property be transferred to or in trust for or vested in the dependant, whether absolutely, for life or for a term of years;

(d) respecting any matter authorized to be ordered under clause 24(1)(a), (b), (c), (d) or (e) (matrimonial home);

(e) requiring that some or all of the money payable under the order be paid into court or to another appropriate person or agency for the dependant's benefit;

(f) requiring that support be paid in respect of any period before the date of the order;

(g) requiring payment to an agency referred to in subsection 33(3) of an amount in reimbursement for a benefit or assistance referred to in that subsection, including a benefit or assistance provided before the date of the order;

(h) requiring payment of expenses in respect of a child's prenatal care and birth;

(i) requiring that a spouse or same-sex partner who has a policy of life insurance as defined in the *Insurance Act* designate the other spouse or same-sex partner or a child as the beneficiary irrevocably;

(j) requiring that a spouse or same-sex partner who has an interest in a pension plan or other benefit plan designate the other spouse or same-sex partner or a child as beneficiary under the plan and not change that designation; and

(k) requiring the securing of payment under the order, by a charge on property or otherwise.

Limitation on jurisdiction of Ontario Court (Provincial Division)

(2) The Ontario Court (Provincial Division) shall not make an order under clause (1)(b), (c), (i), (j) or (k) except for the provision of necessities or to prevent the dependant from becoming or continuing to be a public charge, and shall not make an order under clause (d).

Assignment of support

(3) An order for support may be assigned to an agency referred to in subsection 33(3).

Same

(3.1) An agency referred to in subsection 33(3) to whom an order for support is assigned is entitled to the payments due under the order and has the same right to be notified of and to participate in proceedings under this Act to vary, rescind, suspend or enforce the order as the person who would otherwise be entitled to the payments.

Support order binds estate

(4) An order for support binds the estate of the person having the support obligation unless the order provides otherwise.

Indexing of support payments

(5) In an order made under clause (1)(a), other than an order for the support of a child, the court may provide that the amount payable shall be increased annually on the order's anniversary date by the indexing factor, as defined in subsection (6), for November of the previous year.

Definition

(6) The indexing factor for a given month is the percentage change in the Consumer Price Index for Canada for prices of all items since the same month of the previous year, as published by Statistics Canada.

Domestic contract, etc., may be filed with court

35(1) A person who is a party to a domestic contract or paternity agreement may file the contract or agreement with the clerk of the Ontario Court (Provincial Division) or of the Unified Family Court together with the person's affidavit stating that the contract or agreement is in effect and has not been set aside or varied by a court or agreement.

Effect of filing

(2) A provision for support or maintenance contained in a contract or agreement that is filed in this manner,

(a) may be enforced;

(b) may be varied under section 37; and

(c) except in the case of a provision for the support of a child, may be increased under section 38,

as if it were an order of the court where it is filed.

Setting aside available

(3) Subsection 33(4) (setting aside in unconscionable circumstances, etc.) applies to a contract or agreement that is filed in this manner.

Enforcement available despite waiver

(4) Subsection (1) and clause (2)(a) apply despite an agreement to the contrary.

Existing contracts, etc.

(5) Subsections (1) and (2) also apply to contracts and agreements made before the 1st day of March, 1986.

Existing arrears

(6) Clause (2)(a) also applies to arrears accrued before the 1st day of March, 1986.

Effect of divorce proceeding

36(1) When a divorce proceeding is commenced under the *Divorce Act* (Canada), an application for support under this Part that has not been adjudicated is stayed, unless the court orders otherwise.

Arrears may be included in order

(2) The court that deals with a divorce proceeding under the *Divorce Act* (Canada) may determine the amount of arrears owing under an order for support made under this Part and make an order respecting that amount at the same time as it makes an order under the *Divorce Act* (Canada).

Idem

(3) If a marriage is terminated by divorce or judgment of nullity and the question of support is not adjudicated in the divorce or nullity proceedings, an order for support made under this Part continues in force according to its terms.

Application for variation

37(1) An application to the court for variation of an order made or confirmed under this Part may be made by,

(a) a dependant or respondent named in the order;

(b) a parent of a dependant referred to in clause (a);

(c) the personal representative of a respondent referred to in clause (a); or

(d) an agency referred to in subsection 33(3).

Powers of court: spouse, same-sex partner and parent support

(2) In the case of an order for support of a spouse, same-sex partner or parent, if the court is satisfied that there has been a material change in the dependant's or respondent's circumstances or that evidence not available on the previous hearing has become available, the court may,

(a) discharge, vary or suspend a term of the order, prospectively or retroactively;

(b) relieve the respondent from the payment of part or all of the arrears or any interest due on them; and

(c) make any other order under section 34 that the court considers appropriate in the circumstances referred to in section 33.

Powers of court: child support

(2.1) In the case of an order for support of a child, if the court is satisfied that there has been a change in circumstances within the meaning of the child support guidelines or that evidence not available on the previous hearing has become available, the court may,

(a) discharge, vary or suspend a term of the order, prospectively or retroactively;

(b) relieve the respondent from the payment of part or all of the arrears or any interest due on them; and

(c) make any other order for the support of a child that the court could make on an application under section 33.

Application of child support guidelines

(2.2) A court making an order under subsection (2.1) shall do so in accordance with the child support guidelines.

Exception: special provisions

(2.3) Despite subsection (2.2), a court may award an amount that is different from the amount that would be determined in accordance with the child support guidelines if the court is satisfied,

(a) that special provisions in an order or a written agreement respecting the financial obligations of the parents, or the division or transfer of their property, directly or indirectly benefit a child, or that special provisions have otherwise been made for the benefit of a child; and

(b) that the application of the child support guidelines would result in an amount of child support that is inequitable given those special provisions.

Reasons

(2.4) Where the court awards, under subsection (2.3), an amount that is different from the amount that would be determined in accordance with the child support guidelines, the court shall record its reasons for doing so.

Exception: consent orders

(2.5) Despite subsection (2.2), a court may award an amount that is different from the amount that would be determined in accordance with the child support guidelines on the consent of both parents if the court is satisfied that,

(a) reasonable arrangements have been made for the support of the child to whom the order relates; and

(b) where support for the child is payable out of public money, the arrangements do not provide for an amount less than the amount that would be determined in accordance with the child support guidelines.

Reasonable arrangements

(2.6) For the purposes of clause (2.5)(a), in determining whether reasonable arrangements have been made for the support of a child,

(a) the court shall have regard to the child support guidelines; and

(b) the court shall not consider the arrangements to be unreasonable solely because the amount of support agreed to is not the same as the amount that would otherwise have been determined in accordance with the child support guidelines.

Limitation on applications for variation

(3) No application for variation shall be made within six months after the making of the order for support or the disposition of another application for variation in respect of the same order, except by leave of the court.

INDEXING EXISTING ORDERS

Non-application to orders for child support

38(1) This section does not apply to an order for the support of a child.

Application to have existing order indexed

(2) If an order made or confirmed under this Part is not indexed under subsection 34 (5), the dependant, or an agency referred to in subsection 33(3), may apply to the court to have the order indexed in accordance with subsection 34(5).

Power of court

(3) The court shall, unless the respondent shows that his or her income, assets and means have not increased sufficiently to permit the increase, order that the amount payable be increased by the indexing factor, as defined in subsection 34(6), for November of the year before the year in which the application is made and be increased in the same way annually thereafter on the anniversary date of the order under this section.

Priority to child support

38.1(1) Where a court is considering an application for the support of a child and an application for the support of a spouse or same-sex partner, the court shall give priority to the support of the child in determining the applications.

Reasons

(2) Where as a result of giving priority to the support of a child, the court is unable to make an order for the support of a spouse or same-sex partner or the court makes an order for the support of a spouse or same-sex partner in an amount less than it otherwise would have, the court shall record its reasons for doing so.

Consequences of reduction or termination of child support

(3) Where as a result of giving priority to the support of a child, an order for the support of a spouse or same-sex partner is not made or the amount of the order for the support of a spouse or same-sex partner is less than it otherwise would have been, any material reduction or termination of the support for the child constitutes a material change of circumstances for the purposes of an application for the support of the spouse or same-sex partner or for variation of an order for the support of the spouse or same-sex partner.

Non-application of limitation

(4) Subsection 50(1) does not apply to an action or application for the support of a spouse or same-sex partner in the circumstances set out in subsection (3).

Note: On a day to be named by proclamation of the Lieutenant Governor, subsection (4) is repealed by the Statutes of Ontario, 2002, chapter 24, Schedule B, section 25. See: 2002, c. 24, Sched. B, ss. 25, 51.

Existing orders

39(1) Sections 36 to 38 also apply to orders for maintenance or alimony made before the 31st day of March, 1978 or in proceedings commenced before the 31st day of March, 1978 and to orders for support made under Part II of the *Family Law Reform Act*, being chapter 152 of the Revised Statutes of Ontario, 1980.

Combined support orders

(2) Where an application is made under section 37 to vary an order that provides a single amount of money for the combined support of one or more children and a spouse or same-sex partner, the court shall rescind the order and treat the application as an application for an order for the support of a child and an application for an order for the support of a spouse or same-sex partner.

Existing proceedings

(3) Where an application for the support of a child, including an application under section 37 to vary an order for the support of a child, is made before the day the *Uniform Federal and Provincial Child Support Guidelines Act, 1997* comes into force and the court has not considered any evidence in the application, other than in respect of an interim order, before that day, the proceeding shall be deemed to be an application under the *Family Law Act* as amended by the *Uniform Federal and Provincial Child Support Guidelines Act, 1997*, subject to such directions as the court considers appropriate.

Restraining orders

40. The court may, on application, make an interim or final order restraining the depletion of a spouse's or same-sex partner's property that would impair or defeat a claim under this Part.

Financial statement

41. In an application under section 33 or 37, each party shall serve on the other and file with the court a financial statement verified by oath or statutory declaration in the manner and form prescribed by the rules of the court.

OBTAINING INFORMATION

Order for return by employer

42(1) In an application under section 33 or 37, the court may order the employer of a party to the application to make a written return to the court showing the party's wages or other remuneration during the preceding twelve months.

Return as evidence

(2) A return purporting to be signed by the employer may be received in evidence as proof, in the absence of evidence to the contrary, of its contents.

Order for access to information

(3) The court may, on motion, make an order under subsection (4) if it appears to the court that, in order to make an application under section 33 or 37, the moving party needs to learn or confirm the proposed respondent's whereabouts.

Idem

(4) The order shall require the person or public body to whom it is directed to provide the court or the moving party with any information that is shown on a record in the person's or public body's possession or control and that indicates the proposed respondent's place of employment, address or location.

Crown bound

(5) This section binds the Crown in right of Ontario.

Arrest of absconding debtor

43(1) If an application is made under section 33 or 37 and the court is satisfied that the respondent is about to leave Ontario and that there are reasonable grounds for believing that the respondent intends to evade his or her responsibilities under this Act, the court may issue a warrant for the respondent's arrest for the purpose of bringing him or her before the court.

Bail

(2) Section 150 (interim release by justice of the peace) of the *Provincial Offences Act* applies with necessary modifications to an arrest under the warrant.

Provisional orders

44(1) In an application under section 33 or 37 in the Ontario Court (Provincial Division) or the Unified Family Court, the court shall proceed under this section, whether or not the respondent in the application files a financial statement, if,

(a) the respondent fails to appear;

(b) it appears to the court that the respondent resides in a locality in Ontario that is more than 150 kilometres away from the place where the court sits; and

(c) the court is of the opinion, in the circumstances of the case, that the issues can be adequately determined by proceeding under this section.

Idem

(2) If the court determines that it would be proper to make a final order, were it not for the respondent's failure to appear, the court shall make an order for support that is provisional only and has no effect until it is confirmed by the Ontario Court (Provincial Division) or the Unified Family Court sitting nearest the place where the respondent resides.

Transmission for hearing

(3) The court that makes a provisional order shall send to the court in the locality in which the respondent resides copies of such documents and records, certified in such manner, as are prescribed by the rules of the court.

Show cause

(4) The court to which the documents and records are sent shall cause them to be served upon the respondent, together with a notice to file with the court the financial statement required by section 41, and to appear and show cause why the provisional order should not be confirmed.

Confirmation of order

(5) At the hearing, the respondent may raise any defence that might have been raised in the original proceeding, but if the respondent fails to satisfy the court that the order ought not to be confirmed, the court may confirm the order without variation or with the variation that the court considers proper having regard to all the evidence.

Adjournment for further evidence

(6) If the respondent appears before the court and satisfies the court that for the purpose of a defence or for the taking of further evidence or otherwise it is necessary to remit the case to the court where the applicant resides, the court may remit the case and adjourn the proceeding for that purpose.

Where order not confirmed

(7) If the respondent appears before the court and the court, having regard to all the evidence, is of the opinion that the order ought not to be confirmed, the court shall remit the case to the court sitting where the order was made with a statement of the reasons for doing so, and the court sitting where the order was made shall dispose of the application in accordance with the statement.

Certificates as evidence

(8) A certificate certifying copies of documents or records for the purpose of this section and purporting to be signed by the clerk of the court is, without proof of the clerk's office or signature, admissible in evidence in a court to which it is transmitted under this section as proof, in the absence of evidence to the contrary, of the copy's authenticity.

Right of appeal

(9) No appeal lies from a provisional order made under this section, but a person bound by an order confirmed under this section has the same right of appeal as he or she would have had if the order had been made under section 34.

NECESSITIES OF LIFE

Pledging credit of spouse or same-sex partner

45(1) During cohabitation, a spouse or same-sex partner has authority to render himself or herself and his or her spouse or same-sex partner jointly and severally liable to a third party for necessities of life, unless the spouse or same-sex partner has notified the third party that he or she has withdrawn the authority.

Liability for necessities of minor

(2) If a person is entitled to recover against a minor in respect of the provision of necessities for the minor, every parent who has an obligation to support the minor is liable for them jointly and severally with the minor.

Recovery between persons jointly liable

(3) If persons are jointly and severally liable under this section, their liability to each other shall be determined in accordance with their obligation to provide support.

Common law supplanted

(4) This section applies in place of the rules of common law by which a wife may pledge her husband's credit.

Order restraining harassment

46(1) On application, a court may make an interim or final order restraining the applicant's spouse, same-sex partner or former spouse or same-sex partner from molesting, annoying or harassing the applicant or children in the applicant's lawful custody, or from communicating with the applicant or children, except as the order provides, and may require the applicant's spouse, same-sex partner or former spouse or same-sex partner to enter into the recognizance that the court considers appropriate.

Offence

(2) A person who contravenes a restraining order is guilty of an offence and upon conviction is liable,

(a) in the case of a first offence, to a fine of not more than $5,000 or to imprisonment for a term of not more than three months, or to both; and

(b) in the case of a second or subsequent offence, to a fine of not more than $10,000 or to imprisonment for a term of not more than two years, or to both.

Note: On a day to be named by proclamation of the Lieutenant Governor, subsection (2) is repealed by the Statutes of Ontario, 2000, chapter 33, subsection 22(1). See: 2000, c. 33, ss. 22(1), 23.

Note: Despite the repeal of subsection (2), any prosecution begun under that subsection before its repeal shall continue as if it were still in force. See: 2000, c. 33, s. 22(3).

Arrest without warrant

(3) A police officer may arrest without warrant a person the police officer believes on reasonable and probable grounds to have contravened a restraining order.

Existing orders

(4) Subsections (2) and (3) also apply in respect of contraventions, committed, on or after the 1st day of March, 1986, of restraining orders made under Part II of the *Family Law Reform Act*, being chapter 152 of the Revised Statutes of Ontario, 1980.

Note: On a day to be named by proclamation of the Lieutenant Governor, section 46 is repealed by the Statutes of Ontario, 2000, chapter 33, subsection 22 (2). See: 2000, c. 33, ss. 22(2), 23.

Note: Despite the repeal of section 46, any proceeding begun under that section before its repeal shall continue as if section 46 were still in force, and any order made under section 46, after its repeal, remains in force until it terminates by its own terms or is rescinded or terminated by a court. See: 2000, c. 33, s. 22(4).

Application for custody

47. The court may direct that an application for support stand over until an application for custody under the *Children's Law Reform Act* has been determined.

Appeal from Ontario Court (Provincial Division)

48. An appeal lies from an order of the Ontario Court (Provincial Division) under this Part to the Ontario Court (General Division).

Contempt of orders of Ontario Court (Provincial Division)

49(1) In addition to its powers in respect of contempt, the Ontario Court (Provincial Division) may punish by fine or imprisonment, or by both, any wilful contempt of or resistance to its process, rules or orders under this Act, but the fine shall not exceed $5,000 nor shall the imprisonment exceed ninety days.

Conditions of imprisonment

(2) An order for imprisonment under subsection (1) may be conditional upon default in the performance of a condition set out in the order and may provide for the imprisonment to be served intermittently.

Limitation

50(1) No action or application for an order for the support of a spouse or same-sex partner shall be brought under this Part after two years from the day the spouses or same-sex partners separate.

Idem

(2) If the spouses or same-sex partners provided for support on separation in a domestic contract, subsection (1) does not apply and no action or application for an order for the support of a spouse or same-sex partner shall be brought after default under the contract has subsisted for two years.

Note: On a day to be named by proclamation of the Lieutenant Governor, section 50 is repealed by the Statutes of Ontario, 2002, chapter 24, Schedule B, section 25. See: 2002, c. 24, Sched. B, ss. 25, 51.

PART IV
DOMESTIC CONTRACTS

Definitions

51. In this Part,

"cohabitation agreement" means an agreement entered into under section 53;

"domestic contract" means a marriage contract, separation agreement or cohabitation agreement;

"marriage contract" means an agreement entered into under section 52;

"paternity agreement" means an agreement entered into under section 59;

"separation agreement" means an agreement entered into under section 54.

Marriage contracts

52(1) A man and a woman who are married to each other or intend to marry may enter into an agreement in which they agree on their respective rights and obligations under the marriage or on separation, on the annulment or dissolution of the marriage or on death, including,

(a) ownership in or division of property;

(b) support obligations;

(c) the right to direct the education and moral training of their children, but not the right to custody of or access to their children; and

(d) any other matter in the settlement of their affairs.

Rights re matrimonial home excepted

(2) A provision in a marriage contract purporting to limit a spouse's rights under Part II (Matrimonial Home) is unenforceable.

Cohabitation agreements

53(1) Two persons of the opposite sex or the same sex who are cohabiting or intend to cohabit and who are not married to each other may enter into an agreement in which they agree on their respective rights and obligations during cohabitation, or on ceasing to cohabit or on death, including,

(a) ownership in or division of property;

(b) support obligations;

(c) the right to direct the education and moral training of their children, but not the right to custody of or access to their children; and

(d) any other matter in the settlement of their affairs.

Effect of marriage on agreement

(2) If the parties to a cohabitation agreement marry each other, the agreement shall be deemed to be a marriage contract.

Separation agreements

54. Two persons of the opposite sex or the same sex who cohabited and are living separate and apart may enter into an agreement in which they agree on their respective rights and obligations, including,

(a) ownership in or division of property;

(b) support obligations;

(c) the right to direct the education and moral training of their children;

(d) the right to custody of and access to their children; and

(e) any other matter in the settlement of their affairs.

FORM AND CAPACITY

Form of contract

55(1) A domestic contract and an agreement to amend or rescind a domestic contract are unenforceable unless made in writing, signed by the parties and witnessed.

Capacity of minor

(2) A minor has capacity to enter into a domestic contract, subject to the approval of the court, which may be given before or after the minor enters into the contract.

Guardian of property

(3) If a mentally incapable person has a guardian of property other than his or her own spouse, the guardian may enter into a domestic contract or give any waiver or consent under this Act on the person's behalf, subject to the approval of the court, given in advance.

P.G.T.

(4) In all other cases of mental incapacity, the Public Guardian and Trustee has power to act on the person's behalf in accordance with subsection (3).

PROVISIONS THAT MAY BE SET ASIDE OR DISREGARDED

Contracts subject to best interests of child

56(1) In the determination of a matter respecting the education, moral training or custody of or access to a child, the court may disregard any provision of a domestic contract pertaining to the matter where, in the opinion of the court, to do so is in the best interests of the child.

Contracts subject to child support guidelines

(1.1) In the determination of a matter respecting the support of a child, the court may disregard any provision of a domestic contract or paternity agreement pertaining to the matter where the provision is unreasonable having regard to the child support guidelines, as well as to any other provision relating to support of the child in the contract or agreement.

Clauses requiring chastity

(2) A provision in a domestic contract to take effect on separation whereby any right of a party is dependent upon remaining chaste is unenforceable, but this subsection shall not be construed to affect a contingency upon marriage or cohabitation with another.

Idem

(3) A provision in a domestic contract made before the 1st day of March, 1986 whereby any right of a party is dependent upon remaining chaste shall be given effect as a contingency upon marriage or cohabitation with another.

Setting aside domestic contract

(4) A court may, on application, set aside a domestic contract or a provision in it,

(a) if a party failed to disclose to the other significant assets, or significant debts or other liabilities, existing when the domestic contract was made;

(b) if a party did not understand the nature or consequences of the domestic contract; or

(c) otherwise in accordance with the law of contract.

Barriers to remarriage

(5) The court may, on application, set aside all or part of a separation agreement or settlement, if the court is satisfied that the removal by one spouse of barriers that would prevent the other spouse's remarriage within that spouse's faith was a consideration in the making of the agreement or settlement.

Idem

(6) Subsection (5) also applies to consent orders, releases, notices of discontinuance and abandonment and other written or oral arrangements.

Application of subss. (4, 5, 6)

(7) Subsections (4), (5) and (6) apply despite any agreement to the contrary.

Rights of donors of gifts

57. If a domestic contract provides that specific gifts made to one or both parties may not be disposed of or encumbered without the consent of the donor, the donor shall be deemed to be a party to the contract for the purpose of enforcement or amendment of the provision.

Contracts made outside Ontario

58. The manner and formalities of making a domestic contract and its essential validity and effect are governed by the proper law of the contract, except that,

(a) a contract of which the proper law is that of a jurisdiction other than Ontario is also valid and enforceable in Ontario if entered into in accordance with Ontario's internal law;

(b) subsection 33(4) (setting aside provision for support or waiver) and section 56 apply in Ontario to contracts for which the proper law is that of a jurisdiction other than Ontario; and

(c) a provision in a marriage contract or cohabitation agreement respecting the right to custody of or access to children is not enforceable in Ontario.

Paternity agreements

59(1) If a man and a woman who are not spouses enter into an agreement for,

(a) the payment of the expenses of a child's prenatal care and birth;

(b) support of a child; or

(c) funeral expenses of the child or mother,

on the application of a party, or a children's aid society, to the Ontario Court (Provincial Division) or the Unified Family Court, the court may incorporate the agreement in an order, and Part III (Support Obligations) applies to the order in the same manner as if it were an order made under that Part.

Child support guidelines

(1.1) A court shall not incorporate an agreement for the support of a child in an order under subsection (1) unless the court is satisfied that the agreement is reasonable having regard to the child support guidelines, as well as to any other provision relating to support of the child in the agreement.

Absconding respondent

(2) If an application is made under subsection (1) and a judge of the court is satisfied that the respondent is about to leave Ontario and that there are reasonable grounds to believe that the respondent intends to evade his or her responsibilities under the agreement,

the judge may issue a warrant in the form prescribed by the rules of the court for the respondent's arrest.

Bail

(3) Section 150 (interim release by justice of the peace) of the *Provincial Offences Act* applies with necessary modifications to an arrest under the warrant.

Capacity of minor

(4) A minor has capacity to enter into an agreement under subsection (1) that is approved by the court, whether the approval is given before or after the minor enters into the agreement.

Application to existing agreements

(5) This section applies to paternity agreements that were made before the 1st day of March, 1986.

Application of Act to existing contracts

60(1) A domestic contract validly made before the 1st day of March, 1986 shall be deemed to be a domestic contract for the purposes of this Act.

Contracts entered into before the 1st day of March, 1986

(2) If a domestic contract was entered into before the 1st day of March, 1986 and the contract or any part would have been valid if entered into on or after that day, the contract or part is not invalid for the reason only that it was entered into before that day.

Idem

(3) If property is transferred, under an agreement or understanding reached before the 31st day of March, 1978, between spouses who are living separate and apart, the transfer is effective as if made under a domestic contract.

PART V
DEPENDANTS' CLAIM FOR DAMAGES

Right of dependants to sue in tort

61(1) If a person is injured or killed by the fault or neglect of another under circumstances where the person is entitled to recover damages, or would have been entitled if not killed, the spouse, as defined in Part III (Support Obligations), same-sex partner, as defined in Part III (Support Obligations), children, grandchildren, parents, grandparents, brothers and sisters of the person are entitled to recover their pecuniary loss resulting from the injury or death from the person from whom the person injured or killed is entitled to recover or would have been entitled if not killed, and to maintain an action for the purpose in a court of competent jurisdiction.

Damages in case of injury

(2) The damages recoverable in a claim under subsection (1) may include,

(a) actual expenses reasonably incurred for the benefit of the person injured or killed;

(b) actual funeral expenses reasonably incurred;

(c) a reasonable allowance for travel expenses actually incurred in visiting the person during his or her treatment or recovery;

(d) where, as a result of the injury, the claimant provides nursing, housekeeping or other services for the person, a reasonable allowance for loss of income or the value of the services; and

(e) an amount to compensate for the loss of guidance, care and companionship that the claimant might reasonably have expected to receive from the person if the injury or death had not occurred.

Contributory negligence

(3) In an action under subsection (1), the right to damages is subject to any apportionment of damages due to contributory fault or neglect of the person who was injured or killed.

Limitations of actions

(4) No action shall be brought under subsection (1) after the expiration of two years from the time the cause of action arose.

Note: On a day to be named by proclamation of the Lieutenant Governor, subsection (4) is repealed by the Statutes of Ontario, 2002, chapter 24, Schedule B, section 25. See: 2002, c. 24, Sched. B, ss. 25, 51.

Offer to settle for global sum

62(1) The defendant may make an offer to settle for one sum of money as compensation for his or her fault or neglect to all plaintiffs, without specifying the shares into which it is to be divided.

Apportionment

(2) If the offer is accepted and the compensation has not been otherwise apportioned, the court may, on motion, apportion it among the plaintiffs.

Payment before apportionment

(3) The court may direct payment from the fund before apportionment.

Payment may be postponed

(4) The court may postpone the distribution of money to which minors are entitled.

Assessment of damages, insurance

63. In assessing damages in an action brought under this Part, the court shall not take into account any sum paid or payable as a result of the death or injury under a contract of insurance.

PART VI
AMENDMENTS TO THE COMMON LAW

Unity of legal personality abolished

64(1) For all purposes of the law of Ontario, a married person has a legal personality that is independent, separate and distinct from that of his or her spouse.

Capacity of married person

(2) A married person has and shall be accorded legal capacity for all purposes and in all respects as if he or she were an unmarried person and, in particular, has the same right of action in tort against his or her spouse as if they were not married.

Purpose of subss. (1, 2)

(3) The purpose of subsections (1) and (2) is to make the same law apply, and apply equally, to married men and married women and to remove any difference in it resulting from any common law rule or doctrine.

Actions between parent and child

65. No person is disentitled from bringing an action or other proceeding against another for the reason only that they are parent and child.

Recovery for prenatal injuries

66. No person is disentitled from recovering damages in respect of injuries for the reason only that the injuries were incurred before his or her birth.

Domicile of minor

67. The domicile of a person who is a minor is,

(a) if the minor habitually resides with both parents and the parents have a common domicile, that domicile;

(b) if the minor habitually resides with one parent only, that parent's domicile;

(c) if the minor resides with another person who has lawful custody of him or her, that person's domicile; or

(d) if the minor's domicile cannot be determined under clause (a), (b) or (c), the jurisdiction with which the minor has the closest connection.

68. Repealed.

General

Regulations

69(1) The Lieutenant Governor in Council may make regulations respecting any matter referred to as prescribed by the regulations.

Same

(2) The Lieutenant Governor in Council may make regulations establishing,

(a) guidelines respecting the making of orders for child support under this Act; and

(b) guidelines that may be designated under subsection 2(5) of the *Divorce Act* (Canada).

Same

(3) Without limiting the generality of subsection (2), guidelines may be established under subsection (2),

(a) respecting the way in which the amount of an order for child support is to be determined;

(b) respecting the circumstances in which discretion may be exercised in the making of an order for child support;

(c) respecting the circumstances that give rise to the making of a variation order in respect of an order for the support of a child;

(d) respecting the determination of income for the purposes of the application of the guidelines;

(e) authorizing a court to impute income for the purposes of the application of the guidelines;

(f) respecting the production of income information and providing for sanctions when that information is not provided.

TRANSITION

Application of ss. 5-8

70(1) Sections 5 to 8 apply unless,

(a) an application under section 4 of the *Family Law Reform Act*, being chapter 152 of the Revised Statutes of Ontario, 1980 was adjudicated or settled before the 4th day of June, 1985; or

(b) the first spouse's death occurred before the 1st day of March, 1986.

Application of Part II

(2) Part II (Matrimonial Home) applies unless a proceeding under Part III of the *Family Law Reform Act*, being chapter 152 of the Revised Statutes of Ontario, 1980 to determine the rights between spouses in respect of the property concerned was adjudicated or settled before the 4th day of June, 1985.

Interpretation of existing contracts

(3) A separation agreement or marriage contract that was validly made before the 1st day of March, 1986 and that excludes a spouse's property from the application of sections 4 and 8 of the *Family Law Reform Act*, being chapter 152 of the Revised Statutes of Ontario, 1980,

(a) shall be deemed to exclude that property from the application of section 5 of this Act; and

(b) shall be read with necessary modifications.

Glossary

access the right to visit with the child and to obtain information regarding the child's health, education, and welfare

adjusted cost base the cost at which capital property was acquired

adjusted sale price the value at which capital property is transferred

alimony a common law action by a wife for support from her husband

annulment a declaration that the marriage was never valid

as of right without needing the consent of the other party or an order of the court

attribution of capital gains the decision by the Canada Customs and Revenue Agency to treat the capital gain of one spouse as the capital gain of the other spouse

capital gain the profit made on the sale or other disposition of capital property

cause of action the basis for a legal action

cohabitation agreement an agreement between two persons (of the same or opposite sex) who are cohabiting or intend to cohabit and who are not married to each other in which they agree on their respective rights and obligations during cohabitation, on ceasing to cohabit, or on death

condonation forgiveness of a matrimonial offence by continuing or resuming cohabitation with the guilty spouse, with knowledge of the offence

conference brief a case conference brief (form 17A or form 17B), a settlement conference brief (form 17C or form 17D), or a trial management conference brief (form 17E)

constructive trust a trust imposed on the legal owner of property in favour of another person who has contributed work, money, or money's worth to the acquisition, preservation, or maintenance of the property

contingent liability a liability that is not fixed and absolute but will become fixed and absolute when a specified event occurs

costs of disposition costs of disposing of the property, including real estate commission and legal fees

criminal conversation a tort action by which a husband could claim damages against a man who had sexual intercourse with the husband's wife

custody the rights and responsibilities of a parent, including the right and responsibility to make decisions affecting the well-being of the child

***de facto* custody** actual custody, or custody in fact

divorce *a mensa et thoro* an order of the ecclesiastical courts by which the parties to a valid marriage were relieved of their obligation to cohabit, but were still legally married

divorce *a vinculo matrimonii* an order of the ecclesiastical courts, following a declaration that a marriage was not valid, by which the parties were released from the bonds of marriage

doctrine of constructive desertion a doctrine related to alimony under which it was deemed that the husband had deserted the wife if a wife left her husband because of his misconduct

document exchange a subscription service in which law firms have access to a central facility to deliver and pick up documents, used primarily during postal strikes

domestic contract a marriage contract, separation agreement, or cohabitation agreement

domicile permanent residence

donor one who makes a gift

duress force or threats that cause a person to do something he or she would not ordinarily do

ecclesiastical courts a system of church courts in England

encumbrances mortgages or other liens registered against the property

equalization of net family property a process under the *Family Law Act* under which spouses share equally in the value of most property acquired during the marriage

exclusive possession the sole right to reside in the home to the exclusion of the other spouse

joint custody when both parents share care of and decision-making power over the child

joint tenancy property is owned by two or more people and, on the death of one owner, the property passes to the other(s) automatically and not to the estate of the owner who died

jurisdiction shopping the practice of choosing a jurisdiction in which to start a proceeding based on a party's view of his or her chances of success in that jurisdiction rather than on the jurisdiction's connection with the subject matter of the proceeding

legal capacity to marry legal ability to enter into the contract of marriage

legal formalities of marriage the form a marriage ceremony must take

limitation period a certain time allowed by a statute for the commencement of a court proceeding

marriage contract an agreement between parties who are married or who intend to marry, in which they agree on their respective rights and obligations under the marriage or on separation, annulment, divorce, or death

mediation a method of dispute resolution in which the parties meet with a neutral third party who will help them try to come to an agreement

motion for summary judgment a motion for a final order without a trial

moving party the party who makes the motion

partition divide

presumption of advancement the presumption, created by the *Married Women's Property Act*, that a husband who placed property in the name of his wife intended to make a gift of the property to her

presumption of resulting trust an equitable principle under which it is presumed that a person who places property in the name of another person intends that person to hold the property in trust for the donor

principal residence under the *Income Tax Act*, a residential property in which the taxpayer or other family member has resided during the taxation year

quantum amount

right of physical chastisement the right of a husband to use physical force to discipline his wife

separation agreement an agreement between parties who have cohabited, in or out of marriage, and who have separated, in which they agree on their respective rights and obligations

sole custody when one parent has total care of and decision-making power over the child

stayed temporarily stopped or suspended

substituted service service using a method ordered by the court in circumstances when the usual methods of service provided by the court rules are not effective

support deduction order an order made under the *Family Responsibility and Support Arrears Enforcement Act, 1996*, which allows the Family Responsibility Office to arrange for support payments to be deducted automatically from the payor's income sources

tenants in common two or more people who own property and on the death of one owner the owner's share passes to his or her estate

testator one who makes a will; one who leaves property to another by will

trial record a document that assembles and organizes documents relevant to the trial to be used by the trial judge

unity of legal personality a doctrine by which a husband and wife were considered to be one person in law

void *ab initio* void, or having no legal force, from the beginning

voidable may be declared void but is otherwise not void

Index